SOCIAL INEQUALITY
Comparative and Developmental Approaches

This is a volume in

STUDIES IN ANTHROPOLOGY

Under the consulting editorship of
E. A. Hammel, University of California, Berkeley

A complete list of titles appears at the end of this volume.

SOCIAL INEQUALITY

Comparative and Developmental Approaches

Edited by

GERALD D. BERREMAN

Department of Anthropology
University of California, Berkeley
Berkeley, California

With the assistance of

KATHLEEN M. ZARETSKY
Department of Anthropology
San Jose State University
San Jose, California

ACADEMIC PRESS
A Subsidiary of Harcourt Brace Jovanovich, Publishers
New York   London   Toronto   Sydney   San Francisco

821684

BURG WARTENSTEIN SYMPOSIUM NUMBER 80
Sponsored by the Wenner-Gren Foundation for Anthropological Research
August 25–September 3, 1978

ACADEMIC PRESS, INC.
111 Fifth Avenue, New York, New York 10003

United Kingdom Edition published by
ACADEMIC PRESS, INC. (LONDON) LTD.
24/28 Oval Road, London NW1 7DX

Library of Congress Cataloging in Publication Data
Main entry under title:

Social inequality.

(Studies in anthropology)
Papers presented at a symposium sponsored by the
Wenner–Gren Foundation for Anthropological Research,
and held at Burg Wartenstein, Austria, Aug. 25–
Sept. 3, 1978.
Includes bibliographies and index.
1. Equality––Congresses. 2. Social status––
Congresses. 3. Society, Primitive––Congresses.
I. Berreman, Gerald Duane, Date. II. Zaretsky,
Kathleen M. III. Wenner–Gren Foundation for
Anthropological Research, New York.
GN479.S6   305.5   80–685550
ISBN 0–12–093160–5

PRINTED IN THE UNITED STATES OF AMERICA

81 82 83 84   9 8 7 6 5 4 3 2 1

Contents

PART **III**

DIMENSIONS OF STRATIFICATION

PART **IV**

FORMS OF DOMINATION IN STRATIFIED SOCIETIES

PART **V**

INEQUALITY IN SOCIALIST SOCIETIES

List of Contributors

GERALD D. BERREMAN (3), Department of Anthropology, University of California, Berkeley, Berkeley, California 94720

ANDRÉ BÉTEILLE (59), Department of Sociology, University of Delhi, Delhi, India

JOHN H. BODLEY (183), Department of Anthropology, Washington State University, Pullman, Washington 99164

MINA DAVIS CAULFIELD (201), Department of Anthropology, San Francisco State University, San Francisco, California 94132

SCHUYLER JONES (151), Department of Ethnology and Prehistory, Oxford University, Oxford, OX1 3PP, England

TADEUSZ KRAUZE (337), Department of Sociology, Hofstra University, Hempstead, New York 11550

RICHARD B. LEE (83), Department of Anthropology, University of Toronto, Toronto, Ontario M5S 1A1, Canada

BERNARD MAGUBANE (257), Department of Anthropology, University of Connecticut, Storrs, Connecticut 06268

PHILIP L. NEWMAN (103), Department of Anthropology, University of California, Los Angeles, Los Angeles, California 90024

JOHN U. OGBU (277), Department of Anthropology, University of California, Berkeley, Berkeley, California 94720

MARTIN ORANS (123), Department of Anthropology, University of California, Riverside, Riverside, California 92521

SYDEL SILVERMAN (163), Program in Anthropology, City University of New York, New York, New York 10036

WLODZIMIERZ WESOLOWSKI (337), Institute of Philosophy and Sociology, Polish Academy of Sciences, Nowy Swiat 72, Warsaw, Poland

MARTIN KING WHYTE (309), Department of Sociology, University of Michigan, Ann Arbor, Michigan 48104

ERIC R. WOLF (41), Department of Anthropology, Herbert H. Lehman College, City University of New York, Bronx, New York 10468.

PETER WORSLEY (221), Department of Sociology, University of Manchester, Manchester M13 9PL, England

KATHLEEN M. ZARETSKY (351), Department of Anthropology, San Jose State University, San Jose, California 95192

Preface

This volume is devoted to the anthropology of social inequality. As such, the contributions embody three distinctively anthropological approaches or perspectives not found in the literature on inequality in other disciplines. (1) They are comparative across the full range and variety of human societies around the world. Thus, they include discussions of inequality in unstratified societies (i.e., those organized on the basis of kinship into bands, tribes, and chiefdoms, whose people make their livings by foraging and subsistence food production), as well as in the more frequently analyzed stratified ones (i.e., those organized on the basis of territory, class, occupation, and ethnicity into nation states relying for their livelihoods on surplus food production, industrial and mercantile enterprise, organized in various forms of feudal, capitalist, or socialist economy). (2) They are comparative over time, encompassing the entire period since the emergence of humanity. As such they attend to processes of evolutionary change and development in the social organization and cultural content of systems of human inequality and their concomitants, prehistoric as well as historic and contemporary. (3) They attempt to analyze systems of social inequality in their total sociocultural context and throughout all of their dimensions and attributes. That is, culture is here treated holistically. Inequality is regarded as a major feature of the societies analyzed but not as a separate institution. It is integral with, and inseparable from, the other components that go to make up "that complex whole" which anthropologists have defined culture to be since Edward Burnett Tylor did so more than 100 years ago.[1]

Inequality is therefore analyzed here from an anthropological perspective, considering dimensions and supplying insights almost wholly lacking in the vast sociological literature on stratification, yet also largely overlooked as a subject for systematic inquiry in anthropological works with their focus on kinship, religion, politics, economy, and other categories traditional in ethnographic analysis.

The organization of this volume reflects its anthropological orientation as clearly as does the selection of authors and topics. The initial chapter (Berreman) proposes a conceptual framework for the comparative and evolutionary study of inequality—a framework that is manifest throughout the organization and content of the book. Following are two theoretical and philosophical essays (Wolf, Béteille) which help define the topic and its intellectual context while setting the tone for that which follows. Thereafter are 12 empirically based contributions deriving from a wide range of societies in many parts of the world and focusing on a variety of aspects of inequality: sex roles, social class, race, caste, ethnicity, clientage, social mobility, power, happiness, economic development, energetics, educational policy, and so on. The first three of these chapters analyze the organization of inequality in unstratified societies: in the Kalahari desert (Lee), highland New Guinea (Newman), and Western Samoa (Orans). The remaining nine discuss primarily stratified societies. Three analyze symbolic and material dimensions of stratification: in northeastern Afghanistan (Jones), in central Italy (Silverman), and cross-culturally with special reference to peasant societies (Bodley). The next four analyze forms of domination such as sex, class, race, and caste: Caulfield does so by comparing unstratified and stratified societies, Worsley by comparing "developing" and "developed" societies, Magubane and Ogbu by reference to case-studies of South Africa and the United States, respectively, both of which are rigidly stratified by race and class. The final two empirically based chapters discuss the special characteristics of inequality and social mobility in two socialist societies: China (Whyte), and Poland (Wesolowski and Krauze).

A brief concluding chapter by our rapporteur, Zaretsky, describes the context and dynamics of the discussion that surrounded the presentation of these papers in the symposium out of which this volume grew. That symposium, with the same title as the volume, was organized and chaired by the editor, was sponsored by the Wenner-Gren Foundation for Anthropological Research, and was held at its European conference center in Burg Wartenstein, Austria, on August 25 to September 3, 1978.

[1] Edward B. Tylor, *Primitive Culture* (London: John Murray), 1871, page 1. Harper Torchbook edition: *The Origins of Culture* (New York: Harper and Brothers), 1958 (comprising Vol. I of II), page 1.

Acknowledgments

In his book *The Call Girls*,[1] which is about inveterate conference participants perenially "on call" to attend international symposia not unlike the one which produced this volume, Arthur Koestler remarked that "the main function of a chairman winding up a symposium is to hand out chocolates [Koestler, 1973:100]." Accordingly, I here assume that function.

Four participants in the symposium are not contributors to the volume and therefore deserve special mention. Two, Abdel Ghaffar M. Ahmed of the University of Khartoum and Frank H. Stewart of Oxford University, were prevented from preparing papers by other commitments but were asked to attend in order to participate in discussions. Ahmed gave an enlightening informal presentation on the impact of colonial rule and its implications for social inequality in colonial and postcolonial Sudanese society. Stewart's interest in age-group systems and his unabashed disagreement with the theoretical positions of other participants were major features of his contributions to the discussions. In addition, Wanda Minge-Klevana of Harvard University was a summer resident scholar at Burg Wartenstein at the time of the symposium. Her informal participation reflected her research interest in the effects of the industrial revolution on the European family and household economy. Marshall Sahlins of the University of Chicago contributed, in addition to his characteristically incisive and witty discussion, a substantial paper entitled "Polynesian Riches—with Special Reference to Cooked Men and Raw Women in the Fiji Islands." Having forewarned me that its relevance to the topic at

[1] Arthur Koestler, *The Call Girls: A Tragi-Comedy* (New York: Random House), 1973.

hand would be peripheral, he requested some months after the conference to be excused from appearing in the volume because, in his view, the paper was not fit for publication and in any case had grown to 130 pages. On the latter grounds more than on the former, his request was granted.

Two others' contributions bear explanation. Tadeusz Krauze was regretfully not in attendance, although his paper, coauthored with Wlodzimierz Wesolowski, was an important contribution to the symposium and to this volume. Kathleen Zaretsky was rapporteur for the symposium, which meant that while she did not prepare a paper in advance, she participated in all discussions and in addition helped in the day-to-day organization of the sessions, kept detailed notes on participants' contributions, saw to it that the tape recording (expertly carried out by the Wenner-Gren staff) included all of the sessions and none of the recesses, and listened for and electronically marked on the tapes key points in the discussion for easy identification later. Only if one considers that 7 days were devoted to the discussion can one appreciate the magnitude of her task—a task multiplied exponentially months later when she went over the notes and tapes in detail to prepare the chapter which appears as the conclusion to this volume. During the preparation of the final manuscript, Zaretsky proofread all of the retyped contributions, did final substantive editing, looked up and corrected innumerable incomplete and questionable quotations and citations, and, finally, prepared the index.

The symposium, officially designated "Burg Wartenstein Symposium No. 80," would not have taken place without the encouragement and help of Lita Osmundsen, director of research in the Wenner-Gren Foundation, which supported the conference and provided its salubrious setting in the foothills of the Austrian Alps—a remodeled medieval castle which fairly reeks of its role in the history and evolution of European inequality. Osmundsen was our host at the castle; her administrative staff of Karl Frey, Kristina Baena, Miriam Casanova, and Susan Hogan was a most able, energetic, helpful, and congenial crew.

The Center for Advanced Study in the Behavioral Sciences at Stanford during a fellowship year there in 1976–1977 afforded me the time, encouragement, and the inspiration of colleagues that enabled me to plan and prepare for the symposium as well as to write the initial version of my own paper for it.

The work of preparing the volume itself, after the conference, could not have been adequately accomplished without the help of Grace Buzaljko, part-time editor for the Department of Anthropology at the University of California at Berkeley. She edited the manuscripts into comprehensible, unambiguous, and even felicitous prose and into a consistent style. Her queries, suggestions, revisions, and criticisms were always penetrating, sometimes disconcerting, never frivolous or useless. In many cases they generated lively and extended correspondence with authors.

All of the contributors to this volume, and especially I, as editor, are indebted and grateful to these people and institutions for making it a productive, enjoyable, and rewarding enterprise.

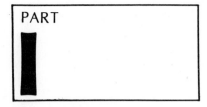

PART

I

CONCEPTS
OF INEQUALITY

1

GERALD D. BERREMAN

Social Inequality:
A Cross-Cultural Analysis[1]

It is always easier to locate an external enemy
than grapple with an internal condition.
— C. Wright Mills (1963b:304)

The enemy is always the total system within
which one lives.
— Jules Henry (1973b:234)

In 1963, Bohannan noted that "probably no range of social phenomena (unless it be the economy) has been so badly observed cross-culturally as that of the institution of inequality [p. 166]." Despite substantial contributions by Fried (1960, 1967), Fallers (1973), Smith (1966), and the authors of essays in collections edited by Béteille (1969) and by Plotnicov and Tuden (1970), that stricture remains largely valid (cf. Cancian, 1976). Two factors seem to have contributed to this situation: (1) lack of interest in, and of systematic attention to, inequality in non-Western societies, and (2) misinformation or biased information about inequality, either because of the projection of observers' categories and evaluations onto the observed or because data have been derived from beneficiaries of the systems observed.

This chapter is an attempt to rectify the problem Bohannan so succinctly identified, and it is presented with the acknowledged risk of exacerbating it. The paper is a product of my cross-cultural study of social inequality, growing out of the premises that inequality is a major social problem in the world and hence is worth understanding, and that no theory of inequality is ade-

[1]This chapter is part of a study undertaken during a year's Fellowship at the Center for Advanced Study in the Behavioral Sciences at Stanford, California, in 1976–1977. I am grateful for the opportunity for study, reflection, and discussion with colleagues provided by that benign environment. An antecedent version of the paper was given at the 1976 Annual Meetings of the American Anthropological Association, Washington, D.C. Another version was presented in 1978 at the Xth International Congress of Anthropological and Ethnological Sciences, Delhi, and was published in 1979 in my book, *Caste and Other Inequities*, by Manohar Book Service of New Delhi, copyright © 1979, by Gerald D. Berreman.

3

ISBN 0-12-093160-5

quate unless it can comprehend all instances. My aim has been to contribute to that understanding by identifying the major dimensions and variations in the social organization of human inequality, and their correlates and implications. The research has been exploratory, and hence the findings remain tentative; their value lies in their degree of utility in organizing and explaining the vast diversity in this area. I do not claim to have discovered God's Truth on the subject, but rather to have engaged in some hocus-pocus that clarifies some important issues. To paraphrase the great Alfred Schutz: Of my results I am not so sure, others may do better; but of one thing I am deeply convinced: here are important problems for social science (cf. Schutz, 1962:xlvii).

Fallers pointed out in his book, *Inequality* (1973), that social inequality is both a moral phenomenon, in the sense that people evaluate one another, and a structural one, in the sense that there is social differentiation in human society. I believe that it is equally importantly: (1) a behavioral phenomenon, in the sense that people *act* on their evaluations; (2) an interactional phenomenon in that these actions occur largely in the context of interpersonal relations; (3) a material phenomenon in that their actions entail differential access to goods, services, and opportunities; and (4) an existential phenomenon in that people experience their statuses and respond to them cognitively and affectively. In short, inequality is a major part of peoples' lives.

In this study I have attended to the relationships among these dimensions of inequality—to how the moral, structural, behavorial, and material aspects are experienced and responded to, cross-culturally and cross-situationally. In sum, I have focused on the regularities, if any, that exist in systems of inequality, and their common and systematic implications for those who experience and enact them.

The Context

It is important to state at the outset that I believe that stratification—the systematic ranking of categories of people, especially in their access to live-lihood and power is pernicious: It is humanly harmful in that it is painful, damaging, and unjust, and it is consistently experienced as such by those who are deprived and oppressed. It is pervasive, being found in various forms in all the socially complex and technologically advanced societies in the world. It is responsible for hunger even when there is plenty, for high mortality, high fertility, and low life expectancy, for low levels of education, literacy, political participation, and other measures of quality of life (see, for example, Eberstadt, 1976; Gavan and Dixon, 1975; Miller, 1977; Ratcliffe, 1978; cf. Nader and Beckerman, 1978). Stratification is also dangerous in that the poverty, oppression, hunger, fear, and frustration inherent in it result in resentment among the deprived and anxiety among the privileged, with the result that overt, perhaps catastrophic, conflict is inevitable. Much of the source of crime in the streets, terrorism, ethnic conflict, civil war, and international war is inequality so organized and the alarm, repression, and competition it engenders (see Berreman, 1980). Inequality between peoples and nations is a major threat to societal and even human survival. Whether or not stratification was inevitable or necessary in the emergence of modern society, as is often maintained, its elimination or drastic reduction appears to be necessary for the continuation of society (see Bodley, 1976: 214-227). Moreover, it is a cultural artifact—hence learned and socially transmitted—and that which is cultural is subject to change. Understanding the phenomenon may be a step, however small, to that difficult, important, and improbable end.

In order to accurately assess and comprehend that which is to follow, a brief history of my own antecedent research will be useful (cf. Berreman, 1979a:xi–xvii). It is presented in order to fulfill my commitment to the all-too-neglected topic of the sociology of anthropological knowledge, rather than for ego gratification. My writings are cited for similar reasons and for their bibliographies and examples, more than for their cogency.

My initial interest in inequality focused on race in the United States and caste in India, deriving from experience in the American deep South in 1953–1955 and in an Indian village in 1957–1958 (Berreman, 1963). I saw striking similarities in the structures, values, interactions, and consequences of the rigid systems of birth-ascribed inequality in these two societies, in both material and experiential terms: in the allocation of livelihood, power, and privilege, in the generation of resentment and anxiety, and in the ways these were acted out. This led me to a comparison of these two instances of birth-ascribed stratification (which I called "caste" stratification), embedded in very different cultures (Berreman, 1960), and later to comparisons with analogous systems elsewhere (Berreman, 1966, 1972a, 1973a).

Having attended to these most rigid systems of inequality, I became interested in comparing them with more open and permeable systems. To do so, I compared caste and race stratification with "class" stratification, relying largely on my own field data from rural, and later urban, India (Berreman, 1972b) and the sociological data on class in Western society. This study entailed making a contrast between stratification by birth ascription and that by characteristics that are acquired or bestowed, that is, primarily the economic situation and its concomitants (Berreman, 1968).

As a result of working through that comparison, I found that the nature of ethnic groups and of ethnic relations loomed as an important and problematic issue. Ranked and/or competing social groups appear repeatedly in the ethnographic literature, groups whose membership is based on cultural heritage rather than on birth ascription alone or on acquired characteristics or activities alone. Such groups are most appropriately termed ethnic groups. I came to regard them as intermediate between class and caste (or race) for reasons to be outlined later (cf. Berreman, 1977).

Having developed my ideas on social stratification, which occurs in societies organized as states or in close connection with states, I have more recently turned to the roots of anthropology: the study of simpler societies wherein stratification does not exist. I have done research in one such society, albeit a heavily Westernized one, the Aleuts (Berreman, 1955, 1964). But for documentation I have had to turn primarily to the anthropological literature: literature on bands, tribes, and chiefdoms. Such nonstate, unstratified societies do indeed exhibit social inequality, but it is organized and experienced quite differently, as I shall describe later.

Part of the outcome of my research has been an analytic framework for the cross-cultural study of inequality. This framework identifies some major structural features of systems of social inequality: features that are important and recurrent and that distinguish significant commonalities and differences in such systems wherever they occur. That is, these features identify types of social inequality that are distinguishable not only in structure, I think, but in behavioral, interactional, psychological, material, and existential consequences for people in the societies that harbor them. The framework entails a typology, but one that I do not regard as an exercise in pigeonholing or simply categorizing systems of inequality. Rather, I see it as a means of identifying, grouping, and analyzing significantly similar phenomena and contrasting them with other such phenomena elsewhere in time, space, and context, in order to comprehend their functioning.

Such a study entails an interest in the experiences and responses of people who live within the various types of systems, for I believe that significantly similar systems of inequality generate similar responses in those who experience them (cf. Berreman, 1966: 308–324) and that these in turn have characteristic social consequences.

The analysis is not a search for origins, nor do I regard the typology as primarily a developmental or evolutionary scheme, although I have benefited from accounts, data, and theories that are of those sorts (e.g., Adams, 1966; Braidwood and Willey, 1962; Childe, 1946; R. Cohen, 1978; R. Cohen and Service, 1978; Flannery, 1972; Fried, 1960, 1967; Service, 1971, 1975). I do, however, incorporate evolutionary processes and sequences in this analysis because I think they are as essential to understanding phenomena of stability and change in systems of inequality as they are to understanding them in other aspects of social, political, and economic organization.

In sum, the typology to be presented is what is often dubbed "a heuristic device"—an aid to inquiry and to understanding the relationships among structure, process, experience, and belief in various systems of social inequality. It therefore has both practical and theoretical implications.

Having described inductively how I came to the interest and materials that underlie this research, I will now turn deductive, and outline the typology that has resulted. There will not be space to make an entirely inductive and therefore convincing case, but a suggestive case can be made which may prove illuminating. For those who do not find it so, perhaps it will provide the challenge that will stimulate a response that will succeed where I have failed, in responding to Bohannan's stricture concerning the inadequacy of cross-cultural studies of inequality.

The typology to be presented identifies ideal types—nodes along a continuum of ways in which people characteristically organize inequality; how people regard and implement differential power, privilege, and prestige. The types are not discrete. There are clearly intergrades and transitional and problematic cases. Particular instances are generally more or less like one of the categories to be described rather than being exactly or exclusively so.

For purposes of communication it would be best if the typology were described inductively, on the basis of the same evidence, at the same tempo, and in the same sequence as it was originally constructed. In written communication, however, this is impossible. Therefore, I must refer the reader not only to the relevant literature but also to the tables that illustrate the text, and ask him or her to attend to their various cells in the order, and at the pace, presented in the text, following the tables from top to bottom and from left to right. It is important to note that characteristics described for each type or "cell" in Table 1.1 are not found exclusively in that cell. Rather, in general, as the discussion moves from the left to the right of the table, it moves along an evolutionary continuum. Moreover, the characteristics tend to be cumulative through processes of accretion and survival. Each type or cell includes features of those to its left *as well as* those described anew for it. An attempt has been made to suggest this by the manner in which the table has been organized.

TABLE 1.1
Partial Typology for a Comparative Study of Social Inequality

			Differentiation	
Equality/ no dominance			Inequality/dominance	
(hypothetical)	Unranked organization		Ranked organization	
		Kin/role ranking	Stratification (see Table 1.3)	
			Sex roles/age roles/stigmatization	
			Servitude	

The Typology

Human *differentiation* is the most general phenomenon to which the typology applies. As Rousseau (1755/1974) has argued at length, people are characterized by both natural differences (of sex, age, strength, etc.) and social differences (such as roles and positions associated with age, kinship, and occupation). These are inherent features of the human condition (see Béteille's discussion in this volume; cf. Dahrendorf, 1968).

Inequality refers to the social evaluation of whatever differences are regarded as relevant in a given society or situation. *Dominance* is the behavioral expression of those differences. "Social inequality" generally refers to the combination of these two processes: inequality and dominance. The absence of inequality and of dominance (i.e., the presence of equality and nondominance) is a theoretical possibility that is apparently not encountered empirically in human society.

The ways in which inequality and dominance are organized in various societies are many, and are a matter for discovery and analysis. I have designated two major ways in which these phenomena seem to me to be organized: *unranked* and *ranked*. These two share the fact that status is unequally distributed within the societies and that this distribution is done in systematic ways. The dimensions of distributed status are privilege, prestige, and power—Weber's classic triumvirate, "class, status and power" (Weber, 1946). In discussing the differences between unranked and ranked systems, I follow closely Fried's discussion in his essay, "On the Evolution of Social Stratification and the State" (1960), and its elaboration in his later book, *The Evolution of Political Society* (1967).

Unranked organization (which Fried calls "egalitarian") is that in which the division of labor is almost exclusively on the basis of age, sex, and personal characteristics. Status differences are based largely on these criteria and, within the family, on familial roles. Fried (1960:715) suggests that "an egalitarian society is one in which there are as many positions of prestige in any given age/sex grade, as there are persons capable of filling them." In addition, of course, interpersonal dominance arises out of interaction occurring in response to particular situations and is sustained as a result of personal characteristics and circumstances. Fallers (1973:4–29), for example, places great emphasis on inequality originating and expressed in dyadic relations. This might be termed *negotiated status* and in some cases *circumstantial status*. It occurs in all societies. Patron–client relations are often of this sort.

In Fried's analysis of egalitarian societies he comments that "at the heart of an egalitarian society is a fundamentally egalitarian economy [Fried, 1967:35]." Accumulation is not valued; generosity and reciprocity are criteria for esteem and high status. Dominance tends to be on the basis of dyadic relationships; status tends to be individual or situational rather than categorical. Prestige is more competed for than power and wealth; that is, in Weber's terms, "status" is more at issue than "class" (cf. Weber, 1968:302–307). Social inequality limited to these criteria is found only in small-scale, nonfood-producing societies organized as bands and tribes. Examples of such societies include most of those generally described as "foraging" or "hunting and gathering" societies and tribes (cf. Service, 1966, 1975:326–329; Sahlins, 1968).

Ranked organization is basically that in which inequality is institutionalized into a hierarchy of statuses—superior and inferior positions of prestige and dominance—that extend beyond age, sex, personal characteristics, and intrafamilial roles.[2]

What are ranked in such systems are social entities or social identities such as categories, groups, and suprafamilial roles. Individuals are ranked and rewarded as a result of the fact that they represent, or are identified with, these ranked entities. In short, when certain social identities beyond age, sex, and familial roles are routinely and categorically more rewarded, more highly regarded, and more influential than others, and when these rewards are explicitly endorsed by those with power in society, then the society is one characterized by *ranked* organization of inequality.

There are two major modes of ranking: *kin/role ranking* and *stratification*.

A *kin/role ranked* system is one wherein ranking depends on position in the kin system and often extends to shared rank within the kin group (e.g., the progeny of the eldest son of an eldest son outrank those of the eldest son of a second son in a patrilineal system based on primogeniture). Ranking may also depend on particular roles—kin roles or activity-based roles (e.g., religious or military roles). These Bohannan (1963:166–168) refers to as "situs," the ranking of roles. Usually kin and role ranking go together in what Fried (1960:717) terms *rank* society. He says that what distinguishes a rank society is the way differential prestige is handled: There are what he calls "additional limitations on access to valued status." (Note that he refers to *status*, not to economic access or power.) Fried further suggests that, in contrast to the "egalitarian" or unranked society, "the rank society is characterized by having *fewer* positions of valued status than individuals capable of handling them. Furthermore, most ranked societies have a fixed number [p. 717]" of these positions. In such societies, generosity and redistribution are valued; political and economic control are absent or minimal.

Kin/role ranked systems are or were characteristic of chiefdoms such as those of Polynesia, parts of Africa, and the American northwest coast, and of smaller scale, food-producing, stateless societies, which means, for the most part, societies with nonagricultural but often horticultural or small-scale

---

[2]Bohannan (1963:164) comments that "rank can be seen as a summary of human modes of dominance." It should be noted that the term *rank* is applied by Bohannan in its generic sense, not in Fried's special usage, to be discussed later.

("subsistence," "unintensive," "nonsurplus producing," "nonaccumulative") agricultural and pastoral economies (cf. Service, 1975:330–331). As Asad has made clear, it is not the particular source of livelihood nor the technical facts of livestock raising or agriculture that determine social and economic organization.

> If we are to understand the principles of economic organization on which structures of inequality are based, we must take into account the *combined effect* of what some Marxists call the relations and forces of production, i.e., the social conditions which facilitate (or inhibit) the systematic production, appropriation and accumulation of production, on the one hand, and the labour process by which natural objects are utilized or transformed into products for human consumption, on the other hand [Asad, 1979:420–421].

It is with this in mind that I emphasize economic "scale" in this context.

I turn now to the second major mode of ranking, that of my principal interest and that experienced by most people in the world today, namely, *stratification*. This is the kind of social inequality that characterizes state-organized societies: those based on large-scale, surplus-generating agriculture and/or animal husbandry, and those in which food production is combined with industry; those exhibiting conspicuous social and cultural diversity and occupational specialization; those with political organization based on territory and economic status rather than kinship; and those that are generally complex and large in size (cf. Berreman, 1978). The greatest distinctiveness to be found—Service (1975:3) calls it a "watershed"—in types of social organization and specifically in types of social inequality is undoubtedly that between stratified and nonstratified societies; between state and nonstate; between surplus food-producing and subsistence food-producing; between agricultural and nonagricultural (cf. Claessen and Skalnik, 1978: Fried, 1967; Service, 1975). Table 1.2 indicates some features of political, social, and economic organization that are frequently associated with this distinction.

Social stratification is the special type of ranking wherein *all* members of society are ranked relative to one another according to certain shared, non-kin characteristics defined by the society as important and used to allocate access to the basic resources that sustain life in the society (cf. Fried, 1967:186). In such systems, people are differentiated by class, status, and power, and the three tend to be highly intercorrelated. People who share significant characteristics share, at least roughly, the same rank and the same access to resources. Categories of people form social layers; hence the term *strata*. From stratum to stratum, there is differential ("shared" and "impaired," Fried [1960] calls it) access to the means of subsistence. Some would prefer to describe such access as a differential relationship to the means of production.

At the same time, *authority* is exercised on the basis of the territorial unit (over those who live in a given area) rather than over the kin group; *prestige* results primarily from accumulation rather than generosity or redistribution;

TABLE 1.2
Some Societal Characteristics Associated with the Typology

Sources:	Unranked	Kin/role ranking	Stratification
	Nonstate Socioculturally *homogeneous*		State Socioculturally *plural*
Service (1971, 1975)	"Band," "tribe"	"Chiefdom"	"Primitive states," "archaic civilizations," "industrial nations"
Sahlins (1968)	"Band"	"Tribe," "chiefdom"	
Fried (1960, 1967)	"Egalitarian"	"Rank"	"Stratification" and "state organization"
Y. Cohen (1968)	"Hunting and gathering (or foraging)," "horticulture," "pastoralism"		"Agriculture" and "industrialism"

power results from control over productive resources and consequently control over persons. As a result, there is exploitation of categories of people—systematic exploitation of one category by and for the benefit of another through application of economic sanctions, threats, and physical force.

It is about stratification that I believe I have the most to say that may be original, and it is on this topic that I will therefore expand in discussing the typology.

Types and Dimensions of Stratification

STATUS VERSUS CLASS

A schematic outline of the major types of stratification that I have found analytically useful is presented in Table 1.3. This table fills in the space under "Stratification" in Table 1.1. It must be noted that this table is so constructed as to be logically clear and empirically accurate, but it is not intended to convey evolutionary sequence as were Table 1.1 and Table 1.2. Nevertheless, as will be evident from the discussion, I do regard caste and estate stratification, where they occur, as evolutionarily prior to class stratification. Therefore, Table 1.3 retains a semblance (but no more than that) of the left–right evolutionary sequence found in the previous tables.

In the typology, stratification is divided into two basic modes; Max Weber called them *status groups* and *classes*. I prefer the terms *status strata* and *class strata* for reasons having to do with use of the term *group*, as will

TABLE 1.3

Typology for a Comparative Study of Social Stratification
(A Continuation of "Stratification" in Table 1.1)

Stratification					
Status strata (Weber's "honor and privilege")				Class strata (Weber's "economic order")	
Caste/race (intrinsic criteria)		Ethnic group ⎯⎯ Estate (criteria intrinsic to stratum, extrinsic to individual)		Social class (extrinsic criteria)	
Caste	Race (*Varna*)			Association (party; sodality)	Class
group	category	group	category	group	category

become clear later. *Status strata* are based on culturally specific criteria of differential honor, prestige,and privilege (which Weber calls *status honor*) shared by members of particular social categories. They are a major feature of the *social order*, and, unlike economic classes, Weber says, they normally constitute *communities* likely to act in their common interests. *Class strata* are based on economic access and economic relationships (which Weber calls the *market situation*, a major feature of the *economic order)* shared in degree and in kind by those within a stratum. In their extreme, ideal–typical form, these two types of social entities are what I have designated, respectively, *caste/race* (which Weber would term *status groups)*, and *social class* (Weber's *classes)*. It must be emphasized that it is *membership* in status strata (caste/race, ethnic group) that is determined by criteria of honor and privilege, whereas membership in class strata (estate, social class) is determined by criteria of economic position. The consequences of *membership* in these two kinds of ranked entities are not limited to the criteria of membership. That is, the consequences (or implications) of ranking in status strata according to criteria of honor and privilege include prominently and importantly economic differentials; the consequences (or implications) of ranking in class strata according to criteria of economic position include prominently and importantly honor and privilege differentials.

Power (control over persons, primarily through control over their livelihood) is the source and the perpetuating force for both high status groups and upper classes (cf. Fogelson and Adams, 1977). It is always and everywhere accompanied by privilege, for the powerful do not tolerate deprivation; power and the experience of oppression are absolutely incompatible. The state is the institutional structure through which power is exercised for privilege in complex societies. Cross-cultural data make clear that no rationale is too tortured, self-serving, or hypocritical to be put foward to justify systems of stratification; no mechanism too bald or brutal to be employed to enforce them (see Berreman, 1972a, 1973a; Pease, Form, and Rytina, 1970). People of deprived strata or groups are rarely (if ever) so credulous as to accept their deprivation without resentment; elites are rarely so perceptive as to recognize the depth (or even the presence) of that resentment (Berreman, 1971; cf. Berreman, 1960, 1973b, 1976, 1977; Freeman, 1979). The social functions of stratification are primarily to maintain the nexus of power, affluence, and privilege in complex societies, and equally to assure that there will be people so vulnerable, poor, and deprived as to have no choice but to occupy occupational roles that are dangerous, dirty, unpleasant, and demeaned (cf. Gans, 1974: 102–126; Lewis, 1978: 155–185).

INTRINSIC AND EXTRINSIC CRITERIA

The critical difference between caste/race, on the one hand, and social class, on the other, is in my opinion the perceived source, or locus, of the criteria by which membership and its associated status are assigned.

Caste/race membership is based on characteristics regarded as *intrinsic* to the individuals comprising the stratum—features of "honor and privilege" thought to inhere in people and therefore constituting the basis for the society's judgments of what I call "differential intrinsic worth." These features are regarded by members of the society, or at least by its elites, as inevitable consequences of birth or ancestry, often described as God-given or genetic (e.g., the caste systems of Hindu India and Islamic Swat and the castelike position in America of Blacks, Whites, and in some regions Indians and Mexican-Americans, in Japan of Burakumin and non-Burakumin, and in Ruanda of Tutsi, Hutu, and Twa) (cf. Berreman, 1973a).

In fact, as I have elaborated elsewhere (Berreman, 1972a, 1973a) *all* systems of birth-ascribed stratification seem to include a claim that the social distinctions are reflected in biological (i.e., "racial") differences revealed in physical make-up or appearance. This is true in Japan, where no actual physical differences can be detected between the pariah "Burakumin" and other Japanese; it is true in India where physical stereotypes about castes abound but actual differences are minimal or absent; it is true in the United States where the physical differences between Black and White are commonly and erroneously thought to be absolute. Associated with these supposed intrinsic and conspicuous physical differences are equally intrinsic and unverifiable traits of character, morality, intelligence, purity, and the like. Because of the absence or unreliability of these putatively intrinsic status-markers, cultural factors such as dress, language, occupation, residence, genealogy, and customary behavior have to be relied upon in addition to whatever biological ones may be present or claimed, in order to make the discriminations upon which ranked social interaction depends. Throughout the world, people who look distinctive are likely to be regarded as socially different; people who are regarded as socially different are consistently thought to look distinctive and to be biologically and psychically different. They are also likely to be required to dress and behave distinctively as affirmation of those differences. Just as societies frequently dramatize the social differences among kin groups (e.g., sibs, clans, phratries) by giving to them totemic names and attributing to them characteristics of animals and plants, thereby identifying the social differences with biological species differences (Lévi-Strauss, 1963), so also societies with intrinsic status hierarchies dramatize and legitimize crucial social differences by identifying them with innate biological, hence "racial" differences. The universality of such "racism" in birth-ascribed stratification can be understood in the fact that the physical differences not only dramatize social stratification but also explain and justify it. The effect is to make social inequality appear to be a natural necessity rather than merely a human choice and hence an artificial imposition. Social distinctions are man-made and learned; what man makes and learns he can unmake and unlearn, he can resist, oppose, and change. What God or biology has ordained is beyond man's influence or control. The former may be defined as artificial, unjust, untenable, and remediable; the latter as inevitable or divinely sanctioned. This is important because stratification by intrinsic criteria is widely or universally resented by those whom it oppresses (at least as it affects them), and advocated by those it rewards. Both categories share the human capability of empathy—can imagine themselves in other circumstances—which in turn inspires envy and resentment, on the one hand, and fear or guilt, on the other. Racism and casteism—the self-righteous rationalization of power and privilege by its beneficiaries in terms of ineluctable biology and divinity—are desperate, costly, and probably ultimately futile attempts to counteract those subversive emotions and the acts to which they lead.

Social class membership and ranking, by contrast, is based on attributes regarded as *extrinsic* to the people who comprise the class. They are individually acquired or bestowed, individually manifest, socially shared, features of the "market situation" of those ranked, or of their "relationship to the means of production." In American society, for example, these include such features as source and amount of income, occupation, education, consumption patterns, and "life-style" as these are used to rank people within a given racial or ethnic category. Extrinsic characteristics are often—but inaccurately, I think—designated as "achieved" in the literature of social science; intrinsic ones are contrastively designated as "ascribed" (cf. Foner, 1979).

Those lowly ranked in a class hierarchy are likely to be regarded as less able or deserving than others—in fact, are consistently so regarded. But the rationale is different from that which underlies a caste/race hierarchy because their status is said to be a result of their abilities and behaviors rather than the reverse (cf. Sennett and Cobb, 1972). That is, in class systems, individuals' statuses are determined by their personal and behavioral attributes; in caste/race systems, individuals' personal and behavioral attributes are determined by their status. By one's behavior and attributes one is assigned one's class; by one's caste or race, one is assigned one's behavior and attributes. Class is, to varying degrees, flexible and permeable; caste/race is rigid and closed. The means to mobility in the former are *prescribed;* in the latter they are *proscribed.* It is often the case, of course, that caste/race groups are internally class-stratified as well, but this is not a necessary condition, and the reverse is only occasionally or rarely true: Most class systems are not associated with caste or race distinctions.

It is important to emphasize that the categories of caste/race and class stratification presented throughout this discussion are clearly and significantly distinguishable but are not mutually incompatible. They co-occur in many societies. But their implications and consequences, both for those who experience them and for the societies in which they occur, are distinctive.

In this context the nature and significance of *ethnic groups* become clearer as a widely occuring and frequently ranked kind of social entity differing from class, caste, and race because based neither on "market situation" nor birth. Ethnicity is instead based on shared cultural heritage, manifest in what Geertz (1963:109–110), following Shils (1957), refers to as *primordial sentiments*. But ethnic groups do share with castes and "races" the fact that those who comprise them share status honor and privilege and the rank that accompanies them. Ethnic groups, therefore, constitute *status strata* (status groups) or *communities*, in Weber's terms. They are defined by criteria of membership that are both *extrinsic and intrinsic*, in some crucial respects one, in other crucial respects the other. Cultural heritage is learned and is therefore *extrinsic* to the individual—it can be relinquished or not learned or unlearned (at least it can be after a generation or more). But cultural heritage also is the product of early socialization and constant reinforcement in the group, where it is often highly valued and therefore tenacious.[3] In fact, it is a defining characteristic of ethnic group membership. It is therefore an *intrinsic* feature of group membership. So long as one identifies with, and is identified with, the ethnic group through exhibiting its culture (i.e., through participating in its culture), he or she shares its status. When one relinquishes or is denied ethnic group membership (through relinquishing its culture or heritage), he or she escapes its status. Examples are to be found in American "ethnics" (those of Irish, Italian, and Polish descent, for example), and regional and linguistic and religious groupings in many societies (cf. Berreman, 1977). To relinquish ethnicity may be, and often is, difficult, requiring more than one generation, but the fact that it can be done without dissimulation is what differentiates this kind of stratification from caste or race. The fact that ethnicity is the product of cultural heritage rather than of social or economic condition is what differentiates it from class.

The American "melting pot" therefore *works* for ambitious ethnic groups because they can assimilate by relinquishing their heritage; it *does not work* for race or caste groups because their status is an unalterable consequence of birth that they cannot relinquish (i.e., are not allowed to relinquish), and hence they cannot assimilate (this is the very essence of racism and casteism); it is *irrelevant* to classes because they are already assimilated.

If one looks at the typology as outlined thus far, one notices an unfilled cell between "ethnic group" and "social class" (see Table 1.3). I will now fill it because it seems to me that there are empirical phenomena which fit there and only there. Thus, I here introduce a fourth category in the typology, one which, like ethnicity, is based on both *extrinsic and intrinsic* criteria, but which, like social class, is based on *economic relations*, that is, on some approximation of the "market situation" rather than on the assumptions of honor and privilege that characterize "status groups" or status strata such as race, caste, and ethnic group.

I venture to apply the term *estate* to this cell in the paradigm. By *estate* I mean a status *intrinsic* to one's structural position (as designated by law and

---

[3]Geertz, (1963:109) comments, with reference to "primordial sentiments," "These congruities of blood, speech, custom, and so on, are seen to have an ineffable, and at times overpowering, coerciveness in and of themselves."

contract) relative to property such as land, and to propertied persons such as holders of land, titles, and offices. Such a status is *extrinsic* to the individual. It is likely to be designated by terms such as vassal, serf, lord, and the like. So long as one maintains the designated relationship to property or the propertied, one's status is fixed; if one relinquishes that relationship, one relinquishes (or escapes from or is deprived of) the status position it implies. As Bloch (1931:208) has noted, "An essential characteristic of the feudal contract was the theory that if one of the two contracting parties broke his pledges he thereby freed the other party of all obligations."

Thus, to summarize the relationships described here among estate, ethnicity, class, and caste/race:

1. Estate and ethnicity share features with one another, namely, the combination of extrinsic and intrinsic criteria.
2. Estate and class share features, namely, that both are based on economic relations and therefore are what I call "class strata."
3. Ethnicity and caste/race share features, namely, that both are based on "honor and privilege," and are therefore "status strata" and "communities."

However, estate and ethnicity *differ* in another and crucial respect, namely, that the former is a *category*, the latter a *group* (or corporate group, Weber's *Verband*). That is, those comprising the former are assigned their commonality; the latter claim it, enact it, even cherish it. The category is only *treated* as an entity; the group *acts* as an entity.[4]

This brings me to the final entries in the typology.

GROUPS VERSUS CATEGORIES

If completeness, symmetry, and logic were to be satisfied in the typology, the criterion that distinguishes ethnic group from estate would be extended. One would expect both category-defined entities and group-defined entities within each of the broader concepts of caste/race and social class. And, indeed, empirically, there are.

Clearly, one can distinguish *race* from *caste* on the basis of this criterion. In earlier publications it has bothered me that, when I roughly equated these two—for in important ways American (and South African) racial stratification is a caste system that is "color-coded"—I had to mention the slightly awkward fact that castes are self-aware and often corporate groups (as *jatis* are in India), whereas races are often only socially designated categories (as in the cases of "Natives" in Alaska, "Negroes" or Blacks in the United States, and Ladinos in Latin America). On the basis of further inquiry and reflection, I

[4]Variation in the degree of group consciousness, corporateness, and concerted action has led James Silverberg, in a personal communication, to advocate substitution of the term *aggregate* for *group* in my typology and analysis.

now propose that this difference be recognized and its implications be attended to by distinguishing the two in this typology: *race* as a social category; *caste* as a social group regarded as such both from within and from without. Note that a purely social definition of race is intended here. In the proposed terminology, a *race* mobilized into a group would thereby and to that extent be termed a *caste* and would be treated as such analytically. Indianists will recognize that *varna* (or "caste category") is an Indian analogue of *race* in this regard: a large ranked social category (composed of internally ranked social groups called *jatis* or castes).

Within "social class" in the typology, it is easy and logical to define "class" as a category, not a group. That is, defined by their economic situation—their relationship to the means of production—classes are found more often to be, in Marx's terms, classes "in themselves," than classes "for themselves" (i.e., self-aware, acting entities). Marxists have long been frustrated by the implications of this fact: workers of the world have generally failed to unite—or even to feel common cause—especially when ethnic, race, or caste differences divide them. Thus, "the great mass of the French nation is formed by simple addition of homologous magnitudes, much as potatoes in a sack form a sack of potatoes [Marx and Engels, 1852/1968: 478–479]." The problem facing those who undertake to make it otherwise is what has been often called consciousness-raising, or the elimination of "false consciousness." A jargonistic anthropologist might say that what they face is the difficult task of making that which is "etic" (here, a class) into something "emic" (here, an interest group) (see Berreman, 1977). "Etic" differences are those that are analytically distinguishable; "emic" phenomena are those defined and treated as significant by the people who manifest them. In a sense, then, "categories" as defined in this typology are etic entities for they are analytically discernible but not bounded, self-aware interest groups: For example, those whose members share their economic situation, here termed *class*, are "classes of themselves" in Marx's terms, an epitome of which is the amorphous, unproductive *lumpenproletariat* which he described. "Groups" in this typology are by definition emic, for they are bounded, self-aware interest groups: For example, those whose members share their economic situation *and* consciousness of their shared interests are "classes for themselves." They may take the form of a variety of organized class or class-based groups such as unions, cooperatives, occupational associations, political parties, or in the case of India, "caste associations" (cf. Rudolph and Rudolph, 1960), and in the case of the People's Republic of China, the various groups encouraged and utilized in economic and political organizations (cf. Schurmann, 1968; Whyte, 1973). Just as etic categories can become emic through "consciousness-raising" activities, efforts, experiences, or situations, events may also lead emic groupings to cease to be significant, and hence no longer extant groups. Thus, categories may be welded into groups; groups may dissipate into categories. This is in the nature of social change.

The discussion thus far has left one cell unfilled in the typology: the space adjacent to "class." Its occupant, if any, would have to be a *group* based on *extrinsic* criteria of *economic (class)* relations. This is precisely the nature of the emic entities discussed in the preceding paragraph, and I therefore place such entities in this final cell in the typology. The generic term I have chosen to designate them is *association*; alternatively, one might choose Weber's term *party* which focuses attention on action orientation and power (Weber, 1946, 1968: 284ff.), or perhaps Lowie's term *sodality* which he used to refer to a voluntary association defined by neither residence nor kinship (Lowie, 1948: 14). Service added to the definition of sodality the criterion of corporate functions or purposes (Service, 1971: 13), thus increasing its similarity to *party*. I shall return to this exceptionally important concept and its cell in the framework shortly.

In considering this final set of concepts in the typology of stratification—race, ethnic group, estate, association, and class—it is important to point out that some of them are *by definition* ranked entities, while others are *not necessarily* ranked. Caste and class are of the former sort, and estate is likely so as well. Race is not necessarily a category of rank, although as the term is generally used in English, it implies ranking, and, of course, *varna* in India is inherently a category of rank. Ethnicity and association are not necessarily ranked, even though frequently they are in fact ranked or are used as bases for ranking. When multiple ethnicities are unranked, we have an instance of ethnic pluralism—something more often advocated than achieved—but possible and worth working toward nonetheless. The same is true for unranked racial differences (i.e., racial pluralism). Associations are the least often ranked and the least closely tied to the rank principle of any of the entities discussed here. This attribute of associations, as I shall point out, is one reason why I attach such importance to them.

FOUR RESIDUAL CATEGORIES

Four features of systems of social inequality that I have not yet dealt with are *sex, age, stigmatization,* and *servitude.* There are doubtless others, but these seem to me especially worthy of comment. I shall first discuss sex and age inequalities and then turn to stigmatization (with which they share some marked similarities) and finally to servitude.

As I have attempted to make clear in Tables 1.1 and 1.4, sex (gender), age, and stigmatization are bases for role differentiation in every cell of the typology. As such, they are potential bases for inequality. There has been considerable debate in the literature of social science, of Marxist theory, and of feminism on the issue of sex as a basis for inequality, specifically on whether or not females suffer universal exploitation and oppression. I agree with Caulfield and Lee (Chapters 10 and 4 in this volume) and with Leacock (1978), among others, that in unranked societies, and to a large extent in kin and role ranked societies as well, role complementarity between the sexes does not (or but rarely does) entail exploitation. In fact, the concept of inequality as it implies disadvantage or degradation is scarcely applicable in such societies. The reason for this is to be found in the fact that in these societies productive activity is for subsistence—for use—rather than for accumulation and exchange, as Caulfield has so clearly pointed out. There is no motive or reward for production exceeding that which is to be used by those who produce and share it. Moreover the unit of production as well as consumption is the family or extended kin group. Roles in production (the division of labor) are familial roles and are functionally complementary as well as cooperative. That is, family and kin relations are congruent with relations of production and therefore are characterized by the mutuality, shared commitment, shared effort, shared responsibility, complementarity, and shared rewards that familial and kin relations imply. Thus, in societies so organized, relations between the sexes and between people of different ages are almost entirely relations between family members and kin who work together and consume together what they produce; who constitute the social and political as well as the economic unit; whose members' interests are common interests. Because kinship is the idiom for virtually *all* relations in nonstratified societies, kin organization is their defining characteristic. Thus, it is in the very definition of nonstratified societies—their organization on the basis of family and kin—that we find the explanation for the absence of systematic exploitation of person by person or category by category within them.

The situation in kin-based societies contrasts sharply with that in stratified societies, for there relations of production are those of patron and client, of owner and worker, of manager and managed, of colonizer and colonized, of ruler and subject, and of class, with the conflict of interest, competition, and exploitation that such relations entail. Sex and age in these societies, accordingly, are characteristically the bases for institutionalized inequality and exploitation. Both are generally regarded as intrinsic and ineluctable attributes of status and role in the hierarchical social and economic system and therefore share many implications of these features with race and caste. However, unlike race and caste neither is the result of ancestry, endogamy, or any other arrangement of marriage, family, or kinship. Both sex and age are based upon actual rather than merely putative physical differences, but the significance of those differences is largely socially defined so that, like race and caste, their expression and consequences are culturally and contextually highly variable. In addition, age changes, as race, caste, and sex do not, but the change is inevitable, irreversible, and wholly predictable. Hence, like race, caste, and sex, age is an intrinsic feature of status. Although sex is unchangeable (or has been until recently), gender (socially defined sexual identity) is not always so.

As a result of significant periods of coresidence and cosocialization of males and females, of old and young, throughout the world, these categories have no distinct ethnic or regional histories nor lifelong separate societies. In this analytically and existentially important respect, therefore, they differ both quantitatively and qualitatively from castes/races, ethnic groups, estates, and social classes. This complicates analysis based on comparisons of sex and age categories with the latter types of categories, and I think it is for such reasons as these that the former have been little analyzed within the framework of social stratification. However, the special characteristics of sex and age categorization do not at all preclude the existence of distinct male and female institutions, age-based institutions, distinct patterns of interaction and communication within and between these categories, or distinctive sub-cultures shared within them—characteristics which when ranked (as they most often are in complex societies) suggest stratification. These similarities, differences, and complexities must be borne in mind in any analysis, and par-ticularly any comparative analysis, of sex and age as criteria for the organiza-tion of inequality.

On the whole, in stratified societies the experiential consequences of sex and age identities seem to be closely allied to those of the most rigid forms of stratification described in this typology: race and caste. Millett (1971: 19), for example, refers to "the most fundamental of society's arbitrary follies, its view of sex as a caste structure ratified by nature." Sex and age deserve careful analysis with reference to such a framework. This is a task that remains largely undone, although Schlegel (1977), Andreas (1971), and Mernissi (1975) have made a start on the subject of comparative sexual stratification as have Caulfield and several other contributors to this volume, together with a number of the Marxist writers cited by Caulfield. Elsewhere I have briefly discussed the issue (Berreman, 1972a: 402–404).

In anthropology, age is far more neglected than sex as a basis for strat-ification, although it is treated extensively by sociologists, for example in Riley *et al.* (1968–1972). Jules Henry was perhaps the first anthropologist to deal with it seriously in American society (see Henry, 1963: 127–321, 391–474, 1973a). Increased social scientific interest in "youth culture," in adult "life-styles," and in the "problem" of the aged promises further analysis of the ine-qualities attached to age in Western societies. Social differentiation and grouping by age have been of considerable interest to anthropologists work-ing in non-Western societies, of course, but inequality has not been an impor-tant feature of that interest (cf. Stewart, 1977).

It seems clear that in American society, among others, females (cf. Ber-reman, 1969), the elderly, and the adolescent (and younger), are all to a sig-nificant extent stigmatized as not fully competent persons or even as nonper-sons (Goffman, 1961: 42), and are accordingly curtailed in their access to society's rewards, lowly ranked in the hierarchy of power, privilege, and esteem. Women have often shared the symbolic diminishment of their adult-hood and personhood experienced by pariah groups in India and the United States (untouchables and Blacks, respectively) who have been traditionally addressed, referred to, and acted toward by the dominant groups as if they were children (Berreman, 1966: 293–295). Jules Henry has observed, with reference to the aged poor in America but with equal relevance for other stigmatized identities including the sexual one, that "individuals are persons to the degree that they are attached to a social system, and this involves the acquisition and retention of certain tangible and intangible symbols of attachment [Henry, 1973a: 38]." The primary symbols of attachment in American society include independent and disposable income and property, and freedom of social and physical movement—prerogatives often withheld from women, the aged, and the young. These prerogatives are also widely withheld from despised or stigmatized races, castes, ethnic groups, and from those socially defined as deviant—to whom I now turn.

Throughout the world, a wide variety of personal characteristics are used to define individuals' social identity as deviant, entailing special (and often curtailed) treatment and experiences. In stratified societies, shared deviant identity, like the disvalued sex and age identities discussed previously, may constitute the basis for stigmatized social categories whose members are denied full realization of their humanity through segregation, derogation, and disadvantage, including impaired access to valued goods, services, and opportunities—to the "tangible and intangible symbols of attachment" to which Henry referred in the aforementioned quotation. That is, such despised or disvalued characteristics are the bases for categorical relegation of persons to some kind of pariah status or stratum (cf. Berreman, 1973b; Goffman, 1963). Such characteristics therefore constitute criteria for the institutionalization of inequality in the sociological sense, and they are likely also to be criteria for institutionalization in the administrative sense of incarceration or, as Romano has aptly termed it, *warehousing* of people (Romano, 1969; cf. Romano, 1971; Goffman, 1961). Short of incarceration, stigmatized status may entail segregation into enclaves, ghettos, or banishment to other forms of shared social isolation. A vivid example is that of lepers in India who, if not concealed by their families, are often relegated, irrespective of their natal castes, to a caste-like pariah status where they can consort freely only with other lepers—people of diverse social origins who share only their affliction (conceived of as a punishment of God) and their stigma. For this reason leprosy is known as "the disease of untouchability," meaning not that it strikes untouchables but that it confers untouchability. In recent times in India as elsewhere, lepers have generally been confined in isolated leper colonies.

Bases for such stigmatized identity and consequent consignment to low status in various complex societies and at various times (although these examples are drawn primarily from American culture) have included: ethnic, linguistic, and "racial" minority affiliation, homosexuality and other culturally-defined anomalies of sex and gender, physical and sensory handicaps (paraplegia, crippling, deafness, blindness), impairment of speech, a physical appearance that is deemed anomalous (dwarfism, obesity, gigantism, albinism, disfigurement, amputation), mental illness (cf. Townsend, 1979), mental retardation, and the like. Also stigmatized have been survivors of stigmatizing experiences ("convicted felons," survivors of nuclear attack or contamination, veterans of unpopular wars), those branded by society as having undesirable habits or character (criminals, delinquents, alcoholics, drug addicts, and addicts of other kinds), those who establish stigmatized relationships (crossing social boundaries), or who forego expected ones (recluses, spinsters, bachelors), those who engage in illegal occupations (drug dealers, pimps, prostitutes), those who engage in other stigmatized occupations (mortuary workers, executioners, scavengers) or who deal in their work with contaminating materials (sewage, cadavers), those who wear unconventional garb, who live in unacceptable dwellings or who live in unacceptable locations (public land, waste land, shanty towns), those who adhere to unconventional political, social, or religious beliefs and commitments, and those who refuse to conform to any of a wide variety of societal demands and expectations of conformity and participation.

The perceived sources of these stigmata range from birth-ascribed to acquired, from accidents of nature and punishments of God to personal perversity. Like age and sex they are generally treated as irrevocable conditions that have ineluctable consequences including denial of full personhood through denial of full participation in society and its rewards. The very fact of socially imposed degradation, deprivation, sanctions, and isolation tends to weld the victims of stigmatized stratification into self-aware, bounded, "emic" entities and often into interest groups and social movements as well. People characteristically react to such status by mobilizing for redress whenever they perceive the opportunity for it through their numbers, legal rights, or other sources of power. In this, as in other respects, such status is similar to low status resulting from other criteria for social stratification. Stigmatized status, however, is so culturally and contextually variable that generalizations and comparisons are difficult to make and in any case require extremely careful analysis when undertaken. Nevertheless, such status is too widespread and important to be overlooked in analyses of social inequality.

Finally, condition of servitude is a recurrent manifestation of inequality that merits consideration within the framework presented here. Aside from routine expectations of involuntary labor based on sex, age, and kin relationships, servitude is limited almost exclusively to stratified societies. The primary exceptions are captives, often described as slaves, in unstratified societies such as those of the aboriginal northwest coast of North America (cf. Fried, 1967:218–223). Servitude, of course, lacks the biological element of differentiation that characterizes sex and age, although it may be imposed upon social categories presumed to be biologically distinctive (e.g., races or castes). It is timely but discouraging to mention that sociobiologists might not agree. In an account of the 1977 annual meeting of the Pacific Division of the American Association for the Advancement of Science, for example, it was reported that sociobiologists used the fact that honeybee workers are born sterile, while only the queen bee reproduces, "as a metaphor for genetically determined caste systems; evolution has created, in effect, a class of honeybee slaves [Perlman, 1977:5]." If the report is accurate, this assertion, coupled with the fact that nourishment, not genetics, determines which bees will be workers and which the queen, would lead me to agree with the quoted observations of Marjorie Green, a critic of sociobiology, that the field is "very crude science" and its proponents are "surprisingly simpleminded" (Perlman, 1977; see Chorover, 1979).

Generally, servitude seems to be an instance of what I have called "estate," based on property and legal rights. When it is birth-ascribed, it becomes an extreme form of caste or race. When it is ethnically ascribed, it becomes an extreme form of ethnic group. When it is the result of economic or political events (e.g., debt or capture), it can be an extreme form of class. Servitude would obviously include indentured labor, "bonded labor" (cf. Hjejle, 1967), serfdom, and slavery—in short, any system wherein an individual is bound to serve another (as a result of birth ascription, or because defined as property, or by contractual agreement) in a status not limited to the particular task or occupation at hand and not subject to the degree of negotiability and independence of action accorded other statuses in the society. Slavery is the most widely remarked and analyzed form of servitude. Although anthropologists have often described slavery in particular societies, little comparative work has appeared. An exception is the excellent volume edited by Watson (1980; see also Siegel, 1945; Fried, 1967:216–223; Finley, 1968).

That sex, age, stigmatization, and servitude have not been analyzed in detail here does not imply that they are unrelated to, or unimportant in, understanding systems and experiences of inequality but only that I am unsure exactly how to handle them in this framework, especially in view of the unsystematic data and analyses available on them as criteria for the organization of inequality.

Caste, Estate, and Evolution

I have indicated that although I do not regard the framework presented here as primarily an evolutionary one, I do incorporate evolutionary processes and sequences within it. It seems appropriate therefore to present an analysis that is explicitly evolutionary within the stratification portion of that framework. To do so I return to the concepts of caste and estate, defined and discussed earlier.

In another paper I have suggested that caste in India originated as an intermediate form of stratification between the prestate, kin-based inequality of bands, tribes, and chiefdoms on the one hand, and the non-kin (or suprakin) class stratification characteristic of modern states (Berreman, 1979b). I there emphasized the peculiar historical circumstances of the South Asian subcontinent, wherein a great number and wide variety of prestate ethnic groups or tribes evidently came under the control of early stratified, state-organized, conquering peoples of Indo-Aryan origin around 3500 years ago (cf. Krader, 1978), following their earlier, less intensive contact with the Indus civilization. Thereafter, the indigenous small-scale ethnic–tribal groups were absorbed into the emerging larger and more complex polity as entities ranked (and hence stratified) relative to one another and to the dominant intruders, whom they supported through labor, rent, taxes, and the land which had been taken from them. During this time labor became occupationally specialized and livelihood for many was derived from wages or shares. These social aggregates were ranked economically but rank was frequently described in terms of ritual evaluation of occupations. In other instances rank was derived from the place of residence (e.g., forests or wastelands as contrasted with productive agricultural areas) or from evaluation of tribal or other ethnic origins and affinities. Control of important productive resources, however, remained the crucial criterion for rank and the basis for power, with the exception of some priestly groups whose rewards were described as otherworldly but included also the patronage of the powerful.

India's castes seem to have arisen, therefore, from a combination of ethnic stratification (cf. Karve, 1961:50–77) and occupationalization of work (cf. Gould, 1971). An essential feature of that combination, and one that makes Indian caste comprehensible in evolutionary terms, is the fact that castes are kin groups—maximal and putative kin groups to be sure, but kin groups nonetheless in the very real sense that they are composed of people who are regarded as actual or classificatory affinal and consanguineal relatives. Each caste constitutes a marriage network, ranked relative to all others. The caste, of course, is made up of smaller kin groupings: extended joint families comprising one or more households and including several nuclear units and often more than one generation. These small kin groups in turn are organized into lineages, the lineages into sibs (or clans), the sibs often into phratries (gotra). Segments of these entities in one village or locality may be organized for many purposes, including ritual ones, in such a manner as to combine principles of lineality and locality in what Murdock (1949:66) has termed compromise kin groups (see also Berreman, 1962). Thus, each caste is a maximal kin group of considerable internal complexity not unlike that to be found in many tribes and chiefdoms. In fact, many castes have a kind of kin-based role ranking and "conical clan" ranking (cf. Sahlins, 1968:20–27) similar to that found in unstratified societies. Such internal ranking no doubt existed in these entities before they became the kin strata (the microstrata composed of putative kinsmen) that we call castes. This internal ranking, however, does not constitute stratification as does the ranking of castes relative to one another. It has an entirely different character precisely because it is a ranking of kinsmen, with all the mutuality that term implies, rather than a ranking of unrelated entities with their conflicting interests and lack of mutuality.

Although a caste is like other prestate social aggregates in that it is a kin-based group in which inequality is organized and expressed in terms of kin-ship, there is this crucial difference: Unlike ranked conical clans found in the chiefdoms described by Sahlins (1968: 20–27) and unlike the ranked kin roles of bands and tribes (Fried, 1960, 1967), castes are in radical disjunction one from another. The members of one caste are not, and cannot be, at all related to those of another. Castes are ranked as disjunctive entities, not as kinsmen.

In social evolution prior to the emergence of the state, kinship and rank or hierarchy were inextricable: Hierarchy *was* a ranking among kinsmen. In fully developed class-stratified states, kinship was replaced by economics as the basis for rank. As caste emerged during the process of state formation in South Asia, kinship and hierarchy *both* were retained as the bases for social organization, but they were separated. The hierarchy became a ranking among unrelated (and, because endogamous, unrelatable) aggregates of kinsmen. In place of such principles of kinship as primogeniture and lineality to determine rank were substituted tribal or ethnic identity, as Karve (1961: 50–77) insists, and occupations, as Gould (1971) insists, and also a variety of other economic relations, including, most importantly, control over land and other productive resources, access to productivity, to income, and to wealth, accumulation of wealth, control over other people, and the like, as I have in-sisted (Berreman, 1979b). In short, society-wide ranking on the basis of in-dividual kin relationships and roles was replaced by the ranking of unrelated categories of people, each of which was bound internally by kin ties. Kin and role ranking was replaced by categorical ranking. The result was the appear-ance of *kin strata* (or kin classes), which is what castes in fact are, as they also constitute emergent stratification.

The Indian caste system comprises a unique congruity among kin, status, rank, occupation, class, ethnicity (culture), and power, creating a powerful, involute, and total system of stratification. It is a system well suited to agricultural production under an early state organization that sharply dis-tinguished between owners and nonowners of major productive resources. But it is *not* well suited to complex, rapidly changing urban–industrial organization (Berreman, 1978). As a result of the emergence of the latter kind of society, we now see changes in Indian caste toward, on the one hand, a familial and narrowly ritual phenomenon, and, on the other, a more broadly defined vehicle for political and economic mobilization in new occupations, technologies, bureaucracies, and politics (cf. Berreman, 1976; Freeman, 1977; Kolenda, 1978; Srinivas, 1966). True class stratification is thus becoming more prominent.

It seems to me likely that in many early states, as in India, ranking of social entities that were identified and held together by bonds of common kin-ship and common culture preceded class strata based entirely on economic, and therefore extrinsic, criteria. Bounded, culturally distinct groups or ag-gregates are better prepared than mere categories to claim and sustain the in-terests of their members in the larger society, whatever their place in the hierarchy of rank, and therefore they may tend more readily to originate or persist as entities.

Marc Bloch has made the point with reference to European feudalism that

> In the absence . . . of a strong state, of blood ties capable of dominating the whole life and of an economic system founded upon money payments there grew up in Carolingian and post-Carolingian society relations of man to man of a peculiar type. The superior individual granted his protection and divers material advantages that assured a subsistence to the dependent directly or indirectly; the inferior pledged various prestations or various services and was under a general obligation to render aid. These relations were not always freely assumed nor did they imply a universally satisfactory equilibrium between the two parties. Built upon authority, the feudal regime never ceased to contain a great number of constraints, violences and abuses. However, this idea of the personal bond, hierarchic and synallagmatic [bilateral, reciprocal] in character, dominated European feudalism [Bloch, 1931:204].[5]

These were relations between vassal and lord ("vassalage")—a defining feature of feudalism (cf. Service, 1975: 81–83). Such relations are in the present analysis collectively termed *estate*. Note that Bloch identifies them as existing "in the absence . . . of a strong state" and in the absence of "blood ties capable of dominating the whole life." These are therefore relations that might be expected to occur in the transition between (a) the stateless, subsistence-based, unstratified, kin-organized society wherein blood ties *are* capable of dominating the whole of life and indeed do so, and (b) the territorially organized, surplus-producing, class-stratified, centrally administered state whose "strength" and economic system dominate. Similarly, because in India castes did not have the mutual isolation found among tribes which had enabled "blood" or kin ties to serve as the basis for ordering relations within them, and because India also did not have a strong state or money economy to regulate stratification, the caste system served these functions there as vassalage did in feudal Europe.

The occupational specialization among castes, together with the *jajmani* system of caste-based patron–client relations in traditional India (cf. Beidelman, 1959; Kolenda, 1963; Wiser, 1936), presents a striking parallel to feudal vassalage in Europe, with the important difference that in India it is kin group or caste vassalage rather than individual vassalage. To paraphrase Bloch, as quoted previously:

> In the absence, then, of a strong state, of blood ties capable of dominating the whole life, and of an economic system founded upon money payments, there grew up in Indian society relations of caste-to-caste (and, between castes, of family-to-family) of a peculiar type called the *jajmani* system. The patron family, of superior caste, grants its

[5]This quote from Bloch, 1931 is reprinted by permission of Macmillan Publishing Company from *Encyclopedia of the Social Sciences*, Edwin R. A. Seligman, editor in chief. Copyright © 1931, renewed 1959 by Macmillan Publishing Co., Inc.

protection and diverse material advantages that assure a subsistence to the dependent, low-caste, client family directly or indirectly; the latter pledges (or is required to make) various prestations and various services and is under a general obligation to render aid. These relations are not always freely assumed, nor do they imply equilibrium between the two parties. Built upon an hereditary caste hierarchy, authority, and power, the caste regime always contains a great number of constraints, violences, and abuses. However, the idea of the intercaste bond, hierarchic, exploitative, and yet bilateral and reciprocal, and hereditary in character, dominates the Indian caste system.

The aptness of Bloch's description of vassalage as a description also of *jajmani* relations between high and low castes suggests that *estate* relations (as I term them) are indeed significantly equivalent to caste relations. They are so not only in function but, I believe, in evolutionary position as well, for both organize and sustain inequality (the former on the basis of individuals and categories; the latter on the basis of extensive kin groups) at the watershed between kin-based, unstratified, prestate institutions of inequality, and class-based, stratified, state-organized institutions of inequality. Under significantly similar conditions, equivalent institutions emerged in India and Europe, each bearing the distinctive stamp of its historical and cultural context, and both bearing also the common stamp of their evolutionary and structural context and of their functional burden. Whether or not one is interested in, or convinced of, this evolutionary status of caste in India it is analytically useful to understand it as structually and functionally intermediate between kin/role ranking and non-kin stratification.

Discussion: Dimensions of Stratification

In the comparative analytic framework presented here, three principal dimensions of stratification have been utilized. The first and most familiar is the contrast in the *criteria* for stratification: by *status* and by *class*, that is, stratification according to social honor and privilege, and that according to economic relations, each of which is closely correlated with, in fact rests upon, the distribution of power. This substantive distinction has enabled me to contrast ranking by ethnicity, race, and caste, on the one hand, with ranking by class, association (party), and estate, on the other. Its implications have been so thoroughly discussed by Max Weber and generations of subsequent sociologists that further elaboration here seems unnecessary, except to point out that there is a high degree of correlation and a functional relationship between the status rank and class rank of the individuals, groups, or categories ranked in these two ways.

A second dimension of stratification introduced here has to do with the *entities* that are ranked, namely, social *groups* and social *categories*. Groups are clearly recognized, significant, and often corporate entities to those who comprise a society—they are "emic." Categories are analytical entities, distinguishable but not necessarily or inevitably self-conscious, recognized, and cohesive in a society—they are usually "etic." In an analysis of social process, groups are empirically easier to identify and delimit, both from within and without, and are more effective and humanly relevant entities than are categories because groups, unlike categories, are consistently recognized, meaningful, acting entities, and they are for their members "reference groups" (cf. Merton, 1968; Berreman, 1964). Thus, associations, ethnic groups, and castes are more commonly and easily mobilized for the perceived interests of their members than are classes, estates, and races.

A third dimension introduced here is that of the presumed *source* or *locus* of the characteristics employed in designating the membership of ranked strata: those that are regarded as *intrinsic* to the people who constitute the ranked stratum, contrasted with those regarded as *extrinsic* to those who make up the stratum. (It should be noted that this presumption of locus is primarily and most consistently adhered to by the powerful and privileged—the elite—and is shared less generally, if concurred in at all, by those of the deprived and denigrated strata.) I suggest, but do not attempt to demonstrate here, that the social–psychological consequences and the social action potential for these two loci are different (cf. Berreman, 1966:308–324, 1972a:404–411, 1973a:14–18, 1973b, 1976). Those strata that are ranked low according to characteristics said to inhere in individuals by birth—which are intrinsic—such as castes and races, are likely to reject the legitimacy of the application of the criteria. They are likely to share resentment of their assigned status, and when opportunity permits, they are likely to resist it, especially if they constitute, or can be made to constitute, a group (cf. Berreman, 1972a:404–411, 1973a:15–18, 1973b, 1976). Such systems of social stratification therefore hold within them the seeds of their own destruction.

Those strata that are ranked low according to characteristics (e.g., income, occupation, life-style) extrinsic to the individuals comprising them—classes and associations, for example—are more likely to accept the societal definition of the legitimacy of their status, and to feel individually inadequate or unfortunate. The contrast here is between the "hidden injuries of class" so well described by Sennett and Cobb (1972), and the all-too-apparent injuries of caste and race. The injuries of class are hidden because their source in the shared experience of economic position may not be apparent to those who suffer them. They may instead perceive the problem to be their own failure to achieve the criteria for high status. The fault, they often believe, lies in themselves. The injuries of caste and race, however, are quite different in that they are evident to those who are injured. The individuals who make up the ranked entities are characteristically aware of their shared situation and its source in their group membership, its corporate activities, and the continuous, pervasive, and blunt sanctions that enforce group identity, group status, and the deprivation and denigration that accompany them. They do not blame themselves but the evaluation put upon them by others by virtue of their birth. They commonly see no fault in themselves, and despite religious, ethical, or genetic rationales propounded by the privileged, they resent and resist what they regard as unjust and iniquitous consequences of birth. In this regard, estate and ethnic groups are intermediate between social class and association, on the one hand, and race and caste, on the other. The specific nature of that intermediacy varies so greatly in specific circumstance that I will not attempt to describe it here.

It is remarkable how consistently, in widely differing social and cultural contexts, these generalizations are confirmed (cf. Berreman, 1973a).

In nonstate (or prestate) societies, the distinctions associated with stratification do not apply, for the most part. There, inequality exists without stratification; status differences exist, but without strata and specifically without class. Economic differences are minimized by the minimization of accumulation as a criterion or prerequisite of elevated status. Status in such societies is primarily a matter of esteem and of symbolic expression rather than of differential access to livelihood.

Prospects for Planned Change: Toward the Elimination or Drastic Reduction of Social Stratification

The comparative investigation and analysis of the full range of systems and principles by which human beings have defined and organized social inequality is an essential step in recognizing and appreciating alternatives to stratification in contemporary industrial and industrializing states. Only then can the social arrangements of particular societies, particular eras, and particular circumstances be distinguished from those of "human nature." Only then can we distinguish between the inevitable and the circumstantial, the universal and the cultural. Only then can we hope to effectively alter the inherently invidious distinctions and iniquitous inequities that constitute social stratification.

If one is interested in contributing to that end, as I am, the most important cell in the typology presented in this chapter (see Table 1.4) may well be that labeled "association (party; sodality)": *groups* defined by *extrinsic* criteria in terms of *economic* relations.

To reduce stratification in contemporary complex societies, measures might best be aimed at the following, perhaps in this sequence from least drastic to most drastic, hence from least to most effective:

1. Emphasis on social groups and individual roles rather than on categories as social, political, and economic units
2. Elimination or minimization of the use of intrinsic criteria in assigning social group and category membership
3. Elimination or minimization of accumulation and privileged economic access as means to, or results of, status achievement, with emphasis

TABLE 1.4
Typology for a Comparative Study of Social Inequality

Differentiation							
Equality/no dominance	Inequality/dominance						
(hypothetical)	Ranked organization						
	Unranked organization	Kin/role ranking	Stratification				
			Status strata (Weber's "honor and privilege")		Class strata (Weber's "economic order")		
			Caste/race (intrinsic criteria)	Ethnic group (criteria intrinsic to the stratum, extrinsic to individuals)	Estate	Social class (extrinsic criteria)	
			Caste / Race (Varna)			Association (party; sodality)	Class
			group / category	group	category	group	category
			Sex roles/age roles/stigmatization				
			Servitude				

31

instead on productivity, sharing, and distribution, and with honor replacing power and economic privilege (i.e., emblems substituting for
emoluments) as rewards

4. Elimination or minimization of economic differentiation among
   groups and categories; in short, elimination of *class* stratification
5. Elimination or minimization of the principle of ranking groups and
   categories of people, in short, of *all* stratification

In social differentiation, therefore, the aim would be to emphasize roles
and group membership, as determined by extrinsic criteria; to de-emphasize
social categories and intrinsic criteria; to maximize equality, sharing, and redistribution; to minimize social ranking, economic accumulation, concentration of power, and the exploitation that is a concomitant of all three.

To accomplish such change would entail an approximation of the kind of
organization of social inequality found in nonstate or prestate societies: one
based on individual and role ranking, on near equality of economic access and
political power, on sharing and redistribution, on a reward system utilizing
primarily honor. It would utilize or co-opt relatively small—even
primary—groups as significant social entities and as the building blocks of
larger organizational units. These groups would be essentially unranked.

The importance of the group over that of the category as the basis for
unstratified activity and commitment cannot be overemphasized, for it is
groups that are likely to be solidary, cooperative, effective social entities
because they are, or can become, real and meaningful ("emic") to their
members in a way that categories are not: foci of commitment, of participation, even of charisma. The consistency with which groups function as effective entities while categories fail has been frequently documented in the
literature of social science (e.g., Berger and Neuhaus, 1977; Berreman, 1978;
Faris, 1932; Geertz, 1963; Homans, 1950; Isaacs, 1975; Sharma, 1969; Shils,
1957; Shils and Janowitz, 1948; Tönnies, 1940; Whyte, 1973). Homans (1950:
456) commented in the little-noted final chapter of *The Human Group:* "At
the level of the tribe or group, society has always found itself able to cohere.
We infer, therefore, that a civilization, if it is in turn to maintain itself, must
preserve at least a few of the characteristics of the group. . . ."And again,
"Brotherhood, of the kind they get in a small and successful group, men must
have [p. 459]."

In effect, what is suggested here as the means to destratification is adoption of principles of social organization consistent only with a reduction in
social scale—reduction in the size and complexity of social institutions (cf.
Berreman, 1978; Barth, 1978). Social stratification, the complex division of
labor that accompanies it, and the hardships that result from it, are universal
concomitants of large scale society as we know it. As Bodley has noted,

> Stratification and specialization are the foundation of the market economy, wealth
> concentration, political centralization, and the frequent conflict between individual

and sub-group self-interest, on the one hand, and societal interest, on the other. All of these cultural arrangements, while they are not in themselves crises, do tend to promote overpopulation, overconsumption and other symptoms of the environmental crisis, and are clearly linked to poverty, war, crime, and many personal crises [Bodley, 1976: 216].

Diamond has addressed this issue too, suggesting that what is required now is to begin the change "with the rational devolution of bureaucracy, the common ownership and decentralization of the basic means of production, for which we have the techniques at hand and for which we must develop the apposite social imagination [Diamond, 1974: 175]." That may not be the only way, but I know of no other, for the gap between rich and poor, powerful and oppressed, privileged and deprived, has so widened and has become so entrenched that only radical solutions have a chance of success in accomplishing destratification.

The obvious question is, could such change occur at all, under any circumstances? Is not stratification an inherent feature of complex societies, and an irreversible one?

Any answer clearly must include acknowledgment that complete equality is impossible; complete elimination of stratification is unlikely in complex societies. Differential authority and reward may be useful, necessary, or inevitable, but I think there is a likelihood that substantial reduction of stratification and its concomitants would be possible within complex social, economic, and political organizations—that stratification is not requisite to such organizations.

Some suggestive evidence is available from the People's Republic of China, especially in the period following the "great leap forward" of 1958–1960. My knowledge comes primarily through the works of such sociologists and historians as Whyte (1973, 1975, and Chapter 14 in this volume) and Schurmann (1968, especially pp. 90–104) and discussions with visitors to China, notably sociologist Alphonso Pinkney (personal communication, 1975) and psychiatrist James P. Comer (personal communication, 1977). In discussing the Maoist critique of the Weberian view of bureaucratic society, Whyte describes Chinese efforts to minimize stratification. Although described in different terms, the Chinese efforts correspond to most of the things I have suggested before: turning from stratification to a kind of role-ranking, the minimization of accumulation, the emphasis on sharing and redistribution, elimination of intrinsic criteria for social differentiation, minimization of class differences and stratification, and focus on the small group (and larger entities composed of small groups) as the economic as well as political and social units in the society. Schurmann (1968:99–100) describes the shift in 1958–1960 as a purposeful one from organic to mechanical solidarity (in the Durkheimian sense) as the basis for cohesion in Chinese society: from specialized interdependent units to more generalized, more self-sufficient units, shifting from reliance on specialists to reliance on generalists in the sociopolitical and economic spheres.

At the same time, the order of magnitude of economic inequality within China and within particular institutions there is reported to be incomparably far below that of prerevolutionary China and far below that of other complex societies today. Social inequality is said to be correspondingly low.

Whether or not the Chinese experiment will prove successful or long-lasting (and recently, as Whyte reports in Chapter 14 in this volume, there has been a return to greater stratification in China), it is interesting and significant that an effort has been made on such a gigantic scale and with a significant degree of success to reduce social stratification in a complex society. Wesolowski (1969) and Wesolowski and Krauze (Chapter 15 in this volume) report less dramatic efforts toward diminished stratification in Poland.

The analytic framework I have outlined has some validity, I think, in that it provides understanding and insight not only into the societies and systems from which the typology was derived but also into China, which constitutes an empirical example of achievement of a goal that also lies behind this analysis: the diminution of stratification. I expect it to have similar utility in examining other societies as well.

The rather unimpressive cell in the typology that I labeled "association (party; sodality)" seems to be especially important as a kind of social entity with characteristics that might be instrumental in effecting fundamental change in the organization and consequences of social inequality in modern societies. Emphasis on the group, emphasis on internal role-ranking, de-emphasis on intrinsic criteria of social identity, de-emphasis on rank itself, and emphasis on social action, all are consistent (but not inevitable, by any means) with organization by association—more so than with any other social entity in the typology or in modern society as I understand it. By elaborating this kind of organization as fundamental to the reorganization of complex society, together with the other principles outlined previously, many of the damaging and dangerous problems of social stratification might be overcome. Other, less promising cells in the paradigm might thereby be replaced or eliminated. In China, such changes seem to have been a large part of the effort toward minimization of inequality and the solution of economic problems, political problems, and problems of class inequities and ethnic conflict.

Conclusion

The aim of the work underlying this chapter has been to understand, on the basis of cross-cultural comparison, the principles according to which social inequality is organized in human societies, and how systems of institutionalized inequality are experienced and responded to by those who live in them. It has been, therefore, an exercise in "the politics of truth," to invoke C. Wright Mills' felicitous phrase—the construction and maintenance of "an adequate definition of reality" about social inequality and its implications

(Mills, 1963a: 611). At the same time, I am cognizant of Mills' warning that "simply to understand is an inadequate alternative to giving in to a sense of . . . tragedy [1963b:300]." Surely, social stratification is a tragedy in itself and a source of tragedy compounded. Mills believed that understanding should lead to responsible action, and suggested that an "effective way to plan the world's future is to criticize the decisions of the present [1963b: 303]." This chapter is offered in that spirit, for I believe stratification to be a product of decisions of the recent past and the present rather than an inevitable feature of the human condition. Decisions can be reversed. A decision to minimize and finally eliminate stratification is urgent and vital, for stratification is the source of invidious advantages and disadvantages among people, and therefore, of the suffering, resentment, fear, and conflict that are their products. Social inequality as presently constituted in the world is at the root of the most immediate, fundamental, and fateful threats facing humankind.

References

Adams, Robert McC.
  1966   The Evolution of Urban Society. Chicago: Aldine.
Andreas, Carol
  1971   Sex and Caste in America. Englewood Cliffs, New Jersey: Prentice-Hall.
Asad, Talal
  1979   Equality in Nomadic Social Systems? Notes Towards the Dissolution of an Anthropological Category. In Pastoral Production and Society. Equipe Écologie et Anthropologie des Sociétés Pastorales, ed. Pp. 419–428. Cambridge: Cambridge University Press.
Barth, Fredrik (ed.)
  1978   Scale and Social Organization. Oslo: Universitetsforlaget.
Beidelman, Thomas O.
  1959   A Comparative Analysis of the Jajmani System. Locust Valley, New York: J. J. Augustin.
Berger, Peter L., and Richard John Neuhaus
  1977   To Empower People: The Role of Mediating Structures in Public Policy. Washington, D.C.: American Enterprise Institute for Public Policy Research.
Berreman, Gerald D.
  1955   Inquiry into Community Integration in an Aleutian Village. American Anthropologist 57:49–59.
  1960   Caste in India and the United States. American Journal of Sociology 66: 120–127.
  1962   Sib and Clan Among the Pahari of North India. Ethnology 1:524–528.
  1963   Hindus of the Himalayas. Berkeley: University of California Press. (Second ed., Hindus of the Himalayas: Ethnography and Change, University of California Press, 1972.)
  1964   Aleut Reference Group Alienation, Mobility, and Acculturation. American Anthropologist 66:231–250.
  1966   Caste in Cross-Cultural Perspective. In Japan's Invisible Race: Caste in Culture and Personality. George DeVos and Hiroshi Wagatsuma, eds. Pp. 275–324. Berkeley: University of California Press.
  1968   Caste: The Concept of Caste. In International Encyclopedia of the Social Sciences. David Sills, ed., Vol. 2. Pp. 333–339. New York: Macmillan and Free Press.
  1969   Women's Roles and Politics: India and the United States. In Readings in General Sociology. Fourth ed. R. W. O'Brien, C. C. Schrag, and W. T. Martin, eds. Pp. 68–71. Boston: Houghton, Mifflin.

1971   The Brahmannical View of Caste. Contributions to Indian Sociology (New Series) 5:18–25.
1972a   Race, Caste, and Other Invidious Distinctions in Social Stratification. Race 13:385–414.
1972b   Social Categories and Social Interaction in Urban India. American Anthropologist 74: 567–586.
1973a   Caste in the Modern World. Morristown, New Jersey: General Learning Press.
1973b   Self, Situation, and Escape from Stigmatized Ethnic Identity. In 1971 Yearbook of the Ethnographic Museum, University of Oslo, Management of Minority Status. Jan Brøgger, ed. Pp. 11–25. Oslo: Universitetsforlaget.
1976   Social Mobility and Change in India's Caste Society. In Responses to Change: Society, Culture, and Personality. George DeVos, ed. Pp. 294–322. New York: D. Van Nostrand.
1977   Social Barriers: Caste, Class, and Race in Cross-Cultural Perspective. Papers in Anthropology, University of Oklahoma 18:217–242. (Special Issue honoring Morris E. Opler.)
1978   Scale and Social Relations. Current Anthropology 19:225–245. (An earlier version appears in Barth, 1978, cited previously, pp. 41–77.)
1979a   Caste and Other Inequities: Essays on Inequality. Delhi: Manohar Books.
1979b   The Evolutionary Status of Caste in Peasant India. In Caste and Other Inequities. Gerald D. Berreman, ed. Pp. 313–325. Delhi: Manohar Books. (Revised version forthcoming: In Social Anthropology of Peasantry. Joan P. Mencher, ed., Durham, North Carolina: Carolina Academic Press.)
1980   Is the Consideration of Human Rights Merely a Politicized Luxury in the World Today? Anthropology and Humanism Quarterly 5: 2–13.
Béteille, André, ed.
1969   Social Inequality: Selected Readings. Middlesex, England: Penguin Books.
Bloch, Marc
1931   Feudalism: European. In Encyclopedia of the Social Sciences. R. A. Seligman, ed. Vol. 6. Pp. 203–210. New York: Macmillan.
Bodley, John H.
1976   Anthropology and Contemporary Human Problems. Menlo Park, California: Cummings.
Bohannan, Paul
1963   Social Anthropology. New York: Holt, Rinehart and Winston.
Braidwood, Robert J., and Gordon R. Willey, eds.
1962   Courses Toward Urban Life: Archaeological Consideration of Some Cultural Alternatives. Viking Fund Publications in Anthropology, No. 32. New York: Wenner-Gren Foundation for Anthropological Research.
Cancian, Frank
1976   Social Stratification. In Annual Review of Anthropology. Bernard J. Siegel, ed. Vol. 5. Pp. 227–248. Palo Alto, California: Annual Reviews.
Childe, V. Gordon
1946   What Happened in History. New York: Penguin Books.
Chorover, Stephan L.
1979   From Genesis to Genocide: The Meaning of Human Nature and the Power of Behavior Control. Cambridge, Massachusetts: MIT Press.
Claessen, Henri J. M., and Peter Skalnik, eds.
1978   The Early State. The Hague: Mouton.
Cohen, Ronald
1968   State Origins: A Reappraisal. In The Early State. H. J. M. Claessen and P. Skalnik, eds. Pp. 31–75. The Hague: Mouton.
Cohen, Ronald, and Elman R. Service, eds.
1978   Origins of the State: The Anthropology of Political Evolution. Philadelphia: Institute for the Study of Human Issues.

Cohen, Yehudi A.
  1968   Culture as Adaptation. *In* Man in Adaptation: The Cultural Present. Yehudi A. Cohen,
        ed. Pp. 40–60. Chicago: Aldine.
Dahrendorf, Ralf
  1968   On the Origin of Inequality Among Men. *In* Essays in the Theory of Society. Ralf Dah-
        rendorf, ed. Pp. 151–178. Stanford, California: Stanford University Press.
Diamond, Stanley
  1974   In Search of the Primitive: A Critique of Civilization. New Brunswick, New Jersey:
        Transaction Books.
Eberstadt, Nick
  1976   Myths of the Food Crisis. The New York Review (February 19) pp. 32–37.
Fallers, Lloyd A.
  1973   Inequality: Social Stratification Reconsidered. Chicago: University of Chicago Press.
Faris, Ellsworth
  1932   The Primary Group: Essence and Accident. American Journal of Sociology 38:41–50.
Finley, M. I.
  1968   Slavery. *In* International Encyclopedia of the Social Sciences. D. L. Sills, ed. Vol. 14.
        Pp. 307–313. New York: Macmillan and Free Press.
Flannery, Kent V.
  1972   The Cultural Evolution of Civilizations. *In* Annual Review of Ecology and Systematics.
        R. F. Johnston, P. W. Frank, and C. D. Michener, eds. Vol. 3. Pp. 399–426. Palo Alto,
        California: Annual Reviews.
Fogelson, Raymond D., and R. N. Adams, eds.
  1977   The Anthropology of Power: Ethnographic Studies from Asia, Oceania and the New
        World. New York: Academic Press.
Foner, Anne
  1979   Ascribed and Achieved Bases of Stratification. *In* Annual Review of Sociology. Alex
        Inkeles, ed. Vol. 5. Pp. 219–242. Palo Alto, California: Annual Reviews.
Freeman, James M.
  1977   Scarcity and Opportunity in an Indian Village. Menlo Park, California: Cummings.
  1979   Untouchable: An Indian Life History. Stanford, California: Stanford University Press.
Fried, Morton
  1960   On the Evolution of Social Stratification and the State. *In* Culture and History: Essays In
        Honor of Paul Radin. Stanley Diamond, ed. Pp. 713–731. New York: Columbia Univer-
        sity Press.
  1967   The Evolution of Political Society. New York: Random House.
Gans, Herbert J.
  1974   More Equality. New York: Vintage Books.
Gavan, James D. and John A. Dixon
  1975   India: A Perspective on the Food Situation. *In* Food: Politics, Economics, Nutrition, and
        Research. Philip H. Abelson, ed. Pp. 49–57. Washington, D.C.: American Association
        for the Advancement of Science.
Geertz, Clifford
  1963   The Integrative Revolution: Primordial Sentiments and Civil Politics in the New States.
        In Old Societies and New States. Clifford Geertz, ed. Pp. 105–157. New York: Free Press
        of Glencoe.
Goffman, Erving
  1961   Asylums: Essays on the Social Situation of Mental Patients and Other Inmates. Garden
        City, New York: Doubleday.
  1963   Stigma: Notes on the Management of Spoiled Identity. Englewood Cliffs, New Jersey:
        Prentice-Hall.
Gould, Harold A.
  1971   Caste and Class: A Comparative View. Morristown, New Jersey: General Learning
        Press.

Henry, Jules
   1963   Culture Against Man. New York: Random House.
   1973a Personality and Aging—With Special Reference to Hospitals for the Aged Poor. In On
          Sham, Vulnerability and Other Forms of Self-Destruction. Jules Henry, ed. Pp. 16–39.
          New York: Random House.
   1973b Ecumenism: An Anthropological View. In On Sham, Vulnerability and Other Forms of
          Self-Destruction. Jules Henry, ed. Pp. 213–234. New York: Random House.
Hjejle, Benedicte
   1967   Slavery and Agricultural Bondage in South India in the Nineteenth Century. Scandina-
          vian Economic History Review 15 (1 and 2):71–126.
Homans, George C.
   1950   The Human Group. New York: Harcourt, Brace.
Isaacs, Harold R.
   1975   Idols of the Tribe: Group Identity and Political Change. New York: Harper and Row.
Karve, Irawati
   1961   Hindu Society—An Interpretation. Poona: Deccan College.
Kolenda, Pauline M.
   1963   Toward a Model of the Hindu Jajmani System. Human Organization 22:11–31.
   1978   Caste in Contemporary India: Beyond Organic Solidarity. Menlo Park, California:
          Benjamin-Cummings.
Krader, Lawrence
   1978   The Origin of the State Among the Nomads of Asia. In The Early State. H. J. M. Claes-
          sen and P. Skalnik, eds. Pp. 93–107. The Hague: Mouton.
Leacock, Eleanor
   1978   Women's Status in Egalitarian Society: Implications for Social Evolution. Current An-
          thropology 19:247–275.
Levi-Strauss, Claude
   1963   The Bear and the Barber. Journal of the Royal Anthropological Institute 93:1–11.
Lewis, Michael
   1978   The Culture of Inequality. New York: New American Library.
Lowie, Robert H.
   1948   Social Organization. New York: Rinehart.
Marx, K.
   1968   The Eighteenth Brumaire of Louis Bonaparte. In Karl Marx and Frederick Engels, Se-
          lected Works. Pp. 97–180. New York: International Publishers. (First ed. 1852.)
Mernissi, Fatima
   1975   Beyond the Veil: Male–Female Dynamics in a Modern Muslim Society. New York: John
          Wiley and Sons.
Merton, Robert K.
   1968   Contributions to the Theory of Reference Group Behavior and Continuities in the The-
          ory of Reference Groups and Social Structure. In Social Theory and Social Structure.
          Robert K. Merton, ed. Pp. 279–440. New York: Free Press.
Miller, Frank C.
   1977   Knowledge and Power: Anthropology, Policy Research, and The Green Revolution.
          American Ethnologist 4:190–198.
Millett, Kate
   1971   Sexual Politics. New York: Avon Books.
Mills, C. Wright
   1963a On Knowledge and Power. In Power, Politics, and People: The Collected Essays of C.
          Wright Mills, I. L. Horowitz, ed. Pp. 599–613. New York: Ballantine Books.
   1963b The Social Role of the Intellectual. In Power, Politics and People: The Collected Essays
          of C. Wright Mills. I. L. Horowitz, ed. Pp. 292–304. New York: Ballantine Books.
Murdock, George P.
   1949   Social Structure. New York: Macmillan.

Nader, Laura, and Stephen Beckerman
    1978   Energy as It Relates to the Quality and Style of Life. *In* Annual Review of Energy. J. M.
           Hollander, M. K. Simmons, D. O. Wood, eds. Vol. 3. Pp. 1–28. Palo Alto, California:
           Annual Reviews.
Pease, John, William H. Form, and Joan H. Rytina
    1970   Ideological Currents in American Stratification Literature. American Sociologist 5:127–
           137.
Perlman, David
    1977   Clash Here Over a Scientific Theory. San Francisco Chronicle. P. 5. June 15.
Plotnicov, Leonard, and Arthur Tuden, eds.
    1970   Essays in Comparative Social Stratification. Pittsburgh: University of Pittsburgh Press.
Ratcliffe, John
    1978   Social Justice and the Demographic Transition: Lessons from India's Kerala State. Inter-
           national Journal of Health Services 8:123–144.
Riley, M. W. *et al.*
    1968–72 Aging and Society. 3 vols. New York: Russell Sage.
Romano, Octavio I., V
    1969   Warehousing. Unpublished manuscript.
    1971   Notes on the Modern State. El Grito 4 (3):78–88.
Rousseau, Jean-Jacques
    1974   Discouse on the Origin and Basis of Inequality Among Men. *In* The Essential Rousseau.
           Lowell Bair, trans. Pp. 125–201. New York: New American Library. (First ed. 1755).
Rudolph, Lloyd I., and Susan H. Rudolph
    1960   The Political Role of India's Caste Associations. Pacific Affairs 33:5–22.
Sahlins, Marshall D.
    1968   Tribesmen. Englewood Cliffs, New Jersey: Prentice-Hall.
Schlegel, Alice
    1977   Toward a Theory of Sexual Stratification. *In* Sexual Stratification: A Cross-Cultural
           View. A. Schlegel, ed. Pp. 1–40. New York: Columbia University Press.
Schurmann, Franz
    1968   Ideology and Organization in Communist China. Second ed. Berkeley: University of
           California Press.
Schutz, Alfred
    1962   The Problem of Social Reality. Collected Papers, Vol. I. Maurice Natanson, ed. The
           Hague: Martinus Nijhoff.
Sennett, Richard, and Jonathan Cobb
    1972   The Hidden Injuries of Class. New York: Random House.
Service, Elman R.
    1966   The Hunters. Englewood Cliffs, New Jersey: Prentice-Hall.
    1971   Primitive Social Organization. Second ed. New York: Random House.
    1975   Origins of the State and Civilization. New York: W. W. Norton.
Sharma, K. N.
    1969   Resource Networks and Resource Groups in the Social Structure. Eastern Anthropolo-
           gist 22:13–17.
Shils, Edward A.
    1957   Primordial, Personal, Sacred, and Civil Ties. British Journal of Sociology 8:130–145.
Shils, Edward A., and Morris Janowitz
    1948   Cohesion and Disintegration in the Wehrmacht in World War II. Public Opinion Quar-
           terly 12:280–315.
Siegel, Bernard T.
    1945   Some Methodological Considerations for a Comparative Study of Slavery. American
           Anthropologist 47:357–392.
Smith, M. G.
    1966   Pre-Industrial Stratification Systems. *In* Social Structure and Mobility in Economic De-
           velopment. N. J. Smelser and S. M. Lipset, eds. Pp. 141–176. Chicago: Aldine.

Srinivas, M. N.
  1966   Social Change in Modern India. Berkeley: University of California Press.
Stewart, Frank H.
  1977   Fundamentals of Age-Group Systems. New York: Academic Press.
Tönnies, Ferdinand
  1940   Fundamental Concepts in Society. C. Loomis, ed. and trans. New York: American
         Book.
Townsend, John Marshall
  1979   Stereotypes of Mental Illness: A Comparison with Ethnic Stereotypes. Culture, Medicine
         and Psychiatry 3: 205–229.
Watson, James L., ed.
  1980   Asian and African Systems of Slavery. Berkeley: University of California Press.
Weber, Max
  1946   Class, Status, and Party. In Max Weber: Essays in Sociology. H. H. Gerth and C. W.
         Mills, eds. and trans. Pp. 180–195. Oxford: Oxford University Press.
  1968   Economy and Society, Vol. 1. Guenther Roth and Claus Wittich, eds. New York: Bed-
         minster Press.
Wesolowski, W.
  1969   The Notions of Strata and Class in Socialist Society. In Social Inequality: Selected Read-
         ings. A. Beteille, ed. Pp. 122–145. Middlesex, England: Penguin Books.
Whyte, Martin King
  1973   Bureaucracy and Modernization in China: The Maoist Critique. American Sociological
         Review 38:149–163.
  1975   Inequality and Stratification in China. China Quarterly, No. 64, Pp. 684–711. Decem-
         ber.
Wiser, William H.
  1936   The Hindu Jajmani System. Lucknow: Lucknow Publishing House.

2

ERIC R. WOLF

The Mills of Inequality:
A Marxian Approach

*It is no longer an accident that capitalist and worker
confront each other as buyer and seller in the
commodity market. It is the rotary mill of the process
itself, which continuously throws back one of them
upon the market as seller of his labor power and
converts his own product into the purchasing power of
the other. Indeed the worker belongs to capital, before
he sells himself to the capitalist.*
—Marx (1867/1923:513)

In this symposium we have been asked to consider social inequality from
a comparative and developmental perspective. Berreman has appropriately
pointed to the relative paucity of such considerations in recent anthropology,
though Stanley Diamond might justifiably argue that the issue of equality and
inequality has constituted the hidden agenda of anthropology since its beginning (see, *inter alia*, Diamond, 1974). Berreman invites us to embark on a
general discussion of the topic, and yet one grounded in empirical evidence. If
anthropology has anything to contribute to an understanding of this topic, it
should be because of the wealth of culturally different situations studied by
anthropologists.

Anthropologists normally attempt a task of cross-cultural comparison by
first assembling "cases," models of societies or cultures constructed from
observed or reported data. These models are then either compared synchronically or seriated with respect to each other, using one or more
diagnostic criteria to order the cases in question. On occasion, the synchronic
or seriated sequence is given a diachronic interpretation and placed in a frame
of elapsed time to arrive at statements of process (e.g., "adaptation" or
"development"). We are all familiar with these procedures, and probably have
employed them ourselves at some time. We know that it can be done and is
done, often with scientifically and aesthetically pleasing results.

41

SOCIAL INEQUALITY
Comparative and Developmental Approaches

I would, however, raise a number of objections to this procedure. First, we often take the data observed or recorded as realities in and of themselves, rather than as more or less tangible results of underlying processes operating in historical time. What we then see and compare are these tangible and observable (and indeed often temporary) precipitates of processes, not the processes themselves. Second, we have known at least since the diffusionists that no society or culture is an island. There are always interchanges and interrelationships with other societies and cultures. What seems less obvious, however, is that these interrelated "cases" appeared in the ken of Europocentric anthropology only because Europeans or Euro-Americans visited them, and these visitors did so because they were propelled by forces that were the outcome of something we call capitalism. Thus, what we explore and observe in the locations anthropologists visit around the world stands in a specific relationship to this process of expansion, which in turn responds to the workings out of a particular structure or relational set.

This process of expansion is historically identifiable, as are the reactions to it. This makes it possible to place our "cases" in an empirically identifiable time-series of contexts. We are then of course no longer dealing with pristine Ojibwa, Ndembu, Bemba, or Ponapeans, but with populations engaged in continuous cultural buildup, breakdown, anabolism, catabolism, rearrangement, organization, reorganization. Once we realize this, we also realize how limiting it is to compare cases without some grip on the underlying processes that govern their interrelationships. It is further limiting to construct conjectural history for our cases, when we now have at our disposal processual histories that situate the cases we study in their variable interchanges with expanding capitalism (see e.g., Wasserstrom [1977] on Chiapas; Miller [1975] on the Congo; Ranger [1968] and Ranger and Kimambo [1972] on East and Central African religious movements; Bishop and Ray [1976] on the Indians trading into Hudson Bay.)

Yet taking advantage of such materials and insights invites a further step, a step toward the construction of adequate theory. Is it possible to construct a theoretical model of the major relationships that motivate capitalist expansion? Would such a construct help us to explain what occurred in the interchanges between the Athabascan speakers and the fur traders, between the East India Company and the cotton growers of Maharashtra, between the inhabitants of the Rhodesian copper belt and the Roan Antelope mine? Is it possible to develop theoretical constructs that would allow us to grasp the significant elements organizing populations not organized capitalistically, but contacted engulfed, or reorganized by advancing capitalism?

Recent discussions among Marxist historians, anthropologists, and *philosophes* have drawn renewed attention to Marx's notion of the mode of production as such a central, unifying, explanatory concept. (See, among the growing number of contributions on this topic, Althusser and Balibar, 1970; Coquery-Vidrovitch, 1969; Godelier, 1970; Meillassoux, 1960, 1967; Sahlins,

1972; Terray, 1969; Tökei, 1966; Töpfer, 1975; and Wittfogel, 1931, 1957.) I will try to show later why this concept has theoretical import for a comparative anthropology, and—specifically—what it has to offer to anthropologists interested in the problem of social inequality.[1]

Outline of the Argument

Since Marx's method differs from those we are accustomed to, I shall first discuss Marx's general approach. I shall then outline three modes of production: (1) the capitalist mode, much as Marx did; (2) a family of modes, variously called Asiatic, African, and feudal, which I will treat as variants of one larger "tributary" mode; and (3) a "kin-ordered" mode, so called to avoid the semantic trap set by the term "primitive." I shall then sum up briefly the implications of the presentation for the topic of this symposium.

Marx's Method

Many of the difficulties with Marx's method flow from the fact that it runs counter to much of what we now accept as the common sense of science. That common sense is of course itself uncommon, and based on presuppositions that need to be clarified. I shall briefly summarize these presuppositions, as they were formulated by David Hume. All we can know, according to Hume, are perceived characteristics. We cannot assume that back of these perceived characteristics there lies any kind of unifying essence or substance that could account for their coherence. Since we cannot assume any such unifying essence, we can say nothing about causality. All we can do is to note the co-occurrence, the conjunction of phenomena. When we assert that two phenomena have taken place together, we cannot assume that they will invariably occur together again in the future, though we may wish to do so. All we can do is to ensure that our technical methods for recording co-occurrence

[1] I am aware that the term *mode of production* (*Produktionsweise* in Marx) sounds awkward today. Yet it enshrines the basic Marxian insights that humans differ from other animals by transforming nature, and that they do this socially. It thus carries a freight of overtones of Marx's confrontation with idealism (Hegel) and contemplative materialism (Feuerbach). For Hegel (as I suppose for Clifford Geertz) the various human transformations of nature were successive concretizations of Spirit ("models of" and "models for"). Feuerbach, in turn, took no account of human sociality and of human socialities in confrontation with nature. Marx was thus interested in stressing the active role of socially organized human kind in the double sense of transforming nature and of creating and recreating (producing and reproducing) the social ties that activate that transformation. I take this to be "what Marx really meant," although I am aware (a) that he was often content merely to indicate the direction he was taking rather than lose himself in terminological battles, and (b) like Hegel, often played with words for fun, in puns familiar to his readers but lost on the "serious doctors" who now interpret him.

or its absence are sound, and not influenced by personal or collective wishes. Only if our methods are sound can they compel consensus. The soundest of methods is to quantify the characteristics of phenomena, for quantification eliminates the element of human subjectivity. (As Kolakowski [1969] notes, this leads to the curious paradox that qualitative features may have to be eliminated in order to compel consensus about the perceived characteristics in question. Yet mathematical ideas can only be said to be valid or invalid; they cannot tell us about the existence of anything.)

This common sense view of science was developed pragmatically by August Comte, the founder of sociology. He added the idea that if our methods for noting co-occurences were sound, they could be used to increase human control over nature and over human social life, thus enhancing man's chances of survival. Truth then is what works.

Now Marx also speaks of his inquiries as science, or, rather, as *Wissenschaft*. This also denotes a process of discovering knowledge, but by a different approach. As against the view that all human beings can do is to note the co-occurence of perceived characteristics through methods they have agreed upon, Marx—and others—begin with what they regard as the undeniable aspects of human experience. These undeniable aspects of human experience are the relation of human beings to nature, the social relations of human beings with one another, the human capacity to transform nature to human use, and the symbolic capabilities of *Homo sapiens*. The names we give to these aspects of human experience, the concepts we apply to them, are products of the historical circumstances in which we pursue understanding; but the aspects themselves are seen as fundamental and real. The task of *Wissenschaft*, then, is to explicate these facets of experience through concepts that will exhibit their interconnections. As Marx puts it, "the hidden substratum of phenomena must first be discovered by science," and, indeed, "science would be superfluous if the outward appearance and the essence of things directly coincided [Marx, 1867/1923:478; 1894/1967:817]."

The thrust of inquiry, however, is from the necessarily abstract formulation that tries to grasp the "essence" of things toward the explication of concrete phenomena. This is what Marx meant by "ascending from the abstract to the concrete." The road from the abstract formulation to the explication of the concrete leads over a series of conceptual approximations to the explication of particular phenomena occurring in particular places and times. Marx clearly characterized the first two steps in approximation: the concept of the *labor process*, and the concept of the *mode* of production. He also attempted to delineate a number of different modes of production. A third step in approximation is to conceptualize a *social formation*, a historically concrete "society," embodying one or more modes of production. Marx and Engels employed the term, but did not account for it theoretically. This task remains unfinished. A fourth step or level of approximation is the observation and interpretation of social interaction and the cultural forms that mediate it, both within and between various social formations.

FIRST STEP: THE LABOR PROCESS

Let us begin with the first step, the step of conceptualizing the labor process. I have said that in this undertaking Marx began with what he considered to be real, fundamental aspects of human existence. The first of these aspects involves the species of *Homo sapiens*, both as a product of nature and as an actor engaged in transforming nature to human use, or—as Marx (1867/1923:133) put it in Hegelian language—"man confronts the material of nature as one of nature's own forces." The spread of ecological thinking has made this a commonplace in anthropology. At the same time, Marx's formulation reminds us that the relation of the species to nature is dual in character: *Homo sapiens* is subject to the imperatives and constraints of the environment; yet also plays an active role in transforming it. This active role is, moreover, predicated not only on the somatic characteristics of *Homo sapiens*, but also on its exosomatic or cultural characteristics.

The next point follows from the first. The way *Homo sapiens* transforms nature for its own purposes is through labor. "The labor process. . . is the general condition for the metabolism between man and nature; it is the everlasting nature-imposed condition of human existence [Marx, 1867/ 1923:139]." This seemingly obvious pronouncement hides a significant theoretical formulation. Marx draws a distinction between work and labor. Work can be the activities of an individual, expending energy to produce energy. But the labor process as a whole is a social phenomenon, carried on by human beings linked to one another through social relationships. This concept of labor in general, as opposed to particular kinds of work, is not self-evident. Marx credited Adam Smith with its formulation, adding that this "immense step forward" became possible only when different kinds of labor had in fact become monetarily interchangeable (1857–1858/1973:104). Once it became possible to talk about labor in general, it also became possible to visualize how human beings forming organized pluralities assign labor to the technical processes of work and share out the products of social labor among themselves. Understanding how human beings transform nature to their use thus does not stop with the description and analysis of how they work. It also requires a description and analysis of the social relations that govern the deployment of social labor and the allocation of the social product that this labor creates. The laborer, the direct producer, is never an isolated Robinson Crusoe, but always someone who stands in relationship to others, as kinsman, serf, slave, or wage-laborer. The controllers of social labor and production are not identical with the technicians who implement the technical operations of work. They are actors in a socially determined and implemented scheme by which social labor is deployed, as elder kinsmen, chiefs, seignorial lords, or capitalists. This perspective allows us to see how the technical division of labor and the processes of work operate in crucial conjunction with social relations of production. Marx thus conceptualized a way in which these two aspects of the human labor process could be thought of together, rather than in separation from each other.

This process by which people in social relationships with one another deploy labor and allocate its products governs both hand *and* head. In contrast to other animals, human beings conceptualize and plan the labor process. Labor thus presupposes intentionality, and therefore information and meaning. As labor is always social labor, so information and meaning are always social, and carried in social ideation. This is not the place to expound at length on Marxian views of ideation, except to underline three recurrent aspects of such views. One is that ideation follows directionality or vectors; it travels along the lines of force generated by the mode in the movement of its elements. A second is that ideation in any given mode encounters external limits, beyond which it cannot go—its horizon (Goldman, 1969). Finally, ideation also encounters internal limits, crucial junctures of the elements constituting a mode, where the current of ideation will be short-circuited and displaced along a "safe" bypass. This creates the phenomenon of "fetishism" or "mystification" (see Godelier, 1973; Taussig, 1977). In what follows I will briefly refer to characteristic modal vectors and mystifications in ideation.

If this relation of human beings' ideation to labor goes unrecognized, thought becomes either completely subjective or wholly independent of people's engagement with the world, "myth thinking itself through men," as Lévi-Strauss (1964:20) has put it. If thought is wholly subjective, there is then no way of assessing its adequacy or inadequacy. If it is wholly independent of what human beings do, change in thought remains unaccounted for, a mere play of the spirit. The emergence of humankind from the matrix of nature, its transformation of nature through social labor, its transformation, indeed, of its own nature all imply change, are historical processes. They are historical processes not in the sense of one event following another, but of changes in relationships between people, labor, and nature. They have changed in the past, they are changing now, and they will change in the future.

SECOND STEP: THE MODE OF PRODUCTION

Given this perspective, we can now conceptualize the major ways in which human beings organize their social relations of production as well as their processes of work. Each such major way constitutes a mode of production, a specific, historically occurring set of social relations through which social labor is deployed to wrest energy from nature by means of tools, skills, organization, and knowledge. To say it again, the concept invites us to consider technics and work and social imperatives in mutual relationship instead of separately.

How many such major ways of interrelating work and guiding social relations are there? In Marx's own writings we find mention of a number of different modes of production: an original, primitive, communitarian mode, conceived after Morgan's model of primitive communism; the slaveholding mode of classical European antiquity; a Germanic mode, supposedly characteristic of the Germanic peoples in their early migrations; a Slavonic mode, said to characterize the early Slavs; a peasant mode; a feudal mode; an Asiatic mode; and a capitalist mode. Not all of these are based on equivalent criteria. Some of them may never have constituted primary modes in their own right, but only accessory or supplementary modes; still others represent extrapolations from historical interpretations now adjudged to have been faulty or erroneous. Nevertheless, Marx indicates how he construed the concept when he says:

> Bourgeois society is the most developed and the most varied organization of production. Hence the categories which express its relations, our understanding of its articulation, at the same time guarantee insight into the articulation and production relations of all past forms of society, with debris and elements of which bourgeois society is built, certain unsubdued remnants of which still survive inside it, and certain mere hints of which it develops to their full significance, etc. The anatomy of man is the key to the anatomy of the ape. The pointers to higher species of animals in the lower species can only be understood if the higher species itself is already known. Thus the bourgeois economy provides the key to the economy of antiquity, etc. [Marx, 1857–1858/1973:105].

The Capitalist Mode

What, then, according to Marx, are the salient characteristics of the capitalist mode of production? For Marx, the mode comes into being when monetary wealth is enabled to buy labor power. This specific capability is not an inherent attribute of wealth as such; it develops historically, and requires the installation of certain prerequisites. Labor power is not a commodity created to be offered for sale in a market. It is a form of human energy, a capability of *Homo sapiens*. As long as people can lay their hands on the means of production (tools, resources, land) and use these to supply their own sustenance—under whatever social arrangements—there is no compelling reason for them to sell their capacity to work to someone else in order to eat. Thus, for labor power to be offered for sale, the tie between producers and the means of production have to be severed for good. This means that holders of wealth must be able to acquire the means of production and deny access to all who want to operate them, except on their own terms. Conversely, people who are denied access to the means of production must come to the holders of wealth who now control them and bargain with them for permission to operate these means of production, in return for wages that will allow them to pay for what they need to sustain themselves.

Indeed, in the capitalist mode production determines distribution. Those who restrict the means of production can also withhold the commodities produced. Those who labor to produce the commodities must buy them back from the owners of the means of production. Means of production, in turn, circulate only among those with capital to acquire them. Hence the way in which the mode commits social labor to the transformation of nature also governs the way the resources used and obtained are distributed among producers and nonproducers. Streams of resources, including income, are not—as one ecologically oriented anthropologist wrote recently (Love, 1977)—the human analogue of the way biological organisms capture energy. Between people and resources stand the strategic relationships governing the mode of allocating social labor to nature.

The holders of wealth who now hold the means of production, however, would have no reason to hire laborers to operate them if the laborers produced only enough to cover the costs of their wage package. In the course of a working day they in fact produce more than is required to cover the costs of their subsistence; they produce a surplus. This surplus, under the conditions of the capitalist mode, belongs to the individual or corporation whose means of production the workers have put into operation. The greater this surplus, the greater the rate of profit obtained by the capitalist when he measures it against his outlays for plant, resources, and labor. There are two ways in which capitalists can increase this surplus. The first is by keeping wages low, or decreasing them to the lowest possible point that is energetically or socially feasible. The other is to raise the level of surplus produced through raising the output of the workers. Such increases in productivity require improvements in the technology of production. These imperatives produce relentless pressures, spurring capitalists to ever-increased accumulation of capital and renewal of technology. The greater the capital at their command, the greater their ability to raise productivity, and hence the greater their ability to accumulate further surplus for additional expansion of production. Conversely, the greater the technological productivity at their command, the greater their ability to outproduce and undersell competitors who either fail to invest in new technology or who attempt to meet competition through placing greater burdens on their labor. The capitalist mode thus shows three intertwined characteristics. First, capitalists control the means of production. Second, laborers are denied independent access to means of production and must sell their labor power to the capitalists. Third, the maximization of surplus produced by the laborers with the means of production owned by the capitalists entails "ceaseless accumulation accompanied by changes in methods of production [Sweezy, 1942:94; see also Mandel, 1972:103–108]."

These characteristics, however, must be understood not only synchronically, operating at any given time, but historically, as developing facets of a mode that has determinate origins in time and develops over time. The point is crucial. Wealth in the hands of holders of wealth is not capital until it controls the means of production, buys labor power and puts it to work, expands and begins to raise surpluses by intensifying productivity through an ever-increasing curve of technological inputs. To accomplish this, capitalism must lay hold of production, must invade the productive process and ceaselessly alter the conditions of production themselves. As long as wealth remains external to the process of production, merely skimming off the products of the primary producers and making profits by selling them, that wealth is *not* capital. It may be wealth obtained and engrossed by overlords or merchants, but it has not yet entered what Marx called "the really revolutionary road" of affecting and transforming the means of production themselves (1894/1967:334). Only where wealth has laid hold of the conditions of production in the ways specified can we speak of the existence or dominance of a capitalist mode. Therefore, there is no such thing as mercantile or merchant capitalism. There is only mercantile wealth. Capitalism, to be capitalism, must be capitalism-in-production.

The capitalist mode, as conceptualized in this construct, therefore enshrines one major inequality that it continuously reproduces: inequality between those who hold the means of production and those who must seek employment in order to gain their subsistence. But it continuously produces further inequalities: a continuous process of differentiation into victors and losers among the owners of the means of production, and another process—equally continuous—of separating the working force into survivors and castaways. The two processes are actually linked, since the shareholders in capital are continuously driven to seek new pools of tractable labor or to replace dear or intractable labor with machines. Marx's model may thus be thought of as a set of relations created among historically developed elements—capital, labor, and machines—that continuously create, recreate, and widen the field of force directing and constraining social relations. Among the social relations thus set in motion is the vaunted and segmented labor market of modern society that continuously recreates real and invidious distinctions among the labor force.

The Tributary Mode

The capitalist mode was historically incubated in societies of a different kind, and encountered other such different societies in the course of its expansion. Among these were societies politically organized to extract surpluses from the primary producers by political and military means. Marx characterized the key attribute of this other mode as follows:

> It is . . . evident that in all forms in which the direct laborer remains the "possessor" of the means of production and labor conditions necessary for the production of his own means of subsistence, the property relationship must simultaneously appear as a direct relation of lordship and servitude, so that the direct producer is not free; a lack of freedom which may be reduced from serfdom with enforced labor to a mere

> tributary relationship. The direct producer, according to our assumption, is to be found here in possession of his own means of production, the necessary material labor conditions required for the realization of his labor and the production of his own means of subsistence. He conducts his agricultural activity and the rural home industries connected with it independently. . . . Under such conditions the surplus labor for the nominal owner of the land can only be extorted from them by other than economic pressure, whatever the form assumed may be. . . [1894/1967:790–791].

In other words, social labor is, under these conditions, mobilized and committed to the transformation of nature primarily through the exercise of power and domination—through a political process. Hence, the deployment of social labor is, in this mode, a function of the locus of political power, and will differ in kind as this locus shifts position.

It is possible to envisage these shifting differentials in the unequal distribution of power by visualizing two alternative situations: one in which power is firmly concentrated in the hands of a ruling elite standing at the apex of the power system, and another in which power is largely held by local overlords and the rule at the apex is fragile and weak.

These two situations are not independent of one another; they operate on a continuum of power distributions. It is clear that a ruling elite of surplus-takers, standing at the apex of the power system, will be strongest when they control: (a) some strategic element in the process of production, such as waterworks (Wittfogel, 1957: passim), and (b) some strategic element of coercion, such as a standing army of superior military capability. Rulers will then be able to deploy their own tribute-gatherers without need of assistance from local powerholders. They will be able to loosen the grip of local overlords over resources, and hence also over the primary producers of surplus, and render them dependent on revenues tended by the rulers, rather than allowing them to attach surpluses themselves. If the rulers are successful in this strategy they can also induce the local overlords to fight among themselves for privileged positions at the source of revenue. Such a ruling elite will also be able to curtail the powers of traders, keeping them from access to the primary producers through controlled investment in the countryside and preventing them from financing potentially rebellious overlords on their own behalf. Finally, such a strong central power will strive with success to inhibit or place limits on translocal "grassroots" organizations, be they guilds, estates, leagues, or religious sects. At the same time, strong central rule often finds support among the surplus-producing peasantry, since central rulers and peasants are linked by a common antagonism against powerholding and surplus-taking intermediaries.

Conversely, the central power will be weak and local powerholders strong where strategic elements of production as well as means of coercion are in the hands of local surplus-takers. Under such conditions, local leaders can intercept the flow of tribute to the center, strengthen their grip over land and the population working it, and enter into local or regional alliances on their own. Such local alliances, however, are frequently directed not only against the center but also against members of the powerholders' own class, with the result that factional struggles ramify throughout the countryside, thus weakening their class position through internecine fights. Factional struggles, in turn, may allow the elite at the center to survive by strategems of "divide and rule." Paradoxically, internecine fights also weaken the position of the primary producers, since they must seek protectors against unrest and predation in the absence of strong central control.

In broad terms, the two situations I have depicted correspond, respectively, to the Marxian concepts of the "Asiatic" and the "feudal" modes of production. These are usually treated as enduring and unchanging polar opposites. One term is usually ascribed by Marxists to Asia, the other to Europe. The preceding exposition should make clear, however, that we are dealing rather with variable outcomes of the competition between classes of nonproducers for power at the top. To the extent that these variable outcomes are all anchored in mechanisms exerting "other than economic pressure," they will also exhibit a family resemblance to each other (Töpfer, 1967; Vasiliev and Stuchevskii, 1967). This family resemblance is best covered by a common term for this mode, suggested by Samir Amin (1972), the "tributary mode of production." Reification of "feudalism" into a separate mode of production merely converts a short period of European history into a type case, against which all other "feudal-like" phenomena must be measured. The concept of the Asiatic mode of production in which a centralized state bureaucracy lords it over unchanging village communities of hapless peasants, in turn, suffers from an ahistorical and ideological reading of Asian history. It has long been customary in the "West" to counterpose Western freedom with Eastern despotism, whether the contrast was made by Herodotus referring to the Greek city-states in their struggles with Persia, or by Montaigne and Voltaire counterposing societies based on the social contract to societies characterized by multitudes groveling under despotic rule. Our use of the term *tributary mode* should permit us rather to specify the politically relevant variables that distinguish one situation from another. Thus ancient China, with a strongly concentrated hydraulic component, clearly represents a different case of "tributary" relationships than India, with its reliance on dispersed tank irrigation, or Iran, with irrigation by underground wells and canals. Moreover, strongly centralized "Asiatic" states frequently break down into political oligopolies resembling "feudalism," or more "feudal" and dispersed controls by local powerholders and landlords yield to more centralized and concentrated power over time. To reify the weak phases of the Sassanian, Byzantine, or T'ang Chinese state into a "feudal-like" mode of production, and the strong phases of these into an "Asiatic" mode falsely separates into two different modes of production a continuum within a single mode.

If it is true, then, that the tributary mode depends on the weak or strong organization of power in particular states, it follows further that its operation

is at least in part determined by whether that state is weak or strong in relation to other states and social constellations. Shifts of state power in the states
of North Africa and western, central, and eastern Asia, for example, were intimately connected with the military and political expansion and contraction
of pastoral nomadic populations, and with the widening or narrowing of
overland trade. If it is true that noncapitalist class-dependent modes depend
on "other than economic means" for the extraction of surplus, it follows that
successful extraction of such surplus cannot be understood in terms of an
isolated "society" alone but is partially a function of the changing organization of the wider field of power within which the particular tributary con-
stellation is located.

Such wider political and economic fields are usually identifiable as "civilizations," or cultural interaction zones pivoted upon some major tributary
formation within it. Usually it is the ideological model or models developed
and carried by a successful centralizing elite of surplus-takers that is copied or
replicated by other similar elites within the wider politico–economic orbit of
interaction. Although one model may become dominant within a given orbit,
as did the Confucian model carried by the Chinese scholar–gentry, the
civilizational orbit is usually an arena in which a number of models or culture
streams compete or coexist.

These ideological models have certain common characteristics that I will
touch on briefly, since they have some bearing on the issue of inequality. The
ideological model paralleling the tributary mode is typically a hierarchical
representation of the cosmos in which the dominant supernatural order,
working through the superior holders of power, encompasses and subjects
humanity to itself. At the same time, the model displaces the real relation
between power-wielding surplus-takers and dominated producers to the
ideological relation between superior deity and inferior "subject" (see
Feuchtwang, 1975). The problem of public power is thus transformed into a
problem of private morality, and the "subject" is invited to win merit by
maintaining order through the regulation of his own conduct. Paradoxically,
the displacement enshrines a contradiction. If public power falters and justice
is not done, the ties linking subject and supernatural are also called into question. The rulers lose legitimacy; the mandate of Heaven may pass to other
contenders, or people may begin to assert the claims of their private morality
against the official apparatus of mediation. The arguments proferred will deal
with the nature of the tie between "subject" and supernatural, not with the
nature of earthly domination, anchored in "other than economic means."

The Kin-Ordered Mode

To construct our third mode of production requires a knowledge of what
kinship is. Empirically, populations vary in the spread and intensity of kinship. Some people seem to have a "lot" of it; others have much "less." Coresidence is often more significant than genealogical position. Task groups con-

tain non-kin as well as relatives. Among some people, kinship primarily governs filiation and marriage, and constitutes only one ordering element among others. Among other populations, kinship looms large and involves jural and political obligations, as well as ecological, economic, and organizational aspects.

Recognizing all this variation, however, still leaves us on the level of defining what kinship does and not what it is. Although anthropologists claim priority over other disciplines because they "do" kinship and the others do not, actually they cannot agree on what kinship is. Some see it primarily as a matter of sex and procreation; others understand it as an "idiom" for discussing social, economic, political, and other matters: still others see kinship as symbolic, the working out of cultural constructs. I shall not try to resolve these differences, but simply refer the reader to the growing literature on this point (see Schneider, 1972), and state peremptorily that kinship is a way of committing social labor to the transformation of nature through appeals to "filiation," "marriage," "consanguinity," or "affinity." Put simply, social labor is here "locked up" in particular relations between people. It can be mobilized only through access to people, such access being defined symbolically. *What* is done unlocks social labor; *how* it is done involves "emic" definitions of kinsmen and affines. Kinship thus involves symbolic constructs ("filiation"/"marriage"; "consanguinity"/"affinity") that place biologically related actors into social relations with another, which permit people to call on the share of social labor possible from each, in order to effect the necessary transformations of nature.

As anthropologists we recognize that populations differ in the degree to which they rely on symbolic constructs of the narrower sphere ("filiation"/"marriage") in contrast to the wider sphere ("consanguinity"/"affinity"). We know that, among some people, rights in other people (or claims to a share of their social labor) are extended in network-like fashion from particular actors or "egos," while, among other people, rights to claim shares of social labor are extended far beyond the primary biological referent to govern political/jural relations between groups.

While in the first case the symbolic constructs of kinship define mainly who has access to whom, in the second case they involve distinctions between pedigreed groups in relation to some "estate." Put in a slightly different way, where symbolic constructs of narrow gauge predominate, claims to social labor and segments of nature remain "open" or potentially extensible. Where symbolic constructs of wide gauge are invoked, they define who has access to whose share of social labor against other possible claimants, as well as who has permission to transform what segment of nature against other possible transformers. Why descent "rather than locality or some other principle forms the basis of such corporate groups" is, as Fortes put it, "a question that needs more study [1953:30]."

Where the symbolic constructs of kinship are thus "extended," we are likely to find that the relations between the producers of social labor and the transformers of nature are structured monopolistically or oligopolistically. They permit or deny people access to strategic goods. They organize exchanges of persons between groups, through marriages or pawning (see Douglas, 1964), turning marriages into alliances or settling issues of outstanding debts. Such exchanges become clearly political. The symbolic charters of kinship, moreover, lay the basis for the unequal distribution of managerial roles in the political and jural field, whether the classifications are between elders and juniors, seniors and cadets, or members of high-ranking and low-ranking lines.

The tendency to feed on external opposition vis-à-vis other groups goes hand in hand with a multiplication of internal oppositions. First, we find oppositions between men and women. Some complementary equilibrium between gender roles can perhaps be maintained, as long as kinship is but one ordering element in a situation of open resources. Yet, with the emergence of pedigreed groups in the political field, affinal relations become political relations and women lose status in relation to men, as they become tokens of alliance. There is also the opposition of elders and juniors, with elders in characteristic positions of managerial command inside and outside the group. Some juniors may indeed come to be seniors and take their place; but others will never succeed to any position of importance. We know that this opposition can break out into open conflict. Ethnographically, we can point to the rebellion of the "boys" against their elders in the transition from settled village life to mounted hunting on the Great Plains (Holder, 1970) and to the formation of slave-raiding non-kin *quilombos* in Angola (Miller, 1975).

Finally, internal ranking creates opposition between original settlers and newcomers, between senior and junior lines of descent from the same ancestor, and indeed between lines rising to prominence and those in a state of decline. The latter may be due to demographic ascendancy or failure; to successful or unsuccessful management of alliances, people, or resources; to success or failure in war. Ups and downs of this kind seem ever present and ever effective in exacerbating oppositions into tension, conflict, and breakdown.

How then do such units cohere at all over time? How is social solidarity possible? The answer is that it is not or, at any rate, not for very long. The kin-ordered mode can regenerate itself only in the absence of any relation or mechanism that can aggregate or mobilize social labor apart from the particular relations set up by kinship. Moreover, its general internal oppositions seem to appear only in myth and ritual, not on the level of "everyday reality." In "everyday reality" the oppositions played out are always particulate, the conjunction of a particular elder with a particular junior or a particular lineage at a particular time and place, and not the general opposition of elder and junior as members of classes. In "everyday life" the kin-ordered mode regenerates itself and its oppositions by particularizing tensions and conflicts.

Paradoxically, formations built upon the kin-ordered mode do the very opposite in myth and ritual, where oppositions fraught with danger in everyday life are played out and elaborated upon on the level of generality and universality. Now they are connected to messages about ways in which these generalities are anchored in the nature of the universe. Explanations, if offered, take the form of universalized verities.

Conflict resolution, however, whether on the particular or general level, must ultimately encounter its limits in the inability of the kin-ordered mode to solve its structural problems. It can do so only by breakup and fission, and it would be surprising if these were not only frequent but—in fact—important sources of change. It is only by maintaining a fiction of the timeless ethnographic present that one can visualize breakup and fission as reconstituting indefinitely the same order over time. Phenomena such as the ecological circumscription noted by Chagnon (1968)—the hemming in of a population by its neighbors—or encounters with societies in the tributary and capitalist mode render replication unlikely at present, and probably have done so over the course of time.

In contrast to others, therefore, who tend to see societies built up in the kin-ordered mode as egalitarian, I argue instead that they are replete with real inequalities and plagued by resulting tensions. They attempt to cope with conflicts by atomizing them, by generalizing and displacing them onto the supernatural, or by breakup and fission. Unlike societies built up on the tributary or capitalist mode, they lack the ability to aggregate and marshall social labor apart from particulate relationships, and therefore they also lack the means of holding society together, internally and externally, by internal and external violence that ensures the continuity of class domination and contradictions.

Summary

In this chapter, I first presented the rationale for introducing the concept of the mode of production, and then attempted to portray three such modes, different ways of committing social labor to change nature and reproducing the social relations governing that commitment in turn. In the course of doing so, I raised the problem of social inequality not as a phenomenon *sui generis*, but as an accompaniment of the workings out of determinant modes. Implied in this approach is that visible and observable social relations, including those of inequality, are in turn predicated upon relations operating at a deeper level. Each mode exhibits a structural causality or dynamic that continuously creates and recreates basic relations of social inequality, upon which other inequalities are then built up.

In this chapter, I have discussed the three modes separately. This represents merely a first approximation. In real space and time, we find particular societies embodying or combining these modes in historically or geographically distinctive forms. Moreover, they do so in combination or conflict (which is also a kind of combination) with one another. In the world studied by anthropologists, some of the most interesting problems concern the ways in which the expansion of one mode may reinforce or alter inequalities in the other.

References

Althusser, Louis, and Etienne Balibar
  1970 Reading "Capital." New York: Pantheon Books.
Amin, Samir
  1972 Underdevelopment and Dependence in Black Africa: Origins and Contemporary Forms. Journal of Modern African Studies 10(4):503–524.
Bishop, Charles A., and Arthur J. Ray, eds.
  1976 The Fur Trade and Culture Change, Resources and Methods. Western Canadian Journal of Anthropology, Vol. 6, No. 1, special issue.
Chagnon, Napoleon A.
  1968 The Culture-Ecology of Shifting (Pioneering) Cultivation Among the Yanomamö Indians. Proceedings, VIIIth International Congress of Anthropological and Ethnological Sciences, Tokyo and Kyoto, Vol. 3. Pp. 249–255.
Coquery-Vidrovitch, Catherine
  1969 Recherche sur un mode de production africain. La Pensée, No. 144. Pp. 61–78.
Diamond, Stanley
  1974 In Search of the Primitive: A Critique of Civilization. New Brunswick, New Jersey: Transaction Books.
Douglas, Mary
  1964 Matriliny and Pawnship in Central Africa. Africa 34 (4):301–313.
Feuchtwang, Stephan
  1975 Investigating Religion. In Marxist Analysis and Social Anthropology. Maurice Bloch, ed. Pp. 61–82. Association of Social Anthropologists Studies, No. 2.
Fortes, Meyer
  1953 The Structure of Unilineal Descent Groups. American Anthropologist 55(1):17–41.
Godelier, Maurice
  1970 Preface. In Sur les Sociétés précapitalistes. Pp. 13–142. Paris: Editions Sociales.
Goldman, Lucien
  1969 The Hidden God. In Society and Religion. Norman Birnbaum and Gertrud Lenzer, eds. Pp. 292–302. Englewood Cliffs, New Jersey: Prentice-Hall.
Holder, Preston
  1970 The Hoe and the Horse on the Plains. Lincoln: University of Nebraska Press.
Kolakowski, Leszek
  1969 The Alienation of Reason: A History of Positivist Thought. New York: Anchor Books.
Lévi-Strauss, Claude
  1964 Le Cru et le cuit. Paris: Plon.
Love, Thomas F.
  1977 Ecological Niche Theory in Sociocultural Anthropology: A Conceptual Framework and an Application. American Ethnologist 4(1):27–41.
Mandel, Ernest
  1972 Der Spätkapitalismus: Versuch einer marxistischen Erklärung. Frankfurt am Main: Suhrkamp.

Marx, Karl
  1923   Das Kapital: Kritik der politischen Okonomie, Vol. 1. Karl Kautsky, ed. Berlin: Dietz. (First ed. 1867).
  1967   Das Kapital: Kritik der politischen Ökonomie, Vol. 3. Friedrich Engels, ed. New York: International Publishers. (First ed. 1894).
  1973   Grundrisse: Foundations of the Critique of Political Economy (Rough Draft). Martin Nicolaus, ed. London: Allen Lane. (First ed. 1857–1858).
Meillassoux, Claude
  1960   Essai d'interprétation du phénomène économique dans les sociétés traditionelles d'auto-subsistance. Cahiers d'Études Africaines, No. 4. Pp. 38–67.
  1967   Recherche d'un niveau de détermination, dans la société cynégétique. L'Homme et la société, Vol. 6. Pp. 95–106.
Miller, Joseph C.
  1975   Kings and Kinsmen: Early Mbundu States in Angola. London: Oxford University Press.
Ranger, Terence O., ed.
  1968   Emerging Themes of African History. Proceedings, International Congress of African Historians, University College, Dar-es-Salaam, 1965. Nairobi: East Africa Publishing House.
Ranger, Terence O., and Isaria N. Kimambo, eds.
  1972   The Historical Study of African Religion. Berkeley: University of California Press.
Sahlins, Marshall D.
  1972   Stone Age Economics. Chicago: Aldine-Atherton.
Schneider, David M.
  1972   What Is Kinship All About? In Kinship Studies in the Morgan Centennial Year. Priscilla Reining, ed. Pp. 32–63. Washington, D.C.: Anthropological Society of Washington.
Sweezy, Paul M.
  1942   The Theory of Capitalist Development. New York: Oxford University Press.
Taussig, Michael
  1977   The Genesis of Capitalism Amongst a South American Peasantry: Devil's Labor and the Baptism of Money. Comparative Studies in Society and History 19(2):130–155.
Terray, Emmanuel
  1969   Le Marxisme devant les sociétés "primitives." Paris: Maspéro.
Tökei, Ferenc
  1966   Sur le Mode de production asiatique. Budapest: Akademiai Kiado (Academy of Sciences).
Töpfer, Bernhard
  1965   Zu einigen Grundfragen des Feudalismus: Ein Diskussionsbeitrag. Zeitschrift für Geschichtswissenschaft, Vol. 13. Pp. 785–809.
Vasiliev, L. S., and I. A. Stuchevskii
  1967   Three Models for the Origin and Evolution of Precapitalist Societies. Soviet Review: A Journal of Translations 8(2):26–39.
Wasserstrom, Robert
  1977   Land and Labour in Central Chiapas: A Regional Analysis. Development and Change, Vol. 8. Pp. 441–463.
Wittfogel, Karl A.
  1931   Wirtschaft und Gesellschaft Chinas. Part I. Produktivkräfte, Produkts-und Zirkulations-Prozess. Schriften des Instituts für Sozialforschung an der Universität Frankfurt am Main, Vol. 3. Leipzig: C. L. Hirschfeld.
  1957   Oriental Despotism: A Comparative Study of Total Power. New Haven: Yale University Press.

3

ANDRÉ BÉTEILLE

The Idea of Natural Inequality[1]

The mind of man is far from the nature of a clear and equal glass, wherein the beams of things should reflect according to their true incidence: nay, it is rather like an enchanted glass, full of superstition and imposture. . . .
—Francis Bacon

When we talk about inequality among people we mean various things. We mean in one sense that human beings are unequally placed, that they have unequal opportunities, and that they are unequally rewarded; this kind of inequality is easily recognized and can easily be shown to exist in any society, simple or complex, past or present. But we also mean in another sense that men and women have unequal abilities, that they are unequally endowed, and also perhaps that they are of unequal worth; the proof of this kind of inequality is difficult, one might say impossible.

Those who make the case for natural inequality will readily concede that people sometimes appear to be unequally endowed because in fact the opportunities available to them are unequal. No society is perfect, and in every society some individuals suffer more than others from a variety of contingent circumstances. But, they will go on to argue, this is not all that there is to it. For, according to them, it should be possible, at least in principle, to remove the existing distortions or imperfections, and when this is done we will still be left with certain irreducible inequalities of endowment. Viewed in this light the main problem of social justice is to bring about a strict correspondence between natural inequality and social inequality.

To an anthropologist, for whom the variety of cultures has a central

[1]This essay was delivered as the thirteenth Auguste Comte Memorial Trust Lecture and is reprinted by permission of The London School of Economics and Political Science from *The Idea of Natural Inequality*, copyright 1980 by The London School of Economics and Political Science.

59

place in the human scheme of things, it would appear that the idea of natural inequality is inherently ambiguous, if not a contradiction in terms. Nature presents us only with differences or potential differences. With human beings these differences do not become inequalities unless and until they are selected, marked out, and evaluated by processes that are cultural and not natural. In other words, differences become inequalities only with the application of scales; and the scales with which we are concerned in talking about inequalities in a social context are not given to us by nature but are culturally constructed by particular human beings under particular historical conditions.

At the same time, the idea of natural inequality is a very durable one, and especially so in a competitive society. People like to believe that the inequalities they see around them—not all of them perhaps, but at least some—are in the nature of things. It would be a mistake to suppose that such beliefs cannot coexist with the rhetoric of equality. There is surely something paradoxical about an age that seems to value equality as such, as an end in itself, and at the same time places so much faith in competition whose result can only be inequality. For no matter how scrupulously we ensure equality of opportunity, there can be equality only before the competition, not after it. Seen from this angle, equality of opportunity appears as the price paid by competitive societies to ensure inequality of reward.

The whole system of competition would lose its legitimacy unless people believed that the results of competition reveal or ought to reveal something basic and fundamental about those who engage in it. And the legitimacy of competition is very widely accepted in the advanced industrial societies, though in different ways in the capitalist and the socialist varieties. I would like to argue that there is in these societies a widespread belief, generally implicit, but sometimes explicit, that there is a natural ordering of individuals that is obscured by the institutions of primitive or traditional societies, and that this ordering can be revealed only through fair and free competition. The orders of rank that obtained in past societies might be capricious and arbitrary, but the one revealed by fair and free competition must correspond to the natural scheme of things.

The point I have in mind may be illustrated by referring to de Tocqueville (1835/1966:423), who believed that it was possible to abolish the privileges granted by law but not those granted by nature. De Tocqueville sought to contrast aristocratic with democratic societies in terms of their morphology as well as their ideology. Democratic societies were based on the principle of equality just as aristocratic societies had been based on the principle of hierarchy. De Tocqueville believed that, while there was something providential about humanity's progress toward equality, there were also certain limits, imposed by nature as it were, to the realization of this equality. This was obviously the case with the three principal races inhabiting the United States, but true as well of the individual members of the more favored race.

It has been a commonplace since de Tocqueville's time to connect equality with individualism. But, though it is commonly held that individualism entails equality (see, e.g., Dumont, 1977 and also 1972), the opposite argument can also plausibly be made. Individualism, when combined with a high value on achievement, creates and legitimizes a structure of unequal rewards. The very fact that individuals vary enormously in their achievements is presented as proof that they are unequally endowed. Indeed, there is a kind of finality about the order established by competition precisely to the extent that the competition is believed to be free and fair; for by this very belief people deny themselves the right of appeal in any other court. The unsuccessful are also inferior, demonstrably and conclusively so; and in a secular, competitive, and achievement-oriented world there can be little hope that their inferiority will be canceled out in a life hereafter.

In modern industrial societies the economic domain is marked out as the preeminent arena of competition and individual achievement. And, as Sir Isaiah Berlin (1978:92) has put it, "The unequal distribution of natural gifts is a well-known obstacle to economic equality." Even if we accept for the moment the idea of natural gifts, clearly not all such gifts have the same relevance to the achievement of economic success. Perhaps we may go a step further and say that while there is a variety of natural qualities, only some of these and not others are transformed into gifts by the operation of the economic system itself.

Not all societies mark out the same qualities for favored attention. Each society chooses from among the multitude of qualities with which human beings are endowed, or potentially endowed, only some, while ignoring others. The conventional character of gifts widely regarded as "natural" is best revealed when we make comparisons between societies whose conventions are markedly different. Such inquiries are in fact the staple of comparative sociology. The difficulty in achieving satisfactory results in them arises from the fact that what is presented as comparative sociology is very often the comparison of all societies in terms of the implicit conventions of one. Nevertheless, comparative sociology, with all its limitations, has succeeded in revealing the "artificial" character of most of what is or was considered "natural" in non-Western societies, and also to some extent in Western society before the modern age.

A system of inequality whose artificial, not to say arbitrary, character is plainly revealed in the light of comparative sociology is the one associated with the Hindu order of castes. This system divided the whole of society into four *varnas* according to one scheme and into innumerable *jatis* according to another, both of which were characterized by a strict order of ranking. And yet all of this, which appears so arbitrary from the outside, was believed by the Hindus to correspond to the natural order of things. It was given its rationale by the Hindu theory of *gunas* or qualities, according to which each individual was endowed with one of three basic qualities (or *gunas*), or some combination of them. In a just and stable society a correspondence was presumed between a person's qualities and his social position, but this correspondence might be disturbed by a variety of circumstances, in which case it was the duty of the just ruler to restore it (see, e.g., Bose, 1975).

It is a far cry from the qualities esteemed among persons in a traditional hierarchical society to those that ensure success in examinations, let us say, or in the job market in an industrial society. There are differences between the two kinds of scales not only in their construction but also in the manner of their application. In the one case, preeminence is assigned to birth, and in the other to competition. We know today that birth as such in a particular family or lineage tells us little about the natural qualities of human beings; but how much more does competition tell us? What I am suggesting is that something may be learned by comparing the reasons people give in support of inequalities in hierarchical societies with those they give in competitive societies.[2]

Rousseau and Locke

The ambiguity underlying the distinction between natural inequality and social inequality is nowhere more evident than in Rousseau's celebrated discourse on inequality. Others before him, notably English political philosophers of the preceding century, had stated that human beings were equal in their natural condition. Rousseau's case is the more interesting because, although he accepted the spirit of this proposition, he was not able to dispose of the idea of natural inequality altogether. It is useful to reconsider Rousseau's arguments because the questions he raised are still important questions, and the distinctions he made explicitly are still implicitly made.

In a general way the contrast is between "the equality which nature has ordained between men" and the "inequality which they have introduced" (Rousseau,1755/1938:157). As one proceeds with the essay, one finds Rousseau struggling to prove that natural inequalities do not really count, that every kind of inequality worth the name is social, not natural. Why then does he feel obliged to begin by making a distinction between natural or physical, and moral or political inequality? Again, why does he say that natural inequality is "established by nature" whereas political inequality is "established, or at least authorized by the consent of men [p. 174]"? If political inequality is merely authorized by the consent of men, then how or by whom is it established?

It may be that, despite his moral commitment to equality, when it came

[2]The contrast is by no means a very clear one. There are strongly hierarchical features in some competitive societies (of which contemporary Britain is a good example), and there is no human society, hierarchical or otherwise, from which competition has been fully excluded. Likewise, the contrast between "birth" and "competition" should not be overdrawn; those who are most strongly committed to competition might also believe that the results of competition are predetermined by birth, particularly for members of different races.

to constructing a social world in his mind, Rousseau found it hard to conceive of all its individual components as being equal in every respect. Many (e.g., Berlin, 1978) have pointed out the difficulty of creating such a world, even in imagination. The simple solution seems to lie in assuming that the individual human components were unequal to begin with, before the construction of the social world began. Rousseau, at any rate, leaves the door open for a wide range of such preexisting inequalities, arising, in his words, from differences in "age, health, bodily strength and the qualities of the mind or of the soul [1755/1938:157]."

Does nature distribute her gifts unequally among men? Rousseau seems to be of two minds about this. On the one hand, he wants to show with almost tender care the evenhanded character of nature's bounty. On the other, he is eager to trace the steps through which "the natural inequality of mankind" became greatly increased by "the inequality of social institutions [p. 204]." Furthermore, it is not merely the great increase of the latter over the former that is irksome, but also the total lack of correspondence between them, the question of such correspondence being, according to Rousseau, fit only "to be discussed by slaves in the hearing of their masters [p. 174]." But, as we shall see, it is this correspondence, real or presumed, that creates much of the interest in the idea of natural inequality in the first place.

It appears that Rousseau is trying to prove two different propositions: first, that there is no correspondence, or no just correspondence, between natural and social inequalities; and second, that there are no significant natural inequalities, or even that there are no natural inequalities as such among human beings. Now, one might argue that if Rousseau were really convinced of the proof of the second proposition, he would not need to prove the first. It may well be asked whether Rousseau did not believe that at least the different races of man were unequally endowed by nature (see Baker, 1974:16–17).

Rousseau seems to be talking at one and the same time about (a) natural inequality among people, and (b) inequality among people in a state of nature. The former is possibly a wider conception than the latter, but one gets very little help from Rousseau in forming a clear idea of the distinction between the two. Presumably, natural inequality among men can exist both in a state of nature and in a state of society. And presumably one can argue about natural inequality in a state of nature only in axiomatic terms, as facts "do not affect the question" (Rousseau, 1938:175). But can one appeal to facts in talking about natural inequality in a state of society? What kinds of facts?

Again, the inequalities in a state of society are not all of the same kind. On the one hand, there are inequalities specific to the state of society, created by it and without any basis at all in the state of nature. On the other hand, the state of society magnifies and transforms, sometimes beyond recognition, natural inequalities that have been carried over into it from a prior state.

Rousseau's name has come to be inseparably linked with the French

Revolution, and he has been hailed as an avatar of equality not only in Europe but in every country that has come under the influence of Western democratic ideals.[3] It may be said that what Rousseau was to the Revolution of 1789, Locke had been to that of 1688 in England. At any rate, it would be difficult to exaggerate Locke's influence on the development of democratic ideals in England and, more particularly, the United States. Locke's writings on equality and inequality in the state of nature, though narrower in scope than Rousseau's, are not themselves free from ambiguity.

Locke begins his *Second Treatise* by presenting the state of nature as a "state also of equality [Locke, 1690/1978:118]," and goes on to reiterate in various contexts "the equality of men by Nature [p. 119]." However, in talking about the subordination of the wife to the husband, he had said already in the *First Treatise* that "there is, I grant, a foundation in Nature for it [p. 34]." And later, in a somewhat uncharacteristic passage on slaves, he says that they "being captives taken in a just war are, by the right of Nature subjected to the absolute dominion and arbitrary power of their masters [p. 158]."

But more important are the qualifications that Locke specifically introduces to restrict his own general propositions about natural equality. "Though I have said . . 'That all men by nature are equal,' I cannot be supposed to understand all sorts of 'equality' [p. 142]." The equality granted by nature is in fact to be understood in a limited political sense, as the equal right of every man to his natural freedom without subjection to the arbitrary will or authority of any other man. Beyond this, nature acknowledges all kinds of distinction, for "age or virtue may give men a just precedency. Excellency of parts and merit may place others above the common level [p. 142]." Locke makes no attempt to examine how distinctions of virtue or merit might arise in a state of nature, but simply leaves his reader to assume that they are there together with a certain equality of condition.

Perhaps we are in a better position today to recognize that the distinction between the state of nature and the state of society, or between nature and culture, is not merely ambiguous but inherently so. The difficulty lies not so much in getting at the facts as in the very act of conceptualizing man's nature independently of his culture. The recovery of this old insight by modern anthropology calls for a fresh examination of the presumed basis of inequality in human societies.

Inequality versus the Division of Labor

There are two broad ways in which social scientists represent inequality among people. They may try to show how certain valued items—whether possessions or qualities—are unequally distributed among individuals con-

[3]For instance, his work inspired the nineteenth-century Bengali writer Bankimchandra Chatterji, who wrote a tract on equality (1977:147–203) in which he placed Rousseau, along with Christ and the Buddha, among the avatars of equality.

sidered independently of any relations that might exist among them. Or they may try to show how elements of inequality, such as deference, superordination, or subordination are entailed in these very relations. This distinction corresponds to what I have elsewhere described as the distinction between the "distributive" and the "relational" aspects of inequality (Béteille, 1969:13; see also Béteille, 1977). They both presuppose the existence of society and culture, although the former does so in a less obvious sense than the latter.

Let us consider first the inequalities entailed in the arrangement of individuals into some kind of an organized whole. If one took a set of blocks, one might find them to be either various in shape and unequal in size, or of exactly the same shape and size. If one took a set of blocks of exactly the same shape and size, one might arrange them in such a way that some would be placed above and others below, without there being anything in the nature of the blocks themselves to determine which ones should be placed above and which ones below. Now, if the blocks were human beings, they would need to find or be given reasons as to why some should be below and others above. I believe that many of the arguments about natural inequality are in fact a response to just this kind of problem. In other words, even if individuals were not naturally unequal, one might have to represent them as such in order to explain or justify their arrangement in an organized whole.

It is, in fact, quite common to view society in morphological terms, as being some kind of a whole comprising an ordered arrangement of parts. In this sense, societies exist not only among humans but also among various animal, notably insect, species. If this kind of order is a necessary condition for the existence of such a society—any society, whether human or animal—then are the inequalities entailed by the order natural or not? There is no reason to believe with either Rousseau or Hobbes that the division of labor and the state of nature are antithetical to each other.

The problem is somewhat simpler in the case of nonhuman species such as ants, bees, and termites, where there is morphological differentiation within the species corresponding to its division of labor. Furthermore, whether simple or elaborate, the division of labor is clear and unambiguous, and the same pattern is replicated from one colony to the next within the species. These two features in combination give such division of labor a fixed and unalterable appearance.

In the human species there is no obvious correspondence between morphological differentiation and the division of labor. The two most manifest forms of morphological differentiation are those that relate to race and to sex. Even if it turns out that the various races are variously endowed, there is no self-evident way of matching racial differentiation with the division of labor; in any case, the division of labor is no less a problem in racially homogeneous societies than it is in racially heterogeneous ones. And, as it is becoming increasingly clear, the biological components of sex provide only the broadest limits within which an almost endless variety of social arrangements is possible.

One important aspect of the division of labor among human beings, an aspect that is related to its variability as well as its flexibility, is that those who participate in it require reasons for its existence. Human beings do not in any society simply fit themselves into the division of labor as they find it; they seek or create reasons that explain or justify it. From this point of view, the division of labor among human beings differs from that among animals probably as much as human language differs from animal language.

The division of labor as it exists in any human society entails certain inequalities of status and power among the differentiated parts or positions. Some positions are more highly esteemed or command more authority than others. Sometimes, as in the Hindu *varna* system, the whole of society is divided up into categories that are serially ordered. Two kinds of arguments are characteristically put forward to explain or justify such differentiation: first, that in its essence it represents the division of labor and not inequality; and second, that the division of labor as such corresponds to the natural scheme of things. These in fact were the arguments of Mahatma Gandhi, who may be regarded as the most important modern interpreter of Hinduism. Indeed, Gandhi's argument (1962) was that the division of labor corresponding to *varnashrama* is natural, hence good, whereas the division of labor corresponding to class is artificial, hence evil.

Gandhi was not the only person to argue that social differentiation in his own society represented the division of labor rather than inequality. Soviet sociologists also maintain that the differentiation of their society into peasants, workers, and the intelligentsia represents the division of labor which they are inclined to contrast with class. Inequalities associated with class are exploitative, and can and should be removed; the division of labor, on the other hand, corresponds to the natural conditions of social existence.

The authors of *The German Ideology* (Marx and Engels, 1932/1968) were much closer to the original insight of Rousseau when they argued that the division of labor, class, and inequality are inseparably linked. Indeed, their argument is more fully developed on this point than Rousseau's. At least in this early phase of their work they saw no real solution to the problems of class and inequality so long as there was division of labor in society. But they did not concede that the division of labor was a necessary condition of social existence; rather, they believed that human society would recover its true nature only when the division of labor was abolished (p. 93).

Is the argument of Marx and Engels in *The German Ideology* tenable that the division of labor is not a necessary (or "natural") condition of social existence? I believe that it is not, although there is something very persuasive about such an argument. Its appeal seems to rest largely on the obvious fact that humans, unlike insects, have divisions of labor that are endlessly variable in both space and time. But to argue that a particular form of the division of labor—any particular form of it—is dispensable (or "artificial") is very different from arguing that the division of labor itself is dispensable.

There is, from this point of view, a certain likeness between the division of labor and language. No human society is conceivable without some division of labor, just as none is conceivable without a language. At the same time, no particular form of either the one or the other can be stipulated as a necessary condition for the existence of society. People are now prepared to concede that their own language is no more natural than any other language, although they have not always or everywhere been prepared to do so. It seems far more difficult for them to be reconciled to a similar view of the division of labor to which they are accustomed.

The division of labor among men and women, and their ordering on a scale, however closely related, are not one and the same thing. It should be possible to order individual items on a scale without there being any preexisting pattern of arrangement among them. In fact, those who talk about inequality among men, particularly natural inequality, do not necessarily presuppose any division of labor among them. Is it possible to order individual human beings without their social division of labor—rights, obligations, shared values—being at all taken into account? By what criteria should one test the adequacy of such ordering?

The basic question centers around the autonomy of the scales that are used for representing or identifying the inequalities among people. If these scales are themselves embedded in the existing social arrangements, then there is an element of fiction involved in the belief that the inequalities they represent are natural as opposed to social.

There obviously is some sense in making a distinction between inequality of merit and inequality of reward, and in pointing out that merit does not always receive its due reward. These are practical problems that concern individuals in every society. But one may wonder whether we clarify or confuse the issue by arguing as if the first (merit) were a creation of nature and the second (reward) an artifact of culture. It is misleading to believe that only the allocation of rewards is a social process; the recognition of merit—and indeed the very definition of what constitutes merit—is equally and as much a social process.

It is the common experience that human beings discriminate and evaluate everywhere, ordering things and persons on scales of various kinds. We do not know very much about the ways in which these scales are constructed, except that they are somehow related to collective experience and, more particularly, to what Durkheim described as collective representations. Some scales evidently are constructed by particular persons for particular purposes, and we can see their "artificial" character easily enough. But there are others that we accept without question, on which there is complete or almost complete agreement within a society because of long usage or for some other reason. Do they then enjoy the special privilege of being beyond the realm of culture?

It would appear that there are such layers in every system of collective representations: those criteria, measures, and standards of evaluation that are tacitly accepted as being "natural," and others whose "artificial" or man-made character is freely conceded. But it is hard to see how discrimination and evaluation of any kind can operate independently of culture. Conversely, it is hard to conceive of a culture that does not discriminate or evaluate, just as it is hard to conceive of a society that has no division of labor; so that we may say that it is in the nature of every culture to order things on its own scales, which is another way of saying that the distinction between "natural" inequality and "social" inequality is inherently ambiguous.

Gandhi

I would like at this point to consider briefly the argument of Mahatma Gandhi about equality and inequality in the context of the natural capacities of individual human beings. I do not expect that you will find it any more convincing than I do. Rather, Gandhi's argument that a particular social arrangement expresses or can express differences of natural ability will be found paradoxical precisely because it is presented in the idiom of another culture.

Gandhi, who commented extensively on Hinduism as well as other religions, was inclined to view the contrast between Hindu society based on *varnashrama* and capitalist society based on classes as a contrast between the natural (or organic) and the artificial (or mechanical). He maintained that the division of society into the four *varnas* of Brahman, Kshatriya, Vaishya, and Shudra was in accordance with the natural order of things, whereas a division into classes whose members were in perpetual competition with each other was the artifact of a mechanical civilization. The first, though corrupt in its current practice, was inherently good; the second was inherently evil because it obstructed the expression of man's real nature.

Gandhi maintained that in *varnadharma* the Hindus had discovered a law of collective life given to man by nature: "It is not a human invention, but an immutable law of nature [1962:13]." As such, it ought to be the organizing principle not merely of Hindu society but of every human society.

> Though the law of Varna is a special discovery of some Hindu seer, it has universal application. Every religion has some distinguishing characteristic, but if it expresses a principle or law, it ought to have universal application. This is how I look at the law of Varna. The world may ignore it today but it will have to accept it in the time to come [p. 8].

In fairness, it ought to be said that Gandhi's conception of *varna* was very different from the representation of it that we get in the usual textbook of sociology.

What is *varna*? The law of *varna*, according to the argument, simply enjoins individual human beings to follow the traditional callings of their fore-fathers in a spirit of duty and service. Gandhi recognized the connection be-tween *varna* and birth, but he did not regard that as a point against it (p. 6). This may sound strange because Gandhi, like Rousseau, was a radical egalitarian. He condemned caste but endorsed *varna* because, according to him, "All Varnas are equal, for the community depends no less on one than on another [p. 7]." Gandhi argued that feelings of superiority and inferiority were a perversion of *varnadharma* and inconsistent with its basic spirit.

Feelings of superiority and inferiority are inherent in the competitive society and, from this point of view, class distinctions are rooted not so much in property as in competition, individualism, and the unlimited pursuit of material gain. As such, they are present under both private and state capitalism. Gandhi's hostility to the dominance of the machine over man is well known. He believed that so long as this dominance prevailed man would remain enmeshed in artificial distinctions and inequalities, unable to recover his true nature as a social being.

De Tocqueville, Marx, and Durkheim

In contrast to all this, nineteenth-century Western liberals and their present-day counterparts maintain that the natural ordering among men can be established and maintained only through fair and free competition. If this ordering reveals inequality, then inequality is to that extent natural, and to suppress such inequality might be to go against both justice and efficiency. Other principles might be invoked to mitigate natural inequality, but one can-not, and indeed should not, cancel it out.

It is not as if there is no awareness in the advanced industrial societies of the negative consequences of unrestricted competition. This awareness has grown steadily over the last 100 years and has led to the introduction of a variety of measures to ensure that society maintains a floor and a ceiling beyond which people do not easily fall or rise. But these measures do not in principle negate the belief that unequal rewards are inevitable in a world in which natural gifts are unequally distributed. Even in the East European coun-tries, social scientists are eager to show that the meritarian principle of remuneration is not really in conflict with the socialist principle (see Chapter 15 by Wesolowski and Krauze in this volume).

In the West the nineteenth century ushered in a new social order and a new consciousness and, along with these, new hopes and new fears. De Tocqueville foresaw the leveling of the old distinctions between high and low and the emergence of a new spirit of equality among men. Marx, who took a closer look at this new society with its inhuman division of labor and its brutal competition, argued that the age of equality would come only with the dissolution, not the consolidation, of the new social order.

A new concentration of intellectual energy was required to make the commitment to equality on one plane consistent with the commitment to inequality on another. Writing in the last decade of the nineteenth century, Émile Durkheim reacted to the paradox of his time in a characteristic manner. He noted, on the one hand, the growing belief among citizens—one might ask, which citizens?—about the increase of equality and, on the other, the inherent tendency of the division of labor to lead to the increase of inequality (Durkheim, 1933, especially Book 3, Chapter 2). How did he seek to resolve the paradox? Durkheim did not deny that the division of labor might lead to the increase of inequality; only, he maintained that such inequality, when established by free competition, would be just and efficient.

Durkheim, like de Tocqueville, was struck by the contrast between the *ancien régime* and the new society. But between de Tocqueville and Durkheim lay the work of Marx, and it was no longer possible to present the contrast between the old and the new orders as simply a contrast between hierarchy and equality. One was now obliged to argue that it did not matter that the new order had its inequality, and that this inequality might in fact increase. What mattered was that the new inequality, quite unlike the old, gave due recognition to merit. But what is merit?

There was, to begin with, the entire panoply of hereditary titles, ranks, and offices whose oppressive and artificial character stood clearly revealed in the light of the new social consciousness. Durkheim had no difficulty in showing that merit, as he and his readers understood it, would be stifled and not given room for play so long as the old distinctions of estate, of caste, and of clan prevailed. The hopeful thing was that these were being steadily and surely effaced as the new division of labor gained ground. But when these became fully effaced, would true merit really come into its own and get its due recognition? What was there to guarantee that, when the veil of artificial social distinctions was removed, a social order based solely on true distinctions of merit would emerge?

Durkheim was a product of the society that first established the myth of careers open to talent, a myth whose power has been on the whole increased rather than diminished by the resources of modern science. It was a society that set great store by merit, viewing merit as somewhat like water which, when left to itself, always finds its own level. The task of social reconstruction lay, then, in removing the obstacles to the free play of merit, so that a "forced" division of labor could be replaced by a "spontaneous" division of labor, and a society that put common faith above everything else could be replaced by one that put justice above everything else. But what is justice without a common faith?

Durkheim's idea of the just society, then, is not that it is one in which all men are equal in every way, or even that it is one in which the inequalities among them are small in extent; as we saw, he believed that the new division of labor might lead inequalities to increase rather than decrease.[4] His idea of the just society is simply that it is one in which "social inequalities exactly express natural inequalities [Durkheim, 1933:377]." But Durkheim, who is otherwise so careful to explain the social origin of everything, including freedom and justice, does not really explain where these natural inequalities come from. They are simply taken to be the fixed points with reference to which the just society—the society that puts justice above common faith—regulates its inequalities. But what if these "natural inequalities" are themselves the creatures of the very society that is presumed merely to express them?

The kind of problem that all this raises—and leaves unresolved—is very well illustrated by the notorious functionalist theory of social stratification. According to this theory, presented in its simplest form by Kingsley Davis and Wilbert Moore (1966), the rewards alloted to individuals are roughly in proportion to the contributions they make to society. Since the theory proposes no independent measures of the values of these contributions, it is in fact perfectly circular. But although the functionalist theory of stratification has been ruled out of court by professional sociologists because of its circularity, it has scarcely been dislodged from its place of importance in the folk wisdom of modern societies.

The problem of an independent measure of ability, merit, or talent is of course the central problem left unresolved in the conception of natural inequality to which Durkheim and others like him take recourse. Suppose for a moment that there are natural inequalities among individuals. By what means are we to determine the degree of correspondence between these and the existing social inequalities? Can the correspondence between the two be subjected to any kind of empirical test? No one has come anywhere near to constructing such a test for any society in its totality, and it is doubtful that we even know what kinds of data would be relevant to such a test.

Instead of starting with a system of natural inequality out there, and then trying to see how society adjusts its positions to correspond to it, suppose we were to start with the order and its existing social inequalities. Would the order then not have to give a reason why particular individuals are placed where they are, and not elsewhere? Is there anything more to the presumed correspondence between "natural" and "social" inequality than just this reason? Suppose there were no natural inequality among men, would society not need to invent it? And would the need for this invention be less compelling in a competitive than in a hierarchical society?

The need for a belief in natural inequality has perhaps a special urgency

[4]As Adam Smith pointed out before him: "the very different genius which appears to distinguish men of different professions, when grown up to maturity, is not upon many occasions so much the cause, as the effect of the division of labour. The difference between the most dissimilar characters, between a philosopher and a common street porter, for example, seems to arise not so much from nature, as from habit, custom, and education [Smith, 1776/1967:19]."

in a modern secular society where people can no longer pretend that the inequalities in this world are unreal or unimportant, since they might be canceled out in a world hereafter. In such a society the individual is given only one chance, as it were, to find his true place in the larger scheme of things. So it is not altogether surprising that the resources of modern science should be used for buttressing the concept of natural inequality, even though the concept is inherently ambiguous.

Huxley and Galton

The science that in the nineteenth century contributed most to the support of folk beliefs about natural equality was biology. What is interesting about this biology is the extent to which, in dealing with the question of human nature, it took for granted the categories of the society of which it was a product. The sociobiology and the bioeconomics of the second half of the present century have become enormously more complex and technical, but it is doubtful that they have succeeded any more in detaching themselves from the categories of a competitive and market-oriented society.[5]

In the closing years of the last century T. H. Huxley published a magazine article, "On the Natural Inequality of Men" (1890:1–23). The article was an attack on Rousseau's discourse on inequality, and carried behind it the whole weight of the author's reputation as one of Britain's leading scientists. Huxley attacked Rousseau for being both inconsistent and disingenuous; he pointed out, moreover, that every one of Rousseau's basic ideas might be traced back to either Locke or Hobbes.

Huxley made no secret of his antipathy for unqualified equality: "Freedom, used foolishly, and equality, asserted in words, but every moment denied by the facts of nature, are things of which, as it seems to me, we have rather too much already [p. 12]." Equality was sanctioned neither by science nor by philosophy; even the equality sanctioned by the great religions, Judaism and Christianity, was a residual kind, "an equality either of insignificance or of imperfection [p. 13]."[6]

Unlike Rousseau, Huxley was convinced that there was a close correspondence between natural inequality and social inequality. The proof of this lay in the evident success of enterprise and skill in every walk of life. Enterprise and skill, moreover, accounted for property rights as they prevailed in nineteenth-century Britain: "so the inequality of individual ownership has grown out of the relative equality of communal ownership in virtue of those natural inequalities of men, which, if unimpeded by circumstances, cannot fail to give rise quietly and peaceably to corresponding political inequalities

[5]For a stimulating recent discussion see Sahlins (1977).
[6]For a recent statement of the same argument, see Joseph and Sumption (1979).

[Huxley, 1890:22]." Echoes of Huxley's words are to be found in the writings of a large number of his contemporaries.[7]

Enterprise and skill were viewed as the basis of property accumulation and occupational achievement, the twin pillars on which nineteenth-century capitalist society rested. Huxley's essay was an attempt to show that the inequalities that fueled the engines of that society were in fact a part of the quiet and peaceable order of nature. There has been a certain shift since his time to the extent that more emphasis appears to be placed now on the natural basis of occupational achievement than of property accumulation.

The arguments Huxley set forth in a magazine article were presented in scientific treatises by Sir Francis Galton who, in the nineteenth century, laid the groundwork for that field of studies that examines the relationship between biological heredity and social achievement. Galton had been greatly struck by the unequal achievements of individuals in various walks of life and sought to prove that much of this was due to heredity. I am not here concerned with showing how far Galton was right or wrong within his own framework of analysis; my concern is with the presuppositions of that framework. And Galton's work is important precisely because it makes little effort to conceal those presuppositions.

Galton begins his book on *Hereditary Genius*, first published in 1869, with the magisterial statement, "It is in the most unqualified manner that I object to pretensions of natural equality [Galton, 1869/1950:12]." And what is the evidence to sustain his objection? He quickly proceeds to provide his most persuasive piece of evidence, which is as follows: "There can hardly be a surer evidence of the enormous difference between the intellectual capacity of men, than the prodigious difference in the number of marks obtained by those who gain mathematical honors at Cambridge [p. 14]." Later in the same work Galton substitutes, for purely technical reasons, success in the classical tripos for success in the mathematical tripos as evidence of superior natural ability.

Galton's line of reasoning seems to be that natural inequalities result in unequal success in examinations, which requires that people be unequally placed in society: Natural inequality is the bedrock on which all inequalities rest. He does not pause to consider the opposite line of reasoning, which might be that men and women have to be certified as naturally unequal because the examination system guarantees their unequal success, and the examination system is what it is because the larger society requires it to be so. On this last point a distinguished contemporary English academic has observed:

> If society insists that individuals be segregated out into categories—first class, second class, third class, upper, middle, lower—then the system will always have to waste an enormous amount of time and energy allocating individuals to the right slots and marking them up with the proper labels [Leach, 1968:73].

[7]Among recent writers perhaps the most notorious is Eysenck (1975).

In this other perspective one sees what is ordinarily described as natural inequality to be largely an artifact of social inequality.

What is striking in Galton, in contrast to his contemporary counterparts, is his disarming candor. Durkheim would argue at most that there was in his society a tendency for social inequalities to express natural inequalties, not that they did so in fact. Galton, on the other hand, took the correspondence between the two for granted: "It follows that the men who achieve eminence, and those who are naturally capable, are, to a large extent, identical [Galton, 1869/1950:34]." Furthermore, men not only get what they deserve, but their desserts are publicly acknowledged: "I feel convinced that no man can achieve a very high reputation without being gifted with very high abilities [p. 43]." With so much trust in the existing system of social rewards, it would take a lot to disturb one's faith in natural inequality.

Nineteenth-century ideas regarding merit, talent, or ability tended to be, on the whole, diffuse and ill-defined. The twentieth century has seen organized and concentrated efforts to make these terms more specific and concrete. There would be little point in talking about careers open to talent if one had only a vague idea of the meaning of talent. The answer to this appears to have been in large measure found in the quality that has come to be identified as intelligence, in particular, intelligence as measured by IQ. As a study entitled *American Beliefs and Attitudes About Intelligence* says,

> measured intelligence today is of higher significance than ever before. . . . In our society there is an increasing value placed on measured intelligence as the basis on which rewards will be allocated, in preference to other characteristics such as honesty, creativity, altruism, leadership, and dramatic, painting, dancing or gardening skills [Brim *et al.*, 1969:3].

This is not to say that other qualities are no longer valued, but only that intelligence has come to acquire a kind of preeminence.

It is difficult not to be impressed by the inputs that have gone into the definition and discussion of intelligence. Psychologists, educationists, biologists, and others have spoken and written about it at length. Scientific skills and political passions have been called into play, together with perhaps a small ingredient of fraud. It is doubtful that any other human quality has been so thoroughly discussed as intelligence, and implicit in much of the discussion is the belief that intelligence is a gift of nature, perhaps her supreme gift.

It is important to appreciate the extent of the preoccupation with intelligence and the testing of intelligence in the modern world. In this, as in so much else, the United States leads the field. Tests of ability have been standardized, and the number of such tests administered each year has grown phenomenally since World War II. It was estimated in the mid-1960s that around 250 million standardized tests of ability were administered each year in the American school system (Brim *et al.*, 1969:1). In a society where schooling is both compulsory and competitive, no child can escape having his or her intelligence tested, directly and indirectly, overtly and covertly, over and over again.

Nor is this all solely for the benefit of children. For the adult, the popular press and the other mass media advertise the manifest virtues of intelligence, and there is now a scientific best-seller which invites people to check their own IQs (Eysenck, 1966). More and more adults take standardized tests of intelligence because they are required to do so in almost every walk of life, in commerce, in industry, in the civil and military branches of government, and, of course, in education (Brim *et al.*, 1969:1). In addition to all this, individuals may administer such tests to themselves in order to keep themselves better informed about their own abilities. A student of comparative sociology might well ask if the notorious Brahmanical obsession with purity can really measure up to this kind of preoccupation with a single human quality.

What makes intelligence particularly appropriate as a quality for the ranking of individuals is the belief that it can be precisely measured, or, rather, that precise measures must be found for any quality if it is to satisfy the requirement of ranking individuals and classes in a modern society. As a result, the experts know much more about measuring intelligence than about what intelligence is. To put it in the words of Arthur Jensen (1965:5), "Intelligence, like electricity, is easier to measure than to define." For most people, in fact, the measure acts as a substitute for understanding, giving them the illusion that by measuring something they bring it within their grasp.

In modern societies achievement and ability are very closely linked together. Achievement is the measure of ability, and ability is reckoned not in the abstract, but in relation to specific standards of achievement. These standards of achievement have their loci in various institutional systems, among which the two most crucial are the educational system and the occupational system. Modern societies are thus most concerned with those variations in human ability that have a direct bearing on scholastic and occupational achievement.

We must appreciate that those, like Arthur Jensen, who argue that heredity contributes substantially to differences in IQ readily concede this. Jensen is careful to make a distinction between "intelligence," which is a narrower concept, and mental ability, which is somewhat wider, pointing out that "intelligence" as measured by intelligence tests is a specific set of abilities, marked out from among the rest because of its correspondence with the traditional system of formal education on the one hand and the established occupational structure on the other. In his own words, "the predominant importance of intelligence is derived, not from any absolute criteria or God-given desiderata, but from social demands [p. 19]." Thus, inequalities here are measured neither on God's scale nor on nature's, but on scales constructed by men with particular ends in view. At the same time, and despite what the experts set down in fine print, these tests strongly confirm folk beliefs that natural inequality is the basis of social inequality as represented by the occupational system.

Sociologists have, in their turn, pointed to the "functional" properties of the quality conceived of as intelligence in modern intelligence tests; in particular, they have pointed out properties that make it functional to the requirements of the occupational system, which, since Durkheim's time, has come to be recognized as the principal locus of prestige in modern societies. This is how one recent sociological study sums it up:

> What we call "occupational prestige" corresponds to an unmistakable social fact. When psychologists came to propose operational counterparts to the notion of intelligence, or to derive measures thereof, they wittingly or unwittingly looked for indicators of capability to function in the system of key roles in society. What they took to be mental performance might equally well have been described as role performance [Duncan, et al., 1972:78].

There is, as one might expect, a strain toward consistency between ability and achievement, or between quality and performance, both of which are socially defined, although the one tends to be thought of as natural in opposition to the other.

It is hardly surprising that psychologists concerned with intelligence ratings and sociologists concerned with the rating of occupations should come up with findings that are in such close agreement with each other. Occupations that rank high in a specific society and the specific abilities required for the performance of those occupations may be seen as two sides of the same coin. Intelligence ratings and occupational ratings are both socially constructed, and are in effect two different applications of the same basic scale. Now, if mental ability were considered to be nature's gift and occupational standing to be society's reward, it is only to be expected that social inequalities will express natural inequalities.

Recent debates on IQ have paid much attention to the relative contributions of heredity and environment to it. Most intelligence testers seem to believe that heredity has a far larger share than environment in determining IQ, although some disagree very sharply (see, e.g., Kamin, 1974). I ought to make it clear that I consider this to be a separate question from the one to which I have tried to address myself.

My argument is not about the fact of individual variations among human beings that are universal and undeniable, but about the significance of these variations. It is difficult to see how one can deny some role to genetic factors in the perpetuation of individual variations. As soon as some of these variations are marked out and transformed into inequalities by being ordered on a scale, such inequalities come rightly to be regarded as hereditary. It is the crucial step by which differences are transformed into inequalities that I consider to be a social construction rather than a gift of nature. What I have tried to argue, therefore, is that intelligence ratings are no more natural than occupational ratings, and when people talk about social inequalities expressing natural inequalities, they are making use of a fiction that even the most acute among them tend to mistake for the truth.

Conclusions

What I have tried to show is that in modern societies there is characteristically a tension between the values placed on equality and on inequality. There is, on the one hand, a strong and somewhat self-consciously virtuous attachment to equality, as in the principle of equal opportunity or of equal consideration of human worth. There is, on the other, a striking preoccupation with sorting individuals out and ranking them according to their natural abilities, aptitudes, and qualities. These two concerns coexist not only within the same culture but often, and perhaps characteristically, within the same personality.

It would be difficult, if not impossible, to assign weights to these two different, and in some sense contradictory, concerns. For one thing, there are enormous variations between individuals within the same society, and between societies that have equal claims to modernity. One important difference seems to lie in the ways in which two modern societies, for example England and the United States, might articulate or give expression to these two contradictory concerns. On the whole the concern for equality is made more widely explicit, whereas the one for inequality is more often left implicit, although here also one may find a good deal of fluctuation, including short-term fluctuation within the life history of the same society.[8]

On the whole people seem reluctant to declare categorically that human beings are by nature made unequal, even when that is the implication of much of what they say. Because the idea of natural inequality is weakly articulated, it is never free from an element of ambiguity. Students of modern societies can follow people in what they say about their belief in equality, but they have to reconstruct people's concept of natural inequality. It can be said that the concept of natural inequality owes some of its strength to its ambiguity, since it enables one to shift from one sense of the term to another in arguing with others or with oneself.

It is not at all clear that when Berlin talks about "the unequal distribution of natural gifts" he has in mind exactly the same sort of thing as when Galton rejects what he describes as "pretensions to natural equality." When pressed to the point, people will often say that what they have in mind is not natural inequality in any absolute sense, but natural inequality relative to a given social arrangement. There is, as it were, a strong thesis about natural inequality and

---

[8]For an attack on egalitarianism by a leading member of the British cabinet, see Joseph and Sumption (1979).

a weak thesis, and people tend to move back and forth between the two. The same person, A. R. Jensen, for instance, might caution his readers that mental tests measure very specific, culturally valued abilities, and then go on to refer to g or generalized intelligence as the "rock of Gibralter" (Jensen, 1965:9; see also Hudson, 1976).

A common source of the ambiguity referred to previously is the tendency to move back and forth, from arguments about natural differences to arguments about natural inequality and vice versa. The following is a char- acteristic example from an essay entitled "The Inequality of Man" by J.B.S. Haldane (1932a:13). "For men are not born equal. No one disputes this fact as regards physical characteristics. Some babies are born black and some white, and very little can be done to alter the colour of the former." From here one moves on to unequal competence in role performance and argues, by analogy, that these *inequalities*, like the *differences* between Black and White babies, are due to nature and not nurture. If the reader feels a little confused as to what exactly is being ascribed to nature, that does not necessarily shake his or her belief in natural inequality.

What Haldane does with the example of Black and White babies is to show that some differences are unalterable, hence, natural. What I have tried to show on the other hand, is that examples of unalterable difference, however numerous or ingenuous, cannot by themselves establish any argu- ment about natural inequality. It is not as if Haldane is unaware that the dif- ference between Black and White babies might vary in significance from one culture to another. Rather, he moves on to examples of other differences that lend themselves more easily to the suggestion that their significance cannot but be the same, no matter what the society or culture is.

The view that the incontestable proof of natural inequality lies in the fact that some differences, of both physical and mental qualities, are hereditary, Haldane (1932b:27–42) has himself elsewhere jocularly described as "scientific Calvinism." The problem is that Calvinism, in both its religious and scientific forms, tends to be strict and narrow in the choice of the qualities it values. Perhaps the very narrowness helps to confirm the view that the choice itself is made for man by nature.

To represent what is socially constructed as something given to man by nature is, according to Roland Barthes, the essence of the art of myth making (Barthes, 1973). The important thing is to seek an anchorage for the social and the historical in something outside of society and history, and that is the broad sense people give to nature when they talk about natural inequality. This being the case, it is not surprising that the idea resists rigorous definition. Myths, as opposed to theories, make their impact less by what they state ex- plicitly than by what they persuade people to take for granted. Two hundred and fifty million test scores serve to make a point more effectively than any formal theory of natural inequality could hope to do.

If the idea of natural inequality has a somewhat shadowy existence, this is because it has little independent value in itself; its value lies in the anchorage it provides, or seeks to provide, to the reality of social inequality. If there had been no social inequality to contend with, it is doubtful that people would give very much thought to natural inequality. From this point of view, Rousseau's professed lack of interest in the correspondence between the two forms or aspects of inequality does appear a little disingenuous, and T. H. Huxley was certainly right in pointing to the hollowness of his rhetoric.

The idea of natural inequality seems to have a special place in the modern world. It is perhaps best viewed as a response to the recognition of the transitoriness and fragility of existing forms of social inequality. Modern societies appear to be animated by the urge to recreate themselves again and again. Through this process modern man seems to recognize instinctively that inequality is an inherent feature of collective life, and at the same time that any particular form of its social expression is not only oppressive but also arbitrary. But if the idea of natural inequality offers some kind of a refuge from the implications of this paradox, it is at best a precarious refuge.

Acknowledgments

The first sketch of the argument of this chapter was presented at the conference in Burg Wartenstein organized by the Wenner-Gren Foundation, which I would like to thank for its hospitality on that occasion. I am grateful to Marshall Sahlins for his comments then. I am grateful also to Meyer Fortes, Edmund Leach, and Alan Macfarlane for their patience and care in reading and commenting on later drafts.

References

Baker, John R.
  1974   Race. London: Oxford University Press.
Barthes, Roland
  1973   Mythologies. St. Albans, England: Paladin.
Berlin, Sir Isaiah
  1978   Equality. In Concepts and Categories: Philosophical Essays. Pp. 81–102. London: Hogarth Press.
Béteille, André
  1977   Inequality Among Men. Oxford: Basil Blackwell.
Béteille, André, ed.
  1969   Social Inequality. Harmondsworth, England: Penguin Books.
Bose, Nirmal Kumar
  1975   The Structure of Hindu Society. New Delhi: Orient Longman.
Brim, Orville, G., Jr., et al.
  1969   American Beliefs and Attitudes About Intelligence. New York: Russell Sage Foundation.
Chatterji, Bankimchandra
  1977   Renaissance and Reaction in Nineteenth-Century Bengal. M. K. Haldar, trans. Calcutta: Minerva Associates.

Davis, Kingsley, and Wilbert Moore
  1966 Some Principles of Stratification. *In* Class, Status, and Power: Social Stratification in Comparative Perspective. Second ed. R. Bendix and S. M. Lipset, eds. Pp. 47–53. New York: Free Press.
Dumont, Louis
  1972 Homo Hierarchicus: The Caste System and Its Implications. St. Albans, England: Paladin.
  1977 From Mandeville to Marx: The Genesis and Triumph of Economic Ideology. Chicago: University of Chicago Press.
Duncan, Otis D., David L. Featherman, and Beverley Duncan
  1972 Socioeconomic Background and Achievement. London: Seminar Press.
Durkheim, Émile
  1933 The Division of Labor in Society. New York: Free Press.
Eysenck, Hans J.
  1966 Check Your Own I.Q. Harmondsworth, England: Penguin Books.
  1975 The Inequality of Man. London: Fontana.
Galton, Francis
  1950 Hereditary Genius. Second ed. London: Watts. (First ed. 1892.)
Gandhi, Mohandas K.
  1962 Varnashramadharma. Ahmedabad: Navajivan Publishing House.
Haldane, J. B. S.
  1932a The Inequality of Man. *In* The Inequality of Man and Other Essays. Pp. 12–26. London: Chatto and Windus.
  1932b Scientific Calvinism. *In* The Inequality of Man and Other Essays. Pp. 27–42. London: Chatto and Windus.
Hudson, L.
  1976 The Cult of the Fact. London: Jonathan Cape.
Huxley, Thomas H.
  1890 On the Natural Inequality of Men. Nineteenth Century 155:1–23.
Jensen, Arthur R.
  1965 How Much Can We Boost IQ and Scholastic Achievement? Harvard Educational Review, Reprint Series, No. 2.
Joseph, K., and J. Sumption
  1979 Equality. London: John Murray.
Kamin, Leon J.
  1974 The Science and Politics of I.Q. Potomac, Maryland: Lawrence Erlbaum Associates.
Leach, Edmund
  1968 A Runaway World? London: British Broadcasting Corporation.
Locke, John
  1978 Two Treatises of Government. London: J. M. Dent. (First ed. 1690.)
Marx, Karl, and Friedrich Engels
  1968 The German Ideology. Moscow: Progress Publishers (First ed. 1932.)
Rousseau, Jean-Jacques
  1938 A Discourse on the Origin of Inequality. *In* The Social Contract and Discourses. Pp. 155–238. London: J. M. Dent (First ed. 1755.)
Sahlins, Marshall
  1977 The Use and Abuse of Biology: An Anthropological Critique of Sociobiology. London: Tavistock.
Smith, Adam
  1967 The Wealth of Nations. Chicago: University of Chicago Press. (First published 1776.)
Tocqueville, Alexis de
  1966 Democracy in America. New York: Harper and Row. (First ed. 1835.)

PART

II

INEQUALITY IN
UNSTRATIFIED SOCIETIES

4

RICHARD B. LEE

Politics, Sexual and Nonsexual, in an Egalitarian Society: The !Kung San[1]

Among the !Kung San, hunter–gatherers of southern Africa, women play an important role in production, in fact providing a greater proportion of the subsistence than do the men (Lee, 1968; L. Marshall, 1960). The same predominance of female over male work productivity has been observed among many other tropical and warm–temperate hunter–gatherers (Lee and DeVore, 1968; McCarthy and McArthur, 1960; Woodburn, 1968). The economic importance of women has led observers to question the male-dominated "patrilocal" model of hunting and gathering society and to revise and upgrade woman's role in human prehistory (Friedl, 1975; Hiatt, 1974; Leacock, 1972; E. Morgan, 1972; Reed, 1975; Rohrlich-Leavitt, 1975; Slocum, 1975; Tanner and Zihlman, 1976). The counterposing of "woman the gatherer" to "man the hunter" has become part of a welcome and long overdue re-examination of the implicit and explicit male biases in anthropological theory (Golde, 1970; Gough, 1970, 1971; Lamphere, 1977; Reiter, 1975, 1977; Rosaldo and Lamphere, 1974; Martin and Voorhies, 1975).

The re-evaluation of women's status in hunter–gatherer society raises the more general issue of the nature of politics in egalitarian societies. Is there a

[1]Field research among the !Kung was conducted in 1963–1964, 1967–1969, and 1973, with support from the National Science Foundation, the National Institute of Mental Health, the Canada Council, and the Wenner-Gren Foundation. Parts of this chapter have been adapted from R. B. Lee, *The !Kung San* (New York: Cambridge University Press, 1979) and in 1978 appeared in *Social Science Information* 17(6):871–895, under the title Politics, Sexual and Non-Sexual in an Egalitarian Society.

83

ISBN 0-12-093160-5

baseline of nonexploitative social relations in the small-scale societies of hunter–gatherers, or is this postulate in error, arising out of a romantic Rousseauian image of the primitive (Diamond, 1975)? Recent writings have sought to discern status inequalities in even the simplest small-scale societies, with males lording it over women and controlling their labor power, and elder males controlling the younger males' and all females' labor power and access to resources (Fox, 1967; Meillassoux, 1973, 1975; Rose, 1968; Tiger, 1969). The issues raised are not simple, and agreement has yet to be reached on even the question of what constitutes the data for resolving the issues.

The more modest purpose of this chapter is to examine male–female relations and the general problem of equality and inequality in hunger–gatherer societies by using data on the !Kung San as an illustrative starting point. Three groups of problems are addressed:

1. By what kinds of criteria—economic, social, ideological—can we evaluate the equality of the sexes or lack of it among the !Kung, so that the results can be cross-culturally applicable? How representative are the !Kung of other hunter–gatherers?
2. What forms of leadership exist in !Kung society, and how do the people handle the apparent paradox of leadership–followership in an egalitarian society?
3. How does equality in the political sphere correspond to the relations of production in the economic sphere? What are the key contradictions between and within these spheres that give a dynamic quality to !Kung society?

Men and Women Foragers: Contemporary Perspectives

Although debate continues on the question of the presence, absence, or degree of male dominance in foraging societies, happily the day is past when learned authorities could simply characterize hunter–gatherer societies as male-dominated and aggressive and contrast them with the female-dominated, fertility-obsessed cultures of the Neolithic horticulturalists. It was not so long ago, for example, that Lewis Mumford could assert:

> Paleolithic tools and weapons mainly were addressed to movements and muscular efforts: instruments of chipping, hacking, digging, burrowing, cleaving, dissecting, exerting force swiftly at a distance; in short every manner of aggressive activity. The bones and muscles of the male dominate his technical contributions. . . .Under woman's dominance the neolithic period is pre-eminently one of containers: it is an age of stone and pottery utensils, of vases, jars, vats, cisterns, bins, barns, granaries, houses, not least the great collective containers like irrigation ditches and villages [1961:25].

Schemes like these echo nineteenth- and early twentieth-century sequences that equated hunters with patriarchy and horticulturalists with matriarchy (e.g., Bachofen, 1861; Freud, 1919; L. H. Morgan, 1877). However, given this long history of controversy, we should be wary of formulas that simply invert the previous sequences and grant all political power to women in early society, or for that matter postulate a perfect equality between males and females in the preagricultural past. Rather than starting with a general assessment of male–female relations in !Kung society, I prefer to deal with the problem piecemeal by discussing in turn the various spheres in which men and women interact to show that dominance of one sex in one sphere does not necessarily mean dominance in another.

HUNTING VERSUS GATHERING

!Kung men hunt and !Kung women gather; gathering provides about two-thirds of the diet and hunting one-third. Behind this simple statement lie some not-so-simple qualifications. For example, there are at least three ways of calculating the relative contributions of hunting and gathering to the foraging diet: (1) by the weight or caloric content of food from each source, (2) by the amount of work effort and productivity per person-hour, and (3) by the value the people themselves place upon the two kinds of subsistence. On the first count, it is clear that gathered foods provide about twice the food value of hunted foods. In a July 1964 study of work, vegetable products yielded 69% of the weight and 71% of the calories of the food eaten in the Dobe camp. At other seasons and other places, such as the temporary late summer and fall camps in Mongongo nut groves or Tsin bean fields, the proportion of vegetable foods may go even higher, as high as 80%. Is there ever a time when hunting predominates over gathering? In late spring and early summer hunting camps, the proportion of meat may rise sharply. In one study, the 4 hunters of a small camp of 12 killed 29 animals in 17 days for a per capita consumption of almost 2 kg of meat per day. These bursts of meat eating tend to be of short duration, however, and overall I estimate that meat comprises between 30 and 40% of the diet and vegetables between 60 and 70%. Of course, not all the plant gathering is done by women. Men gather as well; their work provides almost a fifth of all the gathered food. Therefore, when we sum up the overall contribution of each sex, the disparity is reduced. Men produce about 44% and women 56% of the weight and calories of the food brought into the camp.

Considering work effort and productivity next adds a further dimension to the differences between the sexes. Men put in a longer subsistence work week than do women—about 2.7 days of work for men compared to 2.1 for women—but the productivity of women's work overall and per person-hour is higher than the productivity of men's. A man brings back one game animal for every 4 days of hunting for a success rate of 25%, while the probability of a woman finding food during a day of gathering is 100%. It is true that a single game animal may provide a very large input of food, as many calories as 50 days of gathering in the case of a large kudu. But such kills are few and far between, and for the most part men have to content themselves with smaller kills. Overall each man-day of hunting brings in about 7230 calories compared to 12,000 calories for each person-day of gathering. These differences in productivity account for the fact that women provide a larger share of the food even while they do less of the subsistence work.

In light of the greater importance of gathered food in the diet, it is curious that all !Kung, both men and women, evaluate meat more highly than plant food. When meat is scarce in the camp all people express a craving for it, even when vegetable foods are abundant. The occasions when large animals are killed are usually marked by feasting, dancing, and the giving of gifts of meat. Since game animals are scarce and unpredictable compared to plant foods, it is perhaps not so surprising that hunting is invested with more symbolic significance than gathering; and one should not lose sight of the fact that hunting provides essential nutrients such as high-quality protein, which are not as readily available from plant foods alone.

WOMEN, MEN, AND CHILD CARE

The question of child care and how it should be divided between mother, father, and other caretakers is a key issue in the contemporary West. The saddling of the woman of the modern household with most of the child care responsibilities has come to be regarded as a key symbol of woman's oppression in the capitalist system. In arguing for a more equitable distribution of household labor, feminist anthropologists have turned to data on non-Western societies for evidence of a more just set of child-care arrangements. In some ways the !Kung data offer little support for this point of view, since over 90% of the work involved in caring for young children is borne by the mother aided by other women (Draper, 1976). This is not to say that !Kung fathers ignore their children; they are attentive and loving and spend part of their leisure hours playing with and holding the young infants. But the !Kung father rarely takes sole responsibility for the child while the mother is absent, although the opposite occurs every day (Draper, 1975).

For their part the women do not consider themselves to be oppressed by this state of affairs. They keenly desire children, are excellent mothers, and often complain that they do not have as many children as they would like.

In interpreting these attitudes one should avoid projecting the negative features we associate with child care on an entirely different cultural situation. !Kung women consider childbirth and child care as their sphere of responsibility, and they take steps to guard their prerogatives in this area. For example, the fact that women go to the bush to give birth and insist on excluding men from the childbirth site is justified by them in terms of pollution and taboos, but the underlying reason may be that it simplifies matters if a decision in favor of infanticide is made. Since the woman will commit a considerable amount of her energy to raising each child, she examines the newborn carefully for evidence of defects; if she finds any, the child is not allowed to live and is buried with the afterbirth. By excluding men from the childbed, women can report back to the camp that the child was born dead, without fear of contradiction. But if the child is healthy and wanted by the woman, she accepts the major responsibility for raising it. In this way women exercise control over their own reproduction.

Another important reason why the !Kung woman's share of child care is not oppressive is that she is not isolated from the community in the same way that modern urban mothers are. She is helped by all the other women in the camp and there is no necessity to divide her food-producing work from her child-care work. Gathering and food processing is carried out with her child on her hip. The child is not left at home with babysitters. Also, men do participate in the non-child-care aspects of housework: About 20 to 40% of the housework in a four-person household is done by men (Lee, 1979: Chapter 9). For these reasons it is inaccurate to say that !Kung women are oppressed by the burden of child-care responsibilities.

MARRIAGE, DIVORCE, AND GROUP STRUCTURE

Their contribution to the food supply and their control over reproduction and child care gives !Kung women influence in other areas such as marriage and divorce. For a variety of reasons, including polygamy, there is a scarcity among the !Kung of women of marriageable age. Parents of a girl can afford to be selective about a prospective son-in-law. As a result men usually have to prove themselves worthy by demonstrating their competence in hunting and ritual activities. This task takes many years, so that men are often 7–15 years older than their wives at marriage. For example, the typical age of marriage for the Nyae Nyae !Kung during the 1950s was 14 or 15 for women and 22 to 25 for men (L. Marshall, 1959); in the Dobe area a decade later it was 16 or 17 for women and 23 to 30 for men. At marriage, the girl's people insist that the young couple live with them. The reasons given are of three kinds: first, that it must be seen that the man treats the daughter well; second, that he must prove his hunting abilities by providing meat; and third, that the female is too young to leave her mother. In most marriages, the husband leaves his own group and takes up residence with the wife's group, a stay that may last 3, 5, or 10 years, or even a lifetime. Bride service is found among many of the world's hunter–gatherers and occurs even in northern Australia, an area usually regarded as the heartland of the partrilocal band (Shapiro, 1971).

Thus, there is a central paradox in the idea of Lévi-Strauss (1969:62–65) that in simple societies women are a "scarce good" and that they may have functioned as the original medium of exchange between men in early society.

Their very scarcity actually makes women more desirable and allows them considerable scope to dictate their own terms of marriage. The result is that though among the !Kung most first marriages are arranged, many break up soon after, and the breakup is usually initiated by the wife, not the husband. Furthermore, there is a feedback relationship between the demography of marriage and its ideology. The fewer the women available for marriage, the greater the pressure to marry off girls at a younger age. However, the younger the girl, the longer will be the period of "bride service" necessary for the husband. By the time his bride service is completed, the husband's own parents may be dead, and such a man often decides to continue to stay with his wife's group.

The husband, during the period of bride service, is not exploited or treated as a menial by his wife's family (as was the daughter-in-law in the pre-revolutionary Chinese family). Precisely the opposite is the case. The atmosphere is made as congenial as possible to encourage the son-in-law to stay on after the period of bride service. Usually, in fact, he forms strong ties with other men in the group, especially with his brothers-in-law. Recruiting sons-in-law adds hunting strength to the group and means more meat for the members, a point that will be discussed later.

Bride service and age differences at marriage are two of the factors that explain why women comprise the core of !Kung living groups as frequently as do men (Lee, 1976). Statistically, mother–daughter bonds predominate followed by sister–sister and brother–sister, but father–son and brother–brother bonds are also found. Thus, it would be an overstatement to say that the !Kung group structure is a simple inversion of the patrilocal band model with females replacing males at the group's core. Instead we see that the genealogical core consists of males *and* females, and no single rule of uxorilocal or virilocal postmarital residence will account for the arrangements actually observed.

WOMEN AND POLITICAL POWER

Do women's predominant role in production, their leverage in marriage, and their sharing of core group membership with men lead to power in the political arena as well? The answer in a broad sense is yes: !Kung women's participation in group discussions and decision making is probably greater than that of women in most tribal, peasant, and industrial societies. But the level of their participation is not equal to that of men. Men appear to do about two-thirds of the talking in discussions involving both sexes, and men act as group spokespersons far more frequently than do women.

This disparity between men and women comes into sharper relief when discussions and arguments turn to violence. In 34 cases of fights I observed during the period 1963–1969, 14 involved a man attacking a women, whereas only one involved a woman attacking a man (Lee, 1979: Chapter 13). Since 11 of these 15 cases involved a husband and wife, it is clear that in domestic fights the wife is the victim in the great majority of cases. Similarly, in cases of homicide there were 25 male and no female killers, though it must be noted that 19 of the 22 victims were males as well.

Remarkably, one major form of violence against women, rape, is rare among the !Kung. I know of only two documented cases of rape among the !Kung within living memory, in contrast to its common occurrence in many other societies (Brownmiller, 1975; Webster, 1976).

In summarizing the evidence for male–female relations, we see that women predominate in some spheres of behavior and men in others, while the overall sense of the relations between the sexes is one of give and take. Both sexes work equally hard, with men working longer hours in subsistence and women working longer hours in housework and child care. Women's subsistence work is more efficient and productive than men's, so that they provide more of the food despite their shorter subsistence work week. In marriage arrangements women exercise some control, and they initiate divorce far more frequently than men. On the other hand, because the men are so much older than their wives at marriage, the age factor may tip the balance of influence within the marriage in favor of the males. (It should be noted that in about one out of five !Kung marriages the woman is older than the man—up to 20 years older—and in these unions it is usually the woman's influence that predominates.)

In the political sphere, men do more of the talking than women, and it is my impression that their overall influence in "public" matters is greater, though I cannot present any data to confirm this point. Men exhibit more violent behavior than women, though women are rarely the victims in serious conflicts; rape, a primary form of violence against women in many societies, is not common among the !Kung.

On balance the evidence shows a relatively equal role in society for the two sexes, and there is certainly no support in the !Kung data for a view of women in "the state of nature" as oppressed or dominated by men or as subject to sexual exploitation at the hands of males. However, the comparative evidence suggests that the status of !Kung women may be higher than that enjoyed by women in some other foraging societies such as the Eskimo (Friedl, 1975) and the Australian aborigine (Gale, 1974).

Leadership

How group and individual decisions are made in a society without formal political or judicial institutions is difficult to discern. In egalitarian societies such as the !Kung we see group activities unfolding, plans made, and decisions arrived at, all without a clear focus of authority or influence. Closer examination, however, reveals that patterns of leadership do exist. When a water hole is mentioned, a group living there is often referred to by the !Kung by a single man's or woman's name, for example, Bon!a's camp at !Kangwa, or Kxarun!a's camp at Bate. These individuals are often older people who have lived there the longest or who have married into the owner group, and who have some personal qualities worthy of note as a speaker, an arguer, a ritual specialist, or a hunter. In group discussions these people may speak out more than others, may be deferred to by others, and one gets the feeling that their opinions hold a bit more weight than the opinions of other discussants. Whatever their skills, !Kung leaders have no formal authority. They can only persuade but never enforce their will on others. Even the !Kung vocabulary of leadership is limited. Their word for "chief," //kaiha derived from the word //kai ("wealth"), is applied to Black headmen and chiefs and even to British kings and queens, but only rarely do the !Kung use it of other !Kung and then usually in a derisory manner. One /Xai/xai man nicknamed "//Kaihan!a," meaning "Big Chief," told us it was a joking name, since when he was young he tended to put on airs; people called him "Big Chief" to take him down a peg.

The suffix -n!a ("old or big") is added to any person's name after age 40. When one person of a camp is singled out from other age mates as n!a, it usually means that he or she is the leader of the camp. Lorna Marshall calls the camp leader the k"xaun!a, meaning "big owner" (1976:191).

PATHS TO LEADERSHIP

Analyzing the attributes of the acknowledged leaders of the living groups of the Dobe area, one finds a wide variety of skills, backgrounds, and genealogical positions. Some people are powerful speakers; others say very little. Some leaders are genealogically central; others are outsiders who married a core women. Some have many children and grandchildren in the living group; others have few or no offspring. Most leaders are males, but females also take leadership roles. At least four attributes can contribute to leadership, and most leaders have several of these traits in varying degrees:

1. Seniority in a large family
2. N!ore ("land") ownership
3. Marriage to a n!ore owner
4. Personal qualities

Seniority. Being the oldest member or the surviving member of a sibling group puts one in a position of respect within the family. If the family is large enough, the entire camp may be made up of the senior's descendants, his or her siblings' descendants, and their spouses. Seniority alone, however, does not make a leader, since many of the oldest people do not take leadership roles.

N!ore *Ownership*. This is an important criterion. If one is the senior descendant of a long line of *n!ore* owners, then one's claim to leadership is very strong. For example, Sa//gain!a, who died in 1971, was a descendant of several generations of /Xai/xai owners and though she was a soft-spoken person she was the acknowledged leader of her camp, a position shared with her husband. Her niece Baun!a (d. 1966) had equal claim to *n!ore* ownership, but since she was a strong forceful woman as well she was doubly a leader of her /Xai/xai group. Her son Tsau later became the chief spokesperson for the /Xai/xai San in their relations with the Blacks.

Marriage to a N!ore *Owner*. This is the most frequent route to leadership positions among the !Kung. It usually involves an energetic, capable man from another water hole marrying a woman of the *n!ore*-owning group. The best example of this kind of leader is ≠Toma n!wa, one of Lorna Marshall's main informants at /Gausha (Marshall, 1960, 1976). He married !U, a woman of the *n!ore*-owning sibling group and became the leader of the /Gausha camp, while !U's older brother Gao went to live in the Dobe area. ≠Toma is known to students of anthropology as the senior of the four giraffe hunters in John Marshall's classic film, *The Hunters* (1956). Another example of a leader who married in is ≠Toma//gwe at Dobe, who married //Koka of the *n!ore*-owning group and settled at Dobe to raise a family that by the 1970s had grown to consist of a group of four married children and their spouses and eight grandchildren. ≠Toma//gwe is considered gruff and unreasonable by other !Kung, but his large family plus his connection to the owner group validates his leadership role.

Personal Qualities. Some leaders like ≠Toma n!wa of /Gausha have obvious leadership qualities, being excellent speakers and diplomatic mediators. Others like ≠Toma//gwe are gruff and unreasonable but have strong personalities. ≠Toma Leopard, the young leader of a group at /Xai/xai, is charming but also short-tempered, feisty, and fiercely independent, while Kxaurun!a of Bate and Sa/ / gain!a of /Xai/xai are mellow, grandmotherly, and soft-spoken. No single personality type or personality trait dominates the ranks of leaders. If anything, what the leaders share is *an absence of traits in common*. None are arrogant or overbearing, boastful or aloof. In !Kung terms these traits absolutely disqualify one as a leader and may lead to even stronger sanctions. Some extremely aggressive men have been killed by community agreement (Lee, 1979:Chapter 13).

Another trait emphatically not found among traditional camp leaders is a desire for wealth or acquisitiveness. The leaders of the 15 or so living groups not closely tied to Black cattle posts live in huts no larger, and dress in clothing or ornaments no more lavish, than those of other camp members. Whatever their extravagances in speech, their personal style of living is modest and their accumulation of material goods is minimal. Whatever their personal influence over group decisions, they never translate this into more wealth or more leisure time than other group members. !Kung leaders therefore adhere closely to the image of the "egalitarian redistributor" noted by Harris (1975:289) or the modest band leader noted by Fried (1967:82) as characteristic of egalitarian societies.

SAN HEADMEN?

Whether there are hereditary headmen or chiefs among the San has been a matter of dispute. The existence of San chiefs was clearly stated long ago by Fourie, who wrote:

> At the head of each group is a big man or chief. Though usually considered to be a chief in name only and without any authority over the members of the group, he in fact does exercise considerable influence in the life of the community because in him are vested certain functions, the performance of which are of vital importance to the welfare of his people. The family area with its food and water supply as well as the fire are all looked upon as belonging to him. Among the tribes of the Kalahari he is succeeded by a son or failing such, by the nearest male relative. [1928:86].

Lorna Marshall in her earlier writings also spoke of a hereditary headman in whom resided the ownership of the group's resources and who inherited his position patrilineally (1960:334–352), a view which Fried has questioned (1967:87–89). Marshall has subsequently altered her views and has more recently stated that "'headman' was a misleading and unfortunate paraphrase" for k"xaun!a, meaning "big owner" (1976:191). Her revised thinking on the subject of headman brings the data on the Nyae Nyae !Kung into line with the data from the Dobe area, since in the latter it is clear that the institution of the headman was completely absent among the precontact !Kung. Furthermore, there is good evidence that the concept of headmen came only into currency *after* the arrival of the Blacks.

After reading Marshall's 1960 article and the earlier writings of others, I made inquiries in the Dobe area in 1964 to find out who was the headman or chief (//kaiha) at each water hole. The answers the people gave were almost entirely negative. The younger people did not know who, if anyone, was the headman, and the older people were obviously puzzled by the question. Some people offered up a variety of names, but most answered that the only headman they knew of was Isak, the Botswana headman appointed by the paramount chief. Finally I discussed the question with K"au, a senior /Xai/xai man originally from /Gam.

"Before the Tswana came here," I asked, "did the San have chiefs?"

"No," he replied. "We had no one we set apart like a chief; we all lived on the land."

"What about /Gaun!a? Was he a chief of /Xai/xai?" I asked, citing the name of a man whom the Hereros had mentioned as a former San headman.

"That is not true," K"au responded. "They are mistaken. Because among the Blacks the chief's village is fixed; you come to him, speak, and go away. Others come, speak, and go. But with us San, we are here today, tommorrow over there, and the next day still elsewhere. How can we have a chief leading a life like that?"

"If San have no chiefs," I asked, "then how did /Gaun!a come to be labeled as the chief here?"

"I can tell you that. /Gaun!a was living at /Twihaba east of /Xai/xai when the Blacks came. They saw evidence of his many only campsites and so they called him '//kaiha./ But they named him something that no !Kung person recognizes. But even that is lies," the old man continued, "because /Gaun!a was not even the real owner of /Twihaba! His proper n!ore is N!umtsa, east of /Gam. /Twihaba properly belongs to the people of a ≠ Toma whose descendants now live mostly in the east."

In her early and detailed discussion of the role of the headman, Lorna Marshall (1960:344–52) had used the /Gausha water hole as a prime example. The leader of her /Gausha Band 1 was ≠ Toma n!wa, discussed previously, who had married into the core group. But, she said, the headman at /Gausha was not ≠ Toma but his wife's younger brother, a crippled man named Lame ≠ Gao. The real headman, however, should have been one Gao, who, according to Marshall, "chose to renounce his headmanship and to live with his wife's people in Band 21. . . .However, should Gao change his plan and return to Band 1, the headmanship would automatically fall on him again, as he is the eldest son [1960:350]."

Marshall's Gao turned out to be none other then K"au-Kasupe, a short, lively Dobe resident who had originally come from the Nyae Nyae area. When in 1964 I asked him how it felt to be the absent headman of /Gausha, he expressed surprise, shock, disbelief, and then laughter. With a keen sense of the irony of the situation, Kasupe insisted that he was in no way the headman of /Gausha; that his shrimp of a kid brother, Lame ≠ Gao, certainly was not the headman; that the !Kung do not even have headmen; and that if they did he, Kasupe, would be the headman of / /Karu, not /Gausha, since the former was his father's true n!ore. Finally, asked Kasupe, if he was such a headman how did it happen that he, the boss, was living in rags at Dobe while underlings like his brother and sisters were living in luxury at the South African settlement scheme at Chum!kwe?

Kasupe's genuine surprise at being identified as the headman of /Gausha, along with the abundant corroborating evidence from other informants, convinced me that indeed the !Kung have no headman. Years later I was speaking with /Twi!gum, one of the owners of !Kangwa, and I casually asked him whether the !Kung have headmen.

"Of course we have headmen!" he replied, to my surprise. "In fact, we are all headmen," he continued slyly. "Each one of us is headman over himself!"

!KUNG LEADERSHIP IN THE CONTACT SETTING

Given the conflicting nature of the evidence on the headman question, we may legitimately ask how the illusion of !Kung headmanship came into being. The answer must be sought in the contacts of the !Kung with Blacks and Europeans since the late nineteenth century. The Tswana were a hierarchically organized, expanding people who brought under their rule a number of tribally based societies in western and northern Botswana. By the time they reached the Dobe area in the 1890s, the Tswana had already become part of the British colonial protectorate of Bechuanaland (Sillery, 1952, 1965). Like the British, the Tswana employed a system that combined elements of direct and indirect rule. Around the turn of the century the Tswana Kubu and Mhapa clans were given stewardship of the Dobe area by the Tswana paramount chief, but because the area was vast and their numbers were few, they tried to recruit local !Kung to be spokespeople for the San camps at the various water holes. Later when they moved their cattle up to /Xai/xai, /Gam, and !Kangwa, they put local !Kung men in charge of the livestock. Gradually a system of leaders came into being who were recognized as //kaihas by the Tswana but who had no equivalent standing among the !Kung themselves.

This contradiction between what we might call "inside" leaders and "outside" leaders continues to the present day. Inside leaders achieve their status by being seniors, n!ore owners, or spouses of n!ore owners in combination with personal qualities of leadership. The outside leaders excel in their ability to deal with Blacks and Europeans and in their entrepreneurial skills. Rarely are the two kinds of attributes combined in a single person. For example at Dobe in 1973 there were two camps, the one led by ≠Toma//gwe, who had lived there for many years, and a group led by !Xoma, a vigorous and able man who had long worked for Blacks and Europeans but who had no claim to the ownership of Dobe. Because of his knowledge of and sensitivity to the outside world, !Xoma was highly regarded by government people, anthropologists, and missionaries, but whenever the outsiders were absent, !Xoma's !Kung neighbors would express a great deal of hostility and resentment toward him.

This hostility came to a head in the mid-1970s over a government-sponsored project to dig a well at Dobe to improve and stabilize the water supply and thus make stockraising possible for the Dobe residents. When it came time to register the well in a leader's name, the outside agents favored !Xoma, who was fluent in Setswana and could make a highly articulate case for the !Kung before the district council's land board in Maun, the district capital. To the dismay of the outsiders, the Dobe !Kung chose as their leader a quiet and unaggressive man named ≠Dau, whose main claim to the role was the fact that he was the descendant of ≠Dauhwanadum ("≠Dau licks the river bed"), the senior owner of Dobe 50 years earlier. At the long and contentious meetings held to discuss the issue of the well, ≠Dau would sit quietly to one side listening; only rarely would he interject a comment, compared to !Xoma, who discoursed at length. The fact that the Dobe people chose the former man in preference to the latter indicated that they were not yet fully aware of the threats to the security of their land, and thus were not able to fully mobilize against it.[2] Polly Wiessner has pointed out (personal communication, 1976) that at the Chum!kwe settlement across the border ≠Toma n!wa (the /Gausha leader) was initially elected as the "foreman" to represent the !Kung in their dealings with the South African authorities, but he was defeated at the next election (a fate that has befallen many of his successors as well) after he began to exercise authority in a nontraditional way.

The changing patterns of leadership among the San reveal the existence of two contradictory systems of politics among them. The old system, based on genealogy and n!ore ownership, favored a leader who was modest in demeanor, generous to a fault, and egalitarian, and whose legitimacy arose from longstanding n!ore ownership. The new system required a man who had to deny most of the old virtues. The political arena of district councils, land boards, and nationalist politics required someone who was male, aggressive, articulate, and wise in the ways of the wider world. As antithetical as these characteristics are to !Kung traditional values, the dynamic of their rapid incorporation into the national capitalist system of Botswana makes it inevitable that these new leaders will have to come to the fore.

Social Relations of Production

Central to the foraging mode of production is a lack of wealth accumulation and the social differentiation that accompanies it. This lack of accumulation, even though the means for it—free time and raw materials—are at hand, arises from the requirements of the nomadic life. For people who move around a lot and did not keep pack animals until very recently, it would be sheer folly to amass more goods than can be carried when the group moves. Portability is the major design feature of the items themselves. The total weight of an individual's personal property is less than 25 pounds and can easily be carried from place to place.

---

[2]!Xoma continued to attend the meetings. The outcome of the hearings was that the people did get their title validated, with outside help.

The modest investment in capital goods and the lack of wealth disparities contribute to the distinctive style of San social relations. With personal property so easily portable, it is no problem for people to move as often as they do. There is a similar lack of investment in fixed facilities such as village sites, storage places, and fenced enclosures. When parties come into conflict, it is simpler to part company rather than remain together and resolve differences through adjudication or fighting.

A dynamic of movement informs the daily life of individuals and groups. Land ownership is vested, not in a single individual, but in a collective of *k"ausi*, both males and females, who form the core of the resident camp and who must be approached for permission to use the resources of the area. The right of reciprocal access to food resources is a fundamental principle of land use. If Group A visits Group B in one season, it is expected that Group B will repay the visit in the next. These visiting patterns tend to keep people in circulation from area to area, providing a change of scene and change of company. An individual's primary kin and close affines are always distributed at several different water holes, and through the far-reaching ties of the name relation he or she may establish close ties at a number of others. The outcome of these multiple options is that an individual may utilize the food resources of several water holes as long as he or she observes the elementary good manners of sharing fully with the members of the local camp. Whether an individual will choose to join a given camp depends on the history of his or her relations with the long-term residents. Many men and women who have a reputation for good humor, industry, or curing skills have standing invitations at many different camps. Even less popular individuals have strong primary kinship ties that make them welcome in at least two or three camps and tolerated in others.

This dynamic of movement, coupled with the fact that both males and females form the core of groups, leads to an emphasis in social relations on recruitment rather than exclusion. The older anthropological model of male-centered territorial bands (Fox, 1967; Service, 1962; Tiger, 1969) assumed that the primary requirement of the foraging living group was the maintenance of exclusive rights to land, a task that was best fulfilled by a core of male sibling defenders. In contrast, it is now clear that the *flexibility* to adapt to changing ecological circumstances is far more important in hunter–gatherer group structure than is the maintenance of exclusive rights to land. Flexibility favors a social policy of *bringing in* more personnel rather than keeping them out, and hence the emphasis is on the social principal of *recruitment* rather than *exclusion*. Because of the nature of production in a hunter–gatherer society, the principal way to increase output is to add personnel; therefore, a primary social strategy of many hunter–gatherers is to recruit sons-in-law to augment the group's meat-getting capacity while at the same time trying to retain the sons. The net effect of this strategy is that many of the males in any group are outsiders and unrelated to each other.

THE IDEOLOGY OF EQUALITY

On the political level these characteristics of the foraging life lead to a strong emphasis on egalitarian social relations. It is not simply a question of the *absence* of a headman and other authority figures but also a positive insistence on the essential equality of all people and the refusal to bow to the authority of others, a sentiment expressed in the statement: "Of course we have headmen!. . . Each one of us is headman over himself!" Leaders do exist, but their influence is subtle and indirect. They never order or make demands of others and their accumulation of material goods is never more, and is often much less, than the average accumulation of the other households in their camp.

CONTRADICTIONS IN !KUNG SOCIAL LIFE

Two remarkable cultural practices at the level of consciousness accompany the egalitarian political ideal. They occur among the !Kung and many other hunter–gatherers. The most serious accusations that one !Kung can level against another are the charge of stinginess and the charge of arrogance. To be stingy or "far-hearted" is to hoard one's goods jealously and secretively, guarding them "like a hyena." The corrective for this in the !Kung view is to make the hoarder give "till it hurts," that is, to make him give generously and without stint until everyone can see that he is truly cleaned out. In order to ensure compliance with this cardinal rule, the !Kung browbeat each other constantly to be more generous and not to set themselves apart by hoarding a little nest-egg. The cultural importance of sharing and giving has been ably documented by Lorna Marshall (1961, 1976:287–312).

But as seriously as they regard the fault of stinginess, the !Kung's most scathing criticisms are reserved for an even more serious shortcoming: the crime of arrogance (≠*twi*). While a stingy person is antisocial and irksome, an arrogant person is actually dangerous since according to the !Kung "his pride will make him kill someone." A boasting hunter who comes into camp announcing "I have killed a big animal in the bush" is being arrogant. A woman who gives a gift and announces her great generosity to all is being arrogant. Even an anthropologist who claims to have chosen the biggest ox of the year to slaughter for Christmas is being arrogant. The !Kung perceive this behavior as a danger sign, and they have evolved elaborate devices for puncturing the bubble of conceit and enforcing humility. These leveling devices are in constant daily use, minimizing the size of others' kills, downplaying the value of others' gifts, and treating one's own efforts in a self-deprecating way. "Please" and "thank you" are hardly ever found in their vocabulary; in their stead we find a vocabulary of rough humor, back-handed compliments, put-downs, and damning with faint praise. In fact, the one area in which they are openly competitive is in recounting suffering. They try to outdo each other in tales of misfortune: cold, pain, thirst, hunger, hunting failure, and other hardships represent conversational gold, the obverse of the coin of arrogance, which they so strongly discourage.

To the outsider these cultural preoccupations are disconcerting. We admire the !Kung from afar, but when we are brought into closer contact with their daily concerns, we are alternately moved to pity by their tales of hardship and repelled by their nagging demands for gifts, demands that grow more insistent the more we give.

These contradictions, generosity–stinginess, arrogance–humility, equality–hierarchy, sociability–withdrawal, are central themes in !Kung culture, and they afford us a glimpse into the internal workings of a social existence very different from our own. The essence of this way of life is sharing, a practice that is extended more widely in the foraging mode of production than in any other. People share within the family and between families, and the unit of sharing extends to the boundaries of the face-to-face community and beyond. Visualize the kind of sharing that occurs around the dinner table in a Western household but expanded in scale to include a group of 15–30 people, and you have some idea of the nature of sharing in a !Kung camp.

The principle of generalized reciprocity within the camp, the giving of something without an expectation of equivalent return, is almost universal among foraging peoples (Sahlins, 1965, 1972). In the case of the !Kung, food is shared in a generalized familistic way, while durable goods are exchanged according to the principle of balanced reciprocity; that is, transactions are expected to balance out in the long run. These kinds of reciprocities have their counterpoints in the political sphere. Egalitarian relations are a kind of balanced political reciprocity where giving orders and receiving them balances out. In the same way hierarchical relations correspond to a negative reciprocity at the level of exchange. To give orders from A to B but not from B to A is like taking goods from B to A but not giving anything in return. Conversely, sharing of food and sharing of power seem to go hand in hand.

The fact that communal sharing of food resources and of power is a phenomenon that has been directly observed in recent years among the !Kung and dozens of other foraging groups is a finding that should not be glossed over lightly. Its universality among foragers lends strong support to the theory of Marx and Engels that a stage of primitive communism prevailed before the rise of the state and the breakup of society into classes (Engels, 1884/1972). One should, however, add the proviso that this communism does not extend, as far as we know, to include sexual rights, as Marx and Engels, following L. H. Morgan (1877), originally believed.

Having declared that the foraging mode of production is a form of primitive communism, we would be mistaken if we idealized the foraging peoples as noble savages who have solved all the basic problems of living. Like individuals in any society, foragers have to struggle with their own internal contradictions, and living up to the demands of this strongly collective existence presents some particularly challenging problems. Sharing, for example, is not automatic; it has to be learned and reinforced by culture. Every human infant is born equipped with both the capacity to share and the capacity to be selfish. During the course of socialization, each society channels these impulses into socially acceptable forms, and every society expects some sort of balance between sharing and "selfish" behavior—between the needs of self and the needs of others. Among the foragers, society demands a high level of sharing and tolerates a low level of personal accumulation compared to Western capitalist norms. Living up to these demands, while it has its rewards, also takes its toll. I doubt whether any !Kung ever completely gives up the selfish impulse, and the tension to conform continues through life. Elderly !Kung in particular give voice to the contradictions between sharing and keeping. On one occasion ≠Toma//gwe asked me for a blanket and said, "All my life I've been giving, giving; today I am old and want something for myself." Similar sentiments have been expressed by other oldsters. Perhaps because they are old their departures from the cultural norm are better tolerated than they would be coming from younger adults.

Sharing food is accompanied by sharing space; the second area of communal life that causes stress is the lack of privacy. Daily life goes on in full view of the camp. People rarely spend time alone, and to seek solitude is regarded as a bizarre form of behavior. Even marital sex is carried on discretely under a light blanket shared with the younger children around the family fire. It is considered bad manners for others to look. Sullen, withdrawn behavior is regarded with concern and not allowed to continue. The person showing it is pestered and goaded until he or she loses his temper and the anger that follows helps to clear the air and reintegrate the outsider. When people are depressed or their feelings are hurt, they express it by awaking at night to compose sad songs, which they play for themselves on the thumb piano. These poignant refrains form a counterpoint to the night sounds of the crackling sleeping fires and the calls of the nightjars, and no one tells the players to pipe down or shut up.

Conclusion

It is clear that the demands of the collective existence are not achieved effortlessly, but rather they require a continuing struggle with one's own selfish, arrogant, and antisocial impulses. The fact that the !Kung and other foragers succeed as well as they do in communal living in spite of (or because of?) their material simplicity offers us an important insight. A truly communal life is often dismissed as a utopian ideal, to be endorsed in theory but unattainable in practice. But the evidence for foraging peoples tells us otherwise. A sharing way of life is not only possible but has actually existed in many parts of the world and over long periods of time.

References

Bachofen, Johann J.
  1861   Das Mutterrecht. Basel: Benno Schwabe.
Brownmiller, Susan
  1975   Against Our Will: Men, Women, and Rape. New York: Simon and Schuster.
Diamond, Stanley
  1975   In Search of the Primitive. New York: Dutton.
Draper, Patricia
  1975   !Kung Women: Contrasts in Sexual Egalitarianism in the Foraging and Sedentary Con-
          texts. In Toward an Anthropology of Women. R. Reiter, ed. Pp. 77–109. New York:
          Monthly Review Press.
  1976   Social and Economic Constraints on Child Life Among the !Kung. In Kalahari Hunter-
          Gatherers. R. B. Lee and I. DeVore, eds. Pp. 199–217. Cambridge, Massachusetts: Har-
          vard University Press.
Engels, Friedrich
  1972   The Origin of the Family, Private Property, and the State. E. Leacock, ed. New York:
          International Publishers. (First ed. 1884).
Fourie, Louis
  1928   The Bushmen of South West Africa. In The Native Tribes of South West Africa. C.
          Hahn, L. Fourie, and H. Vedder, eds. Chap. 3. Cape Town: Cape Times.
Fox, Robin
  1967   Kinship and Marriage. Baltimore: Penguin.
Freud, Sigmund
  1919   Totem and Taboo. London: G. Routledge.
Fried, Morton H.
  1967   The Evolution of Political Society. New York: Random House.
Friedl, Ernestine
  1975   Women and Men: An Anthropologist's View. New York: Holt, Rinehart and Winston.
Gale, Fay, ed.
  1974   Women in Aboriginal Society. Second ed. Canberra: Australian Institute of Aboriginal
          Studies.
Golde, Peggy, ed.
  1970   Women in the Field: Anthropological Experiences. Chicago: Aldine.
Gough, Kathleen
  1970   Women in Evolution. Boston: New England Free Press. Pamphlet.
  1971   The Origin of the Family. Journal of Marriage and the Family 33:760–771.
Harris, Marvin
  1975   Culture, People, Nature: An Introduction to General Anthropology. New York:
          Thomas Y. Crowell.
Hiatt, Betty
  1974   Woman the Gatherer. In Woman's Role in Aboriginal Society. Second ed. F. Gale, ed.
          Pp. 4–15. Canberra: Australian Institute of Aboriginal Studies.
Lamphere, Louise
  1977   Anthropology. Signs 2(3):612–627. (Review article.)
Leacock, Eleanor, ed.
  1972   Engels' The Origin of the Family, Private Property, and the State. New York:
          International Publishers.
Lee, Richard B.
  1968   What Hunters Do for a Living, or, How to Make Out on Scarce Resources. In Man the
          Hunter. R. B. Lee and I. DeVore, eds. Pp. 30–48. Chicago: Aldine.

1976 !Kung Spatial Organization: An Ecological and Historical Perspective. *In* Kalahari Hunter–Gatherers: Studies of the !Kung San and Their Neighbors. R. B. Lee and I. DeVore, eds. Pp. 73–97. Cambridge, Massachusetts: Harvard University Press.

1979 The !Kung San: Men, Women, and Work in a Foraging Society. New York: Cambridge University Press.

Lee, Richard B., and Irven DeVore, eds.

1968 Man the Hunter. Chicago: Aldine.

Lévi-Strauss, Claude

1969 The Elementary Structure of Kinship. Revised ed. Boston: Beacon Press.

McCarthy, Frederic D., and Margaret McArthur

1960 The Food Question and the Time Factor in Aboriginal Economic Life. *In* Anthropology and Nutrition. C. P. Mountford, ed. Pp. 145–194. Records of the American–Australian Scientific Expedition to Arnhem Land, Vol. 2. Victoria: Melbourne University Press.

Marshall, John

1956 The Hunters. Somerville, Massachusetts. Center for Documentary Anthropology. Film.

Marshall, Lorna

1959 Marriage among !Kung Bushmen. Africa 29:335–365.

1960 !Kung Bushmen Bands. Africa 30:325–355.

1961 Sharing, Talking, and Giving: Relief of Social Tensions among the !Kung Bushmen. Africa 31:231–249.

1976 The !Kung of Nyae Nyae. Cambridge, Massachusetts: Harvard University Press.

Martin, M. Kay , and Barbara Voorhies

1975 Female of the Species. New York: Columbia University Press.

Meillassoux, Claude

1973 On the Mode of Production of the Hunting Band. *In* French Perspectives in African Studies. P. Alexandre, ed. Pp. 187–203. London: Oxford University Press.

1975 Femmes, greniers et capitaux. Paris: Maspero.

Morgan, Elaine

1972 The Descent of Woman. New York: Stein and Day.

Morgan, Lewis H.

1877 Ancient Society. New York: World Publishing.

Mumford, Lewis

1961 The City in History: Its Origin, Its Transformations, and Its Prospects. London: Secker and Warburg.

Reed, Evelyn

1975 Woman's Evolution from Matriarchal Clan to Patriarchal Family. New York: Pathfinder Press.

Reiter, Rayna R.

1977 Introduction to Special Issue on the Anthropology of Women. Critique of Anthropology 3(9–10):5–24.

Reiter, Rayna R., ed.

1975 Toward an Anthropology of Women. New York: Monthly Review Press.

Rohrlich-Leavitt, Ruby

1975 Peaceable Primates and Gentle People. New York: Harper and Row.

Rosaldo, Michelle Z., and Louise Lamphere

1974 Women, Culture and Society. Stanford, California: Stanford University Press.

Rose, Frederic G. G.

1968 Australian Marriage, Landowning Groups, and Invitations. *In* Man the Hunter. R. Lee and I. DeVore, eds. Pp. 200–208. Chicago: Aldine.

Sahlins, Marshall

1965 The Sociology of Primitive Exchange. *In* The Relevance of Models in Social Anthropology. M. Banton, ed. Pp. 139–236. A. S. A. Monographs, No. 1. London: Tavistock.

1972 Stone Age Economics. Chicago: Aldine.

Service, Elman R.
    1962 Primitive Social Organization: An Evolutionary Perspective. New York: Random House.
Shapiro, W.
    1971 Wawilak: Ontogeny, Phylogeny, and Sexuality in Miwyt ("Murngin") Thought. Paper presented at 70th Annual Meetings of the American Anthropological Association, New York.
Sillery, Anthony
    1952 The Bechuanaland Protectorate. Cape Town: Oxford University Press.
    1965 Founding a Protectorate: History of Bechuanaland, 1885–1895. The Hague: Mouton.
Slocum, Sally
    1975 Woman the Gatherer. *In* Toward an Anthropology of Women. R. Reiter, ed. Pp. 36–50. New York: Monthly Review Press.
Tanner, Nancy, and Adrienne Zihlman
    1976 Women in Evolution. Part I, Innovation and Selection in Human Origins. Signs 1:585–608.
Tiger, Lionel
    1969 Men in Groups. New York: Random House.
Webster, P.
    1976 The Politics of Rape in Primitive Society. Paper presented at 75th Annual Meetings of the American Anthropological Association, Washington, D.C.
Woodburn, James
    1968 An Introduction to Hazda Ecology. *In* Man the Hunter. R. B. Lee and I. DeVore, eds. Pp. 49–55. Chicago: Aldine.

5

PHILIP L. NEWMAN

Sexual Politics and Witchcraft in Two New Guinea Societies

A recent survey of studies on women's status points out that the societies of the New Guinea Highlands, among others, are characterized by certain behaviors, attitudes, and beliefs that have been labeled "sex antagonism." This complex of beliefs attributes to women various innate, dangerous qualities that, in turn, have the effect of subjecting them to behavioral restrictions, a stigmatized position, and physcial abuse that forms part of a pattern of male supremacy (Quinn, 1977:215). Faithorn (1976:87) has characterized the ideological components of this complex as "the three interrelated themes of sexual segregation, male dominance/female subservience, and male purity/female pollution."

The immediate purpose of this chapter is to introduce another theme into this complex, and to suggest that it may have demographic and social correlates. Most anthropolgists who have described and analyzed the complex have focused on menstrual pollution or the polluting influences of sexual intercourse, pregnancy, and birth as the dangerous qualities attributed to women. A less widespread but nonetheless important female attribute is that seen as an innate malevolent quality that can be glossed as "witchcraft." Two contrasting cases will be examined: in one, women are thought to be capable of witchcraft, while in the other, they are not. The more general purpose of this chapter is to focus attention on the study of social inequality in so-called egalitarian societies, especially as it is manifested along sexual lines.

SOCIAL INEQUALITY
Comparative and Developmental Approaches

Background

The two cases to be examined are the Gururumba-Fikese and the Irahkia-Poqna, both of the Eastern Highlands district of Papua–New Guinea. The former are one of the Asaro-speaking groups living on the east and west banks of the upper Asaro River, and are of the East-Central linguistic family as classified by Würm (1964). The Irahkia-Poqna are one of the Awa-speaking groups living on the north and south banks of the lower Lamari River, and are of the Eastern linguistic family by the same classification. Although the two groups are similar culturally, they offer contrasting elaborations of the basic Eastern Highlands cultural configuration.[1]

The total population of the upper Asaro Valley[2] is approximately 13,000 people. This population is organized into nine territorially distinct, socio-political entities each of which comprises a single named phratry, or, in some cases, a pair of phratries. the Gururumba-Fikese are a phratry pair. Each phratry, in turn, is made up of four or five exogamous patriclans. The principal tuber crop is the sweet potato which is cultivated in the valley bottoms or on the sides of ridges in finely worked and neatly laid out plots. After depletion, these plots are allowed to return to fallow cover characterized by natural grasses and reeds as well as deliberately planted casuarina trees. Pigs are tethered, periodically hand-fed, pastured, and, in general, carefully looked after.

The total population of the lower Lamari Valley is approximately 1300 people.[3] The terrain in this area is much more precipitous than in the Asaro Valley, but the amount of land occupied and utilized is about the same, resulting in a much higher population density for the upper Asaro than for the lower Lamari. The Awa population is also organized into territorially distinct phratries that occur either singly or in pairs. There are eight such entities in the Awa case, and the Irahkia-Poqna are one of them, again comprising a pair of phratries. Awa phratries are also divided into named, exogamous patriclans, but there are two or three clans to a phratry rather than four or five as in the Asaro case. Although the internal structure of Gururumba-Fikese and Irahkia-Poqna is similar with respect to levels of segmentation and the number of constituent clans, the number of people within each of these units is very different. Thus, although both units include about the same number of clans, the total population of Irahkia-Poqna, a pair of phratries, approximates that of a single Gururumba clan.

With respect to Awa subsistence patterns, sweet potatoes are grown, but they are secondary in importance to yams and taro among tuberous crops.

[1]See Kenneth Read (1954:1–43) for a general characterization of this configuration and a comparison with the Western Highlands pattern.

[2]Fieldwork was conducted in this region in 1959 and 1960. Although the present tense is used, observations refer to the time of field observations.

[3]Fieldwork was conducted in this region during 1964–1965 and during the summer of 1970.

Awa gardens are principally of two types: gardens in open grassland, some types of which are irrigated, and those cut out of the forest. While the former are tilled, the latter are not, and neither type is characterized by the neatness that comes from the Asaro practices of planting in rows, mounding, and ditching. Casuarinas are unknown as fallow cover and are rarely found in the area. Pigs are not tethered, are fed only occasionally, and are left to run semi-wild.

These background characteristics have been pointed out to indicate that even though the Asaro and Awa peoples share many Eastern Highlands cultural features, including beliefs in female pollution, the men's house complex, and a nucleated, village-type settlement pattern, they are quite different in overall scale. Population density is much lower among Awa speakers, their horticulture is less intensive, local communities are more distant from one another, and the exchange system is not nearly so elaborate, either in amounts of material exchanged or numbers of occasions on which exchanges take place. With respect to the role of women, this chapter examines the possibility that the presence of witchcraft beliefs among Asaro speakers, and its absence among Awa speakers, is the product of social conditions created by these differences.

Women and Witchery

Both the Gururumba-Fikese and the Irahkia-Poqna believe that certain individuals are capable of physically harming others through secret, nonordinary means that do not involve direct physical contact. In both groups there are said to be a number of different techniques that can be utilized, all of which involve learning how to manipulate certain objects and substances. Although any adult can learn to use these techniques, it is generally believed that they are primarily utilized by adult men and are primarily directed at people outside one's own clan or local community. In addition to beliefs of this kind, the Gururumba-Fikese also believe that certain individuals have the innate capacity to harm others by secret, nonordinary means stemming from the presence in them of *gwumu*, an animate substance that drives them to destructive acts and provides them with special powers to accomplish these acts. In this chapter I shall refer to the learned techniques as *sorcery* and the innate capacity as *witchcraft.*

The content of the Gururumba-Fikese belief in witchcraft can be understood more fully, and its contrast with sorcery seen more clearly, by examining five of its major features. First, witches are almost always thought to be women, particularly married women not yet past the age of childbearing. I found a few cases in which men were suspected of being witches, but in each case the person was a somewhat marginal individual, not an active, assertive male representative of the norm. It is also true that some males are thought to have control over a witch who will then do his bidding, but these men are not themselves thought to be witches; their ability to control a witch is said to be a kind of sorcery. Finally, as women grow older and no longer bear children, their behavior shifts slightly toward the male mode. It is at this point that a woman may begin asserting herself more in public by speaking out in group discussions, finding a male trading partner in another group, or becoming the custodian of the male flutes. However, it is not these older women who are most likely to be thought of as witches, but younger women whose families are not yet fully established and whose extrafamilial interests are largely subordinate to those of their husbands.

Second, witches are found among the women of one's own local group and not some distant place. They are to be found among the women one associates with daily in the village, not shadowy figures from places seldom visited or little known. This belief is in marked contrast to those about sorcery. Particular individuals may be accused of being sorcerers, but it much more commonly happens that a village or clan is identified as containing the sorcerer, but the particular individual seldom becomes known.

Third, witchcraft is not a technique, like sorcery, but is a quality of persons. A witch acts because of a substance inside the body known as *gwumu*. Although this substance can be passed from mother to daughter, its transfer is not a matter of intention on the part of either mother or daughter. The Gururumba-Fikese have not developed the idea that there are certain family lines through which the substance characteristically passes. It simply appears or does not appear in an individual, and the individual has no control over its presence or absence. *Gwumu* is sometimes also referred to by a term that means "little sister." This metaphor is informative, as it points to the assumption that what witches do is not so much a matter of their own volition as it is of being driven to act in much the same way one might be driven to respond to the nagging demands of a persistent younger sibling. Consistent with this assumption is the idea that witches are not particularly responsible for their acts. Thus, although a woman who has been accused of witchcraft may suffer severe physical deprivations, these are more the result of attempts to make her admit her deeds or to extract the *gwumu* from her body than they are the result of conscious attempts to punish her. Not only is *gwumu* the main motive force behind the deeds of a witch but it also confers special powers, including powers of flight, of transformation into other living forms (usually insects or bats), and of invisibility, and the ability to enter other physical substances, particularly to eat them from the inside.

Fourth, though witches may attack other women, particularly older women, they are most prone to attack the food, live pigs, and men associated with exchange activities. They get inside men and pigs, bite their livers, and make them sick or cause them to die. They get into cooked pork and eat it from the inside, leaving only a hollow shell to fool the owner. People returning from feasts with food are careful to cover it, saying its sight would attract a witch. Men distributing food at feasts are cautioned to make sure that each woman present gets a small share lest one of them be a witch and attack him for the slight. Witches are said to be attracted by the "smell" of occasions on which food and wealth objects are being given and received. The connotation of "smell" is both olfactory and materialistic in this context; that is, it is both the odor of the cooked food and the excitement of a public occasion on which food and goods are changing hands that attracts the witches. The attacks of a witch are thus thought to be the result of uncontrolled inner desires to consume or destroy the food and wealth of others by secret means.

Fifth, witches are thought to band together over the grave of a recently dead person and make a meal of the flesh—cutting and distributing it in the same manner that pigs are distributed in public exchange activities. This characteristic is particularly interesting in that it again associates witches, as women, with indirect modes of attack. We have already seen that witches use covert means such as physical transformation or invisibility to accomplish their ends, but there is an additional kind of indirection involved in the ghoulish activities of witches. The Gururumba-Fikese assume that witches eat the dead not only because they like the taste of human flesh[4] but also because they know that such desecration of a corpse will cause the ghost of the dead person to attack its living relatives in an effort to get them to compensate it for suffering the horrid act. This point is of importance because it attributes to witches a characteristic also generally attributed to women in certain kinds of situations. Specifically, in situations of interpersonal conflict in which men and women confront one another, it is expected that men will display more directness in dealing with the situation by asserting authority or using physical coercion, while women are expected to attempt control through indirect means such as pleading, taunting, insulting, or withdrawing.[5]

These expectations are interestingly encoded in Gururumba myths, which characteristically concern people confronting threats to themselves arising from the actions of another. In these stories men are depicted as dealing with such situations directly through physical confrontation while women are shown as either giving up, destroying themselves, transforming themselves into animals and thus escaping, or in some way utilizing ghosts as a medium of confrontation.

Witches, then, are thought not only to derive gustatory pleasure from eating the dead but also to derive satisfaction from the knowledge that the relatives of the deceased will probably have to kill more pigs and cook more food than they have already provided in the mortuary feast in order to placate the angry ghost, thereby giving the witches another occasion to exercise their

[4]No cannibalism, mortuary or otherwise, was practiced in this region, and the thought of it is quite abhorrent to the Gururumba-Fikese.

[5]Although these general expectations are manifest in observable behavior, it is also the case the adult women do not hesitate to engage in physical altercations with men (usually their husbands).

voracious appetites. Like women, they utilize covert and indirect means to satisfy their desires to be around food and material wealth.

A final point should be made concerning the incidence of witchcraft and sorcery accusations. The suspicion that sorcery has been used is very common in both the Gururumba-Fikese and Irahkia-Poqna. Almost every death, if it is not that of a small child or a very old person, is attributed at some point to the action of a sorcerer. Illnesses, and to a lesser degree other unfortunate events, are also frequently thought to be the result of sorcery in both groups. In contrast, the suspicion that witchcraft has occurred is much less common. Among the Gururumba-Fikese I actually observed only two accusations during a period of 13 months in which a concerted attempt was made to identify some particular individual as a witch, and I collected five well-documented cases of specific accusations from the recent past history of the community. Casual talk about the possible presence of witches is quite common, however. There is a great deal of half-joking, half-serious conversation during and after food distributions about the likelihood that it will attract witches, about what kinds of precautions should be taken, and about the interpretation of certain signs that can portend their presence. There is also a good deal of "nervousness" after a burial, especially of an important individual, about whether or not the grave will be, or has been, entered by a band of witches. Watches are frequently set around a grave specifically to prevent such an occurrence, although they are not always successful, since witches can transform themselves into insects or become invisible. Concerned relatives may inspect a grave daily for several weeks after a burial, looking for footprints or other signs of a ghoulish visit. Thus, although specific witchcraft accusations are not frequent among the Gururumba-Fikese, witches nevertheless represent a potential threat commonly articulated in everyday life.

Witchcraft and Contrasting Social Environments

In searching for factors that might explain the presence of witchcraft beliefs among the Gururumba-Fikese and their absence among the culturally similar Irahkia-Poqna, I have utilized certain features of the beliefs themselves and a sociological theory of witchcraft proposed by Guy Swanson. In 1960 Swanson published *The Birth of the Gods: The Origin of Primitive Beliefs*, an attempt to modify and expand on the basic Durkheimian thesis concerning the relationship between religion and society. It contains a number of hypotheses predicting associations between various types of supernatural beings or powers and certain aspects of social organization. Swanson then tested these hypotheses cross-culturally on a world sample of societies. His hypothesis (1960:147) concerning witchcraft, which also includes what I have called sorcery, is that it will be found in association with "important but unlegitimated relations among people." He further defines "important but unlegitimated'" contacts as having the following characteristics:

(a) People must interact closely with one another for the achievement of common ends. In this sense, they are intimate. (b) These relations were not developed with the consent, tacit or explicit, of all concerned, or (c) These relations are not such that persons with conflicting objectives and desires can resolve their differences through commonly agreed upon means such as courts or community councils [1960:208–209].

In addition, he cites a number of conditions that fulfill these requirements, two of which are relevant to the cases at hand. They are: "(1) where a person is required to obtain a spouse from an ultimately sovereign group other than his or her own, [and] (2) where strong and persistent conflicts of interest are likely to exist between husbands and wives [p. 209]." Given the fact that Gururumba-Fikese witches are usually thought to be women, especially women as wives rather than as mothers or daughters, Swanson's ideas would suggest three possible areas concerning the position of women in the two Eastern Highland societies as related to their differential attribution as witches. These are: (1) differences with respect to the sovereign groups from which men obtain wives or that women enter on marriage; (2) differences with respect to the mobilization of support by women in conflict situations with men; and (3) differences in the sources of persistent conflicts between husbands and wives.

DIFFERENCES WITH RESPECT TO THE SOVEREIGN GROUPS
FROM WHICH MEN GET WIVES OR THAT WOMEN ENTER
ON MARRIAGE

Swanson defines sovereign groups as follows:

These organizations have original and independent jurisdiction over some sphere of social life. An organization has original jurisdiction if only that organization can legitimately originate a decision in some sphere of social life. It has independent jurisdiction if no other organization and no individual can legitimately abrogate its decisions [1960:202].

Swanson specifies other features as well, but it is clear that for both the Gururumba-Fikese and the Irahkia-Poqna the clan is a sovereign group. The clan is also the most inclusive exogamous group in both cases, and thus fulfills Swanson's condition that a spouse must be obtained from a sovereign group other than one's own. Despite this fundamental similarity with respect to the nature of the sovereign groups from which spouses are obtained, there are also three major differences in the circumstances surrounding marriage that affect the social environment of women when they enter their husbands' local group at marriage.

DIFFERENCES IN DISTANCE BETWEEN THE SOVEREIGN GROUPS FROM WHICH WIVES COME

The women entering a Gururumba-Fikese clan at marriage tend to come from local groups that reside at some distance from the one they enter, whereas Irahkia-Poqna women tend to come from groups close at hand. A tabulation from my genealogies of the largest Gururumba clan reveals that approximately 27% of the in-marrying women came from within Gururumba itself. This means they were within a 20–30-min walk of their natal communities. Fikese, the paired phratry, provided 25% of the wives, who were thus 45 min to 1 hr away from their natal communities. The remaining 48% of in-marrying women came from other upper Asaro groups, from Chimbu groups, or from Gende groups across the Bismark Mountains to the north.[6] If the women were from upper Asaro groups, the distance would involve a walking time of 3–4 hr, whereas if they were from Chimbu or Gende the time would be approximately 6–8 hr.

The Irahkia-Poqna situation is just the reverse of this. Taking the largest Irahkia clan as a point of comparison, I found that 37% of in-marrying women are from within Irahkia phratry itself, 45% are from Poqna, the paired phratry, and 18% were from other Awa-speaking groups. None were from non-Awa-speaking groups.[7] These figures are more meaningful when it is realized that 82% of the women entering this clan were from no greater distance than 10–15 min walk away. It is also significant that the next nearest Awa-speaking group is over 4 hr walk away and that it takes 6–8 hr to walk to half the others from Irahkia. Thus, most Irahkia wives come from near at hand.

These differences in distance are important because, in a situation where walking is the only effective means of communicating between groups, increases in distance between groups will also tend to increase both the degree to which the groups from which wives come will be culturally alien to the one they enter on marriage and group members will be unfamiliar with each other as individuals. It will also tend to increase the degree to which marriage represents a break in social contact between the in-marrying woman and her natal community.

---

[6]The Chimbu and the Gende each speak a language different from that spoken in the upper Asaro valley.

[7]Awa do marry non-Awa-speakers, but the ratio is low compared to the Asaro-speaking peoples. For example, of the six clans within the Irahkia-Poqna phratry, two showed no marriages with non-Awa-speakers in the genealogies collected, and the other four showed marriage with non-Awa speakers at the levels of 2%, 5%, 11%, and 14% respectively.

DIFFERENCES IN THE DEGREE TO WHICH WIVES ARE FAMILIAR WITH THE MEMBERS OF THE SOVEREIGN GROUP THEY ENTER UPON MARRIAGE

Because the women entering a Gururumba-Fikese clan at marriage tend to come from local groups at some distance away, because they enter a community where the married women already resident are from diverse localities, and because they come in their late teens or early twenties, they tend to be unfamiliar with the members of these groups. The majority of women will never have visited the community into which they marry, or at most, will have visited it only infrequently. While it is true that a woman will almost always find someone from her natal community or a closely related group in the community she enters, it is also true that most men and women there will be strangers to her. Furthermore, an entering woman will not even speak the same language as approximately 20% of the other women already there. Finally, although a young girl may be designated as a possible mate for a boy in a particular clan, her actual transfer as a bride does not usually take place until she has reached her late teens or early twenties, so that her period of adjustment to the new community starts relatively late in her life.

The Irahkia-Poqna situation, on the other hand, is one in which the women marrying into a group will almost always be very familiar with its members. Since any given Irahkia-Poqna clan gets most of its wives from the immediate vicinity, a new wife will usually know and be known by the members of the group into which she marries. There is little likelihood that she will encounter anyone who does not speak the same language she does. Finally, it is not unusual for girls to be betrothed in their early or pre-teens, and to be transferred to the clan of their future husbands where they are raised by foster parents, with the result that the period of their adjustment to the new group takes place considerably before marriage occurs.

DIFFERENCES IN THE DEGREE TO WHICH MARRIAGE REPRESENTS A BREAK IN THE SOCIAL CONTACT BETWEEN THE WIFE AND HER NATAL COMMUNITY

Two general areas can be examined for information relating to differences of this sort: the symbolism of bridal transfer at marriage, and the character of postnuptial contact between a women and her patrikin.

The Symbolism of Bridal Transfer

The transfer of a bride in Irahkia-Poqna takes place in the context of ceremonies emphasizing the realignment of nurturant and reciprocal relationships contingent upon the transfer of a woman from one kin group to another. When the relevant adults of two clans have agreed that a marriage should take place between a young man and woman, the groom-to-be must demonstrate his ability to be a provider and show concern for the welfare of his potential affines by supplying the mother of the young woman, and her close male kinsmen, small marsupials and birds he has hunted in the forest. The mother of the young woman collects the bones of these creatures and forms a pendant from them that she wears around her neck. When the pendant becomes heavy and reaches her waist, it is deemed time for the actual transfer of the young woman from the care of her natal kin to those of her husband to take place. The transfer itself stresses the equivalence of the two sides in the new relationship as adult representatives from both the groom's group and the bride's group meet halfway between their places of residence and form a double line through which the young woman passes on her way to the house of a matrikinsman of the groom, where she will stay until her own residence is established.

A prestation of food and goods, arranged by the groom's patrikin for those of the bride, is said to show appreciation for the effort they have expended on raising the girl. This prestation is not thought of as payment for loss of services or future children connected with the transfer of the woman. Indeed, in the early stages of my fieldwork, when Neo-Melanesian was the only mode of communication used in research, it was difficult to talk about these events, as the local people consistently denied that the pidgin idiom of "paying for" or "buying" applied to this case.

The prestation itself is modest in size, consisting of two or three cooked pigs and small amounts of shells, feathers, arrows, and other durable goods. The bride, in turn, brings with her cooked food and goods, and although hers is the lesser amount, the increment of economic loss or gain on either side is negligible. At the subsequent division of both these prestations in the recipient groups, special allotments are set aside for the close female relatives of the two principals, in recognition of the pain and work they have endured in bearing and raising them.

The transfer of a woman as bride in Gururumba-Fikese also emphasizes the realignment of nurturant and reciprocal relationships, but it is overlain by other elements, giving it a different character. The idiom of "payment" for the woman is used freely, and there is considerable discussion of its exact amount. This discussion concerns such things as the past relationship between the two groups, as well as the physical and behavioral characteristics of the woman. The prestation itself is large, consisting of as many as 20 live pigs, plus several cooked ones, and other goods proportionately valuable. The prestation is not so much accepted by the bride's group as it is taken from the groom's group. The bride's male kin, in full battle dress, surround the approaching party of groom's kinsmen bearing the bride price, and "pull" them into the village as if they had been captured. In return, it is not unusual for the groom's group to assert their strength during the exchange by dramatically adding some hitherto hidden wealth to the pile just as the bride's group assumes they have received it all.

The actual transfer of a Gururumba woman from her natal group to that of her husband emphasizes the breaking of old ties. Representatives of the groom's group arrive in her village after the bridewealth has been transferred and after the girl has spent several evenings traveling about the countryside with agemates of both sexes, saying sad farewell to acquaintances and old suitors. The girl stays some distance away from her village on the day of the transfer, protected by her agemates of both sexes, but is eventually wrested from them by her own senior kinsmen in a battle of the generations that may result in considerable physical violence.

When she is finally brought into the village, she is placed with her kin on one side of a food pile while the groom's group is ranged on the opposite side. After some speeches the groom's kinsmen pick her up and carry her to the other side of the pile. After more speeches, in which the groom's group accepts responsibility for her welfare, the food and the girl are carried away. Finally, her incorporation into the new group is dramatically and painfully emphasized when her husband shoots her in the thigh with an arrow as she enters his village, as a reminder of his hegemony over her and the potential consequences of her nonconformity.

The Character of a Woman's Postnuptial Contact with her Patrikin

Both the Irahkia and the Gururumba tend to be patri–virilocal, but differ in the degree and character of a woman's postnuptial contact with her patrikin.

Marriage for a Gururumba-Fikese woman represents a more definitive break from her natal community, particularly from her sibling group, than it does for an Irahkia woman. One of the central themes of the instruction a Gururumba-Fikese woman is given, prior to her being carried away to her new home, emphasizes the energy she must now devote to the concerns of her husband and his patrikin. She is told to stop thinking about her brothers and fathers and to turn her attention to the needs and demands of a new set of males. Young women often find this new situation difficult to deal with, and the high frequency with which they run away from it is indicative of the stress it involves.[8]

The strength of the tie being broken is also indicated by the fact that it is not only the young woman who is upset by this change. It is not uncommon for an unmarried male sibling of a recently transferred woman to have mild anxiety spells in which he is attacked by a ghost who urges him to retrieve his sister lest the unprotected bride be gobbled up by her cannibalistic in-laws or suffer some other horrible fate at their hands. There are a number of myths depicting exactly these happenings. They also frequently depict the suicide of

[8]Some 30% of the women I interviewed reported breaking, or attempting to break, their first marital arrangement, and approximately 20% of these reported reacting similarly to the first two such arrangements.

a brother, a sister, or both, at the time of the bride's transfer, or the killing of a sibling and the bride by a suitor angered at the stress they have displayed on having to part from one another.

After the transfer of a Gururumba-Fikese bride, there are several occasions when she is paid a formal visit by her patrikin and other less closely related members of her clan. The first of these occurs within a month or two after the transfer, when they come bearing large amounts of bast, string, dyes, and other materials related to the making of net bags and other utilitarian items produced by women. The bride is decorated by her affines with feathers and ornaments usually reserved for males, and sits quietly with her husband's group as her patrikin come forward, one by one, to pile the materials in front of her in a presentation clearly emphasizing her separation from one group and incorporation into another. Several months after this, when it has been deemed time to begin gardening with her husband, her patrikin again come as a work party to assist in the initial stages of making the couple's first garden.

There are other occasions for visits as time passes, centering on various life-cycle events, but, like the first two, they tend to be formal public affairs accompanied by food displays and the exchange of goods between the two kin groups. There is little informal or casual contact between a woman and her natal group outside these occasions. Her kin continue to be concerned with her personal welfare, but this concern surfaces primarily in times of severe trouble and takes the form of adjudication designed to settle whatever disput may be involved so that amicable relations may continue between the two groups.

The position of an Irahkia-Poqna woman stands in sharp contrast to that outlined previously. At the time of bride transfer, the instruction given stresses the importance of maintaining a tie between a woman and her patrikin. The young woman is told that she should help her brothers and fathers in their gardens, and that she should not forget to send them food from the new gardens she will make with her husband. To be sure, there are occasions when the two groups for whom she is a link meet to exchange food and other items, but there is also a high incidence of informal contact between a woman and her natal kin. Once a woman has begun to garden, she will personally give small amounts of raw food to her fathers or brothers, or send cooked food, one or more times a week. Furthermore, most women have one or more plots within the gardens of their fathers or brothers in addition to the ones they maintain on their husband's land.

The strength of this tie between an Irahkia-Poqna woman and her natal kin is evident in the ability of a woman to enlist their direct aid in disputes with her husband. Although it does not happen very often, it is recognized that a woman may call on her kin to take punitive action against her husband. If she has enough public support for her position and she cannot on her own deal with the difficulty that has arisen, she may call up her brothers to destroy one of her husband's gardens. They trample the plants, rip out the fences, and otherwise lay waste to it in an action designed to bring public shame to the errant husband. The wife may, in turn, suffer a beating for having initiated the action, but the trampling of the garden is an effective device in that her husband cannot seek compensation or redress for the justifiable damage caused by her kin.

DIFFERENCES WITH RESPECT TO THE MOBILIZATION OF SUPPORT BY WOMEN IN CONFLICT SITUATIONS WITH MEN

There is a marked difference between Gururumba-Fikese and Irahkia-Poqna women in that the latter are better able, both individually and collectively, to enlist the support of others in disputes with their husbands or other men.

A woman married into Gururumba-Fikese is relatively isolated from her natal kin, and thus has limited access to them when she has disputes with her husband. Furthermore, her kin are more apt to show concern for how the dispute might affect relationships between the two groups allied through her than for her own immediate problem. I never observed them to display the kind of specific retaliatory action described previously about the Irahkia-Poqna.

In both the Irahkia-Poqna and the Gururumba, women will physically attack individual men when angered.[9] In addition to this, however, Irahkia-Poqna women will take collective action against men in certain situations on behalf of an individual woman or of the community as a whole. In one case, the women left the village en masse as the result of a dispute between a husband and wife concerning her purported failure to protect him from her menses. The village women felt she had been unjustly accused, and in protest they all went to another village for a few days, depriving their husbands of their services and also putting the men in debt to the host group for the food and gifts given the women while there. In a related case, a woman threatened to initiate such a walkout if her demand for compensation from a group of young men who unintentionally struck her with an arrow was not met. At first they refused, but when it became clear that other women were willing to support her, they met the demand on the advice of older men. In another incident, a dispute arose in the village between two men which threatened to develop into a general fight between clans. The cause was trivial, and although the men were becoming more and more exercised over the matter, the women seemed agreed that their hostility was uncalled for. They succeeded in quelling the fight by threatening to bring all the menstruating women and newborn babies out of the menstrual huts and pollute the men by parading them up and down the village street if they did not stop arguing and go home.

[9]There are also ritual occasions in both groups when the women collectively attack the men physically.

In a final case, there was an occasion when the women were aware of a plot to kill a young man visiting in the village from another Awa group. The women argued that he should not be killed since the group had just gone through a long period of fighting, there had been several deaths, food was low, and this killing would probably mean the resumption of fighting with its attendant hardships. The men were not to be dissuaded, however, and so the women hatched a countermove. They told the visitor of his impending death and provided him a means of escape by dressing him in the cap and knee-length cape characteristic of female attire among the Awa, and walked him out of the village concealed in a group of women.

I did not observe this kind of collective behavior among Gururumba women, and I suggest that its absence is related to the fact that on marriage they enter a community where the women already resident are not familiar to them and are also from a diverse set of home communities. This diversity tends to isolate women from one another because of competing loyalties and unfamiliarity. While it is true that Gururumba women do, over time, establish friendship and support networks among themselves, it also appears that Irahkia women bond with one another more effectively, given their initial familiarity and their proximity to the home group.

DIFFERENCES IN THE SOURCE OF PERSISTENT CONFLICT BETWEEN MEN AND WOMEN

There are numerous sources of persistent conflict between men and women in both groups, but differences in the intensity and importance of ceremonial exchange and the role women play in it causes a certain kind of conflict to be intensified in one of the groups to a greater degree than in the other.

The Gururumba-Fikese, like most other Highland groups, participate in an elaborate exchange cycle, culminating in the congregation of hundreds of people and the killing of scores of pigs. Food and valuables are displayed in impressive piles by the host group, while the guests perform colorful and entertaining dances. In the years between the occurrence of this event, the display and transfer of food and valuables takes place on numerous other occasions. The subclan for which I have the most accurate data hosted 69 such events over a year's time, many of them involving prestations on more than 1 day. More than half these occasions involved killing at least 3 pigs, and the largest involved 40 pigs. This complex of exchange activities can be understood socially as a mechanism for binding groups at various levels of segmentation into a network of alliances, providing both economic and political security for the local group. Concerted participation in these activities is also a major component in the achievement of status among males.

Women are related to this system in two ways relevant to this study. First, transferring a woman in marriage from one group to another is seen by men as a way of opening avenues of exchange between groups. Most of the occasions for exchange concern life-cycle events occurring in the new family established through marriage. Groups thus linked cooperate in trade, in accumulating wealth for prestation to other groups, and in warfare. Second, women play an important role in producing the food and certain classes of goods used in exchange. This is particularly true of pig-tending, as the feeding and care of pigs is a matter of almost daily concern to women.

The association between women and exchange is clearly expressed in a Gururumba myth concerning the origin of women. In this myth two brothers find that a girl has hatched from an egg in the nest of a predatory bird that they had been in the habit of raiding for the small animals that the bird placed there to feed its young. They take her home and tend her while she grows up. The younger brother decides to have sexual relations with her, but discovers that she has no vagina. The older brother creates one with a bamboo knife, and the younger brother and the young woman copulate, producing many female children. When the girls are grown, the older brother makes flutes that, when blown, cause pigs to come up out of the ground. The girls, the flutes, and the pigs are then sent away to other groups that have none of these, and, in gratitude, they return shells and other valuables, thus initiating exchange as a basis of relationship between groups.

While Irahkia-Poqna economic and political structure is fundamentally similar to that of Gururumba-Fikese, the exchange system upon which it rests is far less elaborate. The Irahkia do not participate in the pig festival or any other large-scale ceremonial cycle except as occasional guests of the neighboring but linguistically different Fore. The largest ceremonial gathering, as at male initiation, does not draw more than 200 people. And while the Gururumba will find 8 or 10 separate occasions on which to make formal prestations betwen groups in connection with the betrothal and transfer of a bride, the Irahkia limit these to 2 or 3. As a further index of the difference in the scale and frequency of these activities, it can also be noted that in an equivalent period of time a Gururumba subclan killed 175 pigs for exchange-related purposes while an Irahkia clan killed only 20. Even when these figures are corrected for differences in group size, the Gururumba still killed twice as many pigs as the Irahkia.

No tale in Irahkia mythology has been found that deals solely with the origin of women. In one myth, men and women are depicted as created at the same time; the myth giving the origin of flutes depicts men and women as opponents in that women originally had the flutes and men stole the secret from them. No connection is made in either tale between flutes, pigs, women, and exchange.

The difference in scale of the exchange system of the Gururumba and the Irahkia is, I believe, related to a difference in the kind of bond established between groups allied by this means and, in turn, to the position of women in the two societies. In the elaborate system characteristic of the Gururumba-Fikese, men of different local groups become allied with one another through participation in the intricacies of exchange affairs. As such, they tend to see women as outside the system except insofar as they are producers of exchange items or their transfer in marriage establishes the initial relationship between the groups. The bonds, then, are principally among men, and women are adjuncts to the fulfillment of their interests. Furthermore, Gururumba men tend to see women not only as adjunct to these activities but also as frustrating to their accomplishment. Thus, it is the woman who is habitually identified as the major cause of divorce between young adults. These separations become the source of much difficulty because negotiations concerning retrieval of the bride price often deteriorate into a state of enmity between the groups involved, and the thoughtless or impetuous acts of women tend to be identified as the cause. If a marriage becomes stabilized, trouble may still arise because a woman can become an in-house spokesman for her kin group. She can be bothersome in exerting pressure on her husband to accede to demands for contributions to her kin's exchanges when he may wish to distribute his resources otherwise.

In addition, women are known to harbor hostility toward men because of the secondary role they play to them through most of their lives, and because there is little recognition of the contribution they make to exchange activities. As girls they were decorated in the dazzling style of men and allowed to display themselves on festive occasions to attract suitors, thus emphasizing their importance to the group. As married women, they are allowed little more recognition on public occasions than the right to flap their drab rain capes in time to the drumming at the edge of an all-male dancing group, and they are only secondary recipients of food. Gururumba women are not hesitant to voice their displeasure with this situation. They point out that men control most of the important valuables—valuables they would not have were it not for the efforts of women. Women also fault men for gluttonizing on pork or other delicacies while they themselves must exercise restraint because of food taboos. Men point out that women are not content simply to express these feelings verbally, but also express them through acts that obstruct the accomplishment of male goals; they may fail to tend the pigs carefully, be lazy about gardening, or be careless with their polluting menses.

In Irahkia, on the other hand, women themselves to some degree become transactors between groups through frequent, informal prestations that are possible because of their proximity to their natal kin. The relationship between different local groups allied through marriage emphasizes the continuation of family bonds, and the character of the relationship between individuals thus allied is more personalistic than contractual. Exchange activities are less elaborated as a mode of maintaining alliances between groups. Alliances thus depend less on the exchange activities of men than on the efforts of a man and his wife in carrying out their mutual obligations to their respective affines. This should not be taken to mean that the relationship between Irahkia men and women is any more egalitarian than among the Gururumba, for it is not. It does mean, however, that the part Irahkia women play in maintaining relationships between groups is less submerged and stands out more clearly as a complementary, but different, aspect of the relationship.

Whatever public recognition Gururumba women receive for their role in exchange activities tends to be as individual women associated with prominent males, while Irahkia women also receive recognition as individuals within a collectivity of women. Gururumba women may gain some prominence when they grow older, particularly if they have sons or husbands who are active and successful in exchange affairs. These women may be given a death payment when the pigs they tend are killed, they may come forward to receive the pork their husbands have been given, and they may even be presented with foods and valuables in their own right on certain occasions. In addition to this, however, Irahkia women, as a collectivity, are given recognition at ceremonial distributions. Food is set aside for women in a special display on the more elaborate occasions such as marriage or male initiation. The women come forward as a group to eat, and the men make speeches pointing out that the food is being given to them in compensation for such things as the pain they underwent in bearing children or the work they did in producing food for the ceremony.

It is also relevant to note the difference between Gururumba and Irahkia concerning the role men and women play in food preparation on ceremonial occasions. The success of a Gururumba feast is judged primarily by the amount of food available. While women tend pigs, men are almost exclusively in charge of preparing and cooking them.[10] Men also grow, harvest, and cook yams, taro, and sugarcane, the next most important feast items. Thus, males and the foods associated with them command the limelight at Gururumba feasts. Although pork is important in Irahkia feasts, it is not so abundant or frequently used, and apoya, a taro-based dish cooked inside green bamboo, is its equal in importance. Both men and women are involved with raising taro, and they work together publicly at different but equally important tasks associated with the preparation and cooking of apoya. Irahkia women thereby become publicly associated with a prestigious part of exchange activities in a way Gururumba women do not.

Summary and Conclusions

Witchcraft beliefs among the Gururumba-Fikese assume the existence in one's own local community of women who are driven by an inner force to do things that disrupt or frustrate the exchange activities of men. They display an

---

[10]The only part women play in butchering or cooking pork is to clean the entrails.

acquisitive and greedy desire for the food associated with important prestations between social groups, and will attack prestigious individuals (especially men) or live pigs by eating them from the inside, thus making them sick.

Although this chapter has not attempted to survey the general position and role of women in the two societies, it can be said that they are fundamentally similar. Women perform essentially the same types and range of tasks, their jural and economic rights are much the same, and they stand in the same ritual relationship to men. This chapter has tried to show that there are also certain differences that, while they do not result in a different kind of social order, do create contrasting types of behavioral environments. Specifically, the exchange system of the Gururumba-Fikese is more intensive in its operation and elaborate in its development than that among the Irahkia-Poqna. Further, the conflicts between men and women, which stem from the fact that Gururumba women are barred from access to the rewards of the system in proportion to the contribution they make, not only are more intense but also remain largely unresolved. It is suggested that this is in part because a Gururumba woman is effectively cut off from direct aid by her patrikin in disputes, and in part because other women in her husband's local community do not form an effective support group for her. Women tend to protest their position individually and privately through a kind of nagging contentiousness, and men are disposed to view women as actually or potentially disruptive of their exchange activities. Belief in witches articulates and conceptualizes these attitudes, but since witches can be identified and made to suffer physical deprivations, it also acts to curtail behavior by women that might be interpreted as openly disruptive. Gururumba men say women like to be witches as it allows them to do things they could not otherwise do, but that women are fearful of being thus identified since they have witnessed the public humiliation and physical abuse it can produce.

The security system of the Irahkia-Poqna is much less dependent on a large-scale, socially ramified exchange network than it is among the Gururumba-Fikese. Dominant Irahkia males tend to be what might be called warrior–politicians who act to maintain the security of the local group primarily through physical power and a system of alliances based in large part on giving allies assistance in warfare in return for their assistance at a future time. Dominant Gururumba males tend to be what might be called managerial-warriors. They too operate from a base of physical strength and alliances maintained through assistance in warfare, but the system of alliances is larger in extent, is more widespread spatially, and is more dependent on a complex exchange network.

Women are producers and links in the economic and exchange system in both societies, but because Irahkia women have greater participation and recognition in the exchange system, their attitudes and behaviors are less likely to represent threats to it. Thus, the absence of a belief in witches among the

Irahkia would appear to be related to the absence of a complex exchange system.

References

Faithorn, Elizabeth
   1976   Women as Persons: Aspects of Female Life and Male–Female Relations Among the Kafe.
          In Man and Woman in the New Guinea Highlands. P. Brown and G. Buchbinder, eds.
          Special Publication 8. Pp. 86–95. Washington, D.C.: American Anthropological
          Association.
Quinn, Naomi
   1977   Anthropological Studies of Women's Status. Annual Review of Anthropology 6:181–
          226.
Read, K. E.
   1954   Cultures of the Central Highland, New Guinea. Southwestern Journal of Anthropology
          10:1–43.
Swanson, Guy
   1960   The Birth of the Gods: The Origin of Primitive Beliefs. Ann Arbor: University of Michi-
          gan Press.
Würm, S. A.
   1964   Australian New Guinea Highlands Languages and the Distribution of their Typological
          Features. American Anthropologist 66(4):77–97.

6

MARTIN ORANS

Hierarchy and Happiness in a Western Samoan Community

This chapter is based on fieldwork in progress in the Western Samoan community of Salamumu, and presents my efforts to join the study of hierarchy with that of self-evaluations of well-being. My concern with hierarchy and the experience of hierarchical relationships closely parallels that of Berreman, who has brought us together in this conference. By providing us with the experience of caste relationships in India, particularly from the bottom up, he has done much to dispel the mystifications foisted on us by Brahmanic apologists. Perhaps there is always a top–down justification of hierarchy, and often a conflicting account by those who look upward. But the experience of hierarchy may be equally hidden by both rationalizing presentations. I hope to enrich our understanding of hierarchy in Samoa by a proper attention to the experience of hierarchy as well as its rationalization. To aid in this endeavor I am experimenting with those survey research techniques used to investigate well-being.

Because this report was constructed in the field, it may lack the larger perspective that comes with reflection; it was also impeded by the absence of a computer and extensive references.

My fieldwork has two focuses. The first concerns relationship between the hierarchical system of sociopolitical rank and economic institutions. Despite a pervasive concern for genealogy, Samoa is thought to have maintained considerable political and economic mobility. I want to understand how those with political–economic power have been forestalled from developing institutions that inhibit mobility and how they secure the right to succes-

123

SOCIAL INEQUALITY
Comparative and Developmental Approaches

sion for their close relatives. I am trying to find out who gets what from political–economic institutions; I assume that such benefits and/or perceived benefits constitute the basis of people's support for or opposition to political–economic institutions

My second focus is the development and application of social indicators of "happiness" and "satisfaction," that is, of well-being. This part of the study builds on United States and cross-national survey research studies that ask people for self-evaluations of their well-being (Bradburn and Caplovitz, 1965; Campbell, Converse, and Rogers, 1976; Cantril, 1965). I am joining such survey research with the kind of intensive mode of inquiry characteristic of anthropology. I think that only through such intensive scrutiny can survey results be properly understood, evaluated, and improved.

I first tried such a combination of techniques among students at the University of California, Riverside, over a 2-year period, and the experience strongly confirmed by beliefs. I am now trying a similar approach among Samoans. This research has for one of its objectives the familiar one of differentiating the culturally specific from the culturally universal. For example, older people in the United States generally report themselves as more "satisfied" than younger people except conspicuously in the realm of health; on the other hand, they also report themselves as less "happy" (Campbell, Converse, and Rogers, 1976). Internal survey evidence suggests that "happiness" is closely related to direct experience, pleasant and unpleasant; "satisfaction" seems a more calculated abstraction involving the evaluation of experience against expectations and goals. Thus, older people expect less and are "satisfied," even though they are relatively less "happy." Indeed, it is perhaps this propensity to shift goals and expectations in accordance with estimated probability that had confounded so many studies concerning the experience of hierarchy. Is such a distinction universal or not? If present elsewhere, how are happiness and satisfaction socially distributed?

I am especially concerned with the relationship between wealth–income–economic mobility and happiness–satisfaction. In a very cogent article on this topic, the economist Easterlin (1974) notes that within countries surveyed, income and happiness are strongly correlated, but in comparisons between countries, per capita GNPs are only weakly correlated with cross-national happiness averages. Furthermore, studies within the United States over time show an ambiguous relationship between per capita income and happiness, with rather different trends among subgroups having different incomes. From these reported facts, Easterlin draws the plausible conclusion that it is relative rather than absolute income that makes the happiness difference (one might say its rank pay-off).

Though hierarchy and happiness each have their own valid focus, I have meant from the start to join certain of the findings. My intention, as illustrated in this chapter, is to run the happiness data against the hierarchical data. I am using self-evaluations of well-being to help learn how people experience hierarchy, and since it seems inconceivable that reasonably valid well-being measures could be distributed randomly throughout an hierarchical structure, these measures are being put to the test. Such circularity is not meant as verification, but as the normal kind of dialectic characteristic of the process of discovery.

There are several difficulties connected with self-evaluations of happiness. Because experience is exceedingly varied, one may reasonably doubt the utility of interpersonal ordinal comparison, never mind comparison in a single dimension. I therefore have not ventured into this realm with the assumption that a 3- or 5-point scale in one dimension is likely to measure adequately the quality of life. I am, however, working with these measures because they are the stock-in-trade of the art at this moment, and because I hope to contribute to their evaluation and further development. I have life history data, direct observational data, knowledge of the particular difficulties of individuals—in other words, the stock-in-trade of anthropologists engaged in participant observation.

I am frankly interested in the "good life" and I think it better to discuss it openly and on the basis of data rather than to sneak it in the back door by means of social science gobbledygook. People's own evaluations seem a reasonable starting point for such an inquiry because they are obviously in a privileged position to make such judgments.

Background

Western Samoa, formerly a territory of New Zealand, became an independent nation in 1962. It is composed of two major islands, Upolu (435 square miles) and Savai'i (662 square miles), and seven smaller islands with sparse populations. If the 1971 population projections are nearly right, Upolu, which is the most densely populated island and contains the capital city of Apia, has a population of around 84,957 (excluding the Apia area), the Apia area has 38,500, and Savai'i has a population of about 47,298, for a total of 170,755 on the main islands.

The national government is a kind of constitutional monarchy. It has a one-house Legislative Assembly in which all but two members are elected by *matai* vote, that is, by those holding valid chiefly titles. These legislators are chosen by districts. The two other legislators are elected by nontitled adults not living under *matai* authority; this leaves these two seats, as intended, primarily to non-Samoan Samoan citizens.

The executive consists primarily of a ceremonial Head of State and an active Prime Minister and his Cabinet. Both leaders are du jure chosen by the Legislative Assembly, but back of them lies a complex traditional political system that combines real and fictive kinship and territorial organization. Thus, the first two Heads of State and two of the first three Prime Ministers held the highest traditional titles and were the nominees of the *tama'āiga*, the so-called royal lineages; the third and present Prime Minister is the son of one of the first two Heads of State. This gives some idea of the clout of the traditional system, which coexists with the new legal system.

Finally, there are the courts, including a Supreme Court, with powers to review cases on grounds of constitutionality, and, of more direct importance to the villages, the Land and Titles Court, which deals with the quite frequent disputes in these areas. Salamumu, the village on Upolu where I have been doing my fieldwork, was involved in four such disputes during a recent 6-month period.

Governmental economic policies are very important to the village, which sells almost all its products in Apia and also buys almost everything it needs from there. The government provides aid to agriculture and contributes to education and medical services. The village also participates in the shadowy traditional power structure because of its traditional rights as a *Pule* ("authority–power") village having certain customary rights, a matter which is discussed briefly later. Though such exogenous political connections are important, Salamumu like other Samoan villages maintains considerable autonomy, even when it comes into conflict with the government or the courts. If it were to come to a showdown, the government, which has no armed force and only a small police force, could hardly subdue any determined social entity as large as a village; besides, to subdue an entire village or even an important or large *'āiga* ("kin" or "quasi-kin group") would be regarded as political suicide.

By my own count the village of Salamumu has a population of about 484, with 239 females and 245 males. The village was founded in 1911 by immigrants from the village of Sale'aula, Savai'i, who moved because a volcanic eruption in 1908 had destroyed their village. Some villagers returned to Savai'i to establish a new village of Sale'aula, but others remained on Upolu.

Salamumu lies about 33 miles from Apia; it takes about an hour and a quarter to reach the capital by car, which generally means using one of the two pickups owned by the villagers. The trip takes at least an additional half-hour by bus, which is a service that has just been added. Though road conditions are often difficult and motor transport expensive, the villagers go into Apia frequently to buy and sell and to attend church meetings, court cases, funerals, weddings, state celebrations, and so on. A number of villagers average more than 1 day per week in town. But despite these critical outside connections, the village retains a reputation as a conservative village known for the tight control of its *matai* and for its maintenance of traditional practices.

In national politics and internal structure, Salamumu is tightly linked with Sale'aula on Savai'i. Though separated by land and sea, the two communities form a single district for election of a representative to the Legislative Assembly. Internally, the two villages maintain parallel sociopolitical structures and share a common legendary charter; in fact, in formal speech Salamumu is referred to as Sale'aula, and the formal mode of addressing the villagers (*Fa'alupega*) is shared by both villages. Finally, any title accepted by either village is a title accepted by both.

Internal Structure of Salamumu

Like the rest of Samoa, Salamumu public life is dominated by *matai* (i.e., those holding a title—*suafa*). Such titles are awarded by *'āiga potopoto*, the most extended kin groups. Membership in such a unit may be claimed by all those who trace a blood connection to a common ancestor as well as by those who have been given titles by the unit but are not kin; having attained such a title one becomes kin by virtue of the award, and depending on circumstances one's offspring may or may not also be regarded as kin. Titles are bestowed on the basis of genealogy, age, talent, previous service, and as a result of complex interpersonal intrigue. Normally, the holder of a title has access to land that is traditionally associated with his title; he has also authority over his own household and possibly other related households that have no titled members, such as the households of his sons should they not have titles. If his title is accepted by the village, he has also the right to participate in village meetings (*fono*).

Again as in Samoa generally, Salamumu has two kinds of *matai*: "Chiefs" (*Ali'i*) and "Talking Chiefs" (*Tulāfale*). The most penetrating description of the difference between these statuses have been provided by Shore (1976), who linked the *Ali'i–Tulāfale* contrast with a number of other paired oppositions in which formal power and dignity contrast with instrumental power and action. This does not mean that *Ali'i* generally lack de facto instrumental power, but that their symbolic meaning signifies formal as distinct from instrumental power and often requires therefore that they act instrumentally through a *Tulāfale*.

Though the *Ali'i* of Salamumu would like things to be so arranged in Salamumu, they are not. The village by any measure is dominated in all respects by *Tulāfale*, who jealously restrict *Ali'i* power, prestige, and ceremonial prerogative. One graphic anecdote will convey both this active opposition and the aptness of Shore's generic opposition. As he indicates (1976:285), in some villages it is the custom for *Ali'i* to be served with small, fine china teacups whereas the *Tulāfale* receive theirs in large crude mugs—these vessels neatly symoblizing the formal–instrumental opposition. I had heard of this custom, but had not seen it practiced in Salamumu; I was also dubious about the significance of size and suspected that it was only a question of the *Ali'i* getting the finer cups signifying their higher status.

Because Salamumu is blessed with a lady famous hereabouts for her knowledge of and ministrations on ceremonial occasions, I asked her hypothetically what she would do if she had only fine china in large and small sizes; my thought was that she would say that the larger would then go to the *Ali'i*. But her answer was straight Shore and absolutely contrary to my conjecture. She said she would give the small china to the *Ali'i* because of their "dignity" (*mamalu*) and the large ones to the *Tulāfale* because they have to do the work (*galuega*)! Nevertheless, there is also the story in Salamumu that a certain *Ali'i* recently attempted to make such a serving distinction between *Ali'i* and *Tulāfale* at a gathering in his house of the *matai*, whereupon the presently dominant *Tulāfale* of the village crushed the metal mug in his hand and threw it out on the surrounding rocks! Thus, ever to *Ali'i* in Salamumu! The one *Ali'i* who has considerable influence in the village at this time actually resides in Apia, and his effectiveness stems largely from his knowledge of and participation in urban affairs.

The village of Salamumu is atypical not only in its *Tulāfale* dominance, but also in the way it is differentiated into four structural units ('*aufono* or more formally *fuaiala* or *ala*). No village council meeting (*fono*) consisting of the *matai* of the village is intelligible without an understanding of the four '*aufono*, nor is any other village gathering exempt from its influence. The '*aufono* are based on an original territorial division into four parts in Sale'aula, which was duplicated in Salamumu after the migration. Those titles belonging to individuals residing in a particular section belonged to that section. Through time however, the titled individuals have moved about so that today there is little correspondence between title and place of residence. Nevertheless, the '*aufono* continue to function as though the original territorial basis still pertained.

Each title in the village belongs to one and only one of the units. If there is a problem involving someone with a title or someone serving under a person with a title (virtually everyone), the primary responsibility lies with the unit to which the relevant *matai* belongs. If the problem is not dealt with, the *fono* will hold the whole unit responsible. Furthermore, there is a fixed order for speaking at the onset of a *fono*, beginning with the *Pule 'aufono* and followed by *Atilaufou*, *Vaitu'utu'u*, and *Vaeoleala* in turn. Within each unit, there is also a list of title precedence that governs speaking order. In the ever-delicate decision-making sessions at which a speaker is chosen for a particular occasion (*fa'atau*), those arguing the case will be the senior title holders present for each unit, until all agree as to the speaker; peremptory acquiescence by the *Ali'i* present is then called for. Some *fa'atau* are decided beforehand, in which case the units simply go through the motions of making a decision in public, each politely agreeing to step aside in favor of the prechosen unit. If the performance requiring a speech is not of very great importance there is likely to be no conflict between units, and often the units simply take turns, though a unit may not speak at a function of its own, such as a wedding. On important occasions, however, the contest can be acrimonious and the loser may give way only after lengthy and bitter debate. As in all such matters before the *fono*, agreement must be unanimous, which means that the senior spokesmen from all four units must agree. Unfortunately for some anthropologists, Samoans can sit in uninterrupted or interrupted sessions for unbelievably long and uncomfortable periods. However, the winner of such a contested struggle has gained a public triumph of the most significant kind.

Apart from violations of speaking order that fly in the face of the rules, the only exceptions to speaking order are the occasional efforts of some *matai* to interrupt another's speech by speaking simultaneously. Here the aim is to silence the speaker by either pointing out an error or forcing him into a recitation duel concerning esoteric knowledge in which he may run out of relevant information. Such an interruption is known as "intercepting or trapping a speech" (*seu le lāuga*) and is part of the rhetorical art of the skillful *Tulāfale*.

Clearly the *'aufono* is an essential part of the structure of Salamumu, but it would be entirely mistaken to imagine that the *'aufono* sharply divide one villager from another. Outside the *fono* and public gatherings they have a rather shadowy existence, and there are even instances of a single individual holding titles in more than one unit. Members of a single nuclear family often have titles belonging to more than one unit, not to mention larger kin units, so that any one individual always finds himself under a number of cross-pressures.

The whole structure of the village, including the *'aufono* and its major titles, is justified by legendary charter. And since all Samoan hierarchical relations are in a kind of unstable equilibrium, no two peoples are likely to present the charter in identical form. However, something of a single coherent legend with different emphasis is widely shared among the village leaders and is indeed known beyond the village, at least in part. Some of the complexity of this charter and its ingenuity may be better appreciated if one begins with the recognition that there is an apparent anomaly in the village structure that requires explication. It is widely held that the heroic warrior Le'aula, after whom Sale'aula is named, brought the *Pule* ("power–authority") to the village. He and his illustrious brother Letufuga obtained the *Pule* after a notable victory, and this power extends to the villages associated with them and entitles them to participate in the all-Samoan *fono*. Now, as already indicated, one *'aufono* of the village is known as the *Pule* and indeed has not only the right to open and close a *fono* but also the primary executive function. The anomaly is that the *Le'aula* title does not belong to the *Pule'aufono*, but instead belongs to *Vaitu'utu'u*. The shared legend makes clear why this arrangement is justified and why another title, *Levao Polo*, is associated with the *Pule'aufono*.

According to legend the original village that became Sale'aula was once known as Vaitu'utu'u and was on Savai'i. The chief title and personage was Amuimuia, who was visited by the hero Le'aula, whose mother's people lived there. Thereupon, Amuimuia sent the hero into the forest (*vao*) to get pepper (*polo*) for a kava (*'ava*) ceremony. After several efforts Le'aula brought back some pepper, and Amuimuia announced, "Henceforth you shall be known as [have the title of] *Levao Polo* and I shall take your name-title, *Le'aula.*" Thus, the *Pule* came to the village which was now known as Sale'aula, and because of the switching of titles, *Levao* became associated with the *Pule 'aufono* and *Le'aula* became associated with the *Vaitu'utu'u*—whose function is to *tapua'i*, that is, provide background support for those engaged in action (warriors, contestants in a court action, etc.)[1]

With regard to kinship, the term *'āiga* is used to cover kin units from the smallest to the most inclusive, and even groupings that may include territorial alliances. Sometimes it is qualified, as in *'āiga potopoto*, which indicates the most extensive kin groups, those going beyond the village and functioning only in the allocation of titles as indicated previously.

Within the village there are a number of *'āiga* groups with names like *Sa* + (title) *'āiga*; these include the locally resident core of *'āiga potopoto*. At a less inclusive level there are *'āiga* (normally under control of a *matai*) who have use rights over certain land; these units are the core consumption and production units, and their members reside in one or more houses clustered together and cook their meals in a single oven (*umu*). The *matai* for the unit (or occasionally an untitled male or even a female) may in turn owe service and other economic aid to a higher *matai*; nevertheless, such *umu* groups are the basic units of economic discretion. Wage earners may have obligations similar to the heads of *umu* groups, but they too do not simply turn their income over to higher authorities. With such a complex web of kinship, it is obvious that wealth–income might be examined from a great variety of different viewpoints. In examining income distribution, I am confining myself here to *umu* groups, but this only as an expedient.

Beyond what has been described, Salamumu has the normal complement of Samoan statuses and village organizations. There are the *taule'ala'a*, consisting of untitled men of the village whose age and position allows them to serve a *matai* and join in the organization of such men who collectively serve the *matai* when in assembly. These men, along with similarly situated women, do much of the hard physical labor. As a group they meet when the *matai* meet, but in Salamumu, at least, they choose their own leader and their organization does not parallel the rank positions of the *matai*.

Among the women, the *aualuma*, which would consist primarily of native-born resident women of the village not married to *matai*, does not function as a distinctive unit here. What does operate is "the wives of Chiefs

---

[1]Having thoroughly mastered this legend and the associated *'aufono* system, I was shocked to discover that the de facto top *Tulāfale* before the last one had a title belonging to *Vaitu'utu'u*, not to the *Pule 'aufono*. Apparently he was so senior that no one from the *Pule* unit could challenge him. Thus, despite the very explicit legendary charter and the general precedent of *Pule* rule, there was enough flexibility to permit this aberration. A wise Samoan *matai* responded to my incredulity regarding such matters by exclaiming that the trouble with me was that I wanted everything straight.

(*Ali'i*) and Talking Chiefs (*Tulāfale*)" (*Faletua ma Tausi*). Their organization exactly parallels that of the *matai*—each wife physically occupies the same position at a meeting as her husband does among the *matai*, and her rank obviously derives from his. One serious altercation that came before the *fono* involved a claim of disrespect for the wives of some senior *matai* by the wife of a lower *matai*. Though this particular wife was censured for her behavior, the senior women were also urged to be more considerate and less haughty in dealing with the younger wives.

Like many Samoan villages, Salamumu has grown into a two-section village consisting of an original seaside section (*tai*) and a newer landward section (*uta*). Though obviously based on spatial separation, actual usage relies heavily on social facts as well. The key institution dividing the sections is the church, each section having its own church building and minister. Even though both are Methodist churches, the division is significant. Those who attend the *tai* or *uta* churches may be described as *tai* residents or *uta* residents, even though they may live well into the other section. Since financial support of the churches, including church building, is a major village enterprise, the *tai–uta* distinction is of substantial importance. Also following the *tai–uta* split are the two (female) Brethren ('*auuso*) organizations consisting of women belonging respectively to the *tai* and *uta* church. Similarly, there are two Women's Committees that are government creations designed to cooperate with a District Nurse Program.

HIERARCHY

Having outlined external and internal structure, we must now attend to hierarchy per se. It should be understood that for many Samoans, rank is literally a matter of life and death. Though I have no statistics on suicide, one hears of it frequently, and in most cases it is a matter of honor–dignity (*mamalu*) that is at issue. For example, a *matai* soliciting "fine mats" ('*ie tōga*) for his daughter's marriage finds himself repeatedly forestalled by the action of another *matai*, who wants to make the distribution himself. Following a refusal, the first *matai* hangs himself. Though this incident did not occur in Salamumu, it indicates the deadly seriousness of matters of rank. For Samoans, social gatherings are the spice of life, and all distributions of valuables and speeches that occur on these occasions reflect one's position. This is what charges public action and gives it its consuming interest.

Rank in Samoa, even at the highest level, seems to fall somewhere between Sahlins' (1968:86–95) perceptive distinction between "chiefs" and "big men." Rights, duties, and prerogatives are well formulated and simultaneously under dispute, and the characteristics of the holder of a position are very important in determining how a dispute will be settled. Therefore, any description of the rank order of *matai* in Salamumu is bound to be somewhat arbitrary, and will render an appearance of fixity where unstable equilibrium would be a more accurate appraisal. In addition, there are of course different aspects of rank, such as dignity, influence, and political–economic clout, which are not always perfectly correlated. Nevertheless, I will offer a crude ranking of the *Tulāfale* of Salamumu, putting aside the tricky question of interranking the *Ali'i* titles. I have also confined myself to ranking the titles of those living in Salamumu, and only occasionally will refer to nonresidents attending the *fono* of Salamumu.

The traditional symbolic clues of rank in Salamumu are, as elsewhere in Samoa, importantly represented in seating arrangements, order of *'ava* presentation, and the ceremonial greeting (*Fa'alupega*). Here I shall only briefly touch on these symbols in showing how I have assigned ranks to the *Tulāfale*—or "Talking Chiefs." I am almost entirely avoiding the use of actual title names so that my chapter may not be the cause of any village dispute, nor used as an argument in such a dispute. I have divided the *Tulāfale* into five ranks, each represented by a Roman numeral.

Rank I includes six *Tulāfale* (Tf), three of whom are the first speakers for their respective *'aufono*. The fourth is the second speaker for the *Pule 'aufono* and has special duties concerning the distribution of valuables in the village; his title has a conspicuous part in the legendary founding of the village. The fifth member also has a title intimately linked with the founding of Sale'aula. The last member of this set is a borderline case because of his relative youth, but he too bears a title closely connected with the charter legend of the village. All of these except the last almost invariably sit along the honored long portion of the *Laoa* (Tf meeting house) on the side nearest the *malae* (an open portion of the village). Except in special circumstances, the presiding first speaker for the *Pule* tends to occupy the center post, and all but the last-mentioned *matai* of Rank I sit on both sides of him along adjacent posts. The last member of Rank I is often invited to such a seat, but sometimes modestly declines in view of his age. Clearly, one might rank the presiding first speaker of the *Pule* above the others, but this would entail consideration of other distinctions, and I prefer not to make overlyfine distinctions at this state of inquiry.

Generally sitting on both sides of Rank I along the same edge adjacent to the *malae* are the *matai* of Rank II, of which there are seven. One of these is generally the senior spokesman for one of the *'aufono*, but he has only recently obtained his title and there is a *matai* with the same title received at the same time who lives elsewhere and clearly outranks him when he attends the *fono*. This outside *matai* has potent political connections and economic clout and was deliberately recruited because of these advantages. The other members of Rank II are commonly called upon to speak for their respective *'aufono* in the absence of a more senior *matai*. Further, in the absence of Rank I *matai*, these members are occasionally chosen to speak in some capacity for the village as a whole in meetings beyond the village.

Rank III consists of six Tf who almost always sit along the long edge away from the *malae*, thus facing those of Ranks I and II. Four of them are junior holders of titles belonging to Rank I. Rank IV comprises five titles; its members, who sit among those of Rank III, tend to be the newest recipients of titles. They tend to speak less than those of Rank III and generally receive 'ava later. Rank V consists of three titles, two of which are from elsewhere and by courtesy accepted by the village; the other has an undistinguished title and has done nothing to elevate it. The *Ali'i* or "Chiefs" occupy the shorter rounded sides of the *Laoa* and could by seating, order of 'ava, and so on be similarly ranked. Their ranks with respect to each other would be much clearer than their ranks relative to Tf (see Figure 6.1).

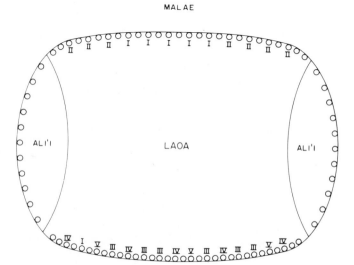

Figure 6.1.   The *fono* by *Tulāfale* rank.

In my concern for how one gets a title and what determines rank at any particular time, I am not content with simply a list of contributing factors; such lists have already been usefully supplied by a number of ethnographers. I want to know in the aggregate how much each factor counts and in as many cases as possible what determined the outcome. One critical factor is simply age; indeed, the correlation between age and Tf rank is $r = .65$ ($n = 27$, sig. .001).[2] Higher titles tend to be given to older people; in addition, younger holders of a title are almost always regarded as lower than older holders of the

---

[2]In this calculation and in the many that follow, I have used Pearson's ~ rather than the more appropriate rank order correlations because of the time saved in hand calculations. Where appropriate I have tested with chi square, but even here I have cut corners by not correcting for lack of continuity, again for computational reasons.

same title, especially if they received the title later. Genealogy is extremely important because close kin to high-ranking Tf are more likely to be considered in the granting of titles.

Though I have a large quantity of genealogical data, I cannot here go into the intricate question of how closeness is counted and how much genealogy counts in a quantitative sense. However, a glance at the list of resident Tf title holders and their respective ages is instructive. In Rank I, one of the younger title holders, besides being quite capable, is by chance the senior title holder in his 'aufono, a factor that has contributed substantially to his high position. The youngest member of Rank I has by advantages of genealogy and talent attained a particularly high title that is not shared with any older person.[3]

The relationships between taule'ale'a and matai are formally, like all Samoan hierarchical relations, up-front unabashed hierarchy (à la Dumont), not a bit shamefaced. A tough matai who demands more than anyone can fulfill is not a tyrant but a noble legendary hero; I have in fact seen the taule'ale'a fined for bringing overcooked rice to a feast even when the fault was clearly not theirs. The taule'ale'a offer service with ceremonial grace, but sometimes one hears muttered epithets when heads are turned. Authority is seldom openly challenged, but there is considerable devious evasion.

Unfortunately, I do not know enough of the relationships between men and women to offer much insight into male–female relationships. Women may obtain titles, and though a number of prominent women have done so (perhaps less than 100 for all of Western Samoa), there are none in Salamumu. In comparative terms, the sexual division of labor is not very sharp and there are important household duties that are normally done by men, such as making the umu ("oven") and assisting in food preparation and cooking, but this is generally confined to the taule'ale'a and younger boys. There is even a ceremonial obligation on the part of brothers to serve their sisters, but I do not know to what degree it is observed in Salamumu. Where young males earn a salary they may not even contribute to food preparation or umu making—but all of these important matters have not yet been properly investigated. I do not think anyone would describe Samoan women as docile creatures submissively participating in their own exploitation. They seem on the whole a jaunty lot with very sharp tongues ready to offer joking derision. Though wife-beating does occur, as it does in Western countries, perhaps more serious is the threat of and actual punishment meted out by brothers to sisters if they are thought to be engaged in even a flirtatious relationship. Brothers always on the alert to defend the family honor may also inflict serious injury and even death on any male thought to look upon their sisters covetously, but of course as male-proving lovers they also find them-

---

[3]There is a continual effort on the part of resident 'āiga to recruit talented, knowledgeable, or wealthy members and to present them with titles. Often these valuable recruits are only distantly related and sometimes totally unrelated even by generous reckoning.

selves on the receiving end. I have heard of several punitive brothers during my stay in Salamumu, and such a situation is a cause of great tension and difficulty for both sexes.

INCOME

The Salamumu income data presently available and sufficiently analyzed cover cash income only, and do not cover products or services that are not sold. Because I do not know the precise relationship between cash income and food production, I cannot tell whether there would be substantial differences in the distribution of income if noncash items were included. In addition, it should be noted that my income data are grossly out of line with previous estimates so far as total income or per capita income is concerned. My figures are based on monthly estimates by *umu* group heads of income received from agriculture and handicrafts, and yearly estimates of returns from wages, businesses, and remittances from abroad. Fish sales were not included because they make a relatively small contribution, though for a few families they may amount to more than I think. There is so much room for error in these figures and the way they have been converted to yearly income that one cannot have much confidence in them in absolute terms. My hunch is that I often got overestimates based on pride. There may also have been some double-counting of wages; some *matai* may have counted wages earned by those who owe them "service" (*tautua*), and the *umu* heads themselves may also have reported these same wages. These duplications can ultimately be sorted out, but I have not done so yet. Though I suspect for the reasons indicated that my figures are too high, the trouble is that they are so much higher than any previous estimates. The highest yearly per capita income estimates for Samoan villages (not just cash income) are about 200 tālā (1 tālā = U.S. $1.39 in 1978). My own figure for just cash per capita income is about 321 tālā.

In a detailed study of four Samoan villages in 1965–1966, Lockwood's data indicate total per capita incomes ranging from 89.80 to 108.60 tālā (Lockwood, 1971).[4] At one extreme, cash sales constituted about 44% of subsistence value and at the other about 233%; if one were to strike a balance and attribute about half of Salamumu's income to cash sales, its per capita income would be about 642 tālā (2 × 321). Obviously, 1978 is not 1965–1966, so that one must allow at least for inflation if not for real increase; however, the price rise over this period of about 250% would still result in a maximum per capita income of only 271.50 tālā, less than half my Salamumu figure. It is also noteworthy that except for the share of cash income derived from agriculture, the pattern in Lockwood's four villages is very close to that of Salamumu (see Table 6.1).

[4]Lockwood uses consumption units varying with age rather than straight per capita income, but the difference in the aggregate is trivial. Also, his figures are given in New Zealand pounds, which I have converted at about the rate that then prevailed (1 £ = 2.00 tālā).

TABLE 6.1
Sources of Income in Five Samoan Villages (in Percentages)

	Agriculture	Handicrafts	Wages	Business	Remittances
Mean from four villages	56	15	21	0	18
Salamumu	39	16	18	4	23

Despite reasonable doubt about the absolute values of per capita income for Salamumu, there is strong reason to believe that rank order between *umu* groups is fairly accurate. Though cash income distribution and wealth distribution are not the same, one would expect considerable correspondence in a community like Salamumu. One wealth item that is easily observable and quite valuable is housing, with the sharpest contrast between Western-style houses and traditional thatched open *fale;* there is also the question of size, tin roofing, and cement versus stone base. There are 13 Western-type houses in the village, of which 2 belong to the churches and are not relevant; of the 11 remaining, 4 belong to *matai* from whom I have not yet obtained income data; of the other 7, 6 belong to *matai* in the upper half of the income ranks. There are 36 ranks in all, with one tie. These comprise ranks 3, 4, 5, 13, 14, and 15; the one falling below is of rank 19. Of the nine *fale* lacking tin roofs, seven belong to the lower half of incomes including ranks 23, 27, 29, 30, 31, 32, and 35; the two in the upper half rank seventh and eighth. Contrasting Western houses with *fale* without tin roofs gives the chi square of 6.349, which corrected for continuity is significant at .05; the correlation would be .59 ($n = 17$, sig. .025). Thus, not only do wealth and income appear to be well correlated, but there is good reason to regard the rank order of incomes as reasonably reliable.

To give some perspective on the income distribution data of Salamumu, I have provided some comparable U.S. and British figures (Tables 6.2 and 6.3).

As the figures indicate, the United States and Salamumu have similar income distributions except at the top, where the United States' upper 20% has 3.15 times the average income of the next to top 20%; in Salamumu, the upper 20% have only 1.53 times the average income of the next to top 20%. Though the ratio of average income of the lowest fifth to the top fifth is almost indentical for the United States and Salamumu (12% and 13%), the range is obviously entirely different. In the United States, within a single community, one family might easily have an income 500 times that of the poorest, whereas in Salamumu the richest family has an income only about 14 times that of the poorest. Clearly, such contrasts are psychologically more meaningful than the average income of a percentile range.

Table 6.3 compares Britain and Salamumu in terms of the percentage of

TABLE 6.2
Average Family Income in the United States and Umu Group Income in Salamumu

United States	Income in 1950 dollars	Salamumu	Income in 1968 tālā
Lowest 20%	1,060	Lowest 20%	828
2nd 20%	2,360	2nd 20%	1,438
3rd 20%	3,440	3rd 20%	2,200
4th 20%	4,690	4th 20%	4,187
5th 20%	14,740	5th 20%	6,388

Source: National Bureau of Economic Research, 1950.
Note: Umu groups average at least twice the population of U.S. households or "families."

TABLE 6.3
Shares of Total Income Received (in Percentages)

	Britain			Salamumu	
	1949	1957	1963	1968	
Top 5%	17.7	14.9	15.7	Top 5%	12
Bottom 30%	14.6	13.4	11.8	Bottom 30%	12

Source: For Britain, Lundberg 1968:7.

after tax-income received by those in the upper and lower ends of the range. It provides a different view of income distribution, showing shares of the total by percentile income ranks. Obviously, Salamumu's distribution in terms of shares of the total is much like that of a Western nation.

Happiness and Hierarchy

The intensive techniques and questionnaire used in Salamumu and our inquiry in the United States were based on previous studies in the United States and elsewhere, including one done by me and my colleague, David Strauss, in 1976. We were particularly influenced by two book-length empirical studies, Bradburn and Caplovitz's *Report on Happiness* (1965) and Cantril's *Pattern of Human Concerns* (1965). With the help of a number of graduate students we spent months getting to know more than a dozen other students through interviews, projective tests, and participant observation; we then tried out questionnaires and discussed the results with them in connection with what was known from our intensive inquiries. I cannot cover here all our major tentative findings, but a few must be mentioned because they were confirmed by our survey at the University of California at Riverside (UCR) or are relevant to the present study. In the first place, our collective judgment was that at best the answers given to any kind of self-evaluation questions were a very crude measure of the quality of life. To give an extreme example, one person who periodically considered suicide consistently gave herself better than mid-point scores; some people had a positive "philosophy" or "looking on the good side" whereas others relied on "looking at things as they are." Some people tried their hardest to tell us the truth so far as they knew it, and others worked hard to make a favorable impression on the investigator.

One of the major findings of Bradburn and Caplovitz (1965:19) was that "positive and negative feeling states correlate individually with happiness, but not with each other. . . ." Our intensive inquiry made us doubt the validity of this finding. Depression seemed occasionally to prevent participation in what were probably pleasant events or to cast a pall over them; similarly, negative feelings might be mitigated by positive ones. In fact, we were able to elicit positive and negative experiential terms that supported this view.

We were extremely intrigued with Cantril's "self-anchoring" "ladder of life." Briefly, it presents one with a ladder having rungs numbered from 0 to 10. One is asked where he or she stands on the ladder today, with the top being the best life as one has defined it oneself and the bottom being the worst life as self-defined. We constructed a similar 5-point ladder and found that it yielded much weaker correlations with affect than did a variety of other devices. Our intensive inquiry suggested that informants thought more of career than affect in answering this question; the ladder did, however, correlate with grade point average (which was not true of our other well-being measures) and thus was consistent with our findings from intensive inquiry.

The Salamumu survey was begun in June 1978 after I had done about 6 months of fieldwork. All my work was conducted with the aid of my field assistant and translator, Elizapeta Eteuati. At the time, my ability to speak and understand Samoan was about that of a dumb 1-year-old, except that I knew many more esoteric words and fewer ordinary ones. I was able to administer about half the questionnaires myself (see Appendix, pp. 144–146 for the questionnaire in Samoan and English), and to explain the meaning of questions that were not clear; sometimes I failed and had to be helped by Mrs. Eteuati. Everyone, except for a few older people, was handed the Samoan version of the questionnaire and was asked to fill it out; almost none were able to do so without any assistance. Often, whole groups assembled together filled out the questionnaires, and I am sure some people were influenced by what they saw others filling in. A few young men seemed chiefly interested in playfully fouling up my results, but the same thing occurred in our UCR survey. We read the questionnaire to those old people unable to read it. After 2 weeks we stopped our survey, having obtained 153 completed question-

TABLE 6.4
Six Nationwide United States Surveys (in Percentages)

Dates	vh	ph	nth	Mean
1957	35	54	11	2.24
1963	32	52	16	2.16
1965	30	53	17	2.13
1971	29	61	10	2.29
1972(a)	26	65	9	2.26
1972(b)	22	68	10	2.24

Source: Campbell, Converse, and Rogers, 1976:26.

TABLE 6.5
Percentage Distribution of Population by Happiness, Nine Countries

Country	vh	"fairly happy"	"not very happy"	Mean
Great Britain	53.0	42.0	4.0	2.48
United States	49.0	46.0	4.0	2.24
West Germany	20.0	66.0	11.0	2.03
Thailand	13.0	74.0	12.0	1.99
Philippines	13.5	73.0	13.5	2.00
Malaysia	17.0	64.0	15.0	1.94
France	12.0	64.0	18.0	1.82
Italy	11.0	52.0	33.0	1.70

Source: Easterlin, 1974:107. Date of surveys was 1965 except for U.S., which was 1958.

naires. The survey was confined to those 12 years of age and older. Though the sample was drawn opportunistically, it constitutes just over half of all those 12 years and older. Every effort was made to get people at different times and locations so as to avoid bias.

The basic Bradburn and Caplovitz "global happiness" question, which is much like our Salamumu question 3, is the following: Taking all things together, how would you say things are these days—would you say you're *very happy* (vh), *pretty happy* (ph), or *not too happy* (nth)? Eighty-two percent of the Salamumu sample placed themselves in the first category, 10% in the second, and 8% in the third. The mean was 2.74. As all the U.S. and cross-national data indicate (Tables 6.4 and 6.5), either Salamumu is the happiest place on earth or the survey question did not work very well. Clearly, Salamumu is out of line in the first category and in the middle category—higher in the former and lower in the latter.[5]

[5]Like any investigator I have become slightly enamoured of my crude instrument, and particularly so when it is scoffed at by wiser folks who know about such things a priori. Thus, an Italian biological scientist on hearing my UCR study report at Stanford remarked that these things might be OK in the U.S., but in Italy almost everyone would report himself very happy—an interesting remark in light of Table 6.5.

Intensive knowledge of Salamumu and additional survey data suggest to me that the Salamumu data are not really comparable in the aggregate to the U.S. data. My impression is that many of my informants reported themselves happier than they knew themselves to be and happier than Americans with the same affectual experience would report themselves. For example, one woman whom I knew relatively well not only reported herself maximally happy and satisfied on every relevant question but also indicated she was never "sad" or "nervous" or "embarrassed–ashamed" (question 4); she also reported maximally good relations with others in every category (questions 10, 11, and 12) and complete support on all three institutional questions (6, 7, 8). I knew, however, that she was having grave family problems that seriously distressed her and I could not believe that she had been neither sad nor nervous during the previous week.

Similarly, a very elderly *matai* also produced a totally positive set of responses though I knew he had suffered considerable physical pain during the previous week. I also knew that he sometimes became quite emotionally upset about village issues and even manifested such discomfort in physical symptoms. There are several other cases about which I have a similar impression, though I am less sure. As for the survey data themselves, 43 (28%) of the 153 informants evaluated themselves as maximally happy and gave no reports of negative affect. There is a conception of the older Samoan, particularly the *matai*—perhaps more particularly the *Ali'i*—as one who maintains at all times a dignified demeanor revealing nothing of inner troubles; this conception is finely portrayed in the novel *Pouliuli* by the Samoan writer, Albert Wendt (1976). I suspect that this is what I have run into, and, as will be shown, some of the data on age and happiness are consistent with this interpretation. Obviously, there are also delicate questions of translation, but a decent discussion of this topic is not possible within the confines of this chapter.

In support of survey validity, three individuals that I know to have ample reason for unhappiness did indeed report this in a variety of appropriate ways; two of these provided me with life history material, and the other is known to me chiefly through remarks by others.

We surely expect that self-evaluations of happiness that mean something like what we intend will be positively correlated with pleasant experience and negatively with unpleasant experience. The sum of the numerical scores for positive feelings (happiness–joy, peace of mind, pride) are indeed correlated with global happiness ($r = .29$, $n = 143$, sig. .01) (question 1). Other happiness questions had more variance of response; they were generally more poorly correlated with other answers. The correlation with negative feeling similarly calculated (sadness, nervousness, ashamed–embarrassed) is $-.16$ ($n = 145$, sig. .1). Though these correlations are a bit reassuring, 8% and 3% of the happiness variance is mighty weak stuff. Judging by a random subsample from my sample, the maximum positive affect–happiness correlation was between "peace of mind" and happiness ($. = .36$, $n = 34$, sig. .05); the maximum negative affect–happiness correlation was with "nervousness" ($r = -.27$, $n = 33$, sig. .20).

We also expect global happiness to be correlated with good social relations (questions 10, 11, 12). Happiness is correlated with good "family" (*'āiga*) relations ($r = .29$, $n = 148$, sig. .01) (question 10) and with a good life in Salamumu (question 12) ($r = .11$, $n = 147$, sig. .2). It is not correlated with "relations with friends" (question 11), perhaps indicating the generally diminished importance of such relations in a Samoan community. Again the correlations are significant, but account for very lttle variance.

As explained earlier, I was particularly concerned to know if happiness and satisfaction would contrast in Samoa as in the United States. Judging by sentences elicited, the term *malie* is a pretty good translation of "satisfied" and contrasts with *fiafia* ("happy"). Furthermore, the correlation between answers to question 1 (happiness) and question 5 (satisfaction) was only .35 ($n = 142$, sig. .001). However, both turned out to yield almost identical correlations with everything else; the one exception was with question 7 (exclusive *matai* vote) in which, surprisingly, happiness was positively correlated ($r = .24$, $n = 148$, sig. .02) and satisfaction not correlated at all; the difference between the two correlations was significant (sig. .05). That global happiness and global satisfaction should be equally related to affect and to social relations and that the former should be more closely related to institutional support (*matai* vote) is quite unexpected and needs to be explained.

Having already noted the strong relation between age and Tulāfale (Tf) rank, we had better have a quick look at age and other variables before turning to hierarchy per se. In general, older people report themselves a bit happier by every measure but not more satisfied: age × happiness ($r = .18$, $n = 147$, sig. .05); age × sum of positive affect ($r = .10$, $n = 146$, ns .20); age × sum of negative affect (0); age × satisfaction (0); age × social relations questions 10, 11, 12 ($r = .12$, $n = 34$, ns), ($r = .17$, n = 34, ns), ($r = 0$), based on a random subsample. These findings are plainly contrary to all U.S. findings that, as indicated, show younger people as happier and older people as more satisfied. Whether difference between the United States and Salamumu is an artifact of demeanor or perhaps a true reflection of the benefits of hierarchy to age is the question to be resolved.

Finally, age is correlated with support for all three institutional questions (6, 7, 8 on *matai* system, *matai* vote, traditional gift exchange) ($r = .29$, $n = 35$, sig. .1), ($r = .28$, $n = 35$, sig. .1), ($r = .30$, $n = 34$, sig. .1). Perhaps this indicates that change is in the cards, but one does not know what the attitudes of presently older people were when they were younger. However, our data do present a baseline for future measures.

We are now in a position to differentiate our sample on the basis of hierarchically relevant variables such as *matai* status versus non-*matai* status, income, *matai* rank, and sex.

Contrasting *matai* and *taule'ale'a*, our radical prejudices are happily supported by the correlation between *matai* status and happiness ($r = .35$, $n = 43$, sig. .05). Perhaps this cannot all be attributed to age, since the correlation between age and happiness among the *taule'ale'a* whose ages range from 19 to 62 is only .10 ($n = 23$, ns .20). Unhappily, however, this correlation between rank and happiness is not supported by the summary scores for positive or negative affect, which are ns. With respect to "feeling proud," where we might most expect a difference, the correlation is only .18 ($n = 51$, ns at .20); on "happiness–joy" the *taule'ale'a* are actually the higher ($r = -.15$, $n = 45$, ns at .20); none of the negative affect differences begin to approach significance. Satisfaction, like happiness, is also correlated with *matai* status ($r = .19$, $n = 52$, sig. .20).

As with age, *matai* versus *taule'ale'a* status is correlated with all three institutional questions ($r = .16$, $n = 55$, ns at .20), ($r = .33$, $n = 54$, sig. .02), ($r = .21$, $n = 55$, sig. .20). I suspect, however, that the *taule'ale'a* may have been holding back a bit on institutional questions.

Because the correlation between cash income and cash per capita income (by "households") is so high (.84), there is no essential difference in their relation with other variables. Cash income is not correlated with global happiness nor with positive affect, which is of course completely contary to experience anywhere else; it is, however, correlated with the sum of negative affect ($r = .43$, $n = 31$, sig. .05). If we take seriously the striking relation between income and negative affect, but not positive affect, we might conclude that for Samoans the income pay-off is avoidance of negative feelings connected perhaps with inability to meet obligations in traditional gift exchange. From that perspective it would be surprising that giving in a grand style is not a positive experience.

As with global happiness, income is not correlated with satisfaction. It is also uncorrelated with institutional questions 6 and 7 concerning the *matai* system and voting, but it is correlated with question 8 regarding traditional gift exchange ($r = .39$, $n = 30$, sig. .02). Clearly, this result again speaks well for the rank order of the income data. Finally, we note that cash income is correlated with the Cantril ladder question (13) ($r = .33$, $n = 30$, sig. .05). Since it is not correlated with global happiness nor satisfaction, as in the UCR study, it again appears that the ladder is more likely to tap life progress or career than affective experience.

The only correlation between *matai* rank and anything else that is significant at even the .20 level (two tails) is the surprisingly negative one between rank and the Cantril ladder ($r = -.35$, $n = 17$, sig. .20). This is, however, consistent with one other weak correlation with rank, that is, rank × satisfaction—which is also negative ($r = -.30$, $n = 17$), but this does not quite make the .20 significance level. Perhaps many lower-ranking *matai*, because they are younger, look upon their careers as more of a success and are more satisfied than older ones, who realize they have reached their zenith. Here is a question that clearly warrants further investigation and finer analysis. Finally, rank of *matai* is positively correlated with income if one wishes to rely on a one-tailed test of significance at the .20 level ($r = .24$, $n = 24$).

As for differences between men and women, no firm statistical results are forthcoming. Wherever there is any measurable difference, women score themselves a little happier or more satisfied, but the differences are seldom statistically significant. The clearest difference is on question 2, which asks about one's happiness over the last 5 years: tested by chi square, women are happier and the result is significant at the .20 level ($\chi^2 = 3.61$, $n = 136$).

Because of Mead's classic study (1928), I could not forego the chance to see how Samoan women over 18 would compare with those 18 and under, though this division was not very sensible in terms of hierarchy. If happiness and satisfaction scores are any measure of stress, adolescents are worse off than their elders. The correlation between age and happiness is significant at .10 ($\chi^2 = 5.15$, $n = 83$) and the correlation between age and satisfaction is significant at .20 ($\chi^2 = 4.00$, $n = 76$).

Conclusions

My judgment at this point is that the questionnaire raises some intriguing questions for further inquiry. Many individuals revealed things about their experience and attitudes that I would not have known without such a survey. I mean to follow such leads in the rest of my fieldwork and to search for better measures of well-being. In particular, I am hopeful that satisfaction evaluations in various domains may prove more revealing than global satisfaction. Naturally, with the aid of a computer, I will be able to explore many relationships that I could not handle with only a statistical calculator. However, given my serious reservations about super-happy Salamumu, I would also be reluctant to take cross-national findings at face value. Perhaps per capita income (especially if income distribution is taken into account) of nations will correlate better with well-being when we learn more about how to standardize the results. At worst let it be said, as Kenneth Boulding once put it, "He left no blind alley unexplored."

Appendix

FESILI E UIGA I LE OLAGA

Igoa Muamua ma Fa'ai'u.........................Tane............Fafine............

Ituaiga A'oa'oga	1	2	3	4	5	6	(Tusi le pusa i le
Faifeau	1	2	3	4	5	6	vasega maualuga)
Primer	1	2	3	4			
Standard	1	2	3	4			
Form	1	2	3	4	5	6	

Fa'aekisi le tali e sili ona lelei mo 'oe!

1. Pe a e fuafuaina itu uma lava, o a mai 'oe i lenei vaitaimi?
   Po'o e—　　　　　　　　　　　　　　　FIAFIA...　LELEI...　FA'ALELELEI...
2. Pe sa fa'apefea lou olaga i le vaitaimi po'o le fa pe lima tausaga ua mavae?
   Pe sa e—　　　　　　　　　　　　　　FIAFIA...　LELEI...　FA'ALELELEI...
3. I le tele o taimi ete—　　　　　　　　　FIAFIA...　LELEI...　FA'ALELELEI...

4. I le vaiaso ua te'a pe masani ona e fa'alogoina ua e—

	Leai se Taimi	Fa'atasi	I nisi Taimi	Aso Uma	Siliatu i le tasi i le aso
FIAFIA	0	1	2	3	4
TO'AFILEMU LOU MAFAUFAU	0	1	2	3	4
MITAMITA	0	1	2	3	4
FA'ANOANOA	0	1	2	3	4
FA'APOPOLEINA	0	1	2	3	4
MĀSIASI	0	1	2	3	4

5. Pe a e fuafuaina itu uma lava, po'o fa'amalieina oe i lenei vaitaimi?
   1. Mātua malie
   2. Malie
   3. Lē mātua malie

	Matua loto i ai	Loto i ai	Le loto i ai	Mātua lē loto i ai
6. E tatau pea ona fa'a-auau le pulega fa'amatai.				
7. E tatau ona palota na o matai.				
8. O le foa'ina ma le taliaina e 'aiga o ietoga, meataumafa ma tupe (fa'alavelave) o se mea lelei.				

	FIAFIA		LELEI		FA'ALELELEI
9. O a mai 'oe i lenei vaitaimi? Po'o e—	1	2	3	4	5

	Silisili ona lelei	Lelei	Feololo	Faalē lelei	Leaga
10. Mafutaga ma lou 'aiga—					
11. Mafutaga ma au uō—					
12. O le olaga i Salamumu e—					

Afai o le 4 o le olaga ua sili ona lelei, 'ae o le O o le olaga ua sili leaga, o fea lea fuainumera o le apefa'i o le a e tuuina iai 'oe?

4

3

2

1

0

TRANSLATION OF HAPPINESS QUESTIONNAIRE

QUESTIONS ON THE MEANING OF LIFE

First name (title) and last or Christian name................................. Male......... Female.........

Kind of education	1	2	3	4	5	6	(Make a box around
Minister (Pastor)	1	2	3	4	5	6	highest grade)
Primer	1	2	3	4			
Standard	1	2	3	4			
Form	1	2	3	4	5	6	

Mark an X next to the answer that best suits you!

1. Considering everything, how are you these times? Are you—
   HAPPY... GOOD... NOT SO GOOD...
2. How was your life during the last 4 or 5 years? Were you—
   HAPPY... GOOD... NOT SO GOOD...
3. Most of the time were you— HAPPY... GOOD... NOT SO GOOD...

4. During the last week, how often did you feel—

	Never	Once	Some of the time	Every day	More than once a day
HAPPY					
PEACE OF MIND					
PROUD					
SAD					
NERVOUS					
ASHAMED–EMBARRASSED					

5. Considering everything, how satisfied are you these times?
   1. Very satisfied
   2. Satsified
   3. Not very satisfied

	Agree completely	Agree	Do not agree	Completely do not agree
6. Matai rule should be continued.				
7. Only matai should vote.				
8. The giving and receiving by 'āiga of fine mats, food, and money ("trouble") is good.				

	HAPPY		GOOD		NOT SO GOOD
9. How are you these times? Are you—	1	2	3	4	5

	The best	Good	Fairly good	Not so good
10. Relations with your 'āiga—				
11. Relations with your friends—				
12. Life in Salamumu is—				

[unnumbered] If 4 is the best life, but 0 is the worst life, what number on the ladder would you attribute to yourself?

4
3
2
1
0

References

Bradburn, Norman M., and David Caplovitz
  1965 Report on Happiness. Chicago: Aldine.
Campbell, Angus, Philip E. Converse, and Willard L. Rogers
  1976 The Quality of American Life. New York: Russell Sage Foundation.
Cantril, Hadley
  1965 The Pattern of Human Concerns. New Brunswick, New Jersey: Rutgers University Press.
Easterlin, Richard A.
  1974 Does Economic Growth Improve the Human Lot? Some Empirical Evidence. *In* Nations and Households in Economic Growth: Essays in Honor of Moses Abramovitz. Paul A. David and Melvin W. Reder, eds. Pp. 89–125. New York: Academic Press.
Lockwood, Brian
  1971 Samoan Village Economy. Melbourne: Oxford University Press.
Lundberg, Ferdinand
  1968 The Rich and the Super-Rich. New York: L. Stuart.
Mead, Margaret
  1928 Coming of Age in Samoa. New York: W. Morrow.
National Bureau of Economic Research
  1950 Report. New York: National Bureau of Economic Research.
Sahlins, M.
  1968 Tribesmen. Englewood Cliffs, New Jersey: Prentice-Hall.
Shore, Bradd
  1976 Incest Prohibitions and the Logic of Power in Samoa. Journal of the Polynesian Society 85(2):275–296.
Wendt, Albert
  1977 Pouliuli. Auckland: Longman Paul.

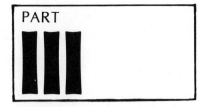

PART

III

DIMENSIONS OF
STRATIFICATION

7

SCHUYLER JONES

Institutionalized Inequalities in Nuristan[1]

This chapter offers examples of institutionalized inequality found today in a congeries of isolated mountain communities in south central Asia.[2] Detailed comparisons between the hierarchically ordered endogamous classes of Nuristan in Afghanistan and the caste system of India—which seem justified in the light of available evidence—will not be made here, though some suggestions concerning such comparisons are offered.

The term *Nuristan* (Persian for "Land of Light") refers to that part of the Hindu Kush mountain range in northeast Afghanistan which until 1900 was known as *Kafiristan* (Persian for "Land of Infidels" or "Heathen Land"). This mountainous region is drained by three main rivers: the Bashgal, the Waigal, and the Pech. Not only do these rivers have branches that are known by other names but at least one river, the Pech, is known by different names along its course. The settlements in these river valleys form clearly defined cultural units.

The Bashgal–Nechingal valleys of northeast Nuristan contain some 25

---

[1]The fieldwork on which this account is based was begun in 1960, but most of the research was carried out at intervals during 1966, 1967, and 1968. Later field visits were made in 1969 and 1970. Between field trips, lengthy interviews with several informants were arranged and tape-recorded in Kabul.

[2]In this chapter the term *institutionalized inequality* is used to refer to those inequalities in a society occurring as a result of rules that act effectively to bar part of the population from social, economic, or political resources. In other words, it is a characteristic of systems that operate to restrict access to resources that might be exploited for the purpose of establishing a power base.

151

SOCIAL INEQUALITY
Comparative and Developmental Approaches

settlements of Kati speakers. The Waigal Valley and its branches in south central Nuristan contain nine villages of Wai-ala speakers, with an additional three outlying settlements that I have included in my analysis for linguistic reasons. Most of what I have to say in this chapter is based on fieldwork carried out in the Waigal Valley (Kalashum territory), home of the Kalash-ala or Wai-ala speaking Kalasha people.[3] The third major river of the region, the Parun or Prasun, which flows through central Nuristan, is known in its lower course as the Pech. This little river, only some 125 km long, flows through no fewer than seven language areas. Three of them are Nuristani (Prasun, Wai-ala, and Ashkuni). In addition, there are Pashai, Ningalami, Wotapur-Katar Qala, and Pashtu areas. If we include the tributaries of this river we get another four language areas: Kati, Grangali, Zamyaki, and Tregami, an example that serves to illustrate the cultural complexity of the region.

In addition to these three river systems, the Ramgal-Kulum rivers in western Nuristan drain a second region occupied by Kati speakers who inhabit a dozen settlements. To the south of these is the Ashkun district, also with a dozen villages. Taken altogether, these many different Nuristani communities occupy an area of approximately 10,000 km², on the southern slopes of the Hindu Kush, between the Kunar River on the east and the Alishang River on the west. The existence of so many different languages in a relatively small area is an indication of the degree and length of isolation experienced by these communities. Even today intervillage communications are, as one might expect, severely restricted by the nature of the relief, the most conspicuous feature being narrow, steep-sided V-shaped valleys separated from each other by high mountains.

Despite the many cultural differences between these communities—linguistic, political, social, and economic—some generalizations are possible. The people of Nuristan live in permanent villages, most of which lie at an altitude of approximately 2000 m above sea level. The 1700–2300-m altitude zone appears to include virtually all Nuristani villages. Generally speaking, this zone also includes the upper limits of the evergreen oak forest and the lower limits of the mixed coniferous forest. Villages are, for the most part, well spaced out, being anything from a 1- to 3-hour walk apart. Each village is economically independent, having its own grazing grounds, arable land, irrigation systems, and timber resources.

The economy of the villages depends upon two main activities: animal husbandry (goats, sheep, and cattle) and arable agriculture (maize, millet, barley, and wheat) on irrigated hill terraces. The division of labor between the sexes is such that men are responsible for taking the livestock to summer pastures and for all the herding, milking, and making of butter, cheese, and

---

[3]The Kalasha of Afghanistan are not to be confused with the Kalash Kafirs of Chitral, Pakistan.

other milk products. The women, staying behind in the villages, spade the terraces, plant the crops, water the fields, weed, and harvest. They also cut hay and firewood in addition to their domestic responsibilities.

In a good year (i.e., one with heavy winter snowfalls and abundant spring rains), the system is capable of producing a substantial surplus over household needs. By the time autumn comes round the storerooms in an average house are well stocked with grain, ghee (clarified butter), walnuts, hazelnuts, honey, and cheese, while the livestock coming down from the mountain pastures to their winter quarters are fat from summer grazing.

Since each village generally produces the same foods as the next, there are no markets nor any organized systems of economic exchange. Each village is entirely self-sufficient. Surplus foods are used to achieve social and political rather than economic ends.

In many parts of Nuristan villages are cut off from each other from December to March, or even longer, first by deep snow and later perhaps by rock slides and spring floods. The use of animals for transport in Nuristan is practical only in the Bashgal Valley, where, since the construction of a jeep track in 1959-1961, there is also a weekly bus service that operates halfway up the valley, as far as the village of Bragamatal. Communications throughout the rest of Nuristan are confined for the most part to narrow and often steep and hazardous foot trails.

For many centuries before 1895 the politically independent and geographically isolated peoples of this region practiced an ancient polytheistic religion (see Jettmar, 1975) which is best known to us from the writings of Dr. George Scott Robertson, who is also the main source of our other information concerning the pre-Muslim period (Robertson, 1896). Between 1895 and 1899 the "kafirs" were invaded by the Afghan armies of Amir Abdur Rahman and converted to Islam (Jones, 1969). As traumatic as this period must have been, it seems to have had relatively little effect on indigenous social and political organization. For a time the economic system was in complete disarray, and its gradual reconstruction involved a change of emphasis, in which herding activities were reduced and arable holdings were expanded. The class system survived intact despite the introduced Muslim ideals of equality, unity, and brotherhood. The main change was in religious institutions and practices.

The political system in Nuristan does not provide a hierarchical structure composed of positions of authority. Neither political authority nor political power are attached to any office, nor do such offices exist. The culture does not accommodate at any level (lineage, clan, village, region) a leader, headman, chief, prince, ruler, or other official. Authority is domestic and vested in the male head of the extended family; it is not political. The politically ambitious man, if he belongs to the privileged class, may succeed in acquiring influence but not authority or power. In Nuristani politics the emphasis is on achieved rather than ascribed status. Although the son of an important man has an advantageous start, a successful career depends upon his personal qualities rather than on anything he might inherit. Certainly he cannot inherit rank or succeed to office.

Dispute Settlement

At the village level the organizational pattern is one in which a group of annually chosen men supervises certain agricultural activities and deals with minor disputes arising therefrom, while an ad hoc "group" (from 1 to 8 or 10 men chosen for the occasion) acts as mediators and tries to settle disputes of a more serious nature (theft, adultery, homicide, etc.). Any adult males, except those of the lower social classes, may act as mediators. Normally the parties involved in a dispute invite one, two, or several men whom they respect to act in this capacity. Once chosen, the mediators take over the problem; "it belongs to them." The aggrieved individuals take no further action except to acquaint the mediators with details of the case and answer questions. The mediators' task is not to judge who is right and who is wrong; they are expected to find a workable solution. Their task is to reestablish peaceful relations between individuals and groups by bringing about a settlement. To this end they listen to accounts of what happened, they question and cross-examine, cite precedence, and then plead, argue, plot, and persuade, using all their wisdom and powers of oratory to get both sides to agree to bring the matter to a peaceful end. This strategy usually involves narrowing the gap, stage by stage, between what one side is willing to give and the other side is willing to accept. Settlement is usually made in valuables or livestock.

Over the years certain men are inevitably invited to act as mediators more frequently than others. They are the men who have gained a reputation for wisdom and objectivity; men with powers of persuasion who are skillful in dealing with others; men who can sort out problems. As their reputations grow, they are invited to mediate more and more frequently. Slowly they acquire influence in village affairs and may in time be invited to act as mediators in neighboring villages. These are the important men in Nuristan today, and their high status is achieved rather than ascribed. However, such men are drawn exclusively from a certain class, membership being ascribed on the basis of birth, and only members of that class have access to high status and the prestige that accompanies it.

The Class System

In Waigal Valley, people regard themselves and are regarded by other Nuristani as belonging to one of four groups or classes. The majority—perhaps as many as 90% of the total population—are *atrožan* by birth;

that is, they are landowners and livestock herders with grazing and water rights and are eligible to compete with other *atrožan* and acquire higher status. It is this class that produces men of influence.

Another group, still within the *atrožan* class but comprising a very small minority, are *ulama*. These are low-status *atrožan* whose family reputations have suffered because in the past they did not enter the competitive arenas of feast-giving and warrior raids in pre-Muslim times and (even worse) they do not today give the obligatory public funeral and coming-of-age feasts required of every self-respecting *atrožan* family. Their failure to do so is attributable to attitude rather than means. While an ambitious *atrožan* man desires wealth (so that he can give it away), he knows that misfortune may reduce a once-powerful lineage to a few impoverished families whose economic circumstances prevent them from fulfilling social obligations. Such families may eventually be adopted by another lineage to restore their social, economic, and political viability. Among other things, such an adjustment ensures that the burden of giving obligatory public feasts marking rites of passage will be shared by a much larger group. These unfortunate families are not regarded as *ulama*, but as less well-off *atrožan*. The term *ulama*, with all its low-status and negative connotations, is applied to those families of *atrožan* who have the means but refuse to use them either for their own feasts or for the feast-giving activities of their fellow lineage members. Of all *atrožan*, they are held in lowest esteem and have the least political influence.

The material culture of Nuristan is produced by a small minority group of socially despised and politically disadvantaged hereditary craftsmen called *bari*. Field investigations indicate that they represent roughly 5% of the total population of Nuristan. *Bari* men are builders, smiths, tanners, potters, carvers, and makers of musical instruments; their wives are weavers.

In Waigal Valley there are two separate classes of craftsmen that one might call skilled (the *bari*) and unskilled (*šewala*), the latter being considered socially inferior to the former. The social inferiority and lack of technical skills of *šewala* are emphasized by the common practice of describing any shoddy piece of work as being so bad that "it looks as if a *šewala* made it." In some villages the *šewala* do most of the basket and leather work, but they are also used as porters and messengers. In a few villages they outnumber the *bari*, while in other villages there are no *šewala* families at all. When referring to the craftsmen classes, *atrožan* may say *brožan* as a general term or, more commonly, *bari-šewala*. One *atrožan* informant explained, "The *bari-šewala* people are quite different from us. They do not belong to our people. There is a story that the *šewala* are descendents of cows."

Maintaining Social Distance

The social distance between the advantaged and the disadvantaged in Nuristan is maintained by attitudes that are expressed in various ways, but particularly by rules and forms of speech designed to prevent the blurring of class lines.

THE RULE OF CLASS ENDOGAMY

Class endogamy is the model that informants offer in response to questions, and, with few exceptions, it is also the discoverable reality. An important aspect of oral tradition among *atrožan* in Nuristani communities is genealogical knowledge of considerable depth. In the early 1960s it was not difficult to find *atrožan* elders who could recite 40 or 50 generations of their ancestors. Such recitations, of course, do not mean that the genealogies are accurate records of biological descent. All of them at various times have been modified or adjusted to accommodate some social reality such as adoption or illegitimate birth. But these genealogies are, or were until very recently, an extremely important part of an *atrožan's* family history. They were there to be recited in order to establish a claim or clarify a point; for one thing, they were needed to determine if a proposed marriage fell within the rules. An *atrožan* man may not marry a woman from his own lineage (*mata*), his mother's lineage, or his father's mother's lineage. *Atrožan* informants often add, "We cannot marry *bari* or *šewala* women. And two people cannot marry if they have drunk milk from the same woman."

In earlier times (i.e., before 1900) there was apparently little or no marriage between *bari* and *šewala*, but in recent years they have begun to do so. *Bari* male informants admitted that they might marry a *šewala* girl, but maintained that they would not want their daughters to marry *šewala* men.

RESTRICTIONS ON COMMENSALITY

Atrožan informants agreed that in pre-Muslim times there were strict rules preventing members of different social classes from eating together, adding that the situation would scarcely have arisen in the first place. Many informants also volunteered the information that "Now we can eat with them. But we don't."

Brožan are invited to public feasts given by *atrožan*, but they sit in a separate place and receive food appropriate to their status, such as the heads of sheep and goats. They also attend feasts in the capacity of musicians to play for *atrožan*.

SPACE INEQUALITIES

The class affiliation, rank, and status of individuals is both acknowledged and reaffirmed on each occasion that a mixed group of individuals gather in a Waigali *atrožan* house. This is because the *ama*, the main room of the house, is regarded by them as being divided into different areas, each of which has a special quality.

The room (see Figure 7.1) is square, the roof being supported by four wooden columns arranged centrally so as to divide the room into smaller squares. The room has no windows; a single door in the center of one wall gives access. The space just inside the door, between the door and the first pair of columns, is low-status; the back wall opposite the door is high-status. The space in between is graded so that as one walks across the room away from the door, each step takes one into an area of higher status. The very high-status area (having a kind of sacred or taboo aspect) is between the second pair of columns and the back wall; especially the space between the hearth and the back wall, a "holy" place where, in pre-Muslim times, a wooden anthropomorphic effigy of a deity stood, at least in some houses.

Space in the *ama* is further conceptually divided into right and left halves. As one enters the room the right half is the men's side. Low-status men and youths are seated or stand near the door on the right; high-status men are seated on the right between the first and second columns. The man of highest status (unless he is the host) will be seated by the second column on the right. Women are seated on the left, ranging from the door to the second column in status order. Lower-status women (since *bari–šewala* women do not normally attend gatherings in an *atrožan* house) are unmarried daughters and daughters-in-law who have yet to bear their first child. They sit between the door and the first column on the left. There is a rule that *brožan* of either sex

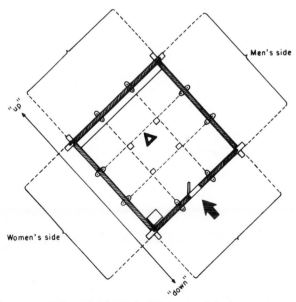

Figure 7.1.   The *ama,* or main room of a Waigali house, contains low-status areas near the door (arrow) and high-status areas (near the back wall). Normally, men sit on the right side of the room, women on the left. The hearth is indicated by a triangle.

may not pass the first columns in an *atrožan* house, as this area is considered to be the "lower" part of the room, just as the back wall is the "upper" part. The doorway does indeed face down the mountain slope, while the opposite wall of the room is always against the upward slope of the mountain.

This same space–status concept is to some extent applied to the situating of houses in a village. *Bari* and *šewala* houses form separate clusters, *šewala* dwellings usually on the lower slopes below *atrožan* houses, while *bari* houses often constitute an entirely separate little hamlet some distance away. It is said that no *bari* or *šewala* may build his house higher on a mountain slope than the lowest *atrožan* house. Thus, as the craftsmen sit in the "lower" part of an *atrožan ama*, so they live in the lower part of an *atrožan* village.

THE TERMINOLOGY OF INEQUALITY

A full account of the complex linguistic and cultural terminology of inequality cannot be given here, as it constitutes a lengthy study in itself. However, it seems that in all "kafir" languages the stems *at-r* ("inner") and *br-* ("outer") are also used to indicate, respectively, "upper" and "down" ("below," "lower"). Thus, *ateram-ganja* ("inner storeroom") and *brom-ganja* ("outer storeroom"), but also *atram-čem* ("upper place"—as upper part of a village) and *brom-čem* ("lower place" or area). It is of sociological interest, then, to note that the privileged class is called *atrožan*, while the *bari–šewala* people are called *brožan*.

In addition to the identification of social classes, many terms also carry with them emotional overtones and value judgments. Such terms are sometimes used as disparaging epithets by *atrožan* in referring to fellow *atrožan* in moments of anger—a dangerous practice, as they are considered to be fighting words. In addition to *bari*, common terms are *dungora*, which means "indigent" and "despicable," and *dungora zaga*, which means son of one is is indigent and dispicable, both terms being synonymous with *brožan* but considerably less polite. Closely linked with these epithets is the term used for those who become debtors and eventually lose their livestock and are forced to work as shepherds for others. Such people are called *lawan* ("slaves").

NONVERBAL EXPRESSIONS OF INEQUALITY

Up until about 1900, *bari* and *šewala* were occasionally bought and sold. Today if one asks the "price" of a *bari* or *šewala*, the answer is usually given as 60 to 120 goats. This statement does not mean that *brožan* are still bought and sold; it means that one would have to pay a certain number of goats to a *brožan* family as compensation if one caused a *brožan* man's death accidentally or deliberately. In contrast, the "price" of an *atrožan* is usually given as 240 goats, though compensation for the death of an important man would be much higher. A very important man is sometimes said to be "worth" 12 times the basic rate of 240 goats.

These values are also reflected in bridewealth and dowry exchanges. The usual *atrožan* bridewealth is stated to be 240 goats, though often the actual exchange involves cattle, "white rupees" (large silver nineteenth-century Afghan coins worth one goat each), and other goods and valuables. An *atrožan* dowry involves very substantial amounts of walnuts, cheeses, and cereals. Bridewealth and dowry exchanges at *brožan* weddings are normally half those of *atrožan*.

In Nuristani culture, horns symbolize strength and wealth. Many of the rank symbols denoting distinguished achievements are abstract representations of goat horns. *Brožan* have no "horns," that is, no strength or wealth.

As in so many cultures, ashes have a special symbolic significance in Nuristan. An individual who is to be severely punished for a breach of the norms may have ashes poured on his head in a public ceremony. This is part of the procedure that reduces an *atrožan* to *šewala* status. It is also sometimes used to punish *brožan*, by way of emphasing their low status. But, for an *atrožan* at least, the punishment is considered extremely harsh, as it is irreversible; that is, it has a permanent effect on the social status of the individual, and is probably rarely done. In this connection there is yet another derogatory term denoting low status, *asä kuna*, which, loosely translated, means "ashes head."

Modes of Livelihood

As mentioned earlier, there is a clear distinction between *atrožan* and *brožan* modes of livelihood. *Atrožan* own livestock, especially goats, have grazing rights, and make milk products. They also own arable land and raise cereal crops. *Brožan* may own a few cattle and perhaps some sheep, but they do not as a rule own goats, and they have little arable land; any they have was earlier granted by *atrožan* as part of the client–patron relationship. *Brožan* are craftsmen and earn their living as such, being paid for their products in measures of grain, ghee, cheese, and other *atrožan* products. Some informants stated that *brožan* are not allowed to own goats. Others said that they *can* own goats, "but they don't." Still others pointed out that they can scarcely own goats, since they have no grazing rights in the alpine pastures. Most frequently, however, both *atrožan* and *brožan* informants explained that a craftsman's duties keep him in the village, while a herdsman must be free to take his livestock to the mountain pastures for some 5 months of the year.

The point here is that the lack of goats effectively bars an ambitious *bari* from ever competing with the *atrožan* for higher status. Culturally, goats represent the ideal form of wealth. Bridewealth is stated in terms of goats;

fines are paid in goats or their equivalent. Debts are expressed in terms of goats. The giving of public feasts requires large amounts of goat meat in addition to other foodstuffs. Goats represent security; they are the means by which social obligations are discharged and political influence is enhanced.

It should be pointed out that *brožan* do not dress differently from *atrožan*, nor are their houses different in appearance, nor do they necessarily eat less well. A casual observer from outside would be unlikely to notice any difference in living standards between *atrožan* and *brožan*. But *brožan* do not own goats, and therefore in this culture they are poor. It is an institutionalized poverty artificially maintained by rules.

Social Mobility and the Distinctions between Groups

Upward social mobility in the sense of passing from a lower social group to a higher one is unknown in Nuristan. Downward social mobility, on the other hand, is possible as an extreme form of punishment. An *atrožan* repeatedly found guilty of gross violations of the norms (homicide and adultery) may eventually—after due deliberation by mediators in consultation with his lineage—be socially destroyed by a public ceremony that changes him to *šewala*. This means, among other things, that he cannot inherit property from his father, that he is forever barred from pursuing rank- and status-enhancing activities, and that he must move to the *šewala-čem*, the *šewala* quarter.

This brings us to a point about which we know all too little: the genetic characteristics of the various social classes in Nuristan. Even superficially one cannot help noticing that *atrožan* in general are rather tall and, although brown eyes and dark hair are common, many of them have light brown, even fair, hair and gray or blue eyes. Physically the *bari* are somewhat different in appearance. They tend to conform to the stereotype expressed by *atrožan*: short, dark, and strong. After even a short period of fieldwork one can usually identify *bari* on sight.

The oral traditions of Nuristan contain many stories that "explain" the origin of *brožan*. Often, after telling one of these stories, an informant will say, "That's just a story. I think they are descended from Muslims [i.e., Afghans] that our ancestors captured in raids," which seems a reasonable suggestion. Another view of *atrožan–bari* stratification is the "conquest theory," which postulates that the skilled craftsmen of Nuristan are the remnants of the original population of the Hindu Kush and that *atrožan* are descended from a people who invaded the area and conquered them.

The observable differences, such as they are, between *atrožan* and *bari* do not apply to *atrožan* and *šewala* peoples; the two groups are visually indistinguishable. This, in connection with what has been said about downward social mobility, may mean that *atrožan* and *šewala* were originally of the same stock and that the šewala group is composed of "outcast" atrožan. This theory would also explain why šewala are unskilled craftsmen and of a lower status than bari: they never had an opportunity to acquire the technical skills of bari craftsmen and were prevented by rules and attitudes from merging with the bari class.

The oral traditions of the Waigal Valley include at least four accounts of the origin of the šewala, all of them variations on a single theme:

1. Mir Kola and Mir Sing were brothers. They were born of a cow. Mir Sing's descendants are Hindus; Mir Kola's descendants are šewala.
2. A shepherd found two infant boys in his stable one day. They had come from the cow dung. All šewala are descended from these two boys.
3. One day a shepherd found two infant boys in his stable. A cow had given birth to them. Their descendants are šewala.
4. A shepherd went to his stable one day and found two infant boys there. He couldn't find their mother. The people decided that an unmarried girl had secretly given birth to the twins and abandoned them. The šewala people are descendants of these two boys.

Sexual Inequalities

Men and women atrožan do not have equal access to such scarce resources as status and prestige. Women do not act as mediators, nor are they seen to take an active part in public affairs. Their daily work is domestic, though it extends to arable agriculture and the practical problems of cereal cultivation. A woman's status in the community is a reflection of her husband's status and, to some extent, that of her father. In pre-Muslim times the wife or daughter of a man of high rank could wear certain symbols on her clothing—cowrie shell decorations, small brass bells, colorful tassels, and so on—but avenues leading to public social and political importance were, and still are, closed to women. However, the social and political influence that women have in Nuristan may be easily overlooked simply because it is not present in an institutionalized form. It is a behind-the-scenes kind of influence that contrasts sharply with the often ostentatious public political activities of the men. The influence that women have in village affairs should not be underestimated, however subordinate their social role may appear. They have influence; they just do not get credit for it.

Women engage in important but relatively low-prestige agricultural activities, mainly cereal production. Men engage in the high-prestige agricultural activities of animal husbandry, especially the breeding and rearing of goats and the making of milk products. Thus, the division of labor in Nuristani society as a whole corresponds with the values assigned to social categories.

Caste

A number of years ago I pointed out the obvious (Jones, 1967:57) when I suggested that the nature and ordering of social classes in Nuristan closely resembled the caste systems of India. Robertson's well-known account of pre-Muslim religious beliefs and practices in Kafiristan (*The Kafirs of the Hindu Kush*, 1896) has been around for over 80 years, but it is only recently that a serious attempt has been made to examine certain aspects of that work in the light of historical and linguistic studies. I refer to Dr. Gérard Fussman's important paper, "Pour une Problématique nouvelle des religions indiennes anciennes," in the *Journal Asiatique* (1977). It would be presumptuous to attempt a summary of Fussman's arguments here, and I merely draw his paper to the attention of scholars who may wish to explore further the implications raised by a comparison of Nuristani class and Indian caste systems.

References

Edelberg, Lennart, and Schuyler Jones
1979 Nuristan. Graz: ADEVA.
Fussman, Gérard
1977 Pour une Problématique nouvelle des religions indiennes anciennes. Journal Asiatique (Paris), pp. 21–70.
Jettmar, Karl
1975 Die Religionen des Hindukusch. Die Religionen der Menschheit, Vol. 4, Part I. C.M. Schröder, ed. Stuttgart: W. Kohlhammer.
Jones, Schuyler
1966 An Annotated Bibliography of Nuristan (Kafiristan) and the Kalash Kafirs of Chitral, Part One. The Royal Danish Academy of Science and Letters, Vol. 41, No. 3.
1967 The Poltical Organization of the Kam Kafirs: A Preliminary Analysis. Copenhagen: Royal Danish Academy of Science and Letters, Vol. 42, No. 2.
1969 A Bibliography of Nuristan (Kafiristan) and the Kalash Kafirs of Chitral, Part Two. Selected Documents from the Secret and Political Records, 1885–1900. The Royal Danish Academy of Science and Letters, Vol. 43, No. 1.
Robertson, Sir George Scott
1896 The Kafirs of the Hindu Kush. London: Lawrence and Bullen.

8

SYDEL SILVERMAN

Rituals of Inequality:
Stratification and Symbol in Central Italy

Anthropologists' inclination to leave the formal study of social inequality to the sociologists has resulted in a fragmentary understanding of the specifically cultural issues in inequality. The intention of this chapter is to invite more systematic attention to the symbolic dimensions of institutionalized inequality. As this symposium looks at inequality in comparative cultural contexts, it may be useful to ask what are the symbolic forms in which unequal distributions of resources and power are phrased, and what is the relationship between symbolic forms and socioeconomic structures of inequality?

As in all areas in which anthropology has been concerned with the relationship between society and symbols, a basic issue is whether symbols reflect, express, or otherwise correspond to social arrangements, or on the other hand, act to mask, obfuscate, or deny social realities, especially the realities of class and power. Most anthropological models proceed from the assumption that symbol and society are two sides of a coin, the view expressed in Clifford Geertz's much quoted phrase about symbols and ritual as a "model of" and a "model for" social reality (Geertz, 1966); but the assumption is rarely treated as a problem in its own right. At the same time, those who consider symbolism essentially as mystification have tended to assume a different kind of direct relationship between society and symbol. They see ideology as emerging from and sustaining a particular structure of power, but they have had little to say about how that happens. In this chapter, I want to turn the assumption of congruence into a question and through this to inquire

163

into some of the ways in which symbolic processes might relate to and affect social inquality.

I propose to approach the problem of symbolism surrounding inequality by considering—in addition to expressed ideology—rituals that depict or define interaction between persons of ranked social categories. By ritual I mean formalized events and actions that carry symbolic charges, whether the context is sacred or secular. This view of ritual takes in both (a) the complex sequences of actions usually structured as performances that may properly be called "events" (ranging from relatively brief acts like lighting a sacred candle to extended festivals), and (b) "ritualized" behavior that may be incorporated into instrumental activity or social encounters (such actions as are spoken of as etiquette or behavioral styles). Such ritual conveys symbolic messages both explicitly, as in the use of terms of respectful address, and implicitly, as in the separations and groupings of actors in a ritual performance. Taking a particular area from my own ethnographic experience (central Italy), I ask how certain rituals "talk about"—or do not talk about or lie about—forms of social inequality, and what the implications are for the persistence of or challenge to such inequality.

If one is to explore the relationship between social inequality and ritual statements *about* inequality, it is essential, first of all, that each of these be described independently. To "read off" social inequality from one's interpretation of ritual symbolism, or on the contrary to "read into" ritual symbolism the particular arrangements one has identified in social analysis, is to preclude an examination of the relationship *between* society and symbol. In the actual research process, of course, the anthropologist encounters the two together and attempts to come to his or her understanding of each in conjunction with the other. But I think it is necessary to try to establish lines of evidence for each if one is to avoid tautology.

The premise of congruence between ritual and social categories is persuasive and has, of course, been enormously productive in anthropology, particularly in the hands of those whose symbolic interpretations are accompanied by full analysis of social processes in their own terms as well. A recent example is Eva Hunt's discussion of the role of ritualism in interactions between ranked groups (Indians and mestizos in Mexico), in which she is careful to treat the sociopolitical relationships of power separately from ritualism before seeking connections between them. Her conclusion is based upon the almost axiomatic notion that ritualism operates in problematic relations between "structurally defined segments of the society" (1974:26). But do we know that the "segments" entering into ritual necessarily correspond to the most significant categories of social organization? And is the most useful understanding always to be gained by looking for the ways in which ritual might be "expressing" the social order?

One dissenting view is offered by Maurice Bloch, who questions the many theories that see ritual as directly expressing or explaining social structure or man's place in the world in general (1974:71). For Bloch, ritual—because of the kind of communication it entails—constitutes "misstatements of reality," and it enters into the exercise of power through its ability to distort events and hide the actual situation (1974:77). Elsewhere Bloch (1977) argues that there is a systematic discrepancy between power (the structure of class) and rank (the subjective representation of hierarchy). He proposes that in evolutionary terms ritualization transforms power into rank, disconnecting rank from its origins in power, and thereby legitimizes and protects authority.

Whether or not one is persuaded by his theory, Bloch's approach is useful heuristically. Suppose that instead of assuming basic congruity between ritual and social categories, one inquires into the disjunction between them. In considering the ritualization of inequality, we might begin by asking about the significant social distinctions that reflect differential power and access to resources, and then consider the extent to which those distinctions appear in ritual and the manner in which they might be obscured. Similarly, if we assume that symbolic statements can distort as well as express social arrangements, we can inquire into the divergence between meanings assigned to relationships of social inequality and the actual content of those relationships. This line of inquiry may throw some light on the processes by which relations of power can be masked. An example of how ritual categories can obscure objectively defined distinctions is suggested by Renato Rosaldo's material on metaphors of hierarchy in a Mayan cargo system (1968). In this case, age is treated symbolically as the defining principle of ritual status, despite the fact that it is wealth (which as an acquired status does not necessarily correspond to age) that determines access to positions of sacred prestige.

A different but related question about the relationship of ritual to social inequality is whether ritual acts to reinforce or to challenge the hierarchical order. The usual anthropological position is of course the former. Hunt, for instance, takes a safety-valve view: "Ultimately ritualism serves to preserve the social order which, metonymically and metaphorically, it expresses, by becoming an instrument which defuses the dramatic situations in which it enters [1974:27–28]." Assumptions of homeostasis seem almost inescapable in anthropological explanation, as much when phrased in the language of adaptation or of conflict resolution as in traditional structural–functionalism. Yet the possibility that ritual can have the opposite effect ought at least to be considered. The historian Natalie Davis has taken such an approach with reference to rituals of reversal in early modern Europe, which are especially interesting for the study of inequality since they depict the structure of power turned topsy-turvy. Davis takes a position contrary to Victor Turner, James Peacock, and others and argues that ritual inversion, by suggesting an alternative to the hierarchy of power, can challenge and undermine it (1965:131). Her historical evidence is drawn from early modern Europe, but she points out that this challenging effect of ritual was reversed with the industrial revolution. This perspective reminds us that ritual processes are not merely fueled by internal cultural dynamics but need to be understood in specific historical contexts. In the latter part of this chapter I will illustrate this point with a historical view of a particular ritual complex, that of the *palio* in Siena.

My ethnographic data are drawn from a stratified state society in which inequality based on class (i.e., differential positions within systems of production) intersects with sex and age; there is little heterogeneity of categories that might be called ethnicity.[1] Sex and age receive ritual treatment in this area as they do in societies at all levels of complexity, and the material presented should therefore have general comparative relevance. However, I believe it would be incorrect to directly equate sex and age here with their counterparts in nonstratified societies. I would suggest that the emergence of class creates a framework that redefines and makes new use of other social distinctions.

I will consider various kinds of social distinctions that are manifested in ritual, in each case attempting to compare the objective inequality it entails with ideological and ritual statements of the distinction. I will first discuss sex and age. Then I will treat class from two points of view: the relationship between socioeconomic class and prestige, and the elaboration of a particular class-based distinction, patronage. Finally, I will examine the ritualization of territorial distinctions in a rather special, but revealing, case. Since I see class as a framework within which other social distinctions exist, the central concern of the chapter will be to show the relationship of various ritual–symbolic categories to class and to explore the implications of the symbolic phrasing of inequality for the class structure.

The Ethnographic Setting

The case material in this chapter is drawn from fieldwork done mainly in the early 1960s in a rural commune (Montecastello di Vibio) in the province of Perugia and from subsequent historical research on central Italy, focusing especially on the area surrounding the town of Todi in south-central Umbria and the city of Siena in Tuscany. The region referred to here as central Italy (which I defined initially on agrarian–economic criteria) extends roughly over the hills and interior plains of Tuscany, Umbria, the Marches, and Lazio.

This region shared in an early urban development, which began in the eleventh century. Multiple cities and towns established themselves as autonomous polities and as centers for controlling and distributing agricultural production in the rural districts they brought under their jurisdiction. Except

---

[1]At the regional level, variation by religion and place of origin (if outside the region) occurs but is relatively unimportant, whereas variation by dialect and cultural patterns attributed to heredity coordinate with the class structure. If one took Italy after 1860 as the unit of analysis, regional variation might be considered as a form of ethnicity.

for Florence and a very few other Tuscan cities that had textile industries, these centers were sustained essentially by agriculture, small-scale artisan manufacture, and services (including, in some instances like Siena, commercial and banking services). The autonomy of the communes of central Italy was short-lived, but the area remained one with a multiplicity of centers, where even small towns retained urban styles and the vestiges of political and civic institutions.

A particular organizational form, the *mezzadria*, became the common means through which the townspeople sponsored agriculture in their surrounding countrysides and brought new lands under cultivation. Originating as a particular kind of agrarian contract in thirteenth-century Tuscany, the *mezzadria* developed as a system through which peasant families worked multi-resource farms, sharing investment and product with landlords who lived in the towns. The *mezzadria* began to break down after World War II, when a modest industrial development in the region expanded the opportunities for wage labor and stimulated rural–urban migration. However, the regional economy retains its basically agrarian character.

Unless otherwise specified, the descriptions that follow refer to Montecastello in the ethnographic present as of 1960.

Social Distinctions

SEX

In Montecastello as throughout central Italy, sex clearly defines differential access to positions of formal authority, to informal power in the public domain, and to control over resources and most valued goods. Although the particular differences between the sexes vary with class, there are commonalities that operate in all classes. Civil law defines different property and personal rights for the two sexes. Family headship (the formal position of *capofamiglia*), which confers exclusive authority over the family and control of its material and labor resources, ordinarily is assigned to men. The separation of customary spheres of male and female activity tends to isolate women from the arenas of formal and informal political life. The structure of education and of access to occupations systematically assigns women to roles subordinate to those of men.

Nevertheless, the realities of actual behavior are more complex. Under circumstances that are defined as "special," women do occupy formal positions of occupation, political life, and family headship that are ideologically the province of men. Women of "unusual" qualities (e.g., a woman with courage "like a man's"), or women in certain family situations (e.g., a daughter tutored to follow in her father's footsteps in the absence of a son) become exceptions with considerable frequency and occasionally achieve real power. Moreover, most women in fact function "like men," managing the family's external affairs, tending to their husbands' economic interests and working alongside them, and influencing the political process. One might suggest that the reality of women's behavior constantly intrudes upon and threatens the ideology of male dominance.

The male–female distinction is underlined symbolically in almost every aspect of daily life. The differentiation of "male" and "female" spaces, activities, and forms of behavior is marked. Language usages, etiquette, and phrases of explanation distinguishing male and female are constant features of social interaction. The distinction expressed both explicitly and implicitly is phrased as one of essence, substance, and inherent quality. To the extent that questions of authority arise, the male is defined as dominant by nature, but in fact dominance is not often at issue. (The matter of "power" is more ambiguous, since different kinds of power are thought to attach to the two sexes.) The basic ideological message is the fact of essential difference. Different qualities inhere in each sex, and these are defined as complementary; each quality (and each sex) has its opposite, and each needs its opposite for its own realization and completion. Actual female behavior that approaches the male ideal is explained as "really" different because of the female's different essence. (For example, girls who aspire to careers explain their ambitions by referring to female qualities, such as nurturance.) Thus, inequality is played down, while complementarity, mutuality, and reciprocal identity are emphasized.

Virtually all ritual activity separates or assigns different roles to men and women. This fact is so unremarkable that it is tempting to neglect it. A more curious version of ritual separation of the sexes occurs in rituals of reversal. The form in which men imitate women (but not the reverse) is fairly common in this area in secular festivities intended to be humorous; the political uses of such inversion, suggested by Natalie Davis, are known for the past but survive in contemporary times only as mild satire. This type of ritual is discussed along with age in the next section, but it does not have the overriding importance of the uses of gender in religious ritual.

An example of the dramatic separation of male and female in ritual is provided by the events of Holy Week, which is the peak of intensity of the annual ceremonial cycle.

On the Friday before Palm Sunday, a procession of women—members of the Confraternity of the Sorrowing Madonna—carry a statue of the Madonna from her niche in the parish church to a little church where the statue of the Dead Christ remains throughout the year. The Sorrowing Madonna statue is an object of great pride to the Confraternity, whose members during the mid-nineteenth century commissioned it and lovingly created its adornment. Virtually all women in the community belong to the Confraternity.

Holy Week is spent in a public reenactment of the death of Christ, and each day's development in the story becomes a vivid part of the community's immediate experience. From Palm Sunday until Wednesday, the women—representing each family of the community—spend a designated hour or more in turn, sitting in the little church with the Mother and Son, "so that they are never left alone in their sorrow." On Wednesday the statues are taken in two processions to the parish church; the women, dressed in mourning, carry the Madonna, and the men carry the Dead Christ. From Thursday until Easter the bells are silent, and a band of boys goes about the town with noisemakers, calling out the messages that the bells would ordinarily impart.

On Good Friday the community spends the day in preparation for the funeral procession of the Dead Christ. Every house along the route is decorated and strung with lanterns, and in the church a Crucifixion scene is prepared. At night, following the priest's sermon on the "Seven Last Words," the populace leaves the parish church and forms a long and solemn procession through the community. Men and women walk in separate sections, the men carrying torches and the women lighted candles, chanting mournfully.

On Holy Saturday, the women of each family prepare a decorated basket containing the ingredients of the Easter meal, which is taken to the church to be blessed. At midnight, there is a Mass that most of the community attends. On Sunday afternoon, in the festive atmosphere of spirited songs and brilliant banners, a statue of the Risen Christ is carried in procession around the town and through the surrounding fields. Easter Monday sees a more elaborate procession, a community pilgrimage to a monastery about 5 km away. In these processions, as in all others throughout the year, there is sharp separation of the sexes. The men precede the focal point of the procession, while women follow; men carry the major objects of the procession and the paraphernalia used by the priest, while women may carry the banners dedicated to the Virgin.

The pervasive message of ritual with regard to sex, like the pervasive message of explicit ideology, is the incommensurability of male and female. The two categories can (and must) be ranked if the issue is forced, but the fundamental assumption is that complementarity rather than ranking is the essence of their relationship. How might this fact relate to the objective nature of sexual inequality? In reality, the differences between men and women are matters of degree. Some women in their formal roles and most women in their actual behavior approach the male domains; to some extent, the reverse is also true. I would suggest that the symbolism surrounding sex serves to prevent the differences of degree from exceeding their limits by pulling both men and women back into identities that are different in kind.

The issue of male–female identities in this case goes beyond the universal processes whereby culture interprets biology. These identities exist within a class structure and, I would argue, are used by it. While the nature of objective inequality between men and women varies with class, the symbolic statement of the gender contrast crosscuts class and social categories of all other kinds. This fact is a conspicuous feature of social life. In interactions between persons of different class or of other potentially opposed interests, it is extremely common for references to be made to male–female differences and for alliances by sex to be called up. Thus, the symbolic contrast between the sexes acts to obscure and defuse socioeconomic cleavages.

AGE

In the material from central Italy, it is possible to distinguish age grades that correspond to a progression of increasing power (until the last). However, the age categories mark a continuum of difference rather than sharp contrasts, and the boundaries between categories are fluid. The age grades differ somewhat for the two sexes, but for both they are marked not by absolute age but by transitions within family cycles. Entrance into adulthood generally comes with marriage; from this point on, a woman's age status changes with her husband's. The peak of dominance for a male does not come until he assumes full headship of a family; in extended families, this occurs only when his father retires or his son marries. Old age comes with the partial relinquishing of active control in family and public affairs, a transition that is gradual and generally voluntary.

Access to positions of authority in the public sphere tends to depend upon familial status. A man who is not yet a *capofamiglia* or who does not yet control family resources (either through inheritance or through having major responsibilities conferred upon him by his father) can take on only a limited political role. For women, increasing age does not usually open up formal authority positions, but it does bring greater freedom, eventually allowing women to talk and act "like men" with impunity. Age also affords women greater informal power, both through their influence over their sons and through the special knowledge that is thought to be possessed by women of middle age and beyond. For both men and women, the status differences attached to age are reflected in forms of language and etiquette.

Among adolescent and young adult males, the age grade takes on a loose organizational form: Bands of youths from a particular locality roam about during leisure hours and occasionally organize games, festivals, or mischief. (Adolescent girls, in contrast, are confined in their movements, increasingly so after engagement and after marriage.) Youthful male bands have been the subject of discussions of *charivari* and other European popular festivities in which there is serious or playful ridicule of unsanctioned behavior or of the social order in general (see Davis, 1965:97–123). Excluded from positions of power and authority both public and private, the youths may use ritual forms to criticize, mock, and sometimes threaten that authority. In the central Italian case, at least, the threat appears to be a cautious one. It is made in the safety of anonymous groups, sometimes in costume, and rarely is it intended seriously to challenge the authority that the young men expect to inherit. Davis's idea that such popular festivities can have political consequences by suggesting alternatives to the existing order (1965:123) is worth pursuing for earlier periods of central Italian history, but the contemporary material does not support such an interpretation.

A traditional skit performed at mid-Lent, the Segavecchia, illustrates both in its organization and its content how age grading can be manifested in ritual. The Segavecchia (literally, the "sawing of the old woman") is a masqueraded comic drama performed by groups of young men who circulate about the community and repeat their performance over a period of days, creating general hilarity, playing pranks, and extracting ransoms in the form of contributions of eggs. The central player is costumed to depict an old woman, the *vecchia*. The content of the play illustrates the interconnection of age, sex, and familial roles, as well as the ritualized mockery of authority both in domestic and public domains.

The Segavecchia acts out the story of an old woman who insists on dancing although it is mid-Lent. Her old husband and her two sons try to stop her and call her to the appropriate Lenten activity—prayer. In response, she only gets wilder, calling for more music and forcing her husband to dance with her. The husband laments her behavior, comparing her youth when he loved her to her ugly old age, and concludes with the wish that she might die. At this, the sons join in; one tells of the sorrow and pain she has always caused them, not even allowing them to take wives. The old woman realizes that they intend to kill her, and she curses her assassin husband and sons. The sons then attack her. One holds her fast while the other proceeds to saw her across the middle, saying that if the sawing does not do the job they will take a hatchet to her. Finally she falls dead.

After some moments of awed silence, the men become alarmed at what they have done, beg pardon of the Lord, and try to call their mother and wife back to life. The old man thinks of calling the doctor and sends a son to fetch him. While the woman is lying on the ground, presumably sawed in half, the son is reporting to the doctor that Mama is very sick and in danger of death, and he asks the doctor for help. The doctor arrives on "horseback," looking serious and important. He examines the body, and then announces that this is no natural illness but someone's evil deed. Everyone denies this, but the doctor threatens to denounce them to the authorities and have them sent to jail for 40 years. The sons beg him not to, saying they will pay him whatever he asks. The doctor suggests that he might be able to set things right, in return for the basket of eggs they are carrying. When they protest that this is asking too much—the fruit of all their labor—the doctor begins to write out the denunciation with great flourishes. Father and sons see that he is serious and plead with him to stop, offering him their basket of eggs plus a large sum of money. The doctor is skeptical that they have the money to pay, but they assure him they will borrow or beg for it. When the doctor is satisfied, he gives the old woman an injection. She begins to stir, whereupon her husband curses her revival! The performance ends as all give thanks to the doctor and to the audience.

The Segavecchia dramatizes the theme of generational conflict, but it is commingled with sexual opposition. The mother, the informal power in the family, becomes the focus of challenge rather than the titular *capofamiglia*. At the climax, all the men, father and sons, unite against the woman; sex overrides age. In the end order is restored, but not before the performers have played out their subversive messages about authority, about generational resentments, and about the underside of the female essence. In this instance, the ritual expression of age-based inequality corresponds to social realities in at least two ways: It is defined by familial role rather than chronological age, and ultimately it is submerged by other forms of inequality, those of sex and class.

The question of class enters into the Segavecchia in the figure of the doctor. In other versions known in the region different authority figures appear, and as in other popular rituals of this sort there is a good deal of room for improvisation and satirical commentary on current social and political issues. The enactment of such rituals also varies in time and place according to whether the actors are drawn from a particular class or category or from across socioeconomic lines. In the not-too-distant past in Montecastello, the Segavecchia was performed by peasant groups, and it forged links of potential alliance not only through the messages it conveyed but also through its support of a network of communication among the scattered farms. In more recent times, the Segavecchia has been domesticated into something of a community event, with the participants drawn from different classes and with townsmen taking a more active, often controlling role. In its more recent manifestations, class-based satire is softened and the focus of criticism is turned against the Church. The *vecchia's* insistence upon dancing at mid-Lent expresses a real controversy between the people and the priest, which is itself an idiom for deeper conflicts over the political role of the Church.

The point to be emphasized is that ritual contains multiple possibilities for symbolic messages, which can be manipulated in various ways in relation to particular historical circumstances. In addition to looking at the content and form of ritual, we must therefore inquire into its use in changing contexts.

Rather than being "a model of" and "a model for" social experience, ritual contains many possible models, and we need to ask why certain possibilities rather than others are elaborated in given conditions.

It appears that as the Segavecchia was co-opted by the town, the themes of youthful rebellion and sexual opposition were emphasized and the issue of class was played down. Yet age and sex have fundamentally different implications for cutting across class lines. While sex defines a fixed contrast, the inequality represented by age is cyclical and the cycle varies by class. Since the young of different classes have different stakes in the social order, the only commonality among all youth is over domestic issues (such as when a son will be allowed to marry). Thus, unlike sex, age has only a limited utility for defueling class antagonisms.

Rosaldo's work in Chiapas (1968) suggests that age can be a metaphor for social hierarchy, translating the realities of incipient socioeconomic power into an idiom of age; the cyclicity of age makes hierarchy phrased in terms of age appear as relatively harmless. However, in the central Italian situation, where class cleavages are strong, this translation is not possible. Here, sex and age articulate with class in basically different ways, and neither can become a metaphor for socioeconomic inequality.

CLASS AND PRESTIGE

The clearest picture of the disjunction between social and symbolic categories of inequality emerges from a comparison of structures of class and of prestige. Elsewhere I have discussed my efforts to inquire into prestige as a separate dimension of stratification, taking prestige to mean differential evaluations by the society and differential capacities to claim deference (see Silverman, 1966). I made the point that the prestige order does not correspond precisely to socioeconomic categories. While it does not contradict objective bases of hierarchy, it reshapes them in accordance with subtle and complex combinations of criteria.

I refer to my field data on Montecastello as of 1960 to illustrate my point. Since from the local perspective this economy is fundamentally agricultural, the basic determinant of class is the relation to land. Most agricultural land is worked under share-farming tenure or *mezzadria*, a system that defines the categories of landlord and *mezzadria*–peasant. Whereas the latter is a relatively uniform category, landlords range from those with very large holdings to those drawing a minute return from a single farm. Landlordship is typically combined with commerical interests, professions, or white-collar jobs. In addition, there is a small but growing category of peasant proprietors. Most families without access to land live in town and work in services, as independent artisans, or as unskilled laborers. A smaller number are agricultural wage laborers.

The class picture is, however, more complex than this, since the local system of agricultural production is embedded in a larger political–economic structure in which the dominant interests are industrial. As a result of shifts at the national level since World War II, the position of all but the largest landlords has steadily eroded. At the same time, external linkages increasingly determine class status. Investments and other interests outside the area, employment and stipends provided by the national government, and access to work in or remittances from family members in industrial regions are all important in socioeconomic differentiation within the community.

The major prestige categories that emerged from my field method, which admittedly have all the limitations of the method itself, may be characterized roughly as follows: those persons considered as legitimate *signori* (the term attached historically to the landed elite), that is, those whose mentality and behavior are thought to reveal them as "true" *signori*; those acknowledged as *signori* by virtue of their economic status or other partial claim; *il popolo di dentro*, the common people of the town ("inside the walls"); ex-*contadini* (peasants) and elite *contadini* (including townspeople still associated with a peasant past and independent peasant proprietors); respected *contadini* families working *mezzadria* farms; and a lower category of *contadini* regarded as ignorant and backward. The criteria used by informants in assigning prestige rank include, in general order of their importance, "civilized" lifestyle and behavior (which correspond closely to urban-associated patterns), occupation, formal education, family history, and financial position. These criteria, however, do not apply uniformly at all ranks; they are weighted differently and combined in varying ways at different points of the hierarchy.

The prestige order is ritualized in forms of encounter and interaction. Particularly between persons of disparate prestige ranks, interaction is marked by specific terms of address, grammatical forms, tones of voice, a fixed order of speech, expressions and gestures of greeting, and various kinds of behavioral etiquette. What is significant in this, for purposes of the present discussion, is that socioeconomic categories—which are not only analytic categories but are culturally recognized—are not directly manifested in ritual. Indeed, in certain instances, the prestige categories rearrange the realities of class and then underline that rearrangement in ritual.

The study of stratification has generally treated prestige as a particular order of inequality whereby esteem (social and moral evaluations) and honor (deference and precedence) are allocated.[2] That is, along with material goods and power, esteem and honor are kinds of valued things that are "given out" differentially. It might be useful, however, to think of prestige not only as the rewards at stake in one form of stratification among others, but also as processes whereby the determinants of socioeconomic and power differences are

[2]Here I disregard those approaches to stratification that merge prestige and class and thus make it impossible to examine their interplay, for instance, definitions of class as a ranking of differentially valued social roles.

partially obscured. The rituals of deference might then be seen as acting to solidify and isolate the prestige categories, which have reordered the facts of class and power.

PATRONAGE

Within the general structure of interclass relationships, a particular kind of personalized, contractual relationship is marked off as a significant social and symbolic distinction: that of patron and dependent. (The social science term *client* is a poor choice in this instance—as in many others described by anthropologists—since that term implies choice, and options are rarely the case. In Italian there is no general term reciprocal to *padrone*. The most frequently used specific term is perhaps *contadino;* that is, the reciprocal for "my patron" in the context of a *mezzadria* relationship is "my peasant.") Up until the time of my fieldwork, the landlord–tenant relationship grounded in the *mezzadria* contract was the most common basis of patronage and was the model for analogous relationships that were sometimes formed between lower-class persons other than *mezzadri* and members of the local upper class (Silverman, 1975:87–105).

Mezzadria relationships are phrased as patronage, whether or not the exchange of goods and services exceeds the terms stipulated by the formal contract and whether or not there is extensive personal contact between landlord and peasant family. Although the term *padrone* connotes elite status, this suggestion is not always accurate, since persons of fairly low class position may own *mezzadria* farms; a peasant may even be a *mezzadro* on one farm while holding another as a *mezzadria* landlord. Furthermore, the term *padrone* may also be used in addressing persons of only marginally higher status (such as a sometime employer), and it may be used in the absence of a continuing relationship (for example, with a bureaucrat or shopkeeper) in the hope of winning some favor. Thus, while the idiom of patronage suggests wide social inequalities between the parties, the actual disparity is not necessarily great.

Ideologically, the distinction between patron and dependent is marked. Forms of interaction between them employ reciprocal symbols of command and deference, concern and respect. The relationship is rationalized in terms of protection and loyalty, and the actual exchange of goods and services is magnified in rhetoric and phrased as generosity and fondness, reciprocally. Implicit in this ideology is the view that patron and dependent are different in basic "mentality" and essence, the one with inherent gentility and capacity to command, the other childlike and close to nature. The symbolic contrast is drawn in much the same way as the male–female distinction (and indeed, the content of the distinction shows parallels as well).

When the ideology of the distinction is pursued in questioning, it is likely to be explained in terms of deep historical accretions rather than biological attributes. Nevertheless, the features associated with each status appear to be what Berreman calls *intrinsic* criteria. Presumably Berreman would assign this kind of situation to his category "estate" (see pp. 16–17), but that concept evades the actual confounding of attributes of the structural position and attributes of the individual.

An example of the manifestation of patronage in ritual is the offering of prestations on ceremonial occasions. Until recently these offerings were written into the *mezzadria* contract, but similar gifts are also made from dependents to patrons outside the *mezzadria* relationship. The gifts are brought to the patron's house and presented formally: capons at Christmas, hens at Carnival, eggs at Easter, and geese or chickens at the local patron saint's festival in mid-August. The dependent's homage may be reciprocated with phrases of affection and an offering of food or drink (which is, however, not shared by the patron).

The implications of this ideology for reinforcing relationships of actual or potential exploitation—by building other claims into them and by couching them in an idiom of reciprocity—are obvious (see Silverman, 1970, 1977). A further interpretation emerges, however. The disjunction between objective and symbolic inequalities in the patron–dependent distinction suggests a process similar to that operating with reference to sex. The symbolic categories define as incommensurability what in reality is a continuum. As in the sex distinction, the symbolism of patronage may act to pull back differences that threaten to become marginal into contrasts of kind. Thus, boundaries are constructed around the *padrone* as a complex of authority, status, and moral claims. If my interpretation is correct, then change in that complex can be expected to come not through gradual inroads into the actual role of the *padrone* but rather through direct attack upon the inherent qualities attributed to him. This is, in fact, what happened in the 1960s, when the political parties of the Left made "exploitation" by *padroni* an ideological weapon at a time when the exploitative capacity of actual *padroni* had greatly deteriorated.

Territorial Distinctions: The *Palio* of Siena

A further social distinction played a historically important role in central Italy, namely that based on territorial divisions within the local political–administrative unit of the commune. This distinction appears in particularly marked form in the city of Siena, where it is the basis of the ritualized horse race, the *palio*. My interest in the *palio* began with an attempt to apply different anthropological theories to the rich historical material on central Italian politics. Social class, which plays no visible role in the *palio*, was not my initial concern. Yet quite unexpectedly, my work has convinced me that class is the central issue in the development of this ritual complex.

The *palio* is run by the 17 *contrade* or wards of the city, who vie for the prize of a banner (*palio*) dedicated to the Virgin. There are two *palio* cycles, which correspond to the festivals of the local Madonna of Provenzano (July 2) and the Assumption of the Virgin (August 16). Although the race lasts only about 90 seconds, each *palio* consists of an elaborate series of events that continue over a period of weeks, including political and religious ceremonies, official negotiations and Byzantine "deals," trial races, processions, and feasts. Indeed, preparations for the *palio* continue all year long. The race is not a sporting event but rather a competition carried out through the politics of alliance, diplomacy, and quasi-military tactics. The horses are drawn by lot and the jockeys are outsiders hired like mercenaries, but in a very real sense it is the *contrade* themselves that run the race, within the structure and control of the overarching commune.

The *contrada* is a corporate unit with ascriptive membership that, in general, is determined by parental identity or birth within the ward boundaries. *Contrada* membership is lifelong, even if there is change in residence. Each *contrada* is named for its totemic symbol (Snail, Goose, Dragon, etc.), and each has a distinctive identity—including colors, numerology, songs, and folklore—that attaches to all its members. The *contrada* has a clearly defined territory and a formal political organization, with officials, administrative and legislative bodies, and ritual positions that are analogous to those of the commune. The *contrada* is a basic reference point for social interaction within the city; each has its own center and age-graded societies that are the major locales of recreational life. Ritual activity of the *contrada* is not limited to the *palio*; for instance, there is a major festival on the *contrada* patron saint's day. However, by far the most important concern of the *contrada* and the main focus of its economic, political, and religious activity the year round is the *palio*.

The *contrada* is internally stratified. Its high-status members are formally designated as "protectors," members of an honorary body of *contrada* dignitaries. However, *contrada* identity attaches equally to members of all ranks, and within the *contrada* there is a marked ideology of equality. Thus, *contradaioli* of different classes use the familiar form of address and an etiquette of intimacy with each other. The ideology is maintained by a sanction against discussing any "divisive" topics, such as national politics, within the *contrada*.

The unitary identity of the *contrada* is played out through contrasts with all other *contrade*. However, inter-*contrada* relationships are differentiated: There are stable paired enmities among *contrade*, which virtually always involve wards adjacent to each other, as well as fluctuating alliances, which generally are formed between enemies of enemies. These identities and these relations, which mimic the external politics of city-states, are endlessly elaborated and reinforced in the *palio*.

The few serious efforts at explaining the *palio* have focused on ritual manifestations rather than on the social processes underlying them. Thus, Dundes and Falassi (1975) treat the *palio* as a metaphor for Sienese world-view, and they draw on psychoanalytic concepts to construct a presumed sematic structure made up of Lévi-Straussian paired oppositions. Another effort, which follows approaches of Geertz and Peacock, regards the *palio* as a cultural performance that uses a historical reenactment to maintain city and *contrada* identity (Pomponio, 1976). In both these studies, direct links are sought between the contemporary *palio* and "medieval" games, warfare, and customs; the reference point for this historical connection is the autonomous, glorious republic of Siena (1260–1555).

My own approach has been to begin inquiry not with the ritual forms of the *palio* but the social and political structure using those forms, namely the *contrade*. The modern Sienese *contrade* have unique characteristics, but they are essentially territorial divisions and as such have counterparts in all phases of the history of all central Italian communes. Similarly, while the Sienese *palio* is unique in its elaboration and continuing vigor, the basic pattern of ritualized competition between territorial units within the commune is endemic in the region.[3] The most significant feature of the Sienese *contrade* as territorial divisions is their corporateness and the strength of their internal organization. Thus, the problem may be rephrased: Under what conditions do strong, corporate territorial units emerge within the commune, and what role do the elaborated symbolic identity and ritual competition play in their emergence or continuity?

In the history of Siena, localized territorial units with political and ritual functions—namely, parishes—existed before the formation of the commune in the twelfth century. In the various phases of communal history these units were transformed, and the problem becomes one of tracing the relationships among parishes (as ecclesiastical units), military companies, guilds, festival units, and *contrade* (i.e., wards or neighborhoods, whose outlines, structure, and functions were quite variable at different times). A general principle that emerges is that corporate, organized territorial divisions appear in inverse relationship to the strength and effective autonomy of the communal organization. It was precisely after the commune was defeated in all but external form, when Siena was conquered and incorporated into the duchy of Tuscany in the

---

[3]An analogous form of ritual competition among territorial divisions is found even in the small commune of Montecastello. The units here, also called *contrade*, are vaguely delimited neighborhoods of the countryside, each centered on and usually named for a chapel or wayside shrine. Every evening during May, the month of the Madonna, women of each *contrada* say rosaries in their chapel. On the last Sunday, a festival "closes" the month. Residents of each *contrada* form a procession carrying their own banner and singing their own favorite songs in praise of the Madonna. As the processions approach each other, they attempt to drown out each other's songs, until all the processions join into a single procession and, in unity, enter the parish church. Significantly for my argument about the *palio*, this festival is not a long-standing tradition but was introduced by the local priest during the Fascist period in a self-conscious effort to encourage religious interest through harmless competition. The territorial divisions existed before this time, but they had been ambiguous and essentially nonfunctional—a situation I would explain by the relative strength of the commune, which itself absorbed all local functions.

mid-sixteenth century, that the *contrade* began to take on their recognizably modern form. The fixity of *contrada* boundaries and the formalization of *contrada* rights and procedures—in other words, the rigidification of the corporate structure of the *contrade*—stems from a 1729 decree by the Tuscan governor, a foreign overlord in the eyes of the Sienese. The development of the modern *palio* goes hand in hand with the history of the *contrade* after the end of the Sienese republic. In my view, it was the *palio* that reinforced the structure and identity of the *contrade* in Siena, while analogous units in most other communes were eclipsed by the administrative reorganizations imposed by territorial states and later by the nation.

Beyond political structure, however, there were socioeconomic processes at work. In tracing the political implications of different kinds of units within the commune over the centuries, I found the most significant factor to be whether such units corresponded to or crosscut class lines. A unit around which class interests could be mobilized was a potential force of which the actors themselves were well aware. For instance, the commune repeatedly acted to guard against the danger of allowing occupational groups—"men holding common economic, social, and political interests"—to become armed (Bowsky, 1972:245). In the thirteenth century the *contrade* themselves were the loci of class interests that were mobilized to successfully challenge the nobles; once the "people's party" took control of the commune, these class interests were institutionalized within the communal apparatus and lost their independent base. The later *contrade* in Siena (unlike those in Florence and some other cities) were always multiclass, incorporating great socioeconomic diversity.

The historical evidence for Siena in the sixteenth century brings into clear focus the connection between the suppression of class alliances, strong *contrada* organization and identity, and the *palio*. The "pageant-loving" Medici princes who conquered Siena followed the Machiavellian prescription to keep the people occupied with festivals and spectacles, while they themselves established mechanisms of political control within a shell of republican governmental forms (see Heywood, 1969:198–199). The process reflects more than a formula of "bread and circuses." As the *contrade* became corporate and sharply bounded—politically, socially, and symbolically—they became a strong counterforce against class-based horizontal alliances. The role of the *palio* in this process is conspicuous. For example, unlike Carnival festivals—which throughout Italy and France sometimes became occasions for the expression of class-based hostilities—disturbances surrounding the *palio* were uniformly concerned with *contrada* interests. This general analysis applies to contemporary Siena as well. Indeed, it is consistent with some of the polemics of the Left on the "regressive" nature of the *palio*.

The superficial resemblance of certain details of the *palio* to "medieval" patterns is therefore misleading. On the contrary, the ritual complex of the *palio* developed along with the corporate territorial divisions only after the autonomous republic came to an end with the Medici conquest. *Palio* and *contrade* persisted in mutual reinforcement and with the active sponsorship of superordinate powers—not only the Florentine merchant princes but also local interests, including the landed elite and the great bank of Siena.

To the ethnographer of Siena, the territorially based *contrada* appears as the single most important kind of social distinction within the commune. The elaborate symbols of identity and the complex events of the *palio* ensure the maintenance of this distinction. The *contrada* formally recognizes distinctions of age and sex, which appear in the recreational societies. However, distinctions of class are bounded by *contrada* lines and absorbed into *contrada* identity, while class alignments cutting across *contrade* are obscured. Yet in Siena as everywhere in cental Italy, it is social class that determines access to resources and power. In this instance, ritual is not a model of or for society; rather, the social distinctions "expressed" in ritual obliterate fundamental socioeconomic realities.

Conclusions

In this chapter I have questioned the assumption that symbols and rituals express society. Instead, I have followed a tactic of inquiring into the disjunctions between structures and symbols of inequality. In a number of instances in the central Italian material, ritual may be seen as reordering, distorting, and disguising objective orders of inequality. In doing so ritual directly impinges upon structures of inequality and affects the course of change. The process through which ritual defines incommensurable categories (as appears in the treatment both of sex and of patronage) counteracts the effects of real variability and incremental changes. Another general process noted is the emphasis upon distinctions that cut across horizontal cleavages. The use of sex (and to a limited extent, age) in this way acts only to soften class relations, but in the case of the Sienese *contrade*, territorial distinctions actively obscure alignments of class and category and prevent such alignments from being transformed into political alliances. Study of the contexts in which these patterns developed suggests that the cultural use of social distinctions in ritual and symbol cannot be understood only in "cultural" terms—as structures of meaning with internal dynamics—but must be seen as determinate results of historically rooted political and economic processes.

References

Bloch, Maurice
   1974   Symbols, Song, Dance, and Features of Articulation: Is Religion an Extreme Form of Traditional Authority? European Journal of Sociology 15:55–81.

1977   The Disconnection Between Power and Rank as a Process. European Journal of Sociology 18:107–148.

Bowksy, William M.
1972   The Anatomy of Rebellion in Fourteenth-Century Siena: From Commune to Signory? *In* Violence and Civil Disorder in Italian Cities, 1200–1500. Lauro Martines, ed. Pp. 229–272. Berkeley: University of California Press.

Davis, Natalie Zemon
1965   Society and Culture in Early Modern France. Stanford: Stanford University Press.

Dundes, Alan, and Alessandro Falassi
1975   La Terra in Piazza: An Interpretation of the Palio of Siena. Berkeley: University of California Press.

Geertz, Clifford
1966   Religion as a Cultural System. *In* Anthropological Approaches to the Study of Religion. Michael Banton, ed. Pp. 1–46. ASA Monographs, No. 3. London: Tavistock.

Heywood, William
1969   Palio and Ponte. New York: Hacker Art Books. (First ed. 1904.)

Hunt, Eva
1974   Ceremonies of Confrontation and Submission: The Symbolic Dimension of Indian–Mexican Political Interactions. Paper prepared for Burg Wartenstein Symposium No. 64. New York: Wenner-Gren Foundation.

Pomponio, Alice
1976   17 Truths: The Palio of Siena as a Life Process. M. A. thesis, Bryn Mawr College, Bryn Mawr, Pennsylvania.

Rosaldo, Renato I., Jr.
1968   Metaphors of Hierarchy in a Mayan Ritual. American Anthropologist 70:524–536.

Silverman, Sydel
1966   An Ethnographic Approach to Social Stratification: Prestige in a Central Italian Community. American Anthropologist 68:899–921.

1970   "Exploitation" in Rural Central Italy: Structure and Ideology in Stratification Study. Comparative Studies in Society and History 12:327–339.

1975   Three Bells of Civilization: The Life of an Italian Hill Town. New York: Columbia University Press.

1977   Patronage as Myth. *In* Patrons and Clients in Mediterranean Societies. Ernest Gellner and John Waterbury, eds. Pp. 7–19. London: Duckworth.

9

JOHN H. BODLEY

Inequality: An Energetics Approach

In this chapter inequality is examined from the viewpoint of the energy consumption patterns of different cultures. The concept of energy inequality is presented as a tool for comparative approaches to inequality that has implications for both social stratification theory and for contemporary energy policymaking. Both primitive cultures and developing nations are considered and the relationship between the form and quantity of energy consumed and inequality within the cultures is examined in detail.

Strictly speaking, energy is not "consumed"; it is merely transformed, according to the first law of thermodynamics (the conservation of energy). As energy changes form, work is done and energy is dispersed in the form of waste heat. With this caveat in mind, this chapter will follow popular usage and continue to speak of energy consumption. My concern here is with energy in its broadest sense. Much of the discussion of the energy crisis tends to focus on the availability of fossil fuels and electricity, but in fact the most critical energy sources are the food and renewable fuels that derive directly from living green plants. For primitive cultures and in much of the developing world today, food and firewood are *the* energy resources. The indirect energy costs of manufactured goods consumed at the household level will also be included in my calculations of energy consumption.

SOCIAL INEQUALITY
Comparative and Developmental Approaches

The Energetics Approach in Anthropology

The concept of energy and the related concepts of biomass and trophic levels have long been central tools for biologists in their attempts to understand natural ecosystems, but social scientists have so far made only limited use of them. Leslie White (1949) viewed culture as humankind's exosomatic means of capturing energy and founded a theory of cultural evolution based on increasing per capita energy use. White's work, however, did not immediately inspire anthropologists to carry out detailed energy-focused research. Fred Cottrell (1955), a sociologist, presented a number of energy-based theories of cultural development in his provocative book, *Energy and Society*, but again, few researchers followed the lead. By the late 1960s, cultural ecologists such as Roy Rappaport (1968) began investigating energy flows in diverse cultures and caloric inputs and outputs, with useful results. At the same time, ecologist Howard Odum (1967, 1971) developed a simple method for diagraming energy pathways through ecosystems that included man and culture. Much of his work has emphasized the enormous energy inefficiencies of the use of fossil fuels. Several investigators have since presented energy-flow analyses of a variety of cultures (for example, Kemp, 1971; Little and Morren, 1976; Rappaport, 1971), and it is fair to say that energetics analysis is now well established in anthropology's tool kit.

Detailed energetics analysis has as yet not been sharply focused on the problem of inequality, however. Increasing energy flow per capita for total societies has of course been treated as a prerequisite for social stratification, but recent writers who have looked at energy in relation to inequality, such as Marvin Harris (1971) and Richard Adams (1975), have worked with concepts of "power" (defined as control over energy) rather than with energy per se. Harris is explicit on this point.:

> A class is a group of people who possess similar amounts of power per capita . . . and who exert similar forms of control (or lack of control) over basic resources, the tools and techniques of production, and the flow of socially available energy [1971:415].

And further,

> We cannot simply add up all the energy in the form of food, chemicals, and kinetic forces that flow through the masses of the Inca commoners as compared with the Inca nobility and arrive at an assessment of their relative power positions [1971:416].

Certainly this distinction between *power* (as control over energy flow) and the actual *rates of flow* through specific pathways is important, but it should not divert attention from the significance of the energy levels themselves and the source of that energy. On the one hand, inequality is unequal control (or unequal power) over energy resources, but this differential power may or may not be expressed in differential energy flow at the household level, where its real impact is likely to be most critical in relation to basic human needs. "Power" is a rather difficult concept to measure, and different observers and even actors might arrive at very different interpretations of the exercise of power in a particular culture. Energy levels of cultures, and details of energy flow through particular households, however, are relatively unambiguous, although they can be plotted only if high-quality data are available.

There are vast differences in both the rates at which different cultures consume energy and the degree of differentiation between different households within a single culture. Many of these differences have been quantified and can provide an obvious measure of inequality, as will be explored later. A second approach might seek to establish a culturally defined minimum comfort or minimum subsistence level as a measure of inequality for specific cultures. This measure would be somewhat akin to officially established "poverty" levels.

An energetics approach does raise some important issues relative to inequality. If, for example, we follow the lead of White (1949) and assume that culture is a means for satisfying man's basic energy needs, we find that increasing the per capita rates for the total population of a given culture beyond a certain level has apparently been achieved only in the face of inequality that in many cases pushes segments of the population below minimum subsistence levels.

The long-established interpretation of advances in cultural evolution is that it has also meant greater adaptive success (Cohen, 1974; Sahlins and Service, 1960; White, 1949). However, in terms of energy inequality, as culture evolves, *more* people may be *less* well off than ever before. Furthermore, shifts to nonrenewable energy sources to support increased inequality may actually threaten the long-run ability of a high-energy culture to satisfy any basic human needs. To the extent that inequality is linked to very high and ever-increasing levels of energy consumption, it may be a fatal flaw in cultural evolution. Luten (1974:26) predicts that the most "advanced" high-energy culture will burn itself and the world out on "Sun Day" 2174—the day that waste heat dissipated equals the incoming heat from the sun. Cultures remaining at low, renewable levels theoretically could last 5 billion years—until the sun burns itself out!

Energy Levels and Inequality

The overall per capita energy level of a culture does seem to be a significant variable influencing the nature of inequality. For our purposes, the concepts of *low-energy culture* and *high-energy culture* provide the most useful categories of energy level. These terms were used by Cottrell (1955) largely to separate fossil-fuel-using societies from nonfossil fuel users. Although this is perhaps their most obvious distinguishing trait, there are other important correlates of high- and low-energy cultures that must be discussed.

As here defined, *low-energy culture* refers to cultures in which the daily per capita energy consumption level is unlikely to exceed 26,000 kilocalories (kcal), and the basic energy sources are solar, renewable, and, for much of the population, noncommercial. This figure is based on an estimate developed by Earl Cook (1971:135) and includes the energy derived directly from plant food, indirectly from plant food fed to animals, and from fuels used for heating and cooking. It applies to northwestern Europe at approximately A.D. 1400 and apparently does not include the energy value of plant and animal materials incorporated in housing and other goods. This figure may be relatively high for low-energy cultures because it does include a minimal use of fossil fuels and assumes state-level political systems. It is clear that a culture limited to plant and animal energy converters will have a relatively low, fixed ceiling of energy available for human consumption. This figure will of course vary for different ecosystems, but lacking political structures designed to stimulate production, low-energy cultures probably seldom exceeded 12,000 kcal per capita per day. This is the estimate that Cook (1971:135) offers for primitive agriculturalists in the Fertile Crescent of 5000 B.C.

High-energy cultures range from consumption levels of 70,000 kcal per capita per day for early industrial cultures to over 200,000 in the modern United States (Cook, 1971:135). Here, energy is largely commercial and non-renewable and flows in pathways that support a highly nonegalitarian social system in which the basic human needs of the entire society may be subordinated to the interests of specialist groups.

The distinction between commercial and noncommercial energy is significant for several reasons. The availability of commercial energy (primarily fossil fuels) is much restricted both because of its limited supply and because of the specialized and often expensive capital required to extract and effectively convert it for use. These limitations automatically imply unequal access and are certainly conducive to energy inequality. In contrast, noncommercial energy (primarily solar energy converted by living plants and animals) is widely and cheaply available as long as land is equitably distributed. Such basic renewable fuels as firewood and dung are still free for the collecting in many countries, and much of the world's fuel supply is still produced by and for subsistence farmers who are largely outside the commercial economy.

Primitive cultures may be taken as ideal prototypes of low-energy cultures. Here, low per capita levels of energy consumption coincide with very low total cultural energy levels. Exclusive use of solar energy means that the energy ceiling is not easily expandable, and use of noncommercial energy means that there are no special interest groups that stand to gain by increasing the energy costs of basic necessities or otherwise elevating consumption levels. Energy conversion decisions remain at the household level with a rather diffuse form of community control (i.e., Sahlins' 1972 concept of "the domestic mode of production"), closely responsive to basic human needs. When there is little energy available, its distribution must be highly equitable; there is simply less energy to go around, and it is unlikely to become concentrated in areas not directly tied to basic needs. Judging from the best descriptions of undisturbed primitive cultures, energy inequality does not exist at this level.

High-energy cultures appear to have elevated the energy costs of subsistence far beyond what would be required to satisfy basic human nutritional needs. Low-energy cultures have proved that these needs can be met at a very low energy cost. In the most "advanced" high-energy cultures such as the United States, it is becoming apparent that the almost total commercialization of food, man's most basic energy source, has created a situation in which special interest groups profit from each increase in the energy costs of food ("value added" in economic terms). As a result, food has effectively been separated from nutrition. Evidence is mounting that energy-intensive foods are often less nutritious than their less expensive, less refined counterparts.

Along these same lines, Ivan Illich (1974) has also argued in a provocative essay that high and expanding energy use destroys equality. As he states, "beyond a certain median per capita energy level, the political system and cultural context of any society must decay [pp. 5–6]." In his view this decay involves an inevitable loss of equality as "technological processes begin to dictate social relations [p. 8]" and as vested interests in the industrial infrastructure increase. The more energy-expensive means of satisfying basic needs often preclude lower-cost alternatives; there is a loss of autonomy for those able to afford it, and it may be too costly for the poor. Illich maintains that "only a ceiling on energy use can lead to social relations that are characterized by high levels of equity [p. 5]." He supports his arguments with an examination of transportation systems, showing how costly fossil fuel systems have displaced more efficient and equitable systems based on foot and bicycle traffic.

Measures of Energy Inequality

Anyone attempting to measure inequality in terms of energy consumption immediately faces a number of difficulties. If the assumption is made that inequality is a function of unequal per capita consumption of energy at the household level within a specified range, then very careful attention must be given to the measurement of energy consumption and some adjustment for the age and sex of various household members may be required. A standard procedure for computing the energy value of various goods that are not food or fuels must be adopted. Given existing data, no great precision can be hoped for, but careful comparisons that follow the same ground rules in examining households within a given culture should yield useful data. Ideally, the energy value of all foods, fuels, and other goods should be considered. But even with the most careful subsistence studies, fully quantified data of this sort are seldom available. Given these limitations, cross-cultural comparisons of energy inequality should be approached with caution.

As a trial formulation, *energy inequality* will be viewed here in terms of both differential net energy consumption and differential input–output efficiencies at the household level. With respect to net consumption, energy inequality will be defined as a wide variation in apparent net annual per capita energy consumption between households in a given culture. Until full comparative data can be compiled, I will not try to gauge the extent to which this variation can occur before declaring energy inequality to exist. I have assumed that in low-energy primitive cultures, variations of this sort will be slight.

A second dimension of energy inequality is energy input–output efficiency. In this chapter *inputs* will be considered to be the energy value of all labor, investments in seeds and tools, kin reciprocity given out, produce marketed, and taxes paid by the household in a given year. *Outputs* will be the total caloric value of all remaining food and fuels consumed and other goods procured annually. The efficiency ratio is simply the outputs divided by the inputs. This value is obviously quite different from but related to the subsistence efficiency ratio used by Harris (1971:203–217), who considers labor inputs in relation to gross food production. The ratio to be adopted here attempts to be more inclusive and stresses final consumption in relation to all energy outputs, whether or not they are directly related to food production.

Energy inequality in terms of the input–output efficiency ratio will be said to exist when households at the lowest per capita energy consumption levels show a conspicuously lower energy efficiency ratio than is the norm for the culture. This lower output efficiency often results from the fact that the lowest-level households may be disadvantaged in a variety of ways so that their energy expenditures are not equally rewarded. The opposite situation obtains in energy-egalitarian societies. The present input–output efficiency definition of energy inequality is designed to reveal those cases of inequality in which household members may actually work harder than average but end up consuming less than the norm.

So far, the discussion has been almost entirely theoretical, but now it is time to confront real data. For this purpose, I have selected three case studies in which household-level energy consumption patterns will be examined. These cases are (1) a Mandinka village engaged in cash-cropping in Gambia; (2) a Chinese farming village; and (3) rural India.

GAMBIAN PEANUT FARMERS

The Gambian data are derived from a 1947–1949 study (Haswell, 1953) of the Mandinka Moslem village of Genieri. From an energetics standpoint, Haswell gives an extremely detailed account of all labor and cash inputs and outputs by extended family compounds for the entire village of 500 people. The ethnographic data described an interesting social stratification pattern that surprisingly was not reflected in the energetics analysis.

According to Haswell, there were three distinct social classes in the village, based in part on their time of arrival. The top group consisted of descendants of the village founders. These individuals held the most influential social positions, owned the prime agricultural lands nearest the village, were able to draw on large kin networks, and paid the lowest rates for work parties. The other two classes were either descendants of slaves or were late arrivals ("strangers") and were at a clear disadvantage in terms of land, access to labor, and social status. The "upper class" included 56% of the population but claimed nearly 70% of the land.

Figures 9.1 and 9.2 outline the energy flows for two sample compounds chosen to represent the "founder" class (compound A) and the "stranger" class (compound Q). These particular households were chosen because they were very similar in size in terms of "adult male equivalents" (AME), a value that controls for age and sex difference. Household A contained 18.3 AME, and household Q contained 20.8 AME. The data were fairly complete, but a few assumptions were still required. For example, the caloric value of cash and purchased goods was computed by converting cash to its caloric equivalent in millet at the market rate of 6 pence = 1 pound (.45 kg) of millet = 1483 kcal. In computing the caloric cost of labor, 6-hour days of 150 kcal per hour were assumed. Labor for Europeans was computed at .61 shillings per hour. It was also assumed that kin labor was on a balanced reciprocal exchange basis. Unfortunately, there was no information on how much paid labor was *given* to other villagers.

The analysis reveals that the "upper-class" compound did indeed come out slightly ahead in terms of apparent annual consumption per AME, with 1,504,000 kcal in compound A to the 1,207,000 kcal of compound Q, but this difference does not seem particularly striking. Compound A held slightly more and presumably higher-quality acres—1.9 per AME to 1.4 for compound Q, but the "poorer" compound actually operated at a slightly higher output/input efficiency—11.9 to 12.3, respectively. It appears that despite its social disadvantages, low-class compound Q was able to raise a larger peanut crop for sale.

While this analysis did not show significant energy inequality between these two households within the village, it did reveal inequality with respect to the national economy. Both households received on the average only .3 kcal of millet kcal equivalents for every kilocalorie of peanuts exported. In terms of food consumption, cash cropping of peanuts appeared to be a losing proposition.

It is obvious that these figures are not comparable with Cook's (1971) caloric consumption estimates cited previously (see p. 186, this volume). The present figures clearly underestimate the total energy consumed. The primary

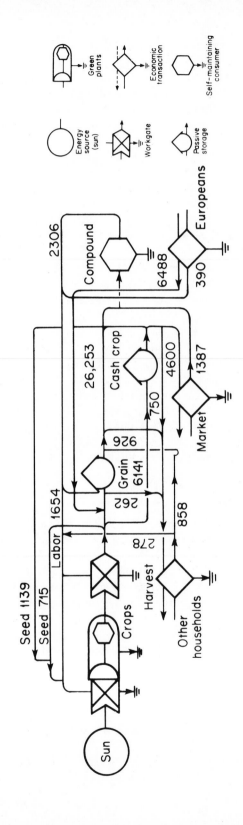

Figure 9.1. Energy flow for Gambian compound A, 1000 kcal per year. (Data are from Haswell, 1953.)

190

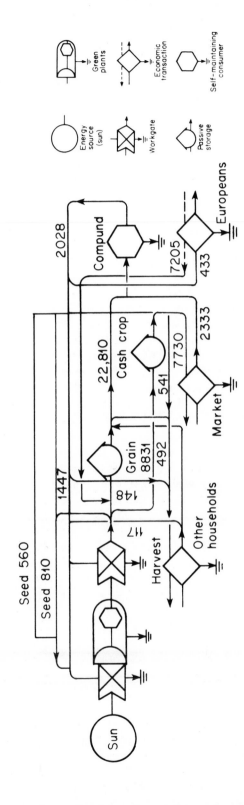

Figure 9.2. Energy flow for Gambian compound Q, 1000 kcal per year. (Data are from Haswell, 1953.)

error is the absence of direct caloric values for fuels and the use of millet equivalent calories. The important consideration, however, is that since the same methodology has been consistently applied, valid comparisons between households within the same society can be made.

CHINESE VILLAGERS

The Chinese data are taken from the work of Hsiao-t'ung Fei and Chih-i Chang (1945), describing the prerevolutionary village of Luts'un in Yunnan as of 1938. The energy consumption patterns of representative households can be outlined in considerable detail using this material. The quality of the data is quite comparable to the Gambian data discussed previously. With a population of 611, the Chinese village is similar in size to Genieri. The social stratification picture, however, is much more extreme.

Three classes are described. There was a landowning leisured class at the top that managed its land resources to produce subsistence and market crops that would ensure a minimum standard of living with the lowest possible workload. The "middle" class was composed of owner–tenants who had to rent most of their land and were left with a slim margin for consumption. At the bottom was the landless class—those who had to survive by hiring out their labor and purchasing basic necessities. In Luts'un 41% of the farmland was owned by 15% of the households, while 31% of the households were completely landless. Nearly half of these nonlandowning households were too poor to even rent any land.

Superficially, the stratification picture here is very similar to that described for Genieri, and some of the dynamics of its formation appear to be the same. The landless class was also composed of immigrants into an already established village. A careful evaluation of the energy picture, however, reveals striking energy inequality that contrasts clearly with the energy patterns of Genieri.

Figures 9.3 and 9.4 present the basic energy flow data that were drawn largely from household budgets provided for specific households representing the landholding and the landless classes. These households differed in size, with five individuals in the landholding family and only two in the landless household. The landowning household actually controlled only 27 *kung* (of approximately 250 m² each), which placed it in the lower range of the landowning class. In this analysis, goods and cash were converted to their rice caloric equivalents as follows: (1.6¢ = 1 kg of rough rice = 3513 kcal, or 83¢ = 1 picual of rice = 50.1 kg). It was further assumed that laborers worked 8-hour days at 150 kcal an hour and received 1000 kcal of food per day in addition to their wages.

Energy inequality was obvious. The landed household showed an apparent per capita food consumption five times that of the landless household (7798 compared to 1610 per capita rice equivalent kcal). It also consumed four

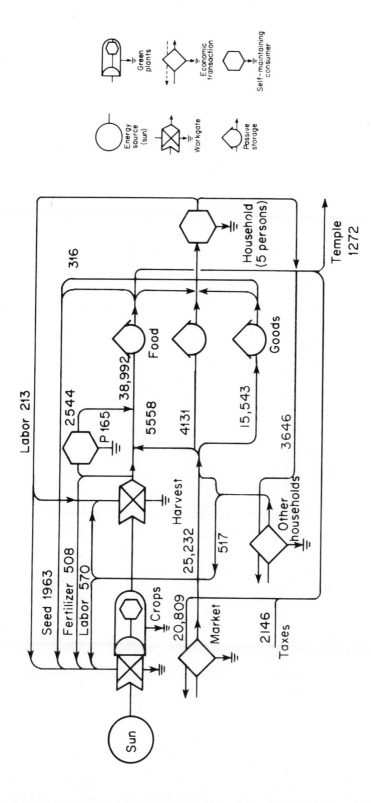

Figure 9.3. Energy flows for a Chinese landowner household, 1000 kcal per year rice equivalent. (Data are from Fei and Chang, 1945.)

193

194

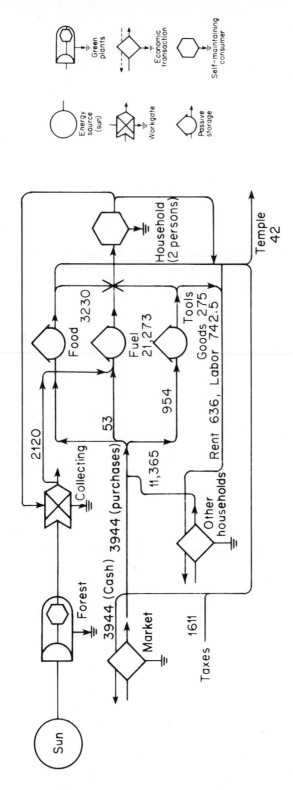

Figure 9.4. Energy flows for a Chinese landless household, 1000 kcal per year rice equivalents. (Data are from Fei and Chang, 1945.)

and one half times the goods and produced at more than twice the energy efficiency rate of the landless household. These consumption figures do not even consider the potential energy stored in savings by the landed household. This stored energy was equivalent to another year's worth of consumption at the same level and, if counted, would have effectively doubled the energy inequality observed. The poor household appeared to be consuming food at just above a minimum subsistence level, with 1,615,000 rice equivalent kcal per capita per year. This figure, however, makes little provision for adequate protein intake. The landed household supported pigs with its garden waste and could easily purchase additional meat. It appears that the poor household was below minimum levels in housing, clothing, and medical care, partly because such a high proportion of its production had to be devoted to food.

RURAL INDIAN HOUSEHOLDS

The data examined for rural India are less detailed than those for the previous examples, but they can still be used to examine the extent of energy inequality in a modern developing country. Sankar (1977) provides national level energy consumption data for India that cover all sources of fuel energy including commercial and noncommercial sources. The noncommerical sources include even the animate energy supplied by cattle and fuels derived from dung, firewood, and vegetable waste. If we assume that everyone was consuming at least 1 million kcal of food annually in addition to the fuel energy Sankar lists, the national daily per capita energy consumption level in 1953 was only approximately 13,000 kcal—barely more than that of primitive agriculturalists by Cook's (1971) estimates (see p. 186, this volume). However, energy inequality means that far fewer calories were actually available to the poorest rural households.

In 1953 only 17% of the commercial energy (largely fossil fuels) used in India was consumed in the domestic and agricultural sector of the country. Much of this actually went to export agriculture or was consumed in the urban sector, but if we apportion the full 17% to the rural area, its apparent energy consumption level drops to approximately 11,000 kcal per capita daily. This is below the level that Cook (1971) ascribes to primitive agriculturalists. Data elsewhere on rural inequality in India (Dandekar and Rath, 1971; Monthly Commentary 1975a, 1975b) suggest that even this meager energy level is not available to many of the rural poor. Even in prosperous Indian states in 1970, it was found that 45–53% of the rural households controlled 94–95% of the farm assets. In poor states, 16% of the households were in control of 70% of the assets. Ninety percent of rural households owned less than one hectare of land. Landless households that were unable to produce their own food had difficulty generating enough cash to purchase it.

In 1960 it was found that one-third of the rural Indian population earned less than that required to purchase a minimum subsistence of 2250 calories a day in food. In such cases, as in China, the bulk of the income was then used to purchase food. Other human needs for shelter, clothing, and medicine were inadequately met.

The overall trend in India since 1953 has been toward an increasing energy inequality. Land has become more concentrated in fewer hands, and noncommercial and renewable energy resources have been steadily eroded as population has increased and as these resources have been replaced by commercial fuels that are not easily accessible to the rural poor.

The Indian energy data document energy inequality somewhat indirectly. They refer to very low absolute levels that must place a large segment of the population below minimum subsistence levels. Unfortunately, comparative data for wealthy households are not at hand. What is also needed is a clear statement of energy consumption in areas other than food in order to establish a minimally adequate subsistence level for India.

Conclusions

These three case studies show that energetics analysis can indeed be an important tool for the study of social inequality. The Gambian example from 1947–1949 revealed that significant energy inequality did not occur, even though the ethnographer described a stratified society. The Chinese village of 1938, which outwardly resembled the Gambian village, actually proved to be highly inequitable in energy terms. The critical difference in Gambia was that even the "lower-class" households had access to land, although it was neither easily accessible nor of high quality. India between the 1950s and 1970s is a case in which the introduction of fossil fuels and industrialization has, if anything, increased inequality to such an extent that much of the population has dropped below the energy levels of primitive agriculturalists and are denied direct access to energy sources.

This work emphasizes the critical importance of access to land and renewable energy sources for the maintenance of energy equality and points to the need for international recognition of a minimum energy allowance as a basic human right.

References

Adams, Richard N.
   1975   Energy and Structure: A Theory of Social Power. Austin: University of Texas Press.
Cohen, Yehudi
   1974   Culture as Adaptation. In Man in Adaptation: The Cultural Present. Second ed. Y.
          Cohen, ed. Pp. 45–68. Chicago: Aldine.
Cook, Earl
   1971   The Flow of Energy in an Industrial Society. Scientific American 225(3):134–144.

Cottrell, Fred
  1955   Energy and Society: The Relation Between Energy, Social Change, and Economic Development. New York: McGraw-Hill.
Dandekar, V. M., and Nilakantha Rath
  1971   Poverty in India. I: Dimensions and Trends. Economic and Political Weekly 6(1):25-33.
Fei, Hsiao-t'ung, and Chih-i Chang
  1945   Earthbound China: A Study of Rural Economy in Yunnan. Chicago: University of Chicago Press.
Harris, Marvin
  1971   Culture, Man, and Nature. New York: Thomas Y. Crowell.
Haswell, M. R.
  1953   Economics of Agriculture in a Savanna Village. Colonial Research Studies No. 8. London: Her Majesty's Stationery Office.
Illich, Ivan
  1974   Energy and Equity. New York: Harper and Row.
Kemp, W. B.
  1971   The Flow of Energy in a Hunting Society. Scientific American 225(3):104-115.
Little, Michael A., and George E. B. Morren, Jr.
  1976   Ecology, Energetics, and Human Variability. Dubuque, Iowa: Wm. C. Brown.
Luten, Daniel B.
  1974   United States Requirements. In Energy, the Environment, and Human Health. A. Finkel. ed. Pp. 17-33. Acton, Massachusetts: Publishing Sciences Group.
Monthly Commentary on Indian Economic Conditions
  1975a   Pattern of Rural Inequality. Vol. 17, No. 1. Pp. 51-60.
  1975b   Indian Destitution and Deprivation: The Changing Picture, 1960-61 to 1970-71. Vol. 17, No. 9. Pp. 59-70.
Odum, Howard T.
  1967   Energetics of World Food Production. In President's Advisory Committee, The World Food Problem: A Report of the Panel on the World Food Supply. Vol. 3. Pp. 55-94. Washington, D.C.: U.S. Government Printing Office.
  1971   Environment, Power, and Society. New York: John Wiley Inter-Science.
Rappaport, Roy
  1968   Pigs for the Ancestors: Ritual in the Ecology of a New Guinea People. New Haven: Yale University Press.
  1971   The Flow of Energy in an Agricultural Society. Scientific American 225(3):117-132.
Sahlins, Marshall
  1972   Stone Age Economics. Chicago: Aldine.
Sahlins, Marshall, and Elman R. Service, eds.
  1960   Evolution and Culture. Ann Arbor: University of Michigan Press.
Sankar, T. L.
  1977   Alternative Energy Development Strategies with a Low-Energy Profile for a Low GNP/Capita Energy-Poor Country: The Case of India. In The Energy Syndrome. Leon N. Lindberg, ed. Pp. 215-254. Lexington, Massachusetts: Lexington Books, D. C. Heath.
White, Leslie A.
  1949   The Science of Culture. New York: Grove Press.

PART
IV

FORMS OF DOMINATION IN STRATIFIED SOCIETIES

10

MINA DAVIS CAULFIELD

Equality, Sex, and Mode of Production[1]

The theme of social inequality is of particular significance to me at this time because of its centrality in a series of ongoing exchanges within the community of feminist anthropologists. In recent years some members of our profession have challenged a number of previously taken-for-granted axioms about the nature of sex roles and the sexual division of labor in a wide range of societies (see, for example, Ardener, 1975; Friedl, 1975; Rohrlich-Leavitt, 1975; Reiter, 1975; Rosaldo and Lamphere, 1974). This questioning has not, of course, been undertaken in a social vacuum; the immediacy of the Women's Movement has been a driving force, and for many of us the central theoretical questions have been those framed by our practice as actual or potential agents of social change. Since social inequality has been the central issue for the Women's Movement as a whole, and since anthropology can logically be expected to bring to the discussion some much-needed cross-cultural data and generalizations on the topic, a great deal of interest has been stimulated in rethinking, reinterpreting data, and in many instances challenging the validity of the observations made by anthropologists who have been shown to be biased by androcentrism.

A number of crucial theoretical questions have been raised in this body of work, questions about the underlying or ultimate causes of male domination. A theme that cuts through many of these theoretical questions is the question

[1]An earlier version of this paper was published under the title "Universal Sex Oppression?—A Critique from Marxist Anthropology," in a special edition on "Feminist Thought," Cynthia Nelson and Virginia Olesen, eds., *Catalyst,* Summer, 1977 (Nos. 10–11).

SOCIAL INEQUALITY
Comparative and Developmental Approaches
ISBN 0-12-093160-5

of the universality of "sex opposition" or "patriarchy," cross-culturally and panhistorically. There is an assumption in the writings of many feminist anthropologists, as in those of feminist theorists generally, that male domination has always and everywhere existed and functioned as a separate system of hierarchy, originating and operating on the basis of a set of social (or biological) laws that are fundamentally different from those that govern other forms of oppression, such as class, race, or imperialist domination. It is this assumption that I wish to address in this chapter.

I will argue that the "inequality" of the sexual division of labor has a totally different and nonoppressive significance in societies that have been organized around what Marx calls the production of use values. It is my further contention that the erosion, distortion, and near annihilation of use value relations by class societies, reaching their height in contemporary capitalism, have resulted in the devaluation and exploitation not only of "women's work," and of women themselves, but also of human relations generally, including those involved in "men's work," the exploitation of the environment, male–female relations, and particularly kinship or family structures and values. Thus, in looking for the origins and causes of male domination, with all the implications which that search carries for political theory and practice in the Women's Movement and other movements, I think it is essential not to seek to isolate the sources of a supposedly universal system of women's oppression, but rather to document the historical changes by which class stratification has operated to change the relations of production for all peoples, incorporating male supremacy as part and parcel of the process of class rule.

The problems with the theory of universal sex oppression are compounded when the concept of equality itself is used uncritically. Equality is, of course, a cultural ideal in modern bourgeois democratic ideology, and feminists as well as other theorists tend to use it without regard for the culture-specific meanings it carries. Cynthia Nelson and Virginia Olesen (1977:24), in a paper critiquing the concept of equality in feminist thought, point out:

> With respect to the distribution of such social rewards as may be at issue, the matter of equality or inequality must be referred to some criterion against which the distribution is analyzed or evaluated. . . . If the criterion for equality is achievement, then the question arises of which achievement and for what purposes. If the criterion for equality is need, then the definitions of needs, most usually articulated by the state come into play. If equality of opportunity is demanded, then the criterion is merit and the consequent processes of change and mobility frequently engender further inequalities.

Historically, equality as a cultural ideal arose with the advent of capitalism, an ideological counter to the feudal notion of divine right and ascribed (unequal) status. In this context, it was inextricable from the concept of individual achievement in "free" competition, and never included (except among socialist theorists) the idea of any kind of equal sharing of societal products. In our society, when we stop to examine what we have always taken for granted, equality means *the right to participate without systematic disadvantage in an individual competition for individual, unequal rewards.* The historical–cultural specificity of this ideal is almost never called into question, though of course the fact that the society has never lived up to the ideal is often pointed out and resented and has been the cause of innumerable social conflicts.

The cultural ideal of equality acts to conceal the reality of powerlessness over the definitions of the rewards, the rules of the competition, and the fact of the competition itself—that is, the relations of production in a capitalist society. Most importantly, this ideal masks the fact that this kind of society is predicated on an extreme inequality, the increasing accumulation of capital in fewer and fewer hands. "Free" labor, in a bourgeois definition, means the freedom to compete for profits and jobs without regard for nonmarket, particularly familistic bonds. Freed of particularistic considerations, and especially "freed" of any rights of property in the forces of production other than his or her labor power, each worker is theoretically "equal," that is, has neither advantage nor disadvantage over competitors by virtue of kinship or any other emotional, personal relation. Thus, the ideal of equality is intimately tied in with the ideology of bourgeois rationality and the denial of affect or collectivity in one's relations to the productive or distributive (market) process.

Inequality, the converse, is naturally seen as a social evil, though it is everywhere apparent in capitalist society. Disadvantages in the labor market because of race, culture, and sex are viewed as imperfections in an otherwise just and harmonious system; yet they are curiously difficult to stamp out. There is evidence of increasing disparity in income between Whites and non-Whites, as well as between men and women, in the United States since the late 1960s.

The standard by which equality is implicitly measured, then, is in relation to the market—precisely that area that has historically been defined as the "man's world." It seems relevant here by way of analogy to note that at least one sociologist has criticized the concept of equality as it is espoused in White society, arguing that it is actually used to perpetuate the oppression of Blacks in the United States. "Equality according to the standards set by whites," says Sidney Willhelm (1974:146 and *passim*), amounts to a new "racist ideology."

Feminist movements in the capitalist world have largely adopted the prevailing ideology of equality, consistently protesting the obvious disadvantages that women have faced in a "man's world"—legal, jural, political, and moral obstacles to equal participation in the competition for societal rewards. Here, as in the case of racist and ethnocentric bias, such obstacles have been

justified by a pervasive ideology of "natural" or biological inferiority or difference, apparently at odds with the cultural ideal of equality. Moreover,
since it is obvious that such obstacles and such ideology did not originate with
capitalism, but on the contrary are immediately apparent in a large number of
other societies, past and present, the tendency has been to address male
domination as a pansocial phenomenon and to seek ultimate causes and
origins in the prehistoric past, even in the prehuman past, in nature itself.

If we assume that social inequality is present in any social formation having some form of division of labor, then clearly all known societies have
embodied forms of inequality. This usage, however, applies the standard of
competitive advantage or disadvantage to all societies, making a universal
principle of it, whereas, as I have argued, it is actually culture-specific. Marx,
in his writings on "primitive communism," dealt with this question quite differently. According to him, the division of labor by sex and age in preclass
societies was a "technical" division, in which social agents were distributed
into socially equivalent places in production. Marx distinguished this division
from the "social" division of labor (between managers and workers) that
characterizes relations of exploitation in class societies (1867/1970:351).
However, Marx and later Engels failed to examine the sexual division of labor
in its socially determined aspects, arguing rather that "within a family, and
after further development within a tribe, there springs up a natural division of
labor, caused by differences of age and sex, a division that is consequently
based on a purely physiological foundation [p. 351]." Since the appeal to
nature or physiology is basically the same as that made by other theorists who
claim sex oppression as a universal, the notion of social equivalence in a
technical rather than social division of labor requires further examination.
Marx's naturalistic explanation for the sexual division of labor has been
criticized by Maxine Molyneux (1977:63):

> It is absurd to talk of the organization of production in terms of a "natural" distribu-
> tion of labour when this organization is maintained by determinate social prac-
> tices—such as, in primitive societies, kinship, mythology and ritual. Moreover, such
> an explanation cannot account for the considerable variation in the ways in which
> agents are allocated along sexual lines. The sexual division of labour is therefore to be
> conceptualized as a social construct, and this is so irrespective of any speculative
> theorizing as to how it might have originated.

Similarly, Eleanor Leacock (1977b:244) argues that

> the sexual division of labor . . . be seen as problematic rather than taken for granted.
> Institutionalized specialization by sex must have been critical somewhere along the
> line of human emergence. A lengthening period of childhood dependency accom-
> panied growing reliance upon tool manufacture, increasing learning capacity, and ex-
> panding cooperation, and this prolongation of childhood had important implications
> for group composition and optimum size.

The division of labor by sex, then, is to be seen not as a biologically determined outgrowth of women's involvement in reproduction, but as a socially
contructed solution to the problems and potentials posed in the evolution of
societies.

The female role in reproduction (or the male role in reproduction, for
that matter) would not necessitate an unequal or devalued status in a society
that was organized around the production of use values. As Bridget
O'Laughlin (1977:21) has argued, production and reproduction are actually a
unified process, since production of consumption goods is also reproduction
of social life, while biological reproduction is also production of use values
(that is, babies). It is only when we conceive of equality in terms of market or
exchange relations that the sexual division of labor appears to carry the
necessary implication of hierarchy.

Several authors have suggested that we start with the idea of complementarity rather than equality/inequality, dominance, or oppression in looking at
the sexual division of labor (Aaby, 1977:34; Edholm, Harris, and Young,
1977:122; Nelson and Olesen, 1977:*passim*; Terray, 1969:96). There are difficulties with this concept, however, that must be kept in mind. As Molyneux
observes (1977:78), Terray's uncritical use of the notion of sexual complementarity is suspect, and for very good reason. Few women is U.S. society are unfamiliar with the mystifications surrounding this idea: The old, old argument
used against feminists is that women's roles are not inferior, just different; the
mothering, nurturant qualities with which women are equipped are said to
"complement" the aggressive, rationalistic qualities with which men go out
and acquire the necessities of life. And indeed, all too often we are presented
with a stereotyped version of "primitive" society (or even ape society) to back
up the whole package. When Nelson and Olesen (1977: 27–34), after criticizing equality as a Western ideal, go on to suggest complementarity as more appropriate, they lose their credibility in my eyes by choosing as their example
the roles of women and men in Muslim society. As Fatima Mernissi makes
clear in her study of male–female dynamics in Muslim society (1975), the kind
of "complementarity" instituted by Islam between men and women was that
of master and slave.

Significantly, Mernissi's work also provides a clue to understanding this
kind of complementarity in the historical changes by which it was brought
about. Pre-Islamic Arab women, far from being controlled and "protected" by
their husbands, had extensive sexual freedom, practiced uxorilocal marriages
that they could terminate at will, and "depended on the tribe (not the husband) for protection and food [1975:34]." As Mernissi says, "The social order
created by the Prophet, a patrilineal monotheistic state, could only exist if the
tribe and its allegiances gave way to the *Umma*. The Prophet found the institution of the family a much more suitable unit for socialization than the
tribe [p. 40–41]." The "complementarity" of female–male relations can be seen
to have undergone a dramatic transformation with the advent of Islam, as in-

deed it did everywhere that state formation and class society were instituted—from the interdependence of group sharing to controlled dependency in a rigid state and family structure. The problem with the concept of
complementarity, just as with that of equality/inequality, is its use as a
universal principle by some theorists, rather than in specific historical-
cultural contexts.

This same tendency to universalize in analyzing women's role in society is
the basic problem in the work of many feminists. Because they fail to deal
with the historical development of the inequalities they criticize, they lead one
to conclude either that women's liberation can be achieved without changing
other aspects of capitalism or that all other kinds of social oppression will
disappear once sex hierarchies are abolished. Both conclusions leave out of
consideration the need to address needed changes in the mode of production
as a means to eliminating all forms of oppression. I will discuss several
theorists within anthropology who propose different forms of the universal
sex-oppression thesis.

Theories of Universal Sex Oppression

Michelle Rosaldo (1974) advances a universal principle to explain what
she assumes to be the universal devaluation, or lack of authority, of women.
She sees a division in all societies between a "public" and a "private" sphere of
social life, with women confined at least to some degree to the private or
domestic sphere, which is devalued in all cultural systems relative to the
public, extra-domestic sphere. This mode of analysis is explicitly ahistorical
and leads, as Rosaldo says, to one or both of two strategies for the Women's
Movement, neither of which deals with the problem of cultural homogeneity
in the Movement, assuming rather that the problems of women in capitalist
society are the same as those of all women. Women, she advocates, should
build their own women's associations and struggle to enter the world of
"public" work (wage labor) and politics; in addition, men must be brought
into the domestic sphere, and the "asymmetry between work and the home
reduced [p. 42]." No historical origins of the public/private split are suggested, despite the fact that Rosaldo cites one society, the Philippine Ilongot,
in which "there is little in everyday . . . life to suggest an asymmetrical relation of the sexes" before the influence of Christian missions (p. 40).

To explain the primary mechanism of the dichotomization, Rosaldo
draws on the work of Nancy Chodorow (1974), who argues that it is the
universal closeness of the mother–infant bond that restricts mothers to the
domestic sphere. Girl children, Chodorow argues, since they need not
distance themselves from their mothers in assuming their adult gender status,
are effectually ensured a social–psychological "embeddedness" in the domestic
nexus, whereas boys must of necessity differentiate themselves in order to
become culturally adult males. Thus, men are psychologically preadapted for

entry into the public sphere, while women remain more oriented toward the private, in all societies.

Another, related argument is proposed by Sherry Ortner (1974) in her paper that asks the question, "Is Female to Male as Nature Is to Culture?" Ortner's answer to her question is a clear "yes": She posits a universal though often unconscious association between women and nature and between men and culture—with the two spheres in a fundamental relation of opposition and hierarchy. This argument is based on the work of Claude Lévi-Strauss, who also assumes that the devaluation of women is a cultural universal, and builds it into his theory of the origins of culture itself. Lévi-Strauss posits the "exchange of women" in marriage as the most fundamental and indeed the definitive cultural act, serving to mark the origins of what is distinctively human rather than "natural." Ortner (1974:78) quotes Lévi-Strauss (1969:479) with approval on this point:

> The universal incest prohibition and its ally, the rule of exogamy, . . . ensure that "the risk of seeing a biological family become established as a closed system is definitely eliminated; the biological group can no longer stand apart, and the bond of alliance with another family ensures the dominance of the social over the biological, and of the cultural over the natural."

Ortner (1974:79) argues that since women are everywhere "associated with, and indeed are more or less confined to, the domestic context, they are identified with this lower order of social–cultural organization," that is, the "biological" family. In contrast, men appear to be more "naturally" suited to the higher-order level of interfamilial relations (politics, religion, warfare, trade) because of their lack of physiological closeness with procreation. Thus, the subjugation and relegation of women to the status of objects of exchange, in the Lévi-Straussian formula, is seen as the basic, necessary step in the formation of social structure and is symbolically linked with the universal cultural process of overcoming nature. In this aboriginal hierarchy, according to Ortner, the linkage of women with nature and of men with culture is both structural and psychological, in that the female, in Simone de Beauvoir's words, "is more enslaved to the species than the male, her animality is more manifest [1953:239; quoted in Ortner, 1974:74]."

Like Rosaldo, Ortner does not assume that what has always been must necessarily continue in the future, despite the "(sadly) efficient feedback system[1974; p. 87]" that the structural and symbolic devaluation of women has set in motion from the beginnings of cultural existence. In view of the apparent enormity of the problem in its pan-cultural scope, Ortner's suggestions for efforts at change are singularly mild and culture-bound, applying quite specifically to contemporary capitalist society. She calls for "institutional" changes such as setting quotas on hiring, passing equal-pay-for-equal-work laws, combined with "efforts directed solely at changing cultural assumptions—through male and female consciousness-raising groups, for example, or through revision of educational materials and mass-media imagery [p. 87]."

Another feminist anthropologist who has advanced a wide-ranging, universal theory of the oppression of women is Gayle Rubin, whose paper "The Traffic in Women" (1975) takes its title from Lévi-Strauss's concept of the "exchange of women." Unlike Rosaldo or Ortner, Rubin identifies herself as a Marxist, but like them she advances an interpretation of sex oppression that is universalistic rather than historical–materialist. She argues (1975:198) that "our [modern capitalist society's] sex/gender system is still organized by the principles outlined by Lévi-Strauss, despite the entirely nonmodern character of his data base." Though she appropriately calls for a Marxian analysis of sex/gender systems and specifies that "a full-bodied analysis of women in a single society, or throughout history, must take *everything* into account: the evolution of commodity forms in women, systems of land tenure, political arrangements, subsistence technology, etc. [p. 209]," her own theoretical stance is quite the opposite. By accepting the Lévi-Straussian concept of kinship as equivalent to the "exchange of women," with all that implies about the devaluation of women or the treatment of women as objects of exchange, she likewise accepts the universality of sex oppression, making her later attempts to reintegrate "sexual systems" into other aspects of particular societies ring rather hollow. If, as she and Lévi-Strauss assume, all known societies have incorporated an oppressive sexual division of labor, then, she thinks, the proper mode of analysis is to "isolate sex and gender from 'mode of production,' and to counter a certain tendency [in Marxism] to explain sex oppression as a reflex of economic forces [p. 203]."

> If Lévi-Strauss is correct in seeing the exchange of women as a fundamental principle of kinship, the subordination of women can be seen as a product of the relationships by which sex and gender are organized and produced. The economic oppression of women is derivative and secondary [p. 177].

What does such an analysis mean for the politics of the Women's Movement? Again, we are offered an answer that assumes that the problems of women as women are essentially the same in all societies, that is, that the task before us is no less than the abolition of kinship and gender themselves. In Rubin's words, her analysis "suggests a conception of the women's movement as analogous to, rather than isomorphic with, the working-class movement, each addressing a different source of human discontent [p. 203]."

Each of these theorists has made important contributions to our understanding of the scope of the tasks confronting us. The major thrust of the contemporary Women's Movement—that issues of sexuality, emotional or "personal" life, reproduction, and socialization must be integrated with efforts at rebuilding society—is given perceptive emphasis and elaboration by Rosaldo, Chodorow, Ortner, and Rubin. But there is a crucial difference between expanding our understanding of public/private dichotomization, symbolic systems of sexual stereotyping, and the mechanisms of enculturation on the one hand, and achieving a historical analysis of how such systems arose and have developed, on the other. The effort to elevate these historically specific systems of sexual oppression to the status of human universals works to obscure the realities of historical–cultural difference and to reinforce the tendency in the Women's Movement to generalize on the basis of our own experience as women in advanced capitalism and apply it to all women. Rather than seeking to *isolate* sex and gender from an analysis of the mode of production, we need to *integrate* the two, and get down to the much more difficult task of concrete historical materialist studies that will help us see how differing relations of production, here and in other societies, embody differing sex and gender systems. In this way we will be able to formulate concrete strategies for change, recognizing that these may well be very different for different historical and cultural situations.

An example of such an historical analysis is the paper by Rayna Reiter (1975), "Men and Women in the South of France: Public and Private Domains." Reiter, a Marxist anthropologist writing of her own field experience, has taken the concept of public–private dichotomization *not* as a universal principle but as an historical phenomenon, a process that can be shown to accompany the social and economic changes involved in state and class formation out of pre-state, kinship-based societies. After documenting the ways in which the public/private split is experienced by women in a modern French village—ways that are quite different from the urban experience—Reiter (1975:279–280) outlines the historical development of public and private spheres in peasant France, showing how both separation and hierarchical valuation between the two realms were part of the penetration of class control:

> In the process of elite classes legitimizing service to their ends, it is the sphere that is extralocal, and male, to which prestige is attached. A distinction that was functionally based on the division of labor by sex and its geographical expression becomes transformed into more distinct public and private arenas. The state then uses the distinction to assert its own legitimacy and to devaluate the authority of kinship groups. . . . Radical restructuring of the peasant economy by modern French capitalism increased the distinction between public and private domains as well as the segregation of the sexes.

By focusing on the historical transformations in a particular sequence, Reiter has shown how the development of a public/private split is an integral part of a larger societal process. Kinship, far from constituting a universally oppressive, separate system of sexual manipulation based on symbolic or psychological imperatives, has different significance in different social formations. By implication, kinship has potentials for further transformations in the future, depending on historical circumstances. As I have argued elsewhere (1974), "the family" among many colonized peoples today can constitute an important force for liberation from oppression, a stronghold of women's and children's power and a crucial element in the cultural resistance to imperialism.

The assertion of the universality of sex oppression is based on anthropological and historical data for a large variety of different societies, and at first glance the evidence appears impressive. In the contemporary, or even the nineteenth-century world, almost every society reported on showed some indication of male domination, or at least of male pre-eminence in the realms of politics, religion, warfare, and trade—the public sphere. Furthermore, the all-too-common practice in anthropology and other Western social sciences is to treat existing colonized peoples as if they were virtually unchanged representatives of the past. This practice, part of a more general tendency to disregard the effects or even the existence of imperialism throughout the world, has allowed generalizations about the devalued status of women "in all cultures" to stand virtually unchallenged. In reality, with very rare exceptions, all the cultures studied by anthropologists have been subject, at the very least, to indirect pressures from the worldwide system of imperialism *for centuries*. If we look at the evidence it is unambiguous as to the kinds of effects European and North American colonialism and neocolonialism have had on male–female roles, family structures, and so forth (Caulfield, 1974; Leacock, 1975). Sex oppression has been one of the major "imports" from Western capitalism.

Unfortunately, few anthropologists, Marxist or otherwise, have looked in depth at this evidence or undertaken the difficult task of reconstructing a true picture of aboriginal sex roles, divisions of labor, or kinship systems. The more common practice has been to separate the "traditional" elements of existing societies from the "Western," or "modern" and to describe a mythical "traditional" society based on these remnants, with a liberal admixture of the male bias that feminist anthropologists are now beginning to document (on male bias in anthropology, see Brown, 1975; Faithorn, 1975; Rohrlich-Leavitt, Sykes, and Weatherford, 1975; Slocum, 1975). As Eleanor Leacock (1974:17) says in this connection:

> The lack of an historical perspective has had serious implications for the cross-cultural study of women, since involvement with a developing capitalist world economy has had profound effects on the relation of women to the production and distribution of basic group needs and to sources of power and decision-making. The practice of stacking contemporary peoples in "historical" layers—as hunter–gatherers, simple agriculturalists, and advanced agriculturalists with domestication—does, it is true, yield some insight into the nature of women's decline in status, since a people's involvement in the world system starts within each "layer" from a different basis. Furthermore, cultural traditions can be remarkably strong, and people can wage stiff battles for those they value. However, . . . socio-economic systems separated from the full economic and political constraints that influence them cannot be treated as directly representing earlier sex role definitions.

Eleanor Leacock's own studies of the effects of the fur trade on the Montagnais-Naskapi (1954, 1955) stand as a prime example of the necessary historical analysis. In these studies and in her Introduction to Engels' *Origin of the Family, Private Property, and the State* (1972), Leacock argues forcefully against the thesis of universal sex oppression, concluding that, in broad outlines at least, Engels' 1891 view was correct: The initial egalitarianism of human society included women; their status relative to men declined as they lost their economic autonomy with the emergence of class stratification and state organization. While recognizing the problems of imperial intrusions, androcentric and ethnocentric biases in the social sciences, and the tendency to lump together all nonstate societies as "primitive," Leacock thinks that by asking new questions of old data, as well as by collecting new kinds of data—as is being done by some feminist anthropologists today, it is possible to outline a category of truly egalitarian societies. In such societies the relations of production and distribution have been such that generalizations about "public" and "private" spheres do not apply, male dominance and exploitation are not present, and even the opposition between "nature" and "culture" has not existed in the value systems of the people.

Rather than attempting to replicate Leacock's examples here (1954, 1955, 1972, 1974, 1975, 1977a, 1977b; Leacock and Nash, 1977), I would like to discuss one nonclass social formation described by the French Marxist Maurice Godelier (1975). In a paper primarily devoted to making an entirely different and (in my opinion) very problematic point, Godelier has done a reconstruction of older data on an Australian hunting–gathering group. These data indicate that the relations of production and the kinship system were one and the same, and raise important questions regarding the "exchange of women," the public/private dichotomy, and the concept of equivalence between female and nature, male and culture. Godelier, though he does not consider these questions himself, has provided a picture, so far as it can be reconstructed, of the mode of production of this group, pointing to a few of the apparent ways in which colonization has affected the operations of a system that can be assumed to have had a very long history indeed.

This society has organized all productive, distributive, kinship, and cosmological relations by the same system. Technical relations of production exist within small bands of related people, in which total cooperation and reciprocity are the guiding principles. Men, women, and children perform different tasks in the productive process, but all are dependent on the total group for survival, and their interdependence is represented and guaranteed in their kinship system by an overlapping set of sections that crosscuts individual bands. Each individual, thus, is a member of a group that travels together; simultaneously, he or she is also a member of a section, with co-members in other bands. Marriage rules mandate that each band contain members of at least three but usually all four sections; this composition guarantees access for the band to the territories and water holes (means of production) of each section. Territory, or "nature," however, does not belong in the property sense to a section, or even to the tribe as a whole; on the contrary, all creatures of nature, including people, belong *in the affiliative sense* to one of the four sections. As Godelier says, "the same principles and the same divisions order nature and society, dividing human beings and all natural creatures into the same categories; nature appears as an enlarged image of society, as its continuation [1975:18]." Just as all people have obligations to share with and care for other people, so have they in their relations with the beings of the natural and supernatural worlds, all belonging to one or another section. The principles of cooperation and reciprocity crosscut group membership, and they also crosscut the nature/culture relationship, which in this value system is one of continuity rather than the opposition that Ortner and Lévi-Strauss assume.

As Godelier notes, the more marginal the land in which such groups live (as with the intrusion of colonialism), the more intricate and complex become their kinship systems, responding to the greater need for flexibility in access to scarce resources. It seems impossible to interpret such a system as "exchange of women," any more than one might interpret it as "exchange of men"; the central principle throughout is the guarantee of interdependence, autonomous cooperation, and reciprocity with as wide a network of kin (human and nonhuman) as possible. Furthermore, there is no suggestion in this arrangement that people see their groups or themselves in any kind of oppositional relation with "nature" in the abstract, or with any specific aspect of nature. If any aspect of nature, such as a kangaroo or rain, must be propitiated, then a member of its section is required to communicate with it, since person and natural phenomenon are perceived to have common bonds of mutual obligation and respect.

As June Nash and Eleanor Leacock have pointed out, the idea that nature must be conquered or "mastered" (with what implications for class and sex?) for the benefit of "society" is a comparatively recent cultural invention.

> The contemporary concept of mastering nature through science in the interest of social benefit is a product of the 17th century. It received its full expression in the hands of Bacon in the period when commercial and technological expansion, linked with colonial exploitation, was laying the foundations for the industrial revolution [1977:621].

This concept, though far from universal, is still very much in use to justify not only the devalued status of women but perhaps more importantly the conquest and "modernization" of so-called "backward" or "underdeveloped" regions of the world, in the ideology of imperialism.

Another aspect of the Australian kinship system described by Godelier that has a bearing on the present discussion is the attribution of what are perceived as the important qualities of human (and natural) character to the members of the different kinship sections. For example, such characteristics as "active," "passive," "fierce," and "sweet" are assumed to inhere to individuals, not according to sex or gender but according to their section. Interestingly enough, the only sex-associated natural feature that Godelier lists as assigned to a section, sperm, belongs to a section designated as "passive" (1975:23).

Anthropologists call such kinship systems "multifunctional"; in Marxist terminology, the relations of production are coterminous with virtually all other relations both in society and in the world of the natural and supernatural. There is no public/private split in this kind of society; each individual is thoroughly "embedded," to use Chodorow's term, in a social world in which he or she has multiple connections, intimacies, rights, and obligations. Domestic or "family" production in such a society *is* public production, and the care and nurturance of children is likewise a right and a responsibility of many adults, male and female (see Leacock, 1977b).

Production for Use Value

It is quite understandable that observers from a culture such as our own would have difficulty understanding a social formation based on principles of reciprocity, interdependence, and autonomy of the individual, socialized as we are to a totally different set of values and practices. Nonetheless, it is worth the effort to understand how these systems have worked, especially if we are committed to building a better society for ourselves. The key concept, in my opinion, is that outlined by Marx in the first volume of *Capital:* the concept of production for use value. As Marshall Sahlins (1972:82) has noted, "the classic distinction between 'production for use' (that is, for the producers) and 'production for exchange' was, from the beginning of an economic anthropology . . . interred in the graveyard of prehistoric concepts." It is high time, as Sahlins implies, it was exhumed. If we are to develop an analysis of sexism in society that deals with the real differences between advanced (or, as I prefer to call it, terminal) capitalism and the varieties of colonized societies, we must take into account the differential retention or disappearance of collective, communal use–value practices and beliefs.

What, then, is meant by production for use value? In the first place, as Leacock has emphasized in her discussion of gathering and hunting societies (1975:608), decision making was dispersed rather than relegated to "leaders" or "managers":

> people made decisions about activities for which they were responsible. Group decisions were arrived at through feeling for consensus. The essential and direct interdependence of the group as a whole both necessitated this autonomy and made it possible as a viable system—*total interdependence was inseparable from real autonomy.* . . . The emphasis was on generosity, on cooperation, on patience and good humor, but also on never forcing one's will on others. This ethic was enforced through ridicule and teasing, often bawdy, behind which lay the threat of great anger at injustice, and the deep fear of starvation.

In Marx' terminology, there was a technical division of labor, but not a social division between thinkers and doers. The complementarity of the sexual division of labor here is not that between master and slave, but between autonomous decision makers.

The different kinds and extents of autonomy and cooperation in different kinds of societies have been discussed by Louise Lamphere (1974). As she makes clear, "the authority structure of the domestic group itself is affected by economic and power relations within the larger society [p. 104]," so that when the domestic and the public spheres are sharply differentiated, as in class societies, women's domestic (let alone their political) autonomy is strictly delimited, and in many cases they must develop strategies of "working through men" rather than focusing on cooperation with women and men, as in the gathering–hunting groups in Lamphere's sample (p. 105).

In capitalist society the division between workers and decision makers has reached immense proportions. The routinization and mindlessness of work when we have no part in the decisions about what is to be produced or how it is to be used and by whom dehumanizes both the activity and the products.

Not only does production for use value involve a unity between thinking and doing, thus making the process of labor a creative, learning experience, but also the appreciation or consumption of products involves the whole person, including the intellect and emotions. Barbara Stuckey and Nancy Welles, writing on the hegemony of commodity fetishism, put it this way:

> Value in use, as opposed to value in exchange, cannot be measured; it can only be experienced. . . . The realization of use value . . . is the result of momentary, subjective evaluation. Use value is not reducible to the bourgeois concept of utility and not at all reducible to a measurement of functionality. . . . The realization of use value means that our intellect and our emotions are engaged simultaneously [1976:306].

By emphasizing the distinction between use value and exchange value, I do not mean to imply that products are never exchanged in societies based on the former principle. On the contrary, "exchange" was a crucial element in all such societies, but not on the basis of measurement or the attempt to achieve an exact equivalence. The principle governing exchange, "generalized reciprocity," is that producers give away their products, thus making a material and spiritual bond between themselves and the group, affirming solidarity, survival, and their own embeddedness. In this process it is not only acceptable but necessary that exact equivalence not be reached, since that would signal a desire to end the relationship, to separate oneself from the group (Sahlins, 1972:193–194). Production for exchange value, in contrast, leads to a sense of nonbelonging, since by attempting to achieve an equivalence (or the appearance of one, as in the sale of one's labor power for a wage), the individual tries to attain a separation. Nothing further is to be expected from the other partner in the exchange once the equivalence is agreed upon; the pleasure, love, or even survival of the other partner is not expected to be a consideration, and any renewal of the relationship is assumed to be on the basis of narrow self-interest. This is called "freedom" in bourgeois ideology.

Despite the near-total suppression of relations based on use value in capitalism, there are still some places where we can see its operation, in grotesquely distorted form. Domestic production or "housework" is a form of use value production, and it is so denigrated and devalued that most women whose lives are devoted to it will tell you "Oh, I don't work; I'm just a housewife." Nonetheless, we can see a glimmer of what could be involved in the testimony of one of the women interviewed by Studs Terkel (1975:401):

> I'll sit here and I'll cook a pie and I'll get to see everybody eat it. This is my offering. I think it's the greatest satisfaction in the world to know you've pleased somebody. . . . I'm doing it for them and they're doing it for me. . . .

The unity of doing, thinking, and feeling, all expressed in the act of working and giving in a solidary, intimate social group, is the essence of use value production.

But in advanced capitalism such activity is not only devalued but in a real sense irrelevant. The housewife may have control over her labor and its products: She can autonomously choose *not* to make a pie, or she can exercise creativity and love in her choice of ingredients, but she cannot assure her own survival or that of her isolated nuclear family by her efforts. It is the "real" world of wage labor, over which neither she nor her husband has control, but in which he works for the family's survival, that dominates and constricts all other activities. Thus housework, though it embodies some of the important characteristics of use value production and represents a heritage from a more humane past, is "turned on its head" in the modern context. Compare the experience of housework quoted previously with the following description recorded by Meredith Tax:

> When I am by myself [in the home], I am nothing. I only know that I exist because I am needed by someone who is real, my husband, and by my children. My husband goes into the real world. . . . I stay in the imaginary world in this house, doing jobs that I largely invent, and that no one cares about but myself [1970:7].

Both descriptions are real, and I think widely representative of how housewives feel. From personal experience I know that the creative, satisfying fulfillment and the degraded, isolated "unreal" feelings can be very powerfully present at one and the same time: This is the contradiction, in everyday experience, of use–value production in capitalist society.

Furthermore, the designation of private, use–value production as "women's work" *and* as irrelevant, silly, or at best secondary to the work of the rational, achieving male in wage labor serves to buttress the ideological system of those who profit from it. The inability of capital to meet *socially determined* needs is obscured by the devaluation of production to fill these needs, by relegating it to the realm of female "nonwork."

Conclusion

Many other societies retain important elements of collective or communal relations and use-value production, often in forms that are much more central to survival, more widely shared than within the isolated nuclear family. Collective agricultural work, extended family reciprocal sharing, mutual aid of many sorts are all examples, some apparently trivial, others of immediate importance to the material lives and value systems of colonized peoples. In most such collective forms women are central figures, largely because of the public/private split that not only characterizes class societies in general but that is also one of the first and most essential impositions accompanying colonial rule. Wage labor, cash cropping, foreign trade, and colonial bureaucracy all constitute "public" arenas, overwhelmingly staffed by men and under the control of Europeans, even where subsistence activities continue in the "traditional" manner. At the same time, older forms that retain at least some features of use-value production are severely distorted, transformed, and disrupted, though not always in the same ways that housework has been transformed.

In the process of building socialist, egalitarian relations of production and politics, such residual forms can be of central importance. People who have had some experience of collective labor, reciprocal sharing, nonbureaucratic decision making, or creative, loving work for the sake of group survival rather than individual profit are much more capable of constructing new collective forms in liberated colonial areas. While male revolutionaries in Third World countries have frequently stressed the importance of building on the basis of older collective forms,[2] there has been little if any recognition of the special skills that women have in these areas as a result of their differential experience of colonial exploitation. The penetration of capitalist relations into the productive systems of colonized peoples has meant, in many parts of the world, that women have been the primary carriers of cultural forms that operate on the basis of collective values. If we keep this fact in mind, then the words of Samir Amin, an Egyptian Marxist, take on a special meaning for the Women's Movement:

> For the developed world as a whole, the main issue is this: how can we broaden the sphere of use value (reduce the fields of commodity relations) without making the

[2] For example, Julius Nyerere (1968:361–362) suggests: "It may be that the way to start under these circumstances [in cash cropping areas] is to operate first on the basis of working groups, but with the individual plots retained—that is, on the basis of mutual help. This would be simply a revival, and perhaps an extension, of the traditional system of joint activity. . . ."

productive forces regress? To the degree that "traditional" use values have already disappeared, buried under the development of commodity relations, we have to invent a culture which is likely to be almost completely new.

For the underdeveloped world as a whole, the main issue is different: how can we develop the productive forces without letting the commodity relations gain ground? In this connection, since the traditional use values still exist here, it will be possible to build a bridge between the past and the future [n.d.:21].

A women's movement dedicated to building a world society that no longer exploits women, children, men, or the rest of the natural world must recognize the historic role that women, in particular women from colonized countries, must play in the process. The myth of universal sex oppression, which acts to isolate women's devaluation from the process of change in modes of production, tends to negate this historic role and to restrict the goals of the movement to a struggle for "equality" of women under capitalist relations.

References

Aaby, Peter
  1977 Engels and Women. Critique of Anthropology, Vol. 3, Nos. 9 and 10.
Amin, Samir
  n.d. Capitalism, Socialism, and Cultural Spheres. Dakar: IDEP.
Ardener, Shirley, ed.
  1975 Perceiving Women. New York: John Wiley.
Brown, Judith K.
  1975 Iroquois Women: An Ethnohistoric Note. In Towards an Anthropology of Women. Rayna Reiter, ed. Pp. 235-251. New York: Monthly Review Press.
Caulfield, Mina D.
  1974 Imperialism, the Family, and Cultures of Resistance. Socialist Revolution, No. 20.
Chodorow, Nancy
  1974 Family Structure and Feminine Personality. In Women, Culture, and Society. Michelle Z. Rosaldo and Louise Lamphere, eds. Pp. 43-66. Stanford, California: Stanford University Press.
de Beauvoir, Simone
  1953 The Second Sex. New York: Knopf.
Edholm, Felicity, Olivia Harris, and Kate Young
  1977 Conceptualizing Women. Critique of Anthropology, Vol. 3, Nos. 9 and 10.
Faithorn, Elizabeth
  1975 The Concept of Pollution Among the Káfe of the Papua New Guinea Highlands. In Toward an Anthropology of Women. Rayna Reiter, ed. Pp. 127-140. New York: Monthly Review Press.
Friedl, Ernestine
  1975 Women and Men: An Anthropologist's View. New York: Holt, Rinehart and Winston.
Godelier, Maurice
  1975 Modes of Production, Kinship, and Demographic Structures. In Marxist Analyses and Social Anthropology. Maurice Bloch, ed. Pp. 3-27. New York: John Wiley.
Lamphere, Louise
  1974 Strategies, Cooperation and Conflict Among Women in Domestic Groups. In Woman, Culture, and Society. Michelle Z. Rosaldo and Louise Lamphere, eds. Pp. 97-112. Stanford, California: Stanford University Press.

Leacock, Eleanor
  1954 The Montagnais "Hunting Territory" and the Fur Trade. American Anthropologist, Memoir 78.
  1955 Matrilocality in a Simple Hunting Economy. Journal of Anthropology, Vo. 11, No. 1.
  1972 Introduction. The Origins of the Family, Private Property, and the State, by F. Engels. New York: International Publishers.
  1974 Women, Social Evolution, and Errors, Crude and Subtle. Paper given at the American Anthropological Association meetings, Mexico City.
  1975 Class, Commodity, and the Status of Women. In Women Cross-Culturally: Change and Challenge. Ruby Rohrlich-Leavitt, ed. Pp. 601–616. The Hague: Mouton Press.
  1977a Women in Egalitarian Societies. In Becoming Visible: Women in European History. Renate Bridenthal, ed. Pp. 11–35. New York: Houghton Mifflin.
  1977b The Changing Family and Lévi-Strauss. Social Research, Vol. 44, No. 2.
Leacock, Eleanor, and June Nash
  1977 Ideologies of Sex: Archetypes and Stereotypes. Annals of The New York Academy of Science 285:618–645.
Lévi-Strauss, Claude
  1969 The Elementary Structures of Kinship. J. H. Bell and J. R. von Sturmer, trans. R. Needham, ed. Boston: Beacon Press.
Marx, Karl
  1970 Capital, Vol. I. London: Lawrence and Wishart (First ed. 1867.)
Mernissi, Fatima
  1975 Beyond the Veil: Male–Female Dynamics in a Modern Muslim Society. New York: John Wiley.
Molyneux, Maxine
  1977 Androcentrism in Marxist Anthropology. Critique of Anthropology, Vol. 3, Nos. 9 and 10.
Nelson, Cynthia, and Virginia Olesen
  1977 Veil and Illusion: A Critique of the Concept of Equality in Western Thought. Catalyst, Nos. 10–11.
Nyerere, Julius
  1968 Freedom and Socialism. London: Oxford University Press.
O'Laughlin, Bridget
  1977 Production and Reproduction: Meillassoux's Femmes, Greniers et Capitaux. Critique of Anthropology, Vol. 3, No. 8.
Ortner, Sherry
  1974 Is Female to Male as Nature Is to Culture? In Woman, Culture, and Society. Michelle Z. Rosaldo and Louise Lamphere, eds. Pp. 67–87. Stanford, California: Stanford University Press.
Reiter, Rayna R.
  1975 Men and Women in the South of France: Public and Private Domains. In Toward an Anthropology of Women. Rayna R. Reiter, ed. Pp. 252–282. New York: Monthly Review Press.
Rohrlich-Leavitt, Ruby, ed.
  1975 Women Cross-Culturally: Change and Challenge. The Hague: Mouton Press.
Rohrlich-Leavitt, Ruby, Barbara Sykes, and Elizabeth Weatherford
  1975 Aboriginal Woman: Male and Female Anthropological Perspectives. In Toward an Anthropology of Women. Rayna R. Reiter, ed. Pp. 110–126. New York: Monthly Review Press.
Rosaldo, Michelle Z.
  1974 Woman, Culture, and Society: A Theoretical Overview. In Woman, Culture, and Society. Michelle Z. Rosaldo and Louise Lamphere, eds. Pp. 17–42. Stanford, California: Stanford University Press.

Rosaldo, Michelle Z., and Louise Lamphere, eds.
1974 Women, Culture, and Society. Stanford, California: Stanford University Press.
Rubin, Gayle
1975 The Traffic in Women: Notes on the "Political Economy" of Sex. In Toward an Anthropology of Women. Rayna R. Reiter, ed. Pp. 157–210. New York: Monthly Review Press.
Sahlins, Marshall
1972 Stone Age Economics. Chicago: Aldine.
Slocum, Sally
1975 Woman the Gatherer: Male Bias in Anthropology. In Toward an Anthropology of Women. Rayna R. Reiter, ed. Pp. 36–50. New York: Monthly Review Press.
Stuckey, Barbara, and Nancy Welles
1976 From Tribe to Multinational Corporation. Manuscript.
Tax, Meredith
1970 Woman and Her Mind. Cambridge, Massachusetts: New England Free Press.
Terkel, Studs
1975 Working. New York: Avon.
Terray, Emmanuel
1969 Marxism and "Primitive" Societies. New York: Monthly Review Press.
Willhelm, Sidney
1974 Equality—America's Racist Ideology. In The Death of White Sociology. Joyce Ladner, ed. Pp. 136–157. New York: Vintage.

11

PETER WORSLEY

Social Class and Development

Though it is heuristically valuable, at a high level of generalization, to take the level of industrialization as marking off "developed" societies from agrarian ones, we need to avoid both the Procrustean logic of those who treat the vast diversity of "preindustrial" cultures as if they constituted a homogeneous category, "traditional" society, and the unilineal naiveté of "convergence" theorists who postulate a unitary "logic of industrialism" (Kerr et al., 1962; Rostow, 1960).

The Varieties of Development

There is no unequivocal, unitary, and universal set of accompaniments to industrialization. Rather, industrialization is a plural phenomenon. Though techniques may be identical, the organization of work, the volume of output aimed at and achieved, the *kinds* of things produced, the uses and distribution of the product, the very nature of "the economy" itself are not given or determined either by technology or even by a system of pure economic logic, but derive from strategies, philosophies, ideologies, and cultural values. Too often, it is true, the genesis and use of values are simply taken as givens also. Structuralists tend to accept the claim of those who exercise decisive power in society that their hegemonic *sub*culture is, in fact, *the* culture of the society as a whole. This imposition is not achieved only by the manipulation of myth; it is usually combined with the deployment or threat of force, if only in the "last

221

SOCIAL INEQUALITY
Comparative and Developmental Approaches

instance." To this dominant subculture other subcultures and countercultures are apposed and opposed. The economy, then, is always a political economy, never exists "in itself," and is always oriented to dominant cultural ends insofar as these are not countervailed by other interest groups.

Economic development has never been simply random, idiosyncratic, or unilineal, but at any one time only a limited range of strategies and models is available. In the contemporary world, there are two major variants (each with subvariants). One is the strategy of capitalist development, oriented to the maintenance of a social order based on private property and its intergenerational transfer through inheritance (Gouldner, 1971:320–326) and, culturally, in ideologies of "possessive individualism" (Macpherson, 1962) and competition, which legitimate an inegalitarian division of power and wealth. The second variant, that of communist societies, is oriented to construction by the state of an egalitarian and collectivistic social order. This type of industrialization now embraces one-third of the world.

The Western world is so saturated with a laissez-faire liberal market ideology that is is necessary to remind ourselves not only that this alternative mode of development exists but also that the liberal ideology no longer makes much sense even in advanced Western economies, first because the state is crucial there too, and, more generally, because both the state and social classes—the critical social components—are not spontaneous "emergences" but *products*. Lest this be thought simply a strident ideological assertion, let me exemplify with a noncapitalist example: John Murra's brilliant and scholarly study of the interdependence between different ecological levels of precapitalist Andean economies (Murra, 1975) nevertheless concentrates on reciprocal exchange as if this were entirely a market phenomenon, taking for granted the systematic violence (military conquest) that was used to incorporate earlier pre-Inca exchange systems into the highly centralized system of the Inca empire, and the continuing use of force to maintain it and to extract and distribute the surpluses (Hemming, 1970; Wachtel, 1973).

As for capitalism, laissez-faire ideology, from Adam Smith onward, has represented its growth in terms of the free and systematically rational interplay on the market between the "holders" of the factors of land, capital, and labor—the ultimate decision-making unit being the individual actor (and not, as in Marx's model, for example, a collective entity, social class).

Yet, as Thompson (1968) has shown in his classic study, the new working class in the period of Britain's Industrial Revolution was *made* as a conative act of *will*. As they say in Mexico, *"Accidentes no nacen; se hacen."* The British working class was brought into being, first, negatively, by being deprived of its previous means of livelihood as tenant farmers or small holders, and, positively, transformed into a new class of urban wage laborers, constantly threatened by the specter of falling into the ranks of the "industrial reserve army" of labor, now commonly called "marginal" (Nun, 1969; Quijano, 1970).

Yet we cannot, as Nun and Quijano do, explain the existence of an involuted tertiary sector in today's Third World cities in terms of their nations' "dependency" on the First World, since exactly the same phenomena were characteristic of nineteeth-century Britain, which was scarcely a "periphery" but rather the world's center (Mayhew, 1949; Stedman Jones, 1971).

The explanation, rather, lies in the incapacity of capitalism—peripheral or central—in its early phases of development to absorb the masses of immigrants created by the "pull" of the living standards of the new cities, and the "push" of losing their land or being displaced by labor-saving machines. In early urban capitalism, those who do not secure stable jobs survive in a number of ways (outlined on pp. 241–242), if they *do* survive. Later capitalism often proves every bit as unable to keep its labor force regularly employed, but it has been able to provide an ever-improving welfare state system of coping with periodic disaster and endemic poverty for the minority, while providing employment for the majority. In the Third World, the welfare state scarcely exists for the mass of the population.

Stability of employment therefore deserves infinitely more attention than it normally receives from social scientists who base their analyses simply on the amount of income received or the differential distribution of wealth. Stability, too, was a major asset for those members of the middle classes who kept their jobs during the Depression of the 1930s and were therefore able to enjoy the enhanced purchasing power caused by low world prices for primary products (Dobb, 1946).

The phrase "developing" societies carries with it not merely the obvious implication that they *are* developing but also that development is akin to a natural process. It needs to be made explicit that development may or may not occur in most Third World countries. In certain important instances it is occurring: In the capitalist world, in Brazil, Argentina, Mexico, South Africa, Taiwan, South Korea, Hong Kong, and Singapore; in the communist world, all East European countries (save, so far, Albania) have already industrialized; China and North Korea will make the shift within a generation (U.S. Congress, 1975). Whether development occurs or not is determined much more by struggles at the level of societal and inter- and supra-national levels of power structures than by the absence or presence of diffuse "traditionalistic" values (Frank, 1967). None of this development is natural or immanent, but is shaped by sociocultural legacies from the past, contemporary interests, and by projects for the future; that is, it is the outcome of social action.

Both the persisting stagnation of the great majority and the industrialization of a significant minority of Third World countries (for whom the label therefore becomes increasingly inappropriate) have to be analyzed within the framework of a world system of political economy that, though still predominantly capitalist (Wallerstein, 1974), also contains a sector that includes one-third of the world's population where capitalism has been rejected both as a growth strategy and as a wider political culture.

In view of recent convergence theory (Goldthorpe, 1964) and the real-life rapprochement between the U.S.S.R. and the United States, it is necessary to emphasize the the *principal contradiction* in the world—to use Mao's term—is still between these two social systems, each dominated by a superpower, with fateful consequences for lesser countries, and with each exerting pressure on the rest of the world—on friends as well as enemies—to conform to its policies, including the strategies for growth it pioneered and that it champions. Such patterns are, in fact, usually inimitable, since "capitalism" and "communism," as sets of general propositions, values, and projects, always have to be translated, interpreted, adapted, and rendered concrete by being applied to a wide variety of quite specific historical and cultural circumstances. Hence, just as developing capitalist countries cannot follow nineteenth-century British or American patterns of growth, neither can small monocultural agrarian countries adopt Soviet strategies. Communism today is consequently a plural phenomenon, with its two major variants locked at each other's throats, while in western Europe a third, reformist variant has emerged.

The ends and directions of development, in sum, tend to diverge further every day along national lines, rather than to converge, despite obvious structural and ideological transnational alignments and professed ideological similarities, which often are at very general levels of abstraction, and therefore more theological than actual. Only in very exceptional circumstances, when faced with an even greater threat, do China and Russia, Nuer-like, tacitly cooperate to assist Vietnam.

Given such diverse processes of social change, the idea that the working class (or any other class) will "in the long run" develop a homogeneous conception of itself and its interests through the dynamics of the class struggle seems to require a Keynesian notion of the "long run." The formation of the working class in the "classical" case of Britain suggests that a class, like any other social entity, is always "becoming," and is highly differentiated internally anyhow. For both British and American sociology, the problem was poverty. In the United States the absorption of immigrants was an additional major problem, not to be experienced on a similar scale in western Europe until after World War II. The United States was not able to solve either the problem of poverty or the problem of cultural absorption of the new White working class until after the Second World War. Then two further problems suggested themselves: Had the working class disappeared—become "bourgeoisified" (Goldthorpe et al., 1969–1971; Marcuse, 1964)—or were poverty and social inequality as endemic as ever, but now transferred to the Black and Hispanic populations?

The allocation of workers, whether by market forces or more forcibly, to a collective occupational structural position (*class situation*, in Weber's term, though only *occupational situation*, really) does not determine how occupants of a structural position respond to and interpret that position or what constructions others seek to put upon it (e.g., as to the rightness of victory going to the strong, the "competent," or the owners of property). As Parkin (1971) has shown, workers may internalize dominant value systems (the "hegemonic" possibility); they may become "oppositional" (radicalized, socialist, and so forth); or, most commonly, they may adapt in a wide range of "accommodational" ways, finding their satisfactions and compensations, rewarding self-compensations and hope, in "other-worldly" forms (religion) or in "this-worldly" forms: in gambling, in interpersonal, familial, and small-group satisfactions; in the production and consumption of art and sport; in sex; and in innumerable other ways.

Which of these possibilities workers do select depends upon a number of conditions: the rate of material improvement in their lives, or otherwise; whether this improvement accures to a minority in the society or is more widespread; the reference groups they compare themselves to, past and present; their future orientations, aspirations, and expectations; their imagination of "possibility" (alternative projects, cognitive maps, utopias, real-world models, and so forth); and, not least, their existential capacity to create countercultures and organizations; and the modalities of political and more generalized social control, external and internalized, that limit their autonomy and prescribe their vertical integration and incorporation or that divide them internally.

"Classical" Industrial Societies

Since modern industrial society ("machinofacture") first began over a century ago, it is worth examining the "classical" experience of some of those countries that did succeed in making the take-off, the variety of ways they did it, and the differences between their situations and those facing later comers, both in Europe and elsewhere.

In the first major capitalist country, Britain, the new working class rapidly generated its own institutions and ideologies. They ranged from millenarist religions through new fundamentalist Protestant sects, to secular Jacobinism and early socialist forms of thought and action. The *autonomy* of working-class ideology is well brought out in Susan Budd's study of nineteenth-century working-class atheism (Budd, 1967), which was only minimally affected by the crises that led intellectuals and the educated middle class to religious despair: Darwinism and the "higher criticism" of the Bible. Until the end of the century, working-class atheists remained firmly wedded to their original theoretical inspiration, the works of Tom Paine.

So wide-ranging and challenging was the array of autonomous and oppositional working-class institutions that resort to force on the part of the ruling class was, as John Foster (1974) has shown, not an "ultimate" but a routine practice. The direct threat represented by thousands of cotton operatives drilling with muskets on the moors around the milltowns of Lancashire was countered by quartering more troops in the northwest than Wellington had used against Napoleon in Spain. Repression was routinely used, too, against trade unionism (the Combination Acts); against terrorism and other forms of economic and political violence: in the countryside (long transformed by capitalist modernization) against Captain Swing (Hobsbawm and Rudé, 1969); and in the cities, against the "plug riots" and outbreaks of Luddism—in in a word, Peterloo.

But political opposition and counter-reaction at the societal and group level of organizations and movements were underpinned by the confrontation between two whole *political cultures* at the "social" level. For the working class the institutional settings for the rites (practices) and beliefs (to use Durkheimian language) of the "congregations" were the pubs, the secular Sunday schools, and the Nonconformist chapels. In a concerted campaign of total relegitimation and reconquest, the ruling classes replaced radical publicans with loyalist and royalist licensees (most pubs today still have monarchist names like the "King George"); mounted a massive campaign to counter Nonconformism with the official ethic of the established church (thus giving rise to the later description of the Church of England as "the Conservative Party at prayer"); and brought into being a system of rudimentary primary education for the children of the masses. Its content was highly functional in economic, political, and ethical terms: little more than the "three R's" and a massive and brutal indoctrination into an ideology of deference, hierarchy, and order that prescribed self-disciplined commitment not only to a Protestant ethic at work but the *acceptance* of one's lot, the internalization of both its rightness and its necessity, the whole being sanctioned by the "sacred canopy" of religion (Berger, 1967).

By the 1840s, the potentially revolutionary situation had been defused, the "physical force" wing of Chartism defeated, and popular energy diverted into the channels of parliamentary-reformist Chartism. Thereafter, in the long epoch "before the socialists" (Harrison, 1965), the working class was to present little serious threat to the established order, nor did the subsequent unionism of the craft and skilled workers. For the best part of a century, then, until the rise of the new mass unionism of the late 1890s, labor was well-contained on the economic front. Politically, the "labor aristocracy" was the first "fraction" to be incorporated into the electoral system, not via the establishment of a party representing the sectional interest of labor, but within the Liberal and Conservative parties (the former inventing the caucus system of controlling its membership, the latter creating "Tory democracy"). These, the first *mass* parties, were underpinned by networks of "social" clubs. And when the (Independent) Labour party did emerge, it did so out of a Liberal matrix. Cultural institutions of this "social" kind are always intrinsic and essential components of a "hegemonic" culture. Without them, force alone stands between the ruling class and chaos. Of course, the latter will also work.

As Marshall has shown, the earlier civic and political incorporation—ideologically expressed as "equality"—was finally complemented in Britain by installments of economic redistribution: the provision of a safety net of economic assistance to individuals to prevent absolute impoverishment (Marshall, 1950).

A new reading is beginning to emerge, then, of the still-mystifying "Whig history" of the first great capitalist society, which takes account of coercion, of the role of the state as partner in a conscious counterattack against the rise of autonomous working-class institutions, and of the crucial importance of political culture, including both hegemonic and "subaltern" cultures and countercultures—in Etzioni's terms, the use of coercive and normative as well as remunerative sanctions (Etzioni, 1964).

In the history of one crucial "late-comer," Germany, the counterpart of British overemphasis on gradualist consent and legitimation has been the overemphasis upon the internal and external use of violence and of the state as an incorporative agency generally. It was Bismarck himself who said that you could do anything with bayonets except sit on them, and who acted on this belief by initiating the welfare state long before Lloyd George. (The incorporative Japanese factory was to perform this function in the other great late-comer.)

In Britain and Germany the working class was effectively incorporated by 1914, with whatever resistance, and the entire edifice cemented together by a virulent nationalism that was to result in the proletariats of each country marching off to fight each other instead of practicing the internationalist solidarity prescribed in Marxist theory. Their paths of development, however, were distinctive, according to different historical processes and cultural legacies. Naturally, the working class and the institutions of labor were not immune to these influences, either. In Britain, the three wings of the labor movement—trade unions, coops, and political party—maintained a wary independence of each other. The incorporation of the working class was much more effective at the parliamentary level (Miliband, 1961) than it ever was on the economic front (in contrast to the United States, say). Symbolically, no unitary ideology emerged in Britain paralleling the formal adhesion to Marxism on the part of the German Social Democratic party.

The latter, the first truly mass working-class party, also exhibited a concomitant high degree of internal *Gleichschaltung*. It was, in Nettl's terms, a *state within a state*, with an elaborate subculture, internally articulated and opposed at every point to the institutions of the dominant class (Nettl, 1966). The clue to the failure of this giant machine, therefore, lies not so much in its incorporation within state and civil society as in the *internal* bureaucratization of the very agency that was perceived as the major means of bringing into being an alternative social order. The bourgeoisification of the German Social Democratic party (SPD), its "hollowness," was noted by a range of perspicacious observers, from Rosa Luxemburg and Lenin in the Marxist camp to Weber and Michels, who saw it as part of a more general process of rationalization. Michels viewed it with optimism as a phase of periodic countermovement; in Weber's bleakly pessimistic model, it was an extension of Marx's analysis of the rationalization of production to include the rationalization and disenchantment of *everything*, including the German SPD—and music. It also foreshadowed an even more ominous future were such a mode of organization to become the pattern of an entire society—state socialism. To counter the trend toward bureaucratization, charisma needed to be institutionalized. Weber succeeded in getting such a device built into the Constitution of the Weimar Republic, and it ultimately contributed to Hitler's election as Chancellor (Mayer, 1956:102,152).

At a more general level, the other main late-comers, Japan and Italy, faced with the task of forced modernization of agrarian societies and confronted with a world largely parceled out among the first-comers (France, Holland, and, above all, Britain), were ultimately to resort to force, as junior partners of Germany, in an attempt to break this monopoly.

Before this mature phase of modern capitalism, world control had not been so effective, and one or two colonial countries had even succeeded in throwing off the European yoke: the United States, "first new nation" (Lipset, 1964), and Haiti (Williams, 1944; James, 1963). In the United States, mature capitalism opened the way to the development of the world's greatest power without any major reliance upon "primary accumulation" abroad. In Haiti, nothing of the sort occurred.

Most of the world, ever since, has been much more like Haiti than the United States. Though the United States, like communist Russia and China later, had the natural resources of nearly a whole continent to exploit, the *technical* possibility became realizable only after a "second revolution"—in the American case, the victory of Northern industrial capital in the Civil War (Moore, 1967).

Internally, Haiti stagnated because no such transformation occurred once slavery had been abolished. Externally, the new world economy determined a fate for most newly independent countries that was little different in formally independent countries from that in formal colonies. It was no technical problem of "communication" that brought about this dependence—inadequate diffusion of values, institutions, technology, capital, or "know-how" from center to periphery, for the center distributed all these factors very effectively when it wished to develop mines or plantations—but it occurred in a way consonant only with the interests of those who owned the "commanding heights." And the commanding heights were outside the frontiers of the peripheric country, in what Mills (1958) sarcastically called the "overdeveloped"world.

Colonialism and Neo-Colonialism: The Creation of Underdevelopment

For the vast majority of former colonial countries, the replacement of the colonial authorities by local elites did not necessarily mean much change in their lives, however much they might now be juridically "citizens," equal to those who ruled and exploited them. The replacement of the Peninsular ruling class by a *criollo* one in the New World was cynically summed up in a popular saying about Ecuadorian independence (Cueva, 1977): *"Ultimo día del despotismo, y primero de lo mismo"* ("The last day of despotism, and the first of the same"). Mills' insistence that the nation-state was the basic unit of analysis retains a great deal of truth, however, despite the integration on a world scale of political blocs, multinational corporations, and other transnational alignments.

We need to avoid dichotomic models of a world reducible to two poles only, which attribute all causality to the "hyper-intentionality" of the center (Anderson, 1974a, 1974b); which deny any autonomy or agency to the dominated; or which reduce the variety of outcomes and responses in different countries to uniformity, even, as Wallerstein (1974) does, treating the Second World predominantly as a special case of "distorted" alternative development in a world still dominated by capitalism. Models of this kind are overintegrated in that they fail to distinguish systems of *production*, which are not necessarily based on *capitalist* relations of production but on a variety of labor systems (e.g., haciendas, with or without parcels of subsistence plots for the workers; debt peonage; serfdom; slavery; indigenous "communitarian" small-holding peasantries, and so on), from capitalist systems of the "realization" or commercialization of the product upon the market (Laclau, 1971). Such models, too, pay scant attention to the phenomenon of unequal development *within* and between colonies, and between regions of the *central* societies. In extreme form, "internal colonialism" (e.g., rural areas supplying labor to mines, food to cities, and so forth) underlies much of the "secondary nationalism" of Catalonia and Scotland, for example. The use of the confusing label "mode of production" to describe both a system of production relations *and* a system of appropriation (to say nothing of a mystifying model of "base" and "superstructure") scarcely makes for clarity, either, and confuses distinctions Weber made between the economic, the economically determined, and the economically relevant.

Apart from denying significant agency to the periphery, the models often treat internal class structure within the colony equally schematically, with little examination of class self-definitions, either in terms of consciousness or of action and struggle. Such models assume, too, that do describe a structure of class *situations* is the end rather than the beginning of analysis of the dynamic interplay between class situation, class consciousness, and class action, and the dialectic, too, of hegemonic cultures, subcultures, and countercultures.

To try to explain the nature of the societies that emerged under colonialism in these denuded, reductionist terms is to fragment classical "political economy" into "economics" and "politics" and to completely omit the realm of culture as informing the entirety—a procedure that would have been thoroughly acceptable to Adam Smith. Thus, Marxist economists in the 1930s correctly emphasized the centralization of the market as the crucial factor in the emergence of the absolutist state. Anderson (1974a, 1974b) has shown, however, that it did require a parallel complex construction of the *state* (a bureaucracy, monopoly of the use of force, fiscal machinery, mercantilist policies, standing armies), all aimed at replacing a form of kingship in which the king was merely *primus inter pares* by one in which he was an absolute monarch. But to this we need to add the construction of a *political culture*, its diffusion, and its penetration of the rest of the cultural order.

The construction of a colonial order equally involved the construction of an integrated market and production system, a new policy, and a political culture. But it was to be a doubly absolutist culture, shaped by the imposition of a mercantilist and still largely feudal system upon a dominated population, a caste system in which Whites from the mother country were superior socially not only to the wretched Indians, Africans, or Asiatics, but also to the settler–criollos.

It was this failure to incorporate the dominant propertied classes within the colony that was ultimately, in the epoch of intensified capitalist colonial exploitation, to generate independence movements that used the language of the new laissez-faire epoch but that refused it in practice, whatever the Constitution said, because it conflicted with a continuing system of economic relations that was usually quite precapitalist.

In more recently colonized countries the consolidation of the state, by definition, was of short duration. Hence, once the colonial gridiron is removed, there is a strong tendency for "unequal development" to express itself politically, both in advanced areas (Biafra, Katanga) seeking to retain their "lead" and in those areas of internal colonialism and "regions of refuge" (Aguirre Beltrán, 1967) inhabited by populations marginalized by the colonial state, who are now given an identity ("the Indian," "the African," or "the native") (Bonfil, 1972) and are collectively "excorporated" by being excluded from participation in national life. Both the "advanced" and the "backward" groups tend to generate claims to ethnic distinctiveness, self-expression, and ultimately autonomy that are variously called "regionalism," "tribalism," or "proto-nationalism."

The new elites that inherit the colonial states have therefore had to repress these tendencies to fission and therefore to the dissolution of the state as a structure (as in Ethiopia) in the name of a conception of either a unitary national identity or a multinational state but, either way, fiercely rejecting "tribalism" and "separatism" and basing national "unity" on the classical capitalist category of the *citizen*, a concept absent in the precapitalist state. Since they are trying at one and the same time to develop economically *and* to build *nations* and *states*, such societies are singularly integrationist in all dimensions. Relying upon labor instead of capital, trying to mobilize even the personalities of their peoples, such states are highly mobilizatory and corporatist. In the great compensatory drive to catch up, Nairn remarks, *people* are "more or less all that the nationalists have going for them [1977:340]."

Hence, they resurrect "past folk-heroes and myths . . . , [looking] desperately back into the past, to gather strength wherever it can be found for the ordeal of 'development' [Nairn, 1977:348–349]."

If the available contemporary models for development are variations upon the themes of capitalism and communism, they take on special forms when applied to specific situations. Westminster simply does not export well, and Cambodia bears little resemblance to the Soviet Union.

This is not to assert, as Chalmers Johnson (1970) does, that the Chinese Communist party is simply the mandarinate writ new, or Maoism a latter-day Confucianism. Legacies of the past also generate innovation and a desire to wipe out the past (China as a "blank sheet" of paper), even if it is still innovation oriented to the dismantling of systems of institutions and ideas. Continuity thus often proceeds from opposition (the underground, Jacobin nature of the Bolshevik party) as much as from lineal continuities. (Anderson [1974b:421] has pointed, too, to the legacy of institutions and ideas at *two* removes to typological time from the present.) But the continuities are now put to new uses: Parcelized sovereignty and the universalist propositions of Roman law and of the Church are transformed into rationales for private property and special kinds of bourgeois freedom.

Nothing like parcelized sovereignty was inherited from colonialism: only a segmental corporatism consolidated in race and caste. The colonial entities were themselves created by feudal societies just beginning to transform *themselves* into absolute states. The colony, then, emerged as a singularly "administrative" entity (Worsley, 1964), only qualified by the incapacity of the colonial power to enforce its rule initially and by the internal segmentation of the colony. Nor were democratic innovations in the mother countries exported, though Napoleonic or Prussian centralism might be. True, constitutional rigidity (emphasized by Wolf [1959:162–164] for the Spanish colonies, for example) ignored the difficulties encountered by Lima, London, or Madrid in actually implementing their will, if only because of communications problems. The formally rigid structures of control, therefore, were often ineffective in practice, allowing latitude for local landowners, mine owners and even bureaucrats to practice a considerable degree of autonomy, even before formal independence (Phelan, 1967). "I obey but do not execute" was the formula of the evasive bureaucrat trying to put *his* policies into practice.

Where mining and agricultural resources were absent or undeveloped, the less dynamic metropolitan states often practiced benign neglect or sold off their assets to the more energetic entrepreneurs, as in Portuguese Africa. In early mercantilism, too, "primitive accumulation" was really either loot ("booty capitalism"), as in India and in New World piracy, or a kind of capitalist hunting and collecting (the hunting of fur-bearing animals or of buffalo for meat, hides, or bones in the North American plains and prairies, of humans and ivory in Africa, the collecting of wild rubber and spices in the Amazon, of bird-of-paradise feathers in New Guinea, of sandalwood in other parts of Melanesia, and so forth) rather than the implanting of capitalist relations of *production*.

Where there was a large population with a complex division of labor (the Aztec and Inca empires, China, West Africa, India, Indonesia), a modernized, "capillary" articulation and intensification of existing internal market production (commonly stimulated by force, including taxation) took place. The introduction of quite novel crops in demand in the West, whether for consumption (tea, coffee, cocoa, sugar, tropical fruits) or as raw materials for manufacturing (cotton), led to new explosions of production based on expanded petty commodity production by peasants. A chain of middlemen usually intervened between producer and ultimate purchaser, usually a multinational corporation in modern times (Unilever in West Africa).

But the direct organization of production in large-scale units, vertically integrated with the metropolis, involved a new level of collective and centralized organization and new relations of employment rewards and conditions of work and extra-work life (in South Africa, the "pass," the compound, the township, and the beer hall). Such enclaves, notably gold, silver, and diamond mines, rubber and sisal plantations, and latterly petroleum, usually dominated the rest of the economy (Cardoso and Falletto, 1969). Unlike, say, extensive pastoral enterprise (Argentina or the American plains) or modern capital-intensive enclaves like oilfields, they called for supplies of labor on a scale that could not often be provided even by the most ruthless mobilization of local rural populations (Hemming, 1970; Van Onselen, 1976) and could not be met either by seasonal mobilization of labor.

Scanty populations, or those thought to be qualitatively unsuitable, had to be replaced by large numbers of imported laborers, whether indentured (Malaya, Kenya, South Africa, California, Hawaii, and so forth) or slaves (the Caribbean, Brazil). Such labor, obviously, had its distinctive cultural attributes, though these are often forgotten in purely economistic models. Free labor *could* be used, and grossly exploited, as on Brazilian coffee estates or Cuban postindependence sugar plantations, but it tended to opt for regions where it could remain free (Siberia, Australia, the American West, non-Andean South America), even when attempts were made to bind it to its employers. As Marx wrote of the colonization schemes of Edward Gibbon Wakefield: He was successful in exporting capital and labor but forgot to export the relations of production (a new version, on the frontier, of the notion that *Stadtluft macht frei*, "the air of the town frees"). Instead, the laborers became small farmers on their own account (Australia's "cocky farmers"), and the pastoral industry reached its apotheosis on the basis of wage labor (including mobile sheepshearers who developed a very proletarian ideology of "mateship" in the great free Australian Southland).

The classical literature of the frontier, especially Turner on the American West, celebrates a major national myth of this kind of colonization, depicting it as the spontaneous self-movement of the homesteader. Other frontier colonization (Siberia, the contemporary Amazon) have a very clear element of State "facilitation," as, actually, did the pioneer colonization of the archetypal West. There, the Indians were killed off or put onto reservations by the State; land was distributed for virtually nothing as part of a conscious social and nationalist expansion policy; an infrastructure of railways was financed in large part out of State loans, also with virtually free land as inducement; and "cow colleges" were established to research appropriate kinds of crops and related technology and management practices, and to educate farmers in their use (Lipset, 1950). Farm credit organizations were a more modern State or parastatal development.

All this is a far cry from those models of "subsistence" or "closed" economies beloved of anthropologists between the World Wars or by populist economists, who treated culture change as a "modern" phenomenon, ignoring precolonial exchange systems or emphasizing principally their ritual dimensions: a conception of an aboriginal, "untouched," timeless, "precontact" "zero situation" that postulated an "ethnographic present" conceived of as the point in time at which direct colonial control became effective—a denial, in effect, of historicity to the non-Western world (e.g., the Asiatic mode of production).

Isolated peoples did exist, of course, and a tiny handful still do. But most have long lived within the kind of framework of ever more inclusive worldsystems of articulation outlined earlier. It is within that kind of framework, then, that we have to examine social class in developing societies. In AngloSaxon countries, unfortunately, other frameworks have been dominant. In particular, "race relations" or "ethnicity" has usually been taken as *the* framework, with the study of prejudice as its central focus, a framework as arbitrarily lopsided as economistic reductionism. And yet as Rex (1970:48) has remarked, "without the power and stratification element there would be no race relations problem," or, in Harris's (1969:204) more general formulation, "a theory of race relations must be a sub-case of a theory of social stratification."

The contrast can best be seen in recent European Marxist studies of Mediterranean immigration that start from very different assumptions: asking the "system" question of how it is that the economy generates a *demand* for labor (Castles and Kosack, 1973), though, like all "system" or functionalist Marxism, it neglects the other side of the dialectic: the active *search* for a better life on the part of the "peasants who travel" (Shanin, 1978), now to Cologne and Paris as they once did to the Nanyang and the Golden West (which the equally mechanistic older language of "push" and "pull" factors did not capture, either).

In the United States, ethnicity, in the form of the general theory of the "melting pot" and the special theory of the "ghetto," had its analogue in anthropology in the stress upon *culture*, in contrast to the austerely structural British *social* anthropology. (The British never asked, therefore, what the lessons of Mundugumor kinship might be for *them*, as Margaret Mead always did.) Now the "culture of poverty" debate has replaced the older approach, which, however, so dominated whole generations of social scientists that, before the recent upsurge of Marxism in the United States, it was left to a handful of ex-Marxists, like Lipset, to remind the nation that it, too, had classes (Lipset, 1960:Chapter 9).

Equally, it took a Third World Marxist (Stavenhagen, 1969) to show British and French anthropologists that Africa, too, had social classes. The transfer of populations on a massive scale implies the incorporation of people who are not simply units of labor or even aggregations of population, in some demographic, presociological sense, but who share social and cultural characteristics that they do not shed overnight or are not allowed to shed. Despite Gluckman, the African in the city is *not* simply a miner but, as Mitchell has shown, is both perceived and treated as a "Bemba," "Ngoni," "Lozi," and so on, categories invested with new meaning, depending, too, on whether it is the work situation, market situation, or status situation that is involved (Lockwood, 1957). Workers, for instance, are commonly recruited along kinship or ethnic lines (Sheth, 1968).

The distinction between "system" sociology and sociologies of action (Dawe, 1970) of course extends more widely than to Marxism alone (it illuminates Parsons' trajectory, for instance), but seems most in evidence today among Marxists, whether they are those who use a functionalist version as part of the hegemonic political apparatus of the U.S.S.R., or are those with reductionist, economistic orientations who treat the "economy" as "structure" and the rest as "subjective" or "social" (Nun, 1969; Quijano, 1970; Singer, 1973). This is to ignore both culture and praxis, the "Promethean" aspects of collective human agency. History, Althusser assures us, is a process with a subject. It is "systems"—like "culture" in structuralist anthropology—that determine social processes. (For Marx, of course, *classes* were the agency of social change; for classical bourgeois political economy, the sovereign individual was.)

Ethnicity and Class

In both market and authoritarian social systems, then, groups and categories of people are allocated to roles and sectors not just in the economic order but in a total societal and cultural division of rights and duties, division of labor, and differential access to valued goods, including power and immaterial goods. Spatially, they find themselves in ghettoes; culturally, they are transformed into new kinds of producers and consumers, under the hegemonic cultural domination of WASP values, which inevitably spread across the capitalist world. In *expanding* economies, the open market and the practice of recruiting according to rational criteria (e.g., qualifications for the job) run counter to and tend to dissolve institutionalized monopolization of occupations according to status criteria (or forcible allocation to such positions), replacing it by intense individual social mobility, the United States and the U.S.S.R. being the most mobile (Miller, 1960). The use of status, notably ethnicity, as an instrument with which to divide and rule is, in a parallel way, countervailed by deliberate "melting pot" policies (denial of ethnicity, deliberate instruction in English in the United States and in Portuguese in Brazil, and, in both, the national "way of life").

It is, however, quite possible to operate even an industrialized society for long periods, as in South Africa, on the basis of ethnic "closure" (Parkin, 1974) (a) if the ideological will is there and (b) if virtually unlimited force is used. Nazi Germany, during World War II, operated its factories with 1.8 million prisoners-of-war. "Every fourth tank, lorry, field gun, every fourth piece of ammunition, was made by the hands of a foreigner in 1944 [Castles and Kosack, 1973:23]."

Employment practices based on market rationality (i.e., recruitment on the basis of appropriate qualifications rather than on the technically irrelevant grounds of kinship connections, ethnic origin, skin color, or religion) have by no means been the exclusive criteria of laissez-faire capitalism. Cheap labor was often preferred to skilled labor, docile to intransigent. And sectional cultural identity was a splendid ready-made basis for policies aimed at dividing and ruling the working class, for example, when newcomers were used in blackleg labor (see Engels [in Marx and Engels, 1870/1953:506] on the Irish/English split in the British working class). Initial cultural attributes of immigrant labor, too, in their attitudes to time, work, earnings, cleanliness, honesty (respect for property), cooperation, obedience, and skills, tend to be used by employers as justification for permanent incapacity by converting them into stereotypes, stereotypes that benefit the indigenous worker, and that therefore become part of his or her perceptions, too. Nor is this necessarily a calculated, Machiavellian strategy; employers actually *believe* in such stereotypes; they are themselves mystified.

Like the Irish, unskilled labor has a habit of coming from somewhere else, usually the internal backlands or from agrarian countries abroad, and hence to be culturally distinct and not very long removed in time from a purely rural environment (with modern buses, sometimes less than 24 hours).

Class and ethnicity, then, are frequently congruent, nor is this process confined to the early stages of capitalist and communist development. In spite of the theory of the changing organic composition of capital, very advanced modern production systems actually use increasing numbers of un-skilled—and commonly *de*-skilled (Paine, 1974)—workers, who carry out operations that are otherwise sometimes performed by much more formally educated labor. There is no apparent *functional* necessity for U.S. foremen to have college degrees; their Argentinian counterparts do not. Eleven million workers from Greece, Italy, Turkey, Morocco, Algeria, Spain, and Portugal man such assembly lines as the Ford plant in Cologne, the Volvo plant in Göteborg, and the Renault plant in Paris. They also sweep the streets, whereas indigenous labor prefers to go on the dole. Many of the immigrants are not *physically* very distinct from the indigenous population, either. Some of the most overt prejudice is directed against Italians in Switzerland (Berger and Mohr, 1975), or against "Pommie bastards" from the "mother" country in Australia and New Zealand. As the Black South African sociologist, Archie Mafeje, observed to me, the "Blacks" in Sweden are the very blond Finnish immigrants.

Such large aggregates could potentially form interest groups, unlike smaller ethnic pockets that can exert political pressure only by allying with fellow-workers of different ethnic background, as Grillo (1967) notes for East African trade unions. But they usually either join trade unions, where permitted, or form "associations" that play a multifaceted role of union, party, club, cooperative, and cultural or "social" entity, providing both mutual aid and a supportive identity (Shanin, 1978). Numbers, anyhow, count for little when political self-expression is inhibited by periodicity rather than permanence of employment (whether because foreign workers are more liable to unemployment or because they are on temporary contracts), and when political controls (ineligibility for citizenship or for public or trade union office, welfare rights, and the vote; liability to deportation; and sheer violent repression) are everyday practice. "The political subculture of the *favela* cannot be understood outside of the context of political repression [Perlman, 1976:191]," nor, one might add, can the subcultures of the working class as a whole. In the more dynamic economies, where urban employment is experienced as improvement, militancy is scarcely likely to develop, especially where the worker is a target worker, waiting only to resume his peasant identity. Most, of course, never will. Ethnic groups occupying inferior roles are not necessarily perceived as any kind of threat to those above them. The analogy drawn by Horkheimer (cited in Castles and Kosack, 1973:448–453) between Jews in Nazi Germany and contemporary working-class immigrants in western Europe is misleading. No mass racism emerges when only one in ten young people of Swiss nationality goes into unskilled or semiskilled jobs, and only 22% of the children of laborers themselves become laborers. The Italians make all this possible in Switzerland.

Ethnicity further acts as a poly-class, vertical force, cutting through horizontal class lines, and institutionalized via mechanisms of clientelism, brokerage, and patronage (Wertheim, 1969; Wolf, 1966:Chapter 3). Whether ethnic divisions are important or not, an expanding economy can offer more to all, however unequally, thereby avoiding a head-on struggle between capital and labor.

Consolidation of wider ranges of class consciousness and action, under such circumstances, is less likely than consciousness and action at narrower or quite different ranges: intraclass, sectional groupings, marked by subcultural closure. Instead of (a) the congruence of class and ethnicity (reinforcing horizontal divisions) or (b) the vertical crosscutting of horizontal identity (e.g., by ethnicity), there is a third option: the proliferation of sectional identities and interest groups that fragments and decomposes class solidarity. Thus, Runciman (1966) has shown that for manual workers, nonmanual workers are commonly their reference group; that workers in one shop, factory, or industry compare their lot with those in other such (known) situations; night workers with dayshift workers; single men with family men; men with women; and so forth.

Only exceptionally, or situationally, do they contrast themselves with more remote occupations, and even more rarely with the richer classes. Only under ideological leadership or under the very bitter experience of repression, or "J-curve" situations of frustrated expectations of continuing improvement (Davies, 1962), and often in a diffuse, resigned, abstract, and often "communal" rather than class way, do they come to view themselves as a collectivity engaged in a zero-sum game with the landlord or capitalist *class*. A striking historical case of a special kind of sectional vision that was, *at the same time*, utterly revolutionary, was the virtual handing back of state power by the Zapatistas, who were only interested in getting back their lands (Womack, 1972).

All this is far removed from Marx's vision of an inevitable and fairly speedy transition to a class conscious "for itself," via class struggle. As Bernstein caustically noted, "Peasants do not sink; middle class does not disappear; crises do not grow ever larger; misery and serfdom do not increase [cited in Hughes, 1958:71–72]." It is a far cry, too, from functionalist ideologies like that of Davis and Moore (1945), itself a special case of the wider ideology of market recruitment to occupational roles of those best fitted to fill them: an image of a culturally neutral unit of labor finding a buyer interested only in his technical attributes. Other qualities of labor, as we have seen, have always been quintessential considerations. Women have been loved not just for their sexual attributes.

The ideology of the atomized culture-free unit of labor, bound only by the cash nexus to his or her employer, looks somewhat inapposite after more than a century of labor's increasingly effective struggle to exert *collective* control, via trade unions, over the market economy, using *political* power, within or without the state. The political equivalent of this atomistic conception of the economic actor, Bendix (1964) has shown, is the concept of *citizenship* as the basic social identity, the counterpart of the sovereign economic individual. Other identities then become impermissible, including collective and corporate ones, when all men are equal before the law or the ballot box, let alone in their right to enter the Hilton Hotel. *"En adelante,"* San Martín grandiloquently declared in the afterglow of independence, *"no se denominará a los aborígines como indios o naturales. Ellos son hijos y ciudadanos del Perú; con el nombre de peruanos deben ser conocidos"* ("From now on the indigenous people should not be called *Indians* or *natives*. They are sons and citizens of Peru and should be called Peruvians") (Arizpe, 1977:13).

In the precapitalist "bureaucratic empires," by contrast, the primary societal identity and loyalty was to some entity intermediate between state and individual—to one's caste, liege lord, or ethnic group—that might even be spatially segregated (in cities like Cairo [Abu-Lughod, 1971]) or institutionalized within the polity as a whole, like the ethnic communities (*millets*) that were recognized under the Ottoman empire and were represented collectively by a religious–ethnic head, whether of the urban ward or the whole community, who mediated between it and the central power. (Archbishop Makarios was precisely the last of these "ethnarchs.") As long as members of these groups paid their taxes and handed over young men for the army or civil service, they could keep their peculiar religions, however much better it might have been for everybody to become a Muslim. Such societies were therefore *segmented states*. Under feudalism, the segments were the "houses" dominated by magnates who owned huge tracts of the country as their fiefs and the "souls" who inhabited them, despite the ideology of the mutual obligations between vassal and lord. In other conquest empires, whole ethnic groups were assimilated simply by changing their former chief or king into a vassal, or by replacing him with a member of the ruling house of the conqueror—the Zulu or Chinese ploy.

Despite arguments to the contrary (e.g., Bennett, 1967:59–87), therefore, nationalism is not simply tribalism writ large, but its opposite: It involves destroying secondary identities, intermediate between individual and state, and replacing them by citizenship. Caste and estate have to go.

Such an individualistic ideology (expressed also in Romanticism) fits ill with modern *corporate* capitalism, however "soulful" the latter might be (Berle, 1960). Yet capitalism cleaves to this classical bourgeois rhetoric both in developed and underdeveloped countries. In the former, the corporate interest has been long with us, together with constitutional divisions of power. In the latter, where sectional interest groups do not exist, they are rapidly conjured into being by the *state*. Now, however, they become peasant organizations, trade union "centrals" "representing" labor, and business chambers, all of these articulated under the overarching umbrella of a *political* organization: the single party (as in Mexico) or the armed forces. Nor does incorporation cease with these levels or with purely class organizations. Popular organizations and associations of all kinds are absorbed, whether of spontaneous origin or otherwise: residential associations, regional groupings, organizations *for* women, youth, ethnic communities, cultural organisms of the intelligentsia, and so on (Eckstein, 1977: Chapter 1). The process, be it noted, is not one of *totalitarian* "congruence" of institutional order (Mills, 1959:45–46), but of articulation and cooption. Hence, the rhetoric of liberal capitalism: the autonomy and rights of the individual, the labeling of the process as "democracy" curiously combined with a more corporatist imagery of "balanced" and "controlled," "organic" representation of legitimate interest groups, even a "higher" form of democracy. As Finer (1962:242) remarks, in underdeveloped countries the word "democracy" is always qualified; it is "national" democracy or "people's" democracy or whatever, but never simply "democracy."

Where there is continuing economic growth, the rhetoric is not without its resonances (Peronism, Getulismo, Ujamaa) and *some* element of redistribution, too. Like all efficacious ideologies, its capacity to mystify has a certain basis in reality. The new urbanites do experience their new existence as improvement, even those living on the Guayaquil rubbish dumps. Hence, the innumerable reports of the optimism of slum and shantytown dwellers, an optimism that has to be examined alongside the statistics of low levels of unemployment and the studies of improved housing in shantytowns. The imposition on this of antinomic categories such as "conservative" or "revolutionary" or the designation of these people as "passive" scarcely catches the complexity of the philosophy of Mangin's Lima shantytown dwellers:

> Work hard, save your money, trust only family members (and them not too much), outwit the State, vote conservatively, if possible, but always in your economic self-interest; educate your children for their future and as old-age insurance for yourself. [They also] aspire toward improvement of the local situation with the hope that their children will enter the professional class [Mangin, 1967:84–85].

Two-thirds of a Mexican slum sample *expected* university-level education for their children (Cornelius, 1975:230). In Perlman's words, the *favela* dwellers of Rio "have the aspirations of the bourgeoisie, the perserverence of pioneers, and the values of patriots [Perlman, 1976:243]." But their experiences more usually generate a calculative acceptance of the limits of possibility that is, however, by no means resigned. When economic expansion slows down or *turns* down and the rural exodus actually increases: some may go back home, like others before them who have failed and a minority who have succeeded and have invested in land, marriage, houses, and consumer durables as well as in traditional symbols of status, though rarely in more modernizing capitalist investment (Paine, 1974). For the great majority who stay in the city, the situation becomes truly a frustration of rising expectations that, if unchecked, threatens to become revolutionary. Some slum dwellers, like the shantytown dwellers whom the MIR in Chile organized, do become radicalized. At this point, they begin to demand redistribution *at the expense of* those who employ, exploit, and rule them. The popularity of the regime withers, vertical incorporation no longer works, and even those who claim to have the interests of the *sans-culottes, descamisados,* and other ill-clothed folk at heart cease to be thought of as fathers of the poor. If they do continue on that tack, they are deposed. Either way, the populist honeymoon comes to an end. To repress the power of organized Labor, force has to be used, even against the "labor aristocracy."

Hence, it is in the "subimperialisms" (like South Africa, Brazil, Argentina, Kenya, Mexico, Taiwan, South Korea, Hong Kong, and Singapore—a list of singularly repressive, even colonial, or at least incorporative regimes all of which exhibit variations of monocentric power) that the most intense industrial growth is taking place, for this is repression *oriented to growth* at the expense of the "popular" classes. Therefore, it has nothing in common with the traditional *caudillismo* practiced into modern times by a Somoza, an Amin, a Duvalier, a Trujillo, or a Stroessner (despite Finer, 1962, and others).

Hence, the use of force by no means signifies the end of expansion. Rather, by depressing consumption and reversing redistribution, and above all by drawing heavily on foreign investment in an economy now free from "labor problems" and where labor is now cheaper, a new phase of industrial growth is launched. The Army ensures that consumption is driven down toward absolute minimum levels for the majority (beans and rice) and that no explosions of popular rage occur. An ever-increasing middle class finds its living standards greatly improved, however curtailed its freedom of speech. Actually, free speech is acceptable; it is action that is not. Meetings and Marxist literature are by no means necessarily taboo; militancy is.

Of course, there are alternative sources of internal capital formation and accumulation: from capital owned by the indigenous bourgeoisie. But this would mean heavier taxation or appropriation by the state (or even the creation of a new state). The natural rejection of this option by the indigenous bourgeoisie drives them to support or at least tolerate the military. The payoff they receive is not negligible; it may be as high as 40% of the national income in the hands of 5% of the population. For foreign capital, private or channeled through state and parastatal development banks, the rates of return are also healthy, consuming as much as two-thirds of the national budget in some cases and yielding much higher rates than can be obtained on investments in the home countries.

The incidence of repression does not fall on all alike, even within the ranks of those who work. What E. V. Walters has called "illth," as well as wealth, is differentially distributed among the masses, too (Walters, n.d.). As Lomnitz shows, there are distinct grades of poverty even in shantytowns (Lomnitz, 1975:77).

There has always been an "aristocracy" of labor even by definition, for in a hierarchical system someone must occupy the lowest slots. In the past this aristocracy ranged from the minority of skilled craft workers in mid-nineteenth-century Britain to the wider "privileged stratum" in Lenin's model, to whom a portion of the superprofits extracted from colonial labor was allocated. Later, Fanon (1965) regarded the *entire* metropolitan working class as privileged, but within the "peripheric" countries it would be wrong to conclude, as he did, that the proletariat there is also a "labor aristocracy." Some are, especially in the extractive "enclaves" such as mining, where, at times, a situation of quasi-hereditary "job-property" in steady, well-paid jobs exists, as in Zambia and Bolivia. It also exists to a lesser extent in South Africa, though there the "labor aristocracy" totally lacks control over working conditions and conditions of employment, including rates of pay, and much, sometimes most, of this labor is impermanent. Certain agrarian enclaves also occasionally approach this condition, as in the nationalized sugar estates in Peru.

More widely, those working in state-owned or state-run enterprises—whether mines, plantations, or factories—or where the state controls the conditions of employment, often constitute a privileged stratum, not necessarily in terms of income so much as in stability of employment and of access to the ridiculously-named "fringe benefits" these jobs carry with them. Ridiculous, because in societies where private medicine costs the earth, medical care, paid holidays, superannuation, some unemployment benefits, severance pay, access to cheaper consumer goods in state-run shops, and other "informal" privileges are scarcely marginal additions to real income. The state, too, becomes a major employer itself, especially of the army of bureaucrats, as in Uruguay. In Japan, however, the corporation has taken over these welfare functions, which are generally a powerful instrument of social control and a conformity-generating device.

It would be ridiculous to classify as "aristocrats" of labor the army of wretchedly paid low-level public servants in societies like Ghana (messengers, porters, cleaners, servants, clerical workers, police, road workers, drivers), who can often survive only by "moonlighting" (Hart, 1973). But even they are often better off than those altogether outside the state sector or the state-regulated sector of the large employers of labor: the "industrial reserve army" of marginals, the would-be workers. The label is clearly unsatisfactory, for it is a residual category, a definition of what they are *not*. Since I, too, have conflated them all in the past, let us distinguish (a) the huge personal service sector (over 60% of working women in Mexico City are domestic servants), whose cheap labor elevates the consumption standards of the middle- and upper-classes, liberating the latter for professional work, dress displays, affairs, and boredom, and, one would think, in terms of some theories of the family, rendering marriage superfluous; (b) a population of hucksters, itinerant salesmen, lottery agents, shoe shiners, street vendors of all kinds (including children), often mediating between kin or "most-favored" partners in the countryside and the urban markets, retailing cheap goods and services to the poor among whom they live; (c) workers in sweatshops that can only compete by paying their workers low wages (Hong Kong, Portugal, and so forth); (d) "putting-out" home employment; (e) domestic production on a family basis; (f) casual laborers (porters, carwashers, and so forth); (g) self-employed artisans, such as shoe repairers, service technicians of all kinds, with informal skills and minimal capital; (h) the "hunters and collectors of the urban jungle," refuse dealers, and so forth (Lomnitz, 1975/1977); (i) criminals and other "deviant" entrepreneurs, notably prostitutes; and (j) beggars and the unemployed.

To label this miscellany of occupations the "informal income-opportunity" sector, as Hart (1973) does, is open to serious question on many counts. Some of these occupations are quite formally articulated to the higher-level manufacturing sector or are actually part of it (e.g., the sales end); others are microcapitalist independent units (what's "informal" about them?); others are workers, at least intermittently. Of course, it is equally schematic to assimilate the street vendor, with no more capital than will buy him a tray of chewing gum, ballpoint pens, or cheap trinkets, to the category "capitalist"—even "penny"—not just because of the minuscule scale of his operations but because relations of production within the micro-enterprise are not necessarily based on the cash nexus at all, or alone. Here McGee's (1973) extension of the Chayanovian model of the peasantry to embrace "urban peasants" makes some sense, at least in terms of the "production machine" aspect of Chayanov's model (Chayanov, 1966). The home, for instance, may be the place where ice cream or cooked foods are produced for sale, using family labor in the making and selling. The family unit among the "industrial peasantry" in the "subsistence transport sector" is also a unit of consumption, à la Chayanov. Even quite sophisticated operations are quite peasantish at times. Leys gives the instance of a Kenya truck owner who employs extended family labor to drive, service, load the vehicle, and so on, but has to practice such inordinate "self-exploitation" in terms of long hours of work for all and makes such a small profit once overhead is met that the family members live at levels little different from wage workers or nineteenth-century Russian peasants (Leys, 1975:161–174, 258–271).

Like rural peasant networks, relations among "urban peasants" are commonly based on kinship, ethnic, or locality ties, not only in production but in finding jobs, buying cheap produce for resale or elaboration, finding customers, and acting as brokers and middlemen who deal not only in material goods but in a variety of services that include delivering votes and mediating with the state (welfare agencies, patronage, and legal assistance).

But the family household is usually a heterogeneous entity, with members who follow a variety of occupations. This heterogeneity is further intensified by the propensity and necessity to move from one kind of occupation to another, from day to day, week to week, or month to month, as jobs dry up or members search for something better. Such volatility naturally makes impossible any stable sense of occupation/class identity or interest, though residential identity may be real.

But there are significant differences from Chayanov-type peasants, too (and there are problems about the model even for his Russian rural peasants). The urban entrepreneurs are oriented entirely to the market, nor do they have fixed wants or levels of wants. If they are "capitalists," they are only so in a very Pickwickian sense, for, having only minute quantities of capital, they are exceptionally vulnerable. They have to buy dear and sell quickly and cheap because they lack credit-worthiness, and therefore withholding power (except in dealing with kin). Familial/kinship relations, as we have seen, constitute a further deviation from the essence of capitalist rationality, the cash nexus.

The differential life chances of the workers in the state or state-regulated sectors reflect the overall structural differences between this kind of state capitalism and the good old days of the "night-watchman state." Naturally, too, the life of the wealthy as well as the *classes laboureuses et dangéreuses* is conditioned by the new centrality of the state. Leys (1975) has shown, indeed, how an entire new elite has been formed in Kenya out of state and party functionaries who have been given abundant land and capital by the state (the Black settlers). The "new class" concept therefore probably applies with greater force to these neocolonial elites than it does even to those of eastern Europe (Djilas, 1957), for there they become wealthy through their monopoly of political power (the state). In Kenya, they own the economy as well, albeit as junior partners to the multinationals.

It is, indeed, perhaps more prudent to use a term like *elite* to describe this Kenyan ruling stratum, not only because of the *political* character of their classness but also because the decisive centers of power, whatever local monopoly the single party exercises, lie outside the country altogether. The real ruling class, which can make decisions within which the local ruling class has to operate, is the class that owns the mines, plantations, factories, and banks: the multinationals. Such is their scale of operation that not just the Third World but even the First World exhibits a dual level of decision making. In the First World, General Motors spends more than the Japanese government (and Japan is the fourth largest industrial power); Ford spends more than the French government spends on defense; and Imperial Chemical Industries has a budget larger than that of Norway. In the Third World, only three Latin American countries—Brazil, Mexico, and Argentina—have a Gross National Product (GNP) superior to the annual sales of General Motors, Standard Oil, Ford, and Royal Dutch Shell, respectively (Borón, 1977:528).

The capacity of "independent" governments in Africa, which, with few exceptions, have a GNP of less than U.S. $100 per head per year with which to exercise sovereign choice, is clearly somewhat limited. Added to this, bilateral "aid" from foreign governments and from multilateral international banks is a major constraint even over the domestic policies pursued by *First* World countries.

Yet the modalities of control and profit take on new forms. Food, for instance, is a singularly powerful weapon, as more and more countries cease to be able to feed themselves. Food exports enable even the United States to improve its negative balance of payments—not steel exports, electronics, or even armaments (Omvedt, 1975). Much of the earnings by the multinationals today does not take the form of old-fashioned return on investment through dividends (now often restricted by local legislation), but is retained for further investment in the periphery. Profits accrue in the form of payments for technical know-how, management expertise, patent rights, and licenses.

Secondly, "transfer pricing" enables the headquarters in the developed country to charge its local subsidiaries in the developing country inordinately high prices for components, chemical and other advanced products, and supplies of all kinds produced abroad. In this way, even a country like Tanzania, which has nationalized practically everything, still experiences a debilitating hemorrhage (Shivjee, 1976).

Political Economy and Cultural Struggle

In this interpenetration of foreign capital, local capital, and state investment, the decisive weight is with the external component. Accompanying the material domination is an ever-increasing cultural, immaterial penetration. True, the "comprador" relationship between foreign, local, and state capital is nothing new, but compradores in nineteenth-century China were primarily conduits for the export of local primary products on the one hand, and the import of manufactured goods on the other. Now manufacturing increasingly occurs *within* the peripheric economies, organized within foreign-owned production systems and increasingly oriented to the *internal* market. Hence, new economic ethics and sets of wants are inculcated not just within an elite, but as *mass* phenomena. I may perhaps be forgiven, therefore, for concentrating on this "wave of the future" rather than on the agrarian stagnation of the Fourth World (or, as V. S. Naipaul said of the West Indies, the "Third World of the Third World"), since in the past too much attention has been paid, in dichotomic models (e.g., Jalée, 1969), to those unfortunate societies that rely on exporting literally peanuts (or cloves), like virtually the whole of sub-Saharan Africa, excluding South Africa and the other mining enclaves.

During the transitional epoch of nationalist "import substitution" in countries like Brazil and Argentina in the 1930s and African states in the 1960s, the assertion of solidarity vis-à-vis external powers necessitated the fostering of transclass vertical solidarities. To achieve this, some limited redistribution was required, and an even richer rhetoric of "social justice" of the "organic" society, including the institutions of labor. In other words, populism was the internal "social" face of the Janus which looked like an intransigent, chauvinist radicalism to powers used to running other continents as their private domain. Without the populist appeal, a lot more force would have been required, together with the manufacture of an ideology justifying repression (as in South Africa). The populist phase, however, is now well over.

During the epoch of dependency of nineteenth-century colonialism, older elites were both economically and politically oriented to the hegemony of the developed powers, and to their cultural hegemony, too. Here the paradigm is perhaps the Soong dynasty of inter-war China: Chiang Kai-Shek, the political controller; T. V. Soong, the banker; and Mme. Chiang: a Christianized ruling family. Even radicals, however, took their ideologies from the developed world. Pandit Nehru went to Harrow, and the Brazilian working class spent itself in wrangles about the superiority of the projects of Bakunin, Trotsky, and Stalin (Dulles, 1973).

Among the masses, cultural nationalism, and even political ideology, has long been displaced by consumerist values. The process Marcuse (1964) lamented for the U.S. working class is now well advanced among the working classes of developing countries, as the deadly serious study of *How to Read Donald Duck*, by Dorfman and Mattelart (1975) shows: Ninety-five percent of the households in São Paulo now have TV sets (Ferreria de Camargo, 1975). Workers are now psychically incorporated, not via a Protestant ethic of work so much as via their transmutation into consumers. If they consume more goods, material and immaterial (though these latter still cost money), they are told, better lives will be possible for them.

Countercultures consume their own diacritical goods though they often reject "materialism" in favor of recovering the primitive, in oriental mysticism, through massage of the body or the personality, in a variety of psychologistic/religious sects, and by contracting out into private worlds of personal satisfaction (e.g., sex) or into artistic forms of self-expression, or out of this world into an hallucinogenic separate reality, options usually only attractive or possible for middle-class intellectuals.

The atomization of society produced by consumerism is now countervailed by new forms of mass identity and solidarity. For a long time now, Lourdes, Guadalupe, and Aparecida have been far less important foci for the passionate expression of personal identification with something greater than oneself than the Aztec Stadium, Maracañã, or Wembley—identifications that may be purely "factional" Simmelian formalism, as when two teams divide a city or Nuer-like unite the populace against other nations. *The* world religion was celebrated in the 1978 pilgrimages to Buenos Aires for the World Cup soccer competition (Villai, 1974). *The* dominant culture is only beginning to feel the need to join in this plebian culture; its pilgrimages are to the shrines that embody other kinds of national values, like money (Las Vegas) or living like a millionaire for a few days (the betting in quarters and not thousands), in Hollywood (the apotheosis of the socially valued young and sexy individual), or the family holiday in Disneyland (where America is given access to a plastic reproduction of the world's cultural diversity and history in a part of the country where these are in short supply).

Increasingly, though, these are also the tourist meccas for those in the Third World who can afford to respond to the TV incentives to visit Disneyland or who take time off from their labors in U.S. field and factory to absorb local culture. The physical flow to and from Tijuana, the Costa Brava, and Hong Kong, where brothels, ballet, punk rock, hamburgers, champagne, jeans, and bikinis are the symbols of modernity, has become almost a mass phenomenon, or at least a middle-class one. Though the rich of the Third

World send their children to local expatriate schools and then to Princeton, and the middle class on a year's *au pair* exchange to Iowa to learn the English that will be vital for their professional careers, the mass media are indirectly transforming the lives of those who will never visit the Middle Kingdom in person. As the world becomes every day more truly a global village, the last remaining "closed corporate" communities and "regions of refuge" are prised open like oysters by tourists and by agribusiness.

The commercialization of agriculture is so far advanced that even on the frontier or on the pocket handkerchiefs or marginal land allocated under land reform, petty farmers are renting their plots to tenants and taking themselves off to the city where they invest in shops (Egypt and the Sudan). Even slum dwellers rent shacks or building sites.

Meanwhile, back at the ranch, there are still peasants, actually increasing in numbers in many countries, despite increasing simultaneous emigration to the cities. Traditional cultural patterns inherited from precolonial, colonial, tribal, or slave society do not simply dissolve. Peasants are the overwhelming majority of the population in India and China, Indonesia, and most of Africa. Only 11% of the population of tropical Africa are in wage employment, including migrant workers (First, 1970:445–81); Cabral (1969) remarked that there was nothing that could really be called a proletariat in Guinea–Bissau.

Ever fewer peasants fit the Chayanov model of the self-sufficient household based on family labor, with fixed wants (and even they produced ancillary wintertime handicrafts and hired themselves out in labor gangs, as Fei [1972] showed for inter-war China). But the days of "agricultural involution" seem numbered, as land and labor become commodities, not sacred trusts and responsibilities falling upon the manager of the family corporation, a link in the long chain from ancestors to descendants, and all become consumers. The intrusion of government speeds up the process via marketing boards, cooperatives, and production campaigns, combined with political mobilization to vote, demonstrate, or go to war. At the end of this road lies the most rationalized entity of all, agribusiness: the vertical integration of production, marketing, financing, and processing by the same corporation whether for the internal market or for sale abroad (Feder's [1977] "strawberry imperialism") or "contract production," retaining the juridical small owner and producer but locking him into a chain linking field with factory, and even making his agricultural decisions for him (the seeds to be used, planting and harvesting times, and so forth).

Other rural development strategies attempt to avoid proletarianization, often for political rather than economic reasons, via land reform. The tiny parcels distributed, without adequate back-up of credit, know-how, and technology, usually end up in the hands of those with the most resources, including skills and education as well as capital. In the Green Revolution, only the better-placed can afford and manage the "package" of fertilizers, machinery, and irrigation required. Even where cooperatives are established, differentiation proceeds apace, by nominating kin as "independent" recipients of land.

Because land reform, under such conditions, often results in *reduced* output, some agricultural modernization strategists have opted to bet on the strong as a conscious decision, letting the weakest go to the wall. For sociopolitical reasons, from the time of the last czar's great minister, Stolypin, onwards, *and* in view of national production needs, they have tried to create a stratum of prosperous farmers as a mass social base for capitalism in the countryside, thus avoiding polarization into an explosive opposition of landless versus magnates. It was precisely to avoid the emergence of a mass class of this kind, which would have been numbered in the millions, and which did emerge as the dominant force in the Russian countryside by the late 1920s, giving rise to the disastrous forced collectivization, that the Chinese followed land distribution with three successive campaigns to "socialize" agriculture, while retaining it as private property: the "mutual aid" teams, two stages of cooperatives, before, ultimately, the transition to communes in 1958.

The penetration of class differentiation into the countryside, however, does not readily dissolve vertical and corporate solidarities, of which ethnic distinctiveness is the expression. The representatives of capitalism in the village, for one thing, are often outsiders (landowners or shopkeepers) and transfer their profits outside. No one is going to get too rich, anyhow, as long as wealth gets converted not into more wealth but into social status via extremely costly rituals that do not redistribute wealth (since the pigs get eaten or the money spent on liquor goes into the shopkeeper's pocket) because high status is preferred to moving up in the class structure. Thus, capital is expended, not accumulated, and individualism and competition is channeled within a conservative cultural institution. The high status, too, is impermanent: Next year is someone else's turn, while last year's incumbent is beginning the 5-year stretch to pay off the debts he incurred. But incurring debts is the name of the game (Arensberg, 1937), since they create new interdependencies between persons and groups with whom one shares a basic condition of endemic, precarious poverty. One needs, then, to cooperate with others, in anticipation of the disasters, big and small, that will surely come. "There are districts," wrote Tawney (1932:77) of rural China in the 1930s, "in which the position of the rural population is that of a man standing permanently up to the neck in water, so that even a ripple is sufficient to drown him."

Disprivilege, therefore, is not very hard for poor people to recognize, but they do not necessarily put a class construction upon their situation. They may see the enemy as Bigness (the populist mode) or as Authority (the anarchist response)—any kind of Bigness, from Big Unions to Big Business, any kind of outsider trying to make us do things. Census takers, medical workers, and teachers risk their lives under these conditions.

The basic strategy for dominant classes, then, is to foster forms of vertical integration, to divide or cross-cut; Durkheim thought so, too. The basic counterstrategy for the exploited majority is precisely the opposite: to build numerical preponderance into an unstoppable horizontal agency. Operating the first is easier, because of control of the economy, the polity, and the means of cultural domination. The latter can be achieved only by an agency like a church or a party, the revolutionary party being by no means the only kind, and rarely successful.

It is useful, therefore, to look at these latter instances. Mao Tse-tung (1954) and Amilcar Cabral (1969) both begin their analyses of the relationship between state and civil society in classical Marxist fashion, with an analysis of the class system. But both do so within the historical and cultural context of their countries' development. Cabral, for instance, emphasizes not only the White/Black cleavage in Guinean society but also the centrality of the state and the *pre*colonial heritage: the incorporation, within the construct of the colony, of a variety of societies with different cultural patterns, some stateless, others state polities; some Muslim, others "animist"; differences in the position of women and of forms of marriage; differences of political authority at the village level (chiefs, lineage elders, secret societies, religious confraternities, and so forth).

Mao (1954) also starts with classes, first at the national level and then in the countryside, recognizing five groups among the "semiproletarians" alone and then moving to the instruments of political dominance by landlords (courts, "bullies"). There follow many more pages on theocratic, lineage/clan, and "masculine" authority, describing how the peasants, though they certainly launched economic and political offensives, also attacked the symbols of cultural domination by landlords, or what Mao calls "bad social customs," mainly forms of conspicuous consumption, such as the use of sedan chairs, the flower drum entertainment, feasts in which ducks, chickens, pigs, and wine were consumed, the use of castanets, and "foolish" customs such as New Year visiting.

Such analysis links past with present and provides a cognitive map, a set of value commitments, and a project of action. It also links the local with the universal, and locates the individual within all this, giving him a new social identity as a member of an oppressed *class*. It gives recognition to the economic, political, and cultural dimensions of social existence, to "civil society" as well as state. Unfortunately, we are so acculturated that we use more primitive models of "base" and "superstructure" imported from the traditional heartlands of Western culture, encoded in a private language of owlish academicism by intellectual mandarins. Antonio Gramsci, the only Western Marxist who did develop a theory of culture, was engaged in non-academic activities and did his writing while in jail. The market for further refurbishings of such inadequate models as those of academic Marxism is, however, distinctly bright in countries where there is plenty of theory, even "theoretical praxis," but little "unity of theory and practice" in changing the world.

In societies like China and Guinea-Bissau, theory has been oriented to successful revolutionary transformation. In the process, theoretical innovation has been called for: the abandonment of old shibboleths and the construction of new concepts. One such central concept is that of culture. But neither Mao nor Cabral, though they used the concept, fully *conceptualized* it. Bourgeois social science, however, did. American anthropologists made it their central concept; symbolic interactionists elaborated the concept of "subculture" and showed, too, how it worked out in everyday life at the level of face-to-face interactions and the small group.

Neither Mao nor Cabral could fully escape from a model that emphasized political and economic relations and treated the rest as "superstructure" and as determined. To be successful in practice, they had to recognize phenomena unaccounted for in their formal theory: Notably, they had to take account of nationalism and to accept the de facto "leading role" of the peasantry rather than the proletariat.

Within the Marxist canon, only Gramsci, condemned to theoretization in prison, developed a *theory* of culture and subculture. Marxist historians like E. P. Thompson and John Foster, too, *use* the concept of culture but do not carry its theoretization very far. Even Thompson's subsequent demolition of Althusser (Thompson, 1978), for all its virtues, does not develop a positive theoretical conception of culture; indeed, he still tries, uneasily, to make creative sense of the base/superstructure division that is at the root of the theoretical mess he is criticizing. If the political practice of the successful revolutionaries was superior to their abstract theory and deviated from it, the superior theorizing of Gramsci may have been due to his very disconnection from the pressures of institutionalized orthodoxy and of everyday practicality. The relationship between theory and practice, therefore, is certainly crucial, but it is rarely a "unity," being mediated in very complex ways. Practice does not dictate theory, nor theory practice.

Conclusion

Until it develops an adequate theory of culture, Marxism, for all its power in the field of the analysis of economic relations, will remain less capable than bourgeois social science of handling the interplay between economic and noneconomic relations. It will continue to be forced to introduce unsatisfactory ad hoc "repairs" and qualifications to the fallacious model of "base" and "superstructure," and despite its claims to be a "historical" theoretical system, it will remain unable to explain the persistence of institutions—from ethnicity to religion—that do not disappear as new modes of production become dominant, but rather adapt themselves to new patterns of economic relations

A more adequate historical treatment of the significance of class in the process of development inevitably has both to draw upon traditional Marxist analysis and to go beyond it, for class struggle occurs in all sociocultural domains, not in some reified and isolated zone of "the economy." Emerging class alignments are nevertheless cut across both by older "vertical" institutions and by new appeals to organic solidarity. A sociology that emphasizes only the latter, neglecting the Marxist emphasis upon class interests and struggle in defense of those interests—like an anthropology that posits an undifferentiated common culture—will be inadequate at best, and at worst merely an endorsement of ideological appeals to societal solidarity.

References

Abu-Lughod, Janet L.
    1971   Cairo: 1001 Years of the City Victorious. Princeton, New Jersey: Princeton University Press.
Aguirre Beltrán, G.
    1967   Regiones de refugio. Mexico City: Instituto Indigenista Interamericana.
Anderson, Perry
    1974a   Passages from Antiquity to Feudalism. London: New Left Books.
    1974b   Lineages of the Absolutist State. London: New Left Books.
Arensberg, Conrad M.
    1937   The Irish Countryman. London: Macmillan.
Arizpe, Lourdes
    1977   El "indio" y las derrotas de la consciencia. Colégio de México, Mexico City. (Mimeographed.)
Bendix, Reinhard
    1964   Nation-Building and Citizenship: Studies of Our Changing Social Order. New York: John Wiley.
Bennett, G.
    1967   Tribalism in Politics. In Tradition and Transition in East Africa: Studies of the Tribal Element in the Modern Era. P. H. Gulliver, ed. Pp. 59-87. London: Routledge and Kegan Paul.
Berger, John, and Jean Mohr
    1975   A Seventh Man. Harmondsworth, England: Penguin Books.
Berger, Peter
    1967   The Sacred Canopy: Elements of a Sociological Theory of Religion. New York: Doubleday.
Berle, Adolf
    1960   Power Without Property: A New Development in American Political Economy. London: Sidgwick and Jackson.
Bonfil Batalla, Guillermo
    1972   El concepto de indio en América: Una categoría de la situación colonial. Anales de Antropología 9:105-124. Mexico City.
Borón, Atilio A.
    1977   El fascismo como categoría histórica: En torno al problema de las dictaduras en América Latina. Revista Mexicana de Sociología 39:481-528.
Budd, Susan
    1967   The Loss of Faith in England: Reasons for Unbelief among Members of the Secular Movement, 1850-1950. Past and Present, No. 36. Pp. 106-125.

Cabral, Amilcar
1969   Revolution in Guinea: An African People's Struggle. London: Stage One.
Cardoso, Fernando Henrique, and Enzo Faletto
1969   Dependencia y desarrollo en América Latina: Ensayo de interpretación sociológica. Mexico City: Siglo XXI.
Castles, Stephen, and Godula Kosack
1973   Immigrant Workers and Class Structure in Western Europe. London: Oxford University Press.
Chayanov, A. K.
1966   The Theory of the Peasant Economy. Homewood, Illinois: Irwin.
Cornelius, Wayne
1975   Politics and the Migrant Poor in Mexico City. Stanford, California: Stanford University Press.
Cueva, Agustín
1977   El proceso de dominación política en el Ecuador. Quito: Ediciones Solitierra.
Davies, James C.
1962   Towards a Theory of Revolution. American Sociological Review 27(1):5-19.
Davis, Kingsley, and Wilbert E. Moore
1945   Some Principles of Stratification. American Sociological Review 10(2):242-249.
Dawe, Alan
1970   The Two Sociologies. British Journal of Sociology 21(2):207-218.
Djilas, Milovan
1957   The New Class. London: Thames and Hudson.
Dobb, Maurice
1946   Studies in the Development of Capitalism. London: Routledge and Kegan Paul.
Dorfman, Ariel, and Armand Mattelart
1975   Para leer al Pato Donald: Communicación de masa y colonialismo. Mexico City: Siglo XXI.
Dulles, John W. F.
1973   Anarchists and Communists in Brazil, 1900-1935. Austin, Texas: University of Texas Press.
Eckstein, Susan
1977   The Poverty of Revolution. Princeton, New Jersey: Princeton University Press.
Etzioni, Amitai
1964   Modern Organizations. Englewood Cliffs, New Jersey: Prentice-Hall.
Fanon, Frantz
1965   The Wretched of the Earth. London: MacGibbon and Kee.
Feder, Ernest
1977   El imperialismo fresa: una investigación sobre los mecanismos de la dependencia en la agricultura mexicana. Mexico City: Editorial Campesina.
Fei, Hsiao-t'ung
1972   China's Gentry: Essays in Rural Urban Relations. Chicago: University of Chicago Press.
Ferreira de Camargo, Candido Procopio et al.
1975   São Paulo 1975: Crescimento and pobreza. São Paulo: Edicões Loyola.
Finer, S. E.
1962   The Man on Horseback: The Role of the Military in Politics. London: Pall Mall Press.
First, Ruth
1970   The Barrel of a Gun: Political Power in Africa and the Coup d'État. London: Allen Lane and Penguin Press.
Foster, John
1974   Class Struggle in the Industrial Revolution: Early Industrial Capitalism in Three English Towns. London: Methuen.

Frank, André Gunder
1967   Sociology of Development and Underdevelopment of Sociology. Catalyst, No. 3. Pp.
       19–72. Buffalo, New York.
Goldthorpe, J. H.
1964   Social Stratification in Industrial Society. In The Development of Industrial Societies.
       Paul Halmos, ed. Sociological Review Monograph, No. 8. Pp. 97–122.
Goldthorpe, John H. et al.
1969–71 The Affluent Worker. Industrial Attitudes and Behaviour, Vol. I; Political Attitudes
       and Behaviour, Vol. II; The Affluent Worker in the Class Structure, Vol. III. Cam-
       bridge: Cambridge University Press.
Gouldner, Alvin W.
1971   The Coming Crisis of Western Sociology. London: Heinemann.
Grillo, R. D.
1967   The Tribal Factor in an East African Trade Union. In Tradition and Transition in East
       Africa: Studies of the Tribal Element in the Modern Era. P. H. Gulliver, ed. Pp.
       297–321. London: Routledge and Kegan Paul.
Harris, Marvin
1969   Review of Race Relations, by Michael Banton. Current Anthropology, 10:204.
Harrison, Royden J.
1965   Before the Socialists: Studies in Labour and Politics, 1861–1891. London: Routledge and
       Kegan Paul
Hart, Keith
1973   Informal Income Opportunities and Urban Employment. Journal of Modern African
       Studies 11:61–89.
Hemming, John
1970   The Conquest of the Incas. London: Macmillan.
Hobsbawm, E. J., and G. Rudé
1969   Captain Swing. London: Lawrence and Wishart.
Hoggart, Richard
1957   The Uses of Literacy: Aspects of Working-Class Life, with Special Reference to Publica-
       tions and Entertainments. London: Chatto and Windus.
Hughes, H. Stuart
1958   Consciousness and Society: The Reorientation of European Social Thought, 1890–1930.
       New York: Knopf.
Jalée, Pierre
1969   The Third World in World Economy. New York: Monthly Review Press.
James, C. L. R.
1963   The Black Jacobins: Toussaint L'Ouverture and the San Domingo Revolution. New
       York: Random House. (First ed. 1938.)
Johnson, Chalmers A.
1970   Peasant Nationalism and Communist Power: The Emergence of Revolutionary
       China, 1937–1945. Stanford, California: Stanford University Press.
Kerr, Clark, et al.
1962   Industrialism and Industrial Man: The Problem of Labor and Management in Economic
       Growth. London: Heinemann.
Laclau, Ernesto
1971   Feudalism and Capitalism in Latin America. New Left Review 67:19–38. London.
Lapidus, Ira M.
1967   Muslim Cities in the Later Middle Ages. Cambridge, Massachusetts: Harvard University
       Press.
Leys, Colin
1975   Underdevelopment in Kenya: The Political Economy of Neocolonialism, 1964–1971.
       London: Heinemann.

Lipset, S. M.
  1950 Agrarian Socialism: The Cooperative Commonwealth Federation in Saskatchewan: A Study in Political Sociology. Berkeley: University of California Press.
  1960 Political Man. London: Heineman.
  1964 The First New Nation: The United States in Historical and Comparative Perspective. New York: Basic Books.
Lockwood, David
  1957 The Black-Coated Worker. London: Allen and Unwin.
Lomnitz, Larissa
  1975 Como sobreviven los marginados. Mexico City: Siglo XXI. (English translation: 1977, Networks and Marginality: Life in a Mexican Shanty Town, New York, Academic Press, 1977.)
McGee, T.
  1973 Peasants in the Cities: A Paradox, A Most Ingenious Paradox. Human Organization 32 (2):135-142.
Macpherson, C. B.
  1962 The Political Theory of Possessive Individualism: Hobbes to Locke. Oxford: Clarendon Press.
Mao, Tse-tung
  1954 Report on Investigation into the Peasant Movement in Hunan. In Selected Works, Vol. I. Pp. 21-59. London: Lawrence and Wishart. (First ed. 1927.)
Mangin, William
  1967 Latin American Squatter Settlements: A Problem and a Solution. Latin American Research Review 2(3):65-98.
Marcuse, Herbert
  1964 One-Dimensional Man: The Ideology of Industrial Society. London: Routledge and Kegan Paul.
Marshall, Tom
  1950 Citizenship and Social Class, and Other Essays. Cambridge: Cambridge University Press.
Marx, Karl, and Friedrich Engels
  1953 Letter from Marx to S. Meyer and A. Vogt, 9 April 1870, in Karl Marx and Friedrich Engels on Britain. Moscow: Foreign Languages Publishing House.
Mayer, Jacob
  1956 Max Weber and German Politics: A Study in Political Sociology. London: Faber.
Mayhew, Henry
  1949 Mayhew's London: Being Selections from "London Labour and the London Poor." Peter Quennell, ed. London: Pilot Press. (First ed. 1851.)
Miliband, Ralph
  1961 Parliamentary Socialism: A Study in the Politics of Labour. London: Allen and Unwin.
Miller, S. M.
  1960 Comparative Social Mobility: A Trend Report and Bibliography. Current Sociology, Vol. IX, No. 1. Oxford: Blackwell.
Mills, C. Wright
  1958 The Causes of World War Three. New York: Simon and Schuster.
  1959 The Sociological Imagination. New York: Oxford University Press.
Moore, Barrington
  1967 Social Origins of Dictatorship and Democracy: Lord and Peasant in the Making of the Modern World. London: Allen Lane and Penguin Press.
Murra, John V.
  1975 Formaciones económicas y políticas del mundo Andino. Lima: Instituto de Estudios Peruanos.

Nairn, Tom
    1977   The Modern Janus. *In* The Break-Up of Britain: Crisis and Neo-Nationalism. Pp. 329–363. London: New Left Books.

Nettl, J. P.
    1966   Rosa Luxemburg. 2 vols. London: Oxford University Press.

Nun, José
    1969   Sobrepoblación relativa, ejército industrial de reserva y masa marginal. Revista Latino-americana de sociología 4(2):178–235.

Omvedt, Gail
    1975   The Political Economy of Starvation. Race and Class 17(2):111–130.

Paine, Suzanne
    1974   Exporting Workers: The Turkish Case. Cambridge: Cambridge University Press.

Parkin, Frank
    1971   Class Inequality and Political Order: Social Stratification in Capitalist and Communist Societies. London: MacGibbon and Kee.
    1974   Strategies of Social Closure in Class Formation. *In* The Social Analysis of Class Structure. Frank Parkin, ed. London: Tavistock.

Perlman, Janice E.
    1976   The Myth of Marginality: Urban Poverty and Politics in Rio de Janeiro. Berkeley: University of California Press.

Phelan, J. L.
    1967   The Kingdom of Quito in the Seventeenth Century: Bureaucratic Politics in the Spanish Empire. Madison, Wisconsin: University of Wisconsin Press.

Quijano, Aníbal
    1970   Redefinición de la dependencia y proceso de marginalización en América Latina. Santiago, Chile: CEPAL. (Mimeographed.)

Rex, John
    1970   The Concept of Race in Sociological Theory. *In* Race and Racialism. S. Zubaida, ed. London: Tavistock.

Rostow, W. W.
    1960   The Stages of Economic Growth: A Non-Communist Manifesto. Pp. 35–55. Cambridge: Cambridge University Press.

Runciman, W. G.
    1966   Relative Deprivation and Social Justice. London: Routlege and Kegan Paul.

Shanin, Teodor
    1978   The Peasants Are Coming: Migrants Who Labour, Peasants Who Travel, and Marxists Who Write. Race and Class 19(3):277–288.

Sheth, Narayan R.
    1968   The Social Framework of an Indian Factory. Manchester, England: Manchester University Press.

Shivjee, I. G.
    1976   Class Struggles in Tanzania. Dar es Salaam, Tanzania: Tanzania Publishing House.

Singer, Paul
    1973   Economía política da urbanizacão. São Paulo: Editora Brasiliense.

Stavenhagen, Rodolfo
    1969   Las clases sociales en las sociedades agrícolas. Mexico City: Siglo XXI.

Stedman Jones, Gareth
    1971   Outcast London: A Study in the Relationship Between Classes in Victorian Society. Oxford: Clarendon Press.

Tawney, R. H.
    1932   Land and Labour in China. London: Allen and Unwin.

Thompson, E. P.
  1968   The Making of the English Working Class. Harmondsworth, England: Penguin Books.
  1978   The Poverty of Theory and Other Essays. London: Merlin.
United States Congress, Joint Economic Committee
  1975   China: A Reassessment of the Economy. Washington, D.C.: U.S. Government Printing Office.
Van Onselen, Charles
  1976   Chibaro: African Mine Labour in Southern Rhodesia, 1900–1933. London: Pluto Press.
Villai, Gerhard
  1974   El fútbol como ideología. Mexico City: Siglo XXI.
Wachtel, Nathan
  1973   Sociedad y ideología: Ensayos de historía y antropología Andinas. Lima: Instituto de Estudios Peruanos.
Wallerstein, Immanuel
  1974   The Modern World-System: Capitalist Agriculture and the Origins of the European World Economy in the Sixteenth Century. New York: Academic Press.
Walters, E. V.
  n.d.   Manuscript, Boston University.
Wertheim, W. F.
  1969   From Aliran Towards Class Struggle in the Countryside of Java. Pacific Viewpoint 10(2):1–17. Wellington, New Zealand.
Williams, Eric
  1944   Capitalism and Slavery. Chapel Hill, North Carolina: University of North Carolina Press.
Wolf, Eric R.
  1959   Sons of the Shaking Earth. Chicago: University of Chicago Press.
  1966   Peasants. Englewood Cliffs, New Jersey: Prentice-Hall.
Womack, John, Jr.
  1972   Zapata and the Mexican Revolution. Harmondsworth, England: Penguin Books.
Worsley, Peter
  1964   The Third World: A Vital New Force in International Affairs. London: Weidenfeld and Nicolson.

Social Inequality:
The South Africa Case[1]

No one reading the evidence can doubt [it]. Nor can it be doubted that blacks and whites had to be taught the meaning of blackness and whiteness. This is not to deny "differences" in color and hair formation, etc. It is only to say that perceptions had to be organized to recognize the differences and that men had to be organized to take advantage of them. The so-called differences were not the cause of racism; on the contrary, men seized on the differences and interpreted them in a certain way in order to create racism. Not only did they exploit "differences," but they also created "differences" and preserved them by force and violence. The differences, in other words, were rationalizations and excuses, not the causes of racism. Once established, however, the ideology of rationalizations assumed a calamitous autonomy and influenced the interests from which they derived.

Who was responsible for this policy?
—Lerone Bennett, Jr. (1975:69)

The scientific study of racial inequality and oppression in the world in general and South Africa in particular has yet to transcend the state of idealist improvisation. To study the evolution of racially based inequalities is not exclusively of academic interest. Without a proper conception of the history of racism in the modern world, it is difficult to see how one can devise strategies for the solution of this burning question of the last quarter of the twentieth century. The plight of the Black people of South Africa is intimately bound up with the history of White settlement in their lands. The South African social

---

[1]This paper is an extract of a book entitled *Race and Class in South Africa*, published by Monthly Review Press, New York, in 1979, and abridged with the publisher's permission. Copyright © 1979 by Bernard Makhosezwe Magubane. Reprinted by permission of Monthly Review Press.

formation represents a stage in the evolution of the world capitalist system. In order to undertake an analysis of racial inequality and exploitation in South Africa, it is indispensable to know its historical roots.

In South Africa the pyramid of wealth and social power exists as a fact of daily experience. Whites, who constitute less than 20% of the population, consume more than 60% of the nation's income, have legal occupancy of 87% of the land, and hold most of the skilled and semiskilled jobs. Inequality of revenue and wealth is not only an economic fact; it also implies inequality of life chances. Infant mortality statistics for Africans have not been disclosed since 1957, but at that time the rate was five times that for Whites and three times that for Asians. Other estimates for Africans are 200–250 infant deaths per 1000 live births. While some experts consider this proportion exaggerated, others suggest that the rate may be as high as 450 infant deaths per 1000 live births. A 1966 survey is reported as indicating that "half the children born in a typical African reserve in South Africa died before reaching the age of five years [Friedman, 1977–1978:33]." This statistic is not surprising given the distribution of physicians for the different "races," which in 1972 was Whites 1:400; Asian 1:900; Coloured 1:6200, and African 1:44,000 (Friedman, 1977–1978).

Every country, of course, is unique, but South Africa is so unique that it almost defies imagination. It seems to have evolved from another planet. Today in South Africa, despite the proclaimed policy of separate development, the African is everywhere: in the fields, in the factories, in the mines, in shops, in offices. Every White person keeps at least one African servant, no matter how poor he is. The Whites in South Africa have reserved for Africans those hard tasks they have refused to mechanize. Thus South Africa as a society, whether we look at its achievement in economic development, sports, or any field of endeavor, cannot be conceived without the existence of the forced labor of Africans.

How then do we conceptualize the inequalities that obtain in South Africa? Today it is not enough just to take stock of the social inequity that exists in each country. It is even more important to take into account the inequality between a small handful of advanced capitalist countries (from the point of view of capital accumulation and industrialization) and the majority of humanity, living in the so-called underdeveloped countries (colonial and semicolonial countries). Social inequality similar to that existing in South Africa has been the fate of other people in Third World countries. Such inequality is rooted in the structure of economic life, by which different economic functions are assigned to particular countries and people and the system is perpetuated and accenuated by the principal social and legal institutions of capitalist hegemony.

While there are many ways to define and study racial inequality, in this chapter it will be conceptualized as an aspect of "imperialism" and "colonialism." These concepts will be used analytically, to refer roughly to the same phenomena—the economic, political, and cultural domination of the African people by White settlers. "Imperialism" will be used, however, to refer more specifically to the relation between a subjugated society and its alien rulers, while "colonialism" will be used to focus more on the typical social structures created within the colonized society by imperialist relationships (Omvedt, 1973:1). Modern colonialism and imperialism established the hegemony of the capitalist mode of production in the world, incorporating various peoples, combining them in the dialectic of "free" development and "forced" underdevelopment: the rapid development of the settlers and the retarded growth of the indigenous peoples.

While colonialism itself has an ancient history, the colonialism of the last five centuries is closely associated with the birth and maturation of the capitalist socioeconomic system. The pursuit and acquisition of colonies (including political and economic domination) was a significant attribute of the mercantile revolution, which contributed to the disintegration of feudalism and the foundation of capitalism (Magdoff, 1972:145).

The Dutch who established a way station at the Cape of Good Hope in 1652 were the typical products of the feudal stagnation in Holland. It is significant that the very establishment of the Cape station was not the result of a government decision but of a trading company, the Dutch East India Company, which was under the direction of 17 rich merchants.

The basic purpose of the joint stock companies of the seventeenth and eighteenth centuries was to produce minerals, spices, and other tropical products, to control trade in them, and to exploit certain forms of unfree labor in mining and plantations. The growth of the Industrial Revolution gave rise to the second phase, imperialism. During this latter period of procurement of raw materials necessitated the opening up of markets for the finished products of the new factories spawned by the Industrial Revolution, as well as areas of outlets for capital investments that would generate superprofits.

The development of capitalism during the past 500 years and the manner in which it affected the relations between Europe on the one hand and Africa, Asia, and Latin America on the other is viewed here as a historical development with certain uniform tendencies. We cannot separate economic from political, much less ideological, motives that have structured capitalist relations of production in the modern world. If capitalism required an expansionist policy of conquest and exploitation, a cumulative process of drives and pressures of various types was set off. These processes produced their own ideology and their own policy, and these became forces capable of autonomously orienting choices and determining decisions.

The ideology of racism, called into life and fed by both expansionist and exploitative socioeconomic relations of the developing capitalist imperialism, became a permanent stimulus for the ordering of unequal and exploitative relations of production along "racial lines" and, further, demanded reasons to justify these relations. The seemingly autonomous development of racism today does not lessen the fact that, as a process seen in historical perspective, it was initiated by the needs of capitalist development and that these needs remain the dominant factor in current racist societies. What is important is to explain racist phenomena as a whole and to clarify their local manifestations in various capitalist societies.

The history of South Africa is an act in the larger drama of the worldwide colonization of Asia, Africa, and the Americans. In South Africa, White settlers elaborated structures for the exploitation of the labor power and the resources of indigenous populations. Just before the start of the twentieth century Hobson (1965:258), looking back at the history of the colonization movement, commented

> Whenever superior races settle on lands where lower races can be profitably used for manual labour in agriculture, mining and domestic work, the latter do not tend to die out, but to form a servile class. This is the case, not only in tropical countries where white men cannot form real colonies, working and rearing families with safety and efficiency, and where hard manual work, if done at all, must be done by "coloured men," but even in countries where white man can settle, as in part of South Africa and of the southern portion of the United States.

Any disquisition on racism and structured inequality that ignores the use of the "lower races," so called by the modern capitalist, inevitably degenerates into banality that only confuses the issues.

The essence of modern capitalism is the ruthless transfer of wealth from the colonized group to the colonizer, from Black to White, from worker to capitalist. An economic system must, however, produce political and ideological systems as well as the transfer of wealth. Thus, as Louis Ruchames (1969:1-2) points out:

> During the Middle Ages and extending into the early modern period, racial thought was used to explain differences between economic and social classes, especially between the peasantry and the nobility. Some thinkers regarded the peasants as descended from Ham, the accursed son of Noah, and the knights from the Trojan heroes, who had presumably settled in England, Germany and France after their defeat. In the seventeenth century, Count de Bougainvilliers, a spokesman for the French nobility, declared the nobles to be descended from their Germanic conquerors and the masses of the people from the subject Celts and Normans.

In the era of imperialism, capitalism grew into a world system of colonial oppression and the financial strangulation of the overwhelming majority of the population of the world by a handful of advanced countries (Lenin, 1917/1969:5). It was this worldwide expansion that, consciously or unconsciously (and indeed very often unconsciously), lay behind the shift of "racial" thought to apply to the people in the colonies. Explaining the change, Ruchames (1969:4) writes:

> With the increase in slavery and the slave trade, and more numerous encounters of Europeans with Indians and Negroes, European scholars began to give greater atten-

tion to race and racial difference. It is interesting to note that it was only during the modern period that the term "race" came into use. The English term was first used at the beginning of the sixteenth century, the Italian *razza* first appeared in the fourteenth century, while the Spanish *raza*, the Portuguese *raca* and the French *race* were first used in the fifteenth century.

The history of colonialism and imperialism was the unfolding of institutions and ideas of class or racial inequality in societies created by early colonists. Almost without exception the gross inequalities in White settler societies demand the claim that the colonized are biological and cultural inferiors. *Everyman's Encyclopedia*, quoted by Hubbard (1968:7), describes the growth of racism as follows:

> The growth of modern racialist theories that hold that there are inherent differences between "superior" and "inferior" races is very recent. It seems to date from the days of slavery in America, when it was necessary to produce reasons for the continued subjection of economically valuable slaves. Much the same is true of South Africa today, where Calvinist doctrines have given such scientifically false beliefs added support. It is noticeable that in many Catholic countries there has been little racialism, since their doctrine has held to the inherent equality of all men. This fact adds support to the view that "race" relations are essentially economic and social and that "race" as such has little to do with the real situation.

Though racial inequality reflects real processes in capitalist society, it must not be understood as simple or mechanical reflections and recurrences. The structures of inequality acquire meaning only through a human definition that includes a wide range of possible mediations and even individual perceptions. Therefore, the study of racist inequality calls for the analysis of a multitude of processes (some historical, some psychological, other religious and philosophical, and even population dynamics), and this analysis requires concepts grounded in history and the rejection of those based on idealistic assumptions about human nature.

Each society, of course, exhibits a particular blend of diverse "racial" groups, a particular mix of their activities, and a particular patterning of their socioeconomic relationships. The ideological instant of racism reflects the specificity of each society as an historical entity. In South Africa, Whites, Coloureds, Indians, and Africans are coordinated in that descending order because the Whites form less than a quarter of the population. In the United States their is no such ordering; if you have an eighth of "Negro" blood you are considered a "Negro."

The concrete peculiarities that distinguish one country from another within the same political epoch must, therefore, be taken into account and explained. Instead of employing general and timeless categories to house social phenomena in different epochs, the methods of abstraction require that we understand the specific dynamics of racism under specific conditions.

For this reason, any realistic verification of racially structured inequality can only be disclosed by studying White settler societies created under varying

conditions, beginning in the sixteenth century. A theory of racially based inequality must grasp the general character of the epoch opened by the so-called
voyages of discovery during the mercantile era. What kinds of societies were
created by European settlers? Only after we have described common elements
in these societies can we deduce the laws that determined modern inequality.

Ruchames (1969:5), in a previously cited essay, writes

> One of the important events in the history of racial thought took place in 1550 and
> 1551 at Valladolid, Spain, in a debate between Juan Genés de Sepulveda and Las
> Casas on the question of whether the Aristotelian theory, that some men are slaves by
> nature, could be applied to the Indians. Sepulveda argued that the Indians were rude
> and inferior beings by nature, with no capacity for political life, whose inferiority re-
> quired that the superior Spaniards rule over them. Las Casas argued that the Indians
> were rational beings, superior to many ancient peoples, even the Greeks and Romans,
> and therefore worthy of freedom. Neither contestant gained a clear-cut victory.
> Although Lewis Hanke argues that Las Casas' publicly stated views strengthened those
> who believed "that all the people of the world are human beings" and represented "one
> more painful and faltering step . . . along the road of justice for all races," he admits
> that during the seventeenth century the Aristotelian view of race "reigned almost
> supreme in Europe and America."

With the advent of capitalism and the colonization movement, Africa, in
particular, experienced slavery and the slave trade, which was soon followed
by the dismemberment and subdivision of the continent—its resources and
people—for the benefit of capitalist Europe. The Aristotelian theory provided
the rationale and apologia for the rape and despoliation of Africa by European colonialism and imperialism. Translated, the theory states that human
society consists of men and women who differ not only in skin color but in
abilities. Some races are masters because their achievements re-echo over the
world. Others are capable of nothing; they may serve, at best, as fertilizer for
history, tilling the soil, digging the mines, and doing other chores for European civilization. Scholasticism was the heir of this theory.

> If Christianity was the only true religion, and Christians the new "chosen people,"
> they could do as they saw fit with the earth and its non-Christian populations.
> Heathens, Jews, Moslems and others were fair game; witness Pope Nicholas V's order
> in 1452 empowering the King of Portugal "to despoil and sell into slavery all Moslems,
> Heathens and other foes of Christ." The Church itself held slaves [Ruchames, 1969:2].

Whether justified as a means of saving the souls of savages or whether as
the extension of a civilization, imperialism changed the entire economic basis
of industrial life in the colonies. In the White settler colonies there were two
sorts of humanity, the superior and inferior. The latter toiled for the former,
and the superior were the real human beings, with opportunities for social and
cultural betterment. Witnessing the rise of imperialism, W.E.B. DuBois
(1915/1970:139–140) concluded in 1915:

> Most persons have accepted the tacit but clear modern philosophy which assigns to
> the white race alone the hegemony of the world and assumes that other races, and par-
> ticularly the Negro race, will either be content to serve the interests of whites or die

out before the all conquering march. This philosophy is the child of the African slave trade and the expansion of Europe during the nineteenth century.

Conceptually and theoretically, the meaning of this development is clear. The structures of inequality that developed during the nineteenth century were attempts to create a coherent system to define relations between Black and White in the era of capitalist hegemony. The incorporation and exploitation of non-White labor in the productive forces of developing European capitalism is the most stable indicator of the nature and character of societies created by White colonization and imperialism over the past 500 years.

Non-Whites have suffered, whether as slaves in the Americas or as colonial subjects in Africa. They have been used, abused, and oppressed to extract the world's riches for the benefit of a tiny handful of exploiters in Europe and America. With the rise of imperialism, Europe proposed or hoped to see the system of exploitation applied on a world scale. This would be done with the "scientific" policy of White supremacy elaborated in a detail of which the world had never dreamed.

In his classic study, *Black Reconstruction in America 1860–1880*, DuBois (1935/1962:15–16) described the world order that imperialism was creating and the role it was assigning to Black, Brown, and Yellow labor in the imperialist scheme of things:

> That dark and vast sea of human labor in China and India, the South Seas and all Africa; in the West Indies and Central America and in the United States—that great majority of mankind, on whose bent and broken backs rest today the founding stones of modern industry—shares a common destiny; it is despised and rejected by race and color, paid a wage below the level of decent living; driven, beaten, prisoned and enslaved in all but name; spawning the world's raw material and luxury—cotton, wool, coffee, tea, cocoa, palm oil, fibers, spices, rubber, lumber, cooper, gold, diamonds, leather—how shall we end the list and where? All these are gathered up at prices lowest of the low, manufactured, transformed and transported at fabulous gain; and the resultant wealth is distributed and displayed and made the basis of world power and univeral dominion and armed arrogance in London and Paris, Berlin and Rome, New York and Rio de Janeiro.[2]

The next section integrates sociological, economic, historical, and political approaches in an effort to comprehend the developments of inequality and racism in South Africa's tragic and complex history. My approach is dictated by the belief that explanation is a statement of process and its historical determination. "Every sociology worthy of the name," writes C. Wright Mills (1959:146), "is historical sociology."

Historical Background

The history of White settler colonists in South Africa (as distinguished from their ideology) clearly illustrates the connection between the imperative of colonization—the desire to take the land—and that of capitalism—the

[2]Copyright 1935, 1963 by W. E. B. DuBois (New York: Russell & Russell, 1956).

desire to exploit Black labor. The dispossession and exploitation of African labor is necessarily objective; it is the material structure on which the structures of inequality can be traced with an element of objectivity. These political–economic practices deprived Africans of their land and then reduced them to instruments for the production of surplus value for their conquerors. Given the complexity of South African history, the scope of this inquiry will have to be severely limited. What I plan to do is to select what Anderson (1964), in analyzing Portuguese colonialism, calls *key* variables that appear to have the most explanatory value as far as the development of South Africa's socioeconomic order is concerned. The key variables defining modern South Africa are (a) its settlement first by the Dutch in the seventeenth century and later by the English in the nineteenth; (b) the subsequent conquest and incorporation of the Africans into the evolving settler society, first in agriculture and later in mining; (c) the discovery of diamonds in 1867 and gold in 1886 and the importance of the gold industry in the monetary system of the capitalist world; (d) the reorganization of agriculture, which caused the depopulation of the countryside and resulted in the "poor white"; (e) the growth of urban-based industry and the competition that ensued between the Black and White proletariat; (f) the granting of political power to unite settlers in 1910 by Britain; (g) the national struggles of the African before and after conquest; and (h) the role assigned to South Africa in the imperialist strategy and division of labor. Through the study of the interaction between these variables, I hope to demonstrate the rigorous coherence between various aspects of South Africa's recent social life—economics, politics, religion, and culture.

It was as a British colony during the latter part of the nineteenth century that South Africa acquired the main structures of inequality that characterize it to this day. These were based on the fact that, first, the African chiefdoms and kingdoms had been conquered. The role of conquest in fostering certain types of class relations was well recognized by classical social scientists.[3]

South Africa, because of its climate, was, like America, Canada,

---

[3]Augustin Thierry in his *History of the Conquest of England by the Normans* (1825/1869:xix–xx) writes:

> The higher and lower classes . . . are in many countries the lineal representatives of the peoples conquering and the peoples conquered of an anterior epoch. . . . The race of the invaders . . . formed a military nobility . . . , the invaded race . . . not living by the sword but by the compulsory labor of their hands. . . .

Karl Kautsky (1972:58) writes in the same vein:

> Different classes may assume the character of different races. On the other hand, the meeting of many races, each developing an occupation of its own, may lead to their taking up various callings or social positions within the same community; race becomes class. Particularly frequent is the case of a poor but warlike nomadic race attacking a prosperous, peaceful population and subjecting it, the former race then assuming the function of a warrior nobility with a monopoly of national defense. This nobility will develop exclusively warlike properties, despite productive labour, and the workers will become poor, badly nourished, defenseless, and unmilitant, which qualities may, in some cases, develop to the point of cowardice.

Australia, and New Zealand, to be a White settler state. African presence was to be tolerated only if it could be reduced to minister to the needs of Whites. Were it not for such use, there would have been no need to spare the lives of the Africans after they were conquered. The development of forced labor in South Africa could only take place after conquest. Karl Marx (1857–1858/1971:29) has explained what happens when a people is conquered:

> A conquering people divides the land among the conquerors, establishing thereby a certain division and form of landed property and determining the character of production, or it turns the conquered people into slaves and thus makes the slave labour the basis of production. . . .Or legislation perpetuates land ownership in large families or distributes labour as a hereditary privilege and thus fixes it in castes.

After conquest African labor was exploited in a constantly changing environment; the development of secondary industries and the growth of towns changed the methods by which the rulers secured surplus value from labor. The legal structure used to incorporate African labor in the political economy is descriptive of race relations as well as of the strategies of controlling African political aspirations. The mountain of labor legislation beginning with the master and slave codes is an indispensable raw material for understanding the politics of racial inequality in changing circumstances.

Though scientific understanding has to confront empirical facts such as labor legislation, the analysis of statutes must not be limited to a cataloguing and a superficial description. Scientific explanations begin with generalizations that culminate in theoretical explanations. Theorists must understand that the forms of labor appropriation change—that there is direct appropriation of surplus labor in slave-owning society, appropriation of the surplus product under feudalism, and appropriation of surplus value under capitalism. Lenin (1972:634) writes that

> The slave-owners . . . regarded the slaves as their property; the law confirmed this view and regarded the slave as a chattel completely owned by the slave-owner. As far as the peasant serf was concerned, class oppression and dependence remained, but it was not considered that the feudal lord owned the peasants as chattels, but that he was only entitled to their labour, to the obligatory performance of certain services. . . .

Looking at South African society and the legal economic relations based on racial classification, one finds hidden behind the racist legal structure the need to cheapen African labor for capitalist exploitation; racial legislation stabilizes the relations of capital and labor. In South Africa racial laws are enacted as much in the immediate interest of the capitalist class as in the interest of White settler society in general. This harmony exists because of the mutual benefits the capitalist class and White settlers derive from African exploitation. There are carefully articulated barriers that institutionally exclude African, Indian, and Coloureds from full consumption of the products of their labor power and force on them a disproportionate share of the inequities of capitalism.

In South Africa there has developed a "distinctive parasitic" relation of White settler groups to what are called backward peoples. Oliver Cox (1964:195) in explaining capitalism as a world system writes: "Indeed the so-called backward peoples are the real exploited proletariat of the capitalist system."

The colonial wars of the nineteenth century in South Africa were not intended to "clean the lands" of the original inhabitants as happened in America. Actually, the colonial wars were a process that gave the White settlers both the best lands and a considerable measure of control over African labor. DeKiewiet (1966:180) writes, "The land wars were also labor wars. In other words, the natives lost free access to the land, but were permitted to draw sustenance from it as laborers, herdsmen, tenants or renters."

South Africa today lives within the tension of a historic contradiction: the presence of large numbers of the indigenous population in a country that the settlers meant to make their permanent home. Herein lies the content of the ideological instance of territorial apartheid that superficially seems to run counter to the economic system. Caught in the contradiction between wanting to exploit African labor but not wanting the physical presence of the African himself, the settlers evolved the apartheid system not merely as ideology but as myth that Whites have a prior claim to parts of South Africa. Accordingly, racism in South Africa can no longer be examined apart from the historical context of social development and the territorial claims that Whites make to a piece of South Africa's soil.

All previous attempts at conquest had pursued the aim of dominating and exploiting the country; none was aimed at robbing the people of their productive forces and destroying their social organization for the purpose of incorporating them as cheap units of labor to "eternity." When the British invested both men and capital, they meant to usurp African rights to their ancient land and to use them as cheap labor. In no time the blight of capitalist civilization succeeded in disrupting the entire social organization of the African people.

The structure of the state bequeathed to White settlers in South Africa by the British in 1910 was quite unique. It was projected within the structure of White minority power and adjusted to the requirements of cheap labor. British imperialism, in its heyday, developed a peculiar pattern of international relations with its colonies. The "White" dominions represented "colonial" settlements in the old Roman sense. In the British scheme of things these dominions were to be a set of economies dependent on and complementary to the British. Each would exchange the primary products for which its geographical situation fitted it: wool in Australia, meat and dairy products in New Zealand, wheat and beef in Canada, gold and diamonds in South Africa.

Behind the South African political economy in the last quarter of the nineteenth century lay a world order conforming to the dictates of a world economy dominated by Britain. Though South Africa's development has experienced some modifications, it was until recently conditioned to a large extent by the objective circumstances of its dependence on gold mining which was controlled by British imperialist interests. Among the things that need analysis are other industries in South Africa most deeply penetrated by foreign capital attracted by cheap African labor. To fail to consider how this hidden dimension of South African history forms the structure present racist reality is to ignore those forces that reinforce racism and inequality.

The gold mining industry, in terms of international capital behind it, clearly demonstrates the motive of the imperialist chain and the complex network of connections that sustains this industry, described by one writer (Green, 1968:58) as a "state within a state."

As financial backers of Cecil Rhodes, the Rothschilds were part of the very foundation of the South African mining industry, and they have remained so ever since. Around the Anglo-American Corporation, formed in 1917, have been such American corporations as Morgan Guarantee Trust and the Rockefeller interests. Every important South African company involved in nonferrous metals is penetrated by foreign capital, and the diamond industry is completely controlled by it through DeBeers, in which the Rothschilds also had a strong interest. The mining industry in South Africa sets the standard for the exploitation of African labor. This seemingly obvious history requires emphasis because South African race relations theory is cursed by the narrow focus of its assumptions: It usually focuses on the character of the Afrikaners and their historical experience rather than on the systemic aspects of imperialism that foster inequality and racism. Before Afrikaner racism acquired a structure and consciousness of itself, the social processes that it would take advantage of were already operating.

The point here is that the relations between White settlers and Africans took a definite and structural form during the last quarter of the nineteenth century. After a series of wars, Britain had total power over both Africans and Boer settlers (the latter whom she subjugated in the Anglo–Boer War of 1899–1902), and installed a White supremacist society for specific social and economic reasons.

The era of unchallenged British hegemony in South Africa saw many arbitrary acts imposed on the African people. The 1908 Constitution disposed of the African politically without his consent, like the trees and wildlife on a private estate. The British government, by agreeing to be a one-sided, racist political settlement, created institutional circumstances in which Whites tested the benefits of political power. Wittfogel (1957:101–102) observes that "under absolutist conditions, the holder of the strongest positions, benefiting from the cumulative tendency of unchecked power, tends to expand his authority through alliances, maneuvers, and ruthless schemes until, having conquered all other centers of supreme decision, he alone prevails."

The political developments in South Africa in the years since the Constitution have seen the development among Whites of a single quality—racist chauvinism at the expense of all other human qualities. White settler rule over Blacks has not been checked by any effective constitutional, societal, or cultural counterweight. The plundering of the African peoples by ill-concealed military means and by outright violence has continued, and no moral preaching has been of any avail. After South Africa secured its "independence" from Britain in 1910, no White political party, Boer or British, would extend franchise rights to the Africans. In fact, attempts were soon to be made to abolish even the qualified franchise for Africans in the Cape Province. First introduced in the middle of the nineteenth century, this franchise had been retained in 1910 as a constitutional fraud to hoodwink the world. In a confidential memo to General Jan Christiaan Smuts dated July 19, 1908, J. X. Merriman, then British agent on the scene, had made this Manichean comment:

> To me personally, the idea of a Native franchise is repellent but I am convinced that it is a safety-valve and the best safety-valve, and that so far from its leading to any immediate danger it will be generations before the European political supremacy will be menaced, while it does undoubtedly not only safeguard the rights of the inferior race but also gives them a content which puts an end to the poltical unrest that any unrepresented population always will have [Hancock and Van der Poel, 1966:448].

The political history of South Africa since 1910 has been an unending series of diminutions of African rights achieved by White settlers through constitutional maneuvers. It is a catalogue of racial laws that have institutionalized inequality and exploited African labor. In *Notebooks on Imperialism*, Lenin (1915–1916/1960:211) quoted Lincoln's remarkably frank words, "When the white man governs himself and also governs others, it is no longer self-government, it is despotism."

Perhaps the first step in formulating a theory of inequality and racism as it operates in South Africa is to recover some sense of the British legacy as a colonial power against which we can compare the thrust of contemporary development. Without some notion of what British imperialism left behind, we tend to lose perspective on how such a system developed. Deliberately structured by racial laws and socioeconomic arrangements and propelled by past and present exploitation, the system continues inexorably to reproduce racial inequality.

The practice of using Africans as cheap labor was openly encouraged by British representatives before 1910. For instance, in a speech on the use of African labor, Earl Grey, British Secretary of State for War and Colonies in the 1880s, told the mine owners of South Africa to dismiss from their minds the idea of developing their mines with White labor. Means had to be sought to induce the natives to spontaneously seek employment in the mines and to work willingly for long terms of more or less continuous service. In time, he predicted, the education of the "natives" would cause them to seek work to gratify those growing wants that were the certain result of increasing contact with civilization. Meanwhile, an incentive to laborers had to be provided by the imposition of a hut tax of at least £1, in conformity with the practice in Basutoland, and also of a small laborer tax, which those able-bodied natives should be required to pay who were unable to show a certificate of 4 months of work a year (cf. Hobson, 1900:234).

This was not just an isolated recommendation. In a memo to Smuts entitled "Notes on a Suggested Policy Towards Coloured People and Natives," Lord Selborne, High Commissioner for South Africa and Governor of the Transvaal and Orange River Colony from 1908 to 1910, spelled out his thinking on a political structure for the Union of South Africa that would ensure cheap labor:

> *Coloured people.* Our object should be to teach the Coloured people to give their loyal support to the white population. It seems to me sheer folly to classify them with Natives, and by treating them as Natives to force them away from their natural allegiance to the whites and into making common cause with the Natives. If they are so forced, in the time of trouble they will furnish exactly those leaders which the Natives could not furnish for themselves. It is, therefore, in my opinion, unwise to think of treating them as Natives; and it would be as unjust as unwise. There are many Coloured people who are quite white inside, though they may be coloured outside. There are some, indeed, who are quite white outside also. The problem of the treatment of the Coloured people is, indeed, sadly complicated by the fact that they vary in every shade of character and colour from pure white inside and outside to pure black inside and outside.
>
> I suggest that the wise policy is to give them the benefit of their white blood—not to lay the stress on the black blood, but to lay the stress on the white blood, and to make any differentiation of treatment between them and whites the exception and not the rule. A case for such differentiation would only arise when a coloured man showed by his manner of living, e.g., by the practice of polygamy, that he had reverted to the tribal type [Hancock and Van der Poel, 1966:375].

For the African, Lord Selborne recommended:

> *Natives.* The objects which the Government must have in view in their Native policy are:
>> (i) to preserve the peace of the country, for nothing is so demoralizing or injurious to its true welfare as a native war;
>> (ii) to promote the steady development of Christianity and civilization among the Natives,
>> (iii) to ensure the gradual destruction of the tribal system, which is incompatible with civilization.
>
> An important feature of this policy will be teaching the Natives to work. A large proportion of them do work now, but mostly in a desultory and inefficient manner. The object must be to teach them to work as continually and effectively as the whites are supposed to but do not always do [Hancock and Van der Poel, 1966:377].

These observations by Earl Grey and Lord Selborne reveal a callous disregard of African interests by British officials. Their recommendations were incorporated in the Union Constitution which was endorsed by the

British Parliament and determined the actions of almost all future South African governments. As a colonial metropolis, Britain was a "center of determination" for the South African social and economic structures affirmed in the Act of Union.

The racial Constitution agreed to by Britain in 1908 and the play on color differences concealed the needs of capitalist and imperialist to exploit cheap labor. The manner in which this need was to be met meant the creation of social relations, attitudes, and habits corresponding to those found in slave societies. The important point here is the process of social engineering that lay behind the disenfranchisement of the African rather than the racial attitudes that developed in the process. Once the exploitative capitalist structures had been installed, they continued to develop, accentuating their typical features. Perry Anderson (1964:400) has observed:

> Imperialism automatically sets up a premium on a patrician political style: as a pure system of alien domination, it always, within the limits of safety, seeks to *maximize the existential difference* between the ruling and the ruled race, to create a magical and impossible gulf between two fixed essences. This need everywhere produces a distinctive colonial ceremonial and a colonial Vice-regency. Domestic domination can be realized with a "popular" and "egalitarian" appearance, alien domination never.

The ideological argument for a White supremacist state was admirably summed up by Lord Selborne at a degree-giving day at the University of Cape Town in 1908. Typcially, Lord Selborne emphasized the unbridgeable difference between Africans and Whites:

> It is impossible for us, who once sprung from races which were in contact with the Roman Civilization before the Christian Era, to look to the question from the same point of view as the Bantu races who are totally different. So far as we can form an opinion, our forefathers, 2,000 years ago . . . were distinctly less barbarous than were the Bantu races when they came into contact with white men less than 100 years ago. Nor has the Bantu hitherto evinced any capacity from their first contact with it . . . . Speaking generally . . . so far as we can foresee, the Bantu can never catch up with the Europeans, whether in intellect or in strength of character. As a race, the white race has received a superior intellect and mental endowment. . . . The white man is the racial adult, the black man is the racial child.

Race and Class: An Analysis

Space limitations do not permit a further discussion of the role of Britain in creating racist structures in South Africa. Such a synopsis of the ideas of those who determined British policy in South Africa cannot possibly do justice to the processes that accrued from the structures they set up. Suffice it to say that imperialism was necessary and sufficient for the Anglo–Boer War which led to the formation of the Union of South Africa as a White-dominated state, but it also caused much racial hatred. That being said, it must, however, be pointed out that the British were able to establish their domination because of historical and other social circumstances. The elevation of all Whites into a racial aristocracy happened in the aftermath of conquest, when the Africans could only look back at a series of debacles and when it seemed that all other alternatives were futile. Even more important than this negative outlook, the society that had won the war (against both the Africans and Boers) was possessed of a most formidable battery of cultural symbols and weapons with which to justify its superiority and mystify its victims.

The structures of racial inequality in South Africa were a creation of men who systematically fashioned conditions that separated Blacks from Whites in order to exploit the former. The men who were the architects of the Constitution of the Union of South Africa directed that political, economic, and social power was to be the exclusive preserve of Europeans. Their decisions foreclosed the possibilities of building a nonracial society and fraternal cooperation between the races. No doubt, the latter would have required consummate patience and an abandonment of the peculiar nineteenth-century European assumption that Whites were the lords of creation, entitled to appropriate the resources and labor power of Black and Brown "races."

R. Hilferding (quoted in Sweezy, 1942:310) drew attention to the relations between colonialism, conquest, imperialism, and racism:

> Since the subordination of foreign nations proceeds by force, that is to say in a very natural way, it appears to the dominant nation that it owes its mastery to its special natural qualities, in other words to its racial characteristics. Thus in racial ideology there emerges a scientifically-cloaked foundation for the power lust of finance capital, which in this way demonstrates the cause and necessity of its operations. In place of the democratic ideal of equality there steps the oligarchical ideal of mastery.

Karl Liebknecht (1972:2-3) discussed how the monopolization of power and its use by the ruling class can be a decisive factor in mediating the politics of class oppression:

> The deciding factor in every social relation of power is, in the last resort, the superiority of physical force, which, as a social phenomenon, does not appear in the form of the greater physical strength of some individuals. . . . On an average, one human being equals another, and a purely numerical proportion decides who is in the majority. . . .
>
> Economic superiority helps directly to displace and to confuse the numerical proportion, because economic pressure not only influences the height of the intellectual and moral stage and, thereby, the recognition of class interest but also produces a tendency to act in conformity with more or less well understood class principles. *That the political machinery of the governing class lends its increased power to "correct" the numerical proportion in favor of the ruling group of interests is taught us by all the well-known institutions* such as: the police, justice, schools, and the church which must also be included here. These institutions are set up through the political machinery and employed in an administrative capacity. The first two work chiefly by threats, intimidation and violence; the schools chiefly by blocking up all those chan-

nels by which class-consciousness might reach the brain and the heart; the church most effectively by blinding the people to present evils and awakening their desire for the joys of a future life, and by terrifying them with threats of the torture chambers in hell [emphasis added].

Insofar as military power was inherited by the Whites only, they soon translated it into political and economic power, which has since emerged as a crucial factor in entrenching and mediating class and racial inequality. The inheritors of the colonial estate used this power to deprive Africans of the economic, political, and other cultural attributes that the Whites provided for themselves, creating a classic vicious circle. The oppressed "racial" groups and classes are denied the chances of development and growth and then cursed for being backward and primitive. The strength of South African racism rests on the monopoly of power in White hands and its use to deliberately foster inequalities between the various ethnic groups. As Africans make advances, the legislation of inequality assumes ever more dramatic, if ridiculous, dimensions. General Smuts, quoted in a biography by his son (1952:303), was refreshing in the bluntness with which he stated the problem facing Whites in South Africa:

Though the problem of mixed populations is not a new one in history, it nevertheless presents certain novel aspects in South Africa and the rest of the continent. Normally, it takes the form of a minority living in the midst of an overwhelming mass of other people, often under conditions of some disability. Here in South Africa, however, the small minority of whites lives not under the normal conditions of sufferance, but actually rule the majority with an iron hand. *They have retained in their possession full initiative insofar as tactical power and intellectual advantage is concerned and they have clung aggressively to what they consider their rights to wealth and leadership* [emphasis added].

The development of racism was not based on natural law but on given historical circumstances. The White settlers never created a sense of "legitimacy" but only exercised dominance. The tendency of power in such a situation (because it lacks "legitimacy") is to spread and occupy an ever larger place in society; the conjuncture of events and the struggles of the oppressed cause the rulers to create "security" behind a barrage of laws.

To put my thesis this way is to open myself to the charge that the power equation and nothing else is important. However, there are methodological and theoretical advantages to analyzing racial inequality in South Africa in terms of power in its various manifestations. Domination and coercion are the means whereby imperial capital violates and rapes those from whose labor it is derived. Racial laws are the means by which potentially violent class relations are contained and masked.

Fanon (1965:Chapter 1) demonstrated that a colonial society by its very nature functions because the colonists monopolize coercive violence, which facilitates the exploitation and submission of the colonized. The use of violence aims to keep the "native" enslaved and at arm's length; it seeks to dehumanize him.

No matter from what angle race inequality is observed, the usefulness of the theory of racial inferiority of those it brutalized was indispensable. Not only was racism useful for the superexploitation of Black labor but the social degradation of Blacks embodied in the inequities of social, political, and economic impoverishment made racism imperative.

In South Africa the form and shape of racial violence is further dictated by the numerical minority of White settlers, its purpose being to uphold the White order of society, to prop up the White minority state and its exploitative capitalist institutions against the struggle of the majority for freedom. The growing militarization of the state is directly related to the escalating class and national struggles of the African people. To the extent, then, that bourgeois theories of racial oppression neglect or minimize the role of violence in the exploitation and oppression of the African, they must be judged inadequate.

Between the White settlers as a conquering and ruling national class and the Africans as a conquered national class, there exist fundamental national and class conflicts. The basis of the conflicts is not race but results from the violation of the national integrity of the Africans and their class oppression. The Africans are faced with a brute fact: monopoly of power in its various forms in the hands of the settler minority, which is supported by the world imperialist system. The seriousness of the South African situation results from the conflicting claims to land and the means of production by Africans and White settlers. How the war will be resolved between the two groups claiming the same territory and bound together so intimately in the capitalist economy is a question of far-reaching theoretical and practical interest.

The struggle between Black and White is a conflict to the finish. Its dimensions are of more than local and historical significance, for they stem from the fact that many of the corporations that control the commanding heights of the American, British, European, and Japanese economies are also predominant in South Africa. Therefore, the national and class warfare in South Africa is the great class struggle raging in the world before our eyes.

South African society has posed a theoretical challenge to those social scientists interested in racial inequality. For some, the challenge appears to be that of identifying a key factor between race and class; some seek out the underlying causes of racism. For some, no one "factor" predominates over any other; "live and let live" is supposed to play its part. For other individuals, the issue seems to be one of showing in correct order and sufficient detail the sequence of events that have led to the present state of affairs. For others, the issue is one of nomenclature, that is, of finding a suprahistorical category that supposedly catches, as in a snapshot, the structual relationships of South African society. For still others, the problem is one of exhaustive description of every fact and every event. And for a final group, the problem is a "moral dilemma" that urgently cries out for some sort of solution without apportioning blame.

In the study of racist inequality, especially in a capitalist society, the task of social inquiry is to disclose historical facts not directly perceived; that is, social theory must contribute to an identification of the basic stages of the development of the structures of race inequality within the continuum of capitalist evolution; it must explain the specific ways in which racism has been used in this socioeconomic formation. For most bourgeois social scientists, it is the ideological assertions and cultural aspects of the problems of race that have claimed the most attention.

Alternatively, social scientists substitute merely a description of the facts of racial inequality for a theory of racism. And that is totally unscientific. It is essential to understand how ideological racism emerges, both from the economic uses of the labor power of the oppressed and from the need to justify oppression even as it reacts upon and helps determine its precise form.

South African society is a living organism in a state of constant development. Only an historical explanation can produce a verifiable theory capable of encompassing the dynamics of racial conflict. Racism is not abstractions, nor is it its own justification. Anyone who wants to change the structure of racial oppression must understand its fundamental nature, its historical formation, and its manipulation by the rulers. That is, the correct view of ruling class practice should constitute the point of departure for a theory of racism.

The problem of racism in South Africa is not one of simple cultural differences between groups but arises from the fact that Africans are exploited, enslaved, and despised by Whites. This condition makes easier their exploitation by a capitalist society. Racial oppression and class exploitation are inextricably intertwined in the modern world; they cannot be neatly separated as some have done for the sake of theoretical purity.

Fundamental analysis must grasp the dialectics between race and class as historical configurations. In the study of racism we must seek its foundation and not select symptoms and phases of manifestation casually and superficially, as it suits our ideological predisposition. For this reason we need a concept that is grounded in history and capable of grasping the dynamics of capitalist oppression in all its nuances. The concept of class is useful not because it is "true" but because it correctly identifies the basis of exploitation in the development of capitalist society. The concept of class directs scientific inquiry to the fundamental of racism as an instrument for extracting surplus value and keeping working people divided.

Conclusions

The fundamental feature that produces the problems we encounter in South Africa and is, accordingly, critical to our conception of that society as a distinctive social order is its capitalistic economy and the fact that Whites are a settler society. Though the divisions in South Africa appear superficially to be racial in form, the economic content of its racism is characteristic of all capitalist and settler societies, namely, that one class or else a coalition of classes with some common interest constitutes the dominant class or classes and stands in partial or complete antagonism to the nonpossessing classes. This is true for South Africa whether we look at land ownership, ownership of industry and commerce, or the distribution of income between Black and White. What is happening in Ireland should suffice as an example in Europe.

The maldistribution of wealth and power between White and Black imposed a political system that enhanced the interest of the former, since the coalition of classes that are socially and politically dominant use their power to preserve and extend the mode of production on which their income depends. The economic relations between Black and White are fundamental arrangements that constitute class conflict, national oppression, and struggle. Although for the White rulers the African exists only as a labor power, the White workers consider the African (rightly or wrongly) a threat to their economic security that is partly derived from and guaranteed by the superexploitation of the African.

Capitalism was responsible for the exploitation of the African, not because he was of a different "race" but because capitalism placed him in a peculiar economic situation. Racism as a formal ideological system had to be cultivated by the politically conscious classes to subvert class unity between Black and White labor. It is thus clear that the sequence of motivation has been predominantly from the system to society and the individual: The internal societal and political organization seems to depend upon demands and imperatives arising chiefly from a play of circumstances peculiar to the capitalist system.

Since their violent incorporation within the expanding capitalist–imperialist system, African societies suffered what can be called the calamity of an epoch. They fell into a condition of "forced retardation," both in the development of their technological skills and in the satisfaction of their social needs, such as food, shelter, and education.

References

Anderson, Perry
    1964   The Origins of the Present Crisis. New Left Review, No. 23.
Bennett, Lerone, Jr.
    1975   The Shaping of Black America. Chicago: Johnson Publishing Company.
Cox, Oliver C.
    1964   Capitalism as a System. New York: Monthly Review Press.
DeKiewiet, C. W. D.
    1966   A History of South Africa, Social and Economic. London: Oxford University Press.
DuBois, W. E. B.
    1962   Black Reconstruction in America 1860–1880. New York: Russell & Russell Publishers.
            (First ed. 1935.)
    1970   The Negro. New York: Oxford University Press. (First ed. 1915.)

Fanon, Frantz
    1965   The Wretched of the Earth. New York: Grove Press.
Friedman, Julian R.
    1977-78   Basic Facts on the Republic of South Africa and the Policy of Apartheid. Objective:
              Justice. New York: United Nations Office of Public Information. Vol. 9, No. 4.
Green, Timothy
    1968   The World of Gold. New York: Walker.
Hancock, W. K., and Jean Van der Poel, eds.
    1966   Selections from the Smuts Papers, Vol. II. Cambridge: Cambridge University Press.
Hobson, J. A.
    1900   The War in South Africa. London: Nisbet.
    1965   Imperialism: A Study. Ann Arbor: University of Michigan Press. (First ed. 1902.)
Hubbard, H. J. M.
    1968   Race and Guyana: The Anatomy of a Colonial Enterprise. Georgetown, Guyana:
           H. J. M. Hubbard.
Kautsky, Karl
    1972   Are the Jews a Race? Westport, Connecticut: Greenwood Press. (First ed. 1926.)
Lenin, V. I.
    1960   Notebooks on Imperialism. In Collected Works, Vol. 39. Pp. 27-768. Moscow: Progress
           Publishers. (First ed. 1915-1916.)
    1969   Imperialism, the Highest Stage of Capitalism. Moscow: Foreign Language Press. (First
           ed. 1917.)
    1972   Marx, Engles, Lenin: On Historical Materialism. Moscow: Progress Publishers.
Liebknecht, Karl
    1972   Militarism and Anti-Militarism. New York: Dover Publications.
Magdoff, Harry
    1972   Imperialism without Colonies. In Studies in the Theory of Imperialism. Roger Owen and
           Bob Sutcliffe, eds. Pp. 144-170. London: Longman.
Marx, Karl
    1971   The Grundrisse. David McLellan, ed. New York: Harper & Row. (First ed. 1857-1858.)
Mills, C. Wright
    1959   The Sociological Imagination. New York: Oxford University Press.
Omvedt, Gail
    1973   Toward a Theory of Colonialism. Insurgent Sociologist 3(3):1-24.
Ruchames, Louis
    1969   Introduction: The Sources of Racial Thought in Colonial America. In Racial Thought in
           America. Vol. I. Louis Ruchames, ed. Pp. 1-23. Amherst, Massachusetts: University of
           Massachusetts Press.
Smuts, J. C.
    1952   Jan Christian Smuts. London: Cassel.
Sweezy, Paul M.
    1942   The Theory of Capitalist Development. New York: Monthly Review Press.
Thierry, Augustin
    1869   History of the Conquest of England by the Normans, Vol. I. London: Bell and Daldy.
           (First ed. 1825.)
Wittfogel, Karl A.
    1957   Oriental Despotism: A Comparative Study of Total Power. New Haven: Yale University
           Press.

13

JOHN U. OGBU

Education, Clientage, and Social Mobility: Caste and Social Change in the United States and Nigeria[1]

Social mobility—the movement of groups or persons between ranked positions—is a major concern of students of social stratification. Most often we focus narrowly at the societal level on *rates* or *amounts* of mobility and at the individual level on *distances* between status positions into which people were born and those which they attain. Our emphasis on rates and distances is motivated partly by our concern for the degree of "openness" of different types of societies. Essentially we want to know how structural and normative features of societies affect the amount of upward and downard mobility. From this point of view, our research results to date are disappointing: Studies of generations of humans within hierarchies defined in terms of occupational prestige indicate that there are no major differences in rates of mobility among contemporary nation-states. Furthermore, there appear to have been no marked differences in rates of mobility *within* individual societies in the last 40 or 50 years. (See Coxon and Jones, 1975:7–8; Duberman, 1976:96–97; Kraus, 1976:32; Muller and Mayer, 1973:7–8; Tumin, 1970:294.)

Major differences in rates of social mobility are found, however, when we compare different groups within a single society, such as Blacks and Whites in the United States. Here a large occupational gap remains when we compare Blacks and Whites with similar schooling and family background (Duncan, 1975; Duncan and Blau, 1967; HEW 1969; Newman *et al.*, 1978; Rogoff, 1953; Rossi and Ornstein, 1973; U.S. Commission on Civil Rights,

[1]This paper is based on research supported financially by Faculty Research Funds, University of California, Berkeley; and NIMH Research Grant 1-RO3-MH25130-01.

1978). Our most common explanation of these discrepancies is racial discrimination in the labor market. This is, for example, the position of the U.S. Department of Health, Education and Welfare, which concludes that the discrepancy "is surely attributable in part to racial discrimination in hiring, promotion, and other job-related opportunities [HEW, 1969:25]."

The consequences of racial discrimination are, however, not confined to lower rates of social mobility. Of equal importance is its influence on the strategies of mobility developed by Blacks. My study of both historical and contemporary economic, political, and social "realities" of Black Americans indicates that, faced with barriers against effective use of conventional strategies for status mobility, they developed a number of supplementary or alternative strategies for "survival' and self-advancement. Among these strategies are collective struggle (Newman, 1978; J. W. Scott, 1976), clientage (Drake and Cayton, 1970; Powdermaker, 1939/1968), "hustling" (Haley, 1966; Heard, 1968; Milner and Milner, 1976; Valentine, 1978), "passing" (Burma, 1946; Eckard, 1947; Warner, et al. 1941), and mutual exchange (Stack, 1974). *Alternative stategies for social mobility* are an important tactic that Black Americans share with other subordinate groups similarly faced with limited effective use of their society's conventional strategies (Adams and Laurikietis, 1977; Epstein, 1971; Sjoberg, 1960; Whitaker, 1973).

Not all strategies developed by members of a subordinate group lead to status positions valued by the dominant group. In this chapter I am concerned with those strategies that do and on their interaction with the conventional strategies of the society in general. Specifically, I shall focus on one such alternative strategy among Black Americans—*clientage.* I shall argue that clientage emerged as an alternative or supplementary strategy to White conventional strategy. Although its role was diffuse at first, clientage subsequently became the *additional qualification* required of Blacks when educational credentials crystalized as the society's main institutionalized strategy for job placement and remuneration. I shall further argue that although in the early phase of Black–White interaction, clientage was more important than educational credentials for Black occupational placement and remuneration, a number of forces—among them pressures from civil rights groups, civil rights legislation, executive orders, court enforcement of anti-discrimination laws—have acted to modify the relative roles of clientage and education. I hypothesize that because of changes in the type and role of clientage since the early 1960s, educational credentials are becoming the primary criterion or strategy for Black occupational placement and remuneration; and that if this development continues, Blacks and Whites will eventually be participating in one status mobility system dominated by a single institutionalized strategy—educational credentials—a situation that will eliminate the social mobility gap between the two racial groups. Toward the end of the chapter I shall describe how similar changes in institutionalized mobility strategies occurred among the Igbo caste groups in Nigeria, and I shall hypothesize about the possible long-term effects of this change.

In addition to being preoccupied with rates to the neglect of strategies of social mobility, current approaches have the following shortcomings: They do not pay sufficient attention to the multiple nature of stratification systems in contemporary societies like the United States. They ignore, that is, the coexistence of stratification systems based on socioeconomic status, race/caste, and gender, a situation that should warn us against trying to fit everyone's status position into a single mobility model. Since there appears to be some ideological resistance to recognizing the multiple nature of the stratification system (Maquet, 1970), I shall begin by distinguishing those factors that affect Blacks and their status mobility, namely caste and class.

Caste and Class Stratification in the United States

In the opinion of some scholars, the overall position of Blacks in the United States approximates that of a caste group and the United States should therefore by studied as stratified both by class and racial castes (Berreman, 1960, 1967; Davis, Gardner, and Gardner, 1941/1965; Dollard, 1937/1957; Myrdal, 1944; Warner, 1936; Warner et al., 1970). Others, however, reject this suggestion partly on the assumption that caste is a phenomenon unique to the Indian subcontinent and partly because of an assimilationist ideology (Cox, 1945; Dumont, 1961; Johnson, 1966). Ethnographic and historical evidence seems to overwhelmingly support the class–caste model. Berreman (1960, 1967:295–304) has amply shown that features often said to be unique to India are also found elsewhere, including the United States. Every careful historical analysis of the structural position of American Blacks shows that they do not become "assimilated" into the dominant White group as do White immigrants. The dividing line between the two racial groups, as Myrdal pointed out long ago, is permanent even though the relationship between them has been changing, especially in recent decades (Myrdal, 1944:668, 675; see also Bullock, 1970; Katzman, 1973; Thernstrom, 1973).

Black–White stratification in the United States satisfies Berreman's definition of a caste system as a hierarchy of endogamous groups whose membership is determined permanently at birth (Berreman, 1967:279). The basis of rankng the White caste as superior and the Black caste as inferior is skin color or socially defined race. As Berreman adds, however, to say that American society has a caste stratification, like India, does not mean that the American caste system is the same as the Indian caste system. Similarly, to say that modern Nigeria, like American society, is stratified by class does not mean that the Nigerian class system is the same as that of the United States. In this chapter I am using class and caste simply as analytical categories with which to study similar features characteristic of two different societies (see Maquet, 1970:94; Myrdal, 1944).

Caste stratification is often said to differ from class stratification because it permits *no individual vertical social mobility*. This is not necessarily true, especially for modern caste societies in which caste groups may be internally stratified by class. However, caste stratification does affect the strategies, distances, and rates of social mobility in the component castes. Perhaps noting a few points of differences between class and caste stratification will aid our subsequent discussion of the impact of caste stratification on mobility strategies.

One distinguishing feature of class stratification is that it is based on economic relations, whereas caste stratification is based on what Weber calls "status honor" (Weber, 1946, cited in Berreman, 1977:12). Another is that attributes (such as education, occupation, income, marriage, and so on) that determine a person's class position can be acquired during the individual's lifetime, but caste membership cannot be so acquired. Thus, individual mobility between strata is characteristic of a class but not caste system. Such mobility occurs *within* the caste groups internally stratified by class. Intercaste mobility can, of course, occur through the painful process of "passing" but it is rare. Berreman has also suggested two other features that distinguish class stratification in modern industrial societies, namely, low status summation and low class consciousness (Berreman, 1977). By low status summation is meant that people's social, political, and occupational roles are primarily determined by their training and ability, not by their classes of origin. By low class consciousness is meant that members of a given social class do not necessarily perceive themselves as a people subject to similar collective experience. For example, lower-class Americans usually do not blame the economic system but rather their individual selves or luck for their failure to achieve self-betterment. Subordinate castes like Black Americans, in contrast, traditionally have a high status summation that contributes to their highly developed caste consciousness and "system-blaming" attitudes.

As already noted, Black and White castes are internally stratified by class. But their class systems are not equal because the two groups do not have equal access to education, jobs, income, and other resources that facilitate class mobility (see pp. 281–282). Moreover, the institutionalized strategies for obtaining available resources are not the same, since lower castes do not often control the resources associated with social differentiation and mobility within their own class system. The consequence of this situation is that similar class positions in the White and Black castes are not products of the same circumstances: A White person who is lower class is lower class by virtue of his or her attained education, job, income, and the like. But a Black person who is lower class is also a member of a subordinate caste whose education, occupation, income and other resources may have been limited by prior existing caste barriers. In order to overcome the prior existing barriers he or she requires at least one additional strategy or "qualification," namely the sponsorship of a White patron or *clientage*.

Job Ceiling and Unequal Status Systems

The term *status* refers to a position that entitles its incumbent to certain rewards and that demands of him or her certain ways of behaving. The statuses of a society must be ranked if social mobility is to take place, and these rankings constitute a system of social rewards for certain behaviors (LeVine, 1967:17).

The social goods that make up the content of the status system of modern societies include political power, occupation, wealth, prestige, and privilege. Conventional studies of social mobility usually focus on occupation as the most important social good partly because it provides the best access to other forms of social goods, and partly because it is the easiest to measure quantitatively and qualitatively (Duberman, 1976:100; Hodges, 1964:248; S.M. Miller, 1960:4–6). Fallers (1964:118–119) and H.P. Miller (1971:18) both say that occupation plays the primary role in determining a person's position in the American status system. Fallers (p. 119) adds that the study of American social stratification and social mobility is essentially the study of the ranking of occupations.

If occupation is the chief determinant of social status, we can use the concept of a *job ceiling* to describe unequal status systems of Blacks and Whites. That there is a job ceiling against Blacks means that they are not permitted to compete freely as individuals for any types of jobs to which they aspire and for which they possess the qualifications considered sufficient for other members of society; they are prevented from obtaining their proportional share of the more desirable jobs where education is a prerequisite; and they are, as a result, over-represented in menial jobs.

In the current job classification in the United States, the professional, technical, office, proprietory, clerical, sales, and skilled jobs are the jobs *above the job ceiling*. These constitute, in American cultural idiom, the most desirable jobs in terms of wages, social prestige, and the like. *Below the job ceiling* and associated with lower wages and less social prestige are semiskilled operative work, personal and domestic service, and various forms of laboring jobs.

The job ceiling against Blacks was at first very low. For example, at the beginning of the twentieth century about the only places Blacks could secure jobs above the job ceiling were in the segregated Black communities and in public institutions such as hospitals and schools. Here there were opportunities for a limited number of workers in entrepreneurial, religious, literary, entertainment, and professional activities. The pool of jobs above the job ceiling was also increased by the growth of urban ghettos in the North and South (A. M. Ross, 1967).

Three other factors have also contributed to the increase in the pool of jobs above the job ceiling since the beginning of the century. One is the periodic occurrence of labor shortages in the wider society due to war and other national crises. Such was the case during the economic growth of 1900–1908, the restriction of immigrant labor between 1922 and 1929, and World War I, World War II, the Korean War, and the Vietnam War.

Another factor in raising the job ceiling has been the pressure from civil rights groups that, since the 1920s has forced many private businesses and public agencies to hire Blacks in many jobs previously closed to them. Civil rights activities have also forced some local and state governments in the North and the federal government to use their legislative and executive powers to encourage or force public and private employment of Blacks and similar minorities in the coveted positions above the job ceiling. The courts, too, have contributed to the raising of the job ceiling by upholding the laws against discrimination in employment, promotion, and wages (Adams, 1972; Burkey, 1971; Huff, 1974; National Advisory Commission on Civil Disorders, 1968).

Status Mobility Strategies

EDUCATION

Conventional studies of mobility usually focus on education as the primary institutionalized strategy or channel of social mobility in terms of occupational status. The importance of family background is also recognized, as it directly affects occupational placement and indirectly affects it through education. Other factors like motivation and ability (the latter as measured IQ) are often discussed with regard to their influence on educational attainment (Crockett, 1966: Duncan and Blau, 1967; HEW, 1969; Muller and Mayer, 1973).

Formal education is closely linked to occupation, and hence to social mobility, in two ways. First, occupations, especially the technical, specialized, and generally high-level ones, require some knowledge, skills, and other personal attributes that are acquired through formal schooling. It is possible to acquire such knowledge, skills, and attributes in other settings, but present-day social, political, and economic realities make it virtually certain that most people will acquire them in school. To suggest that this kind of technical linkage exists does not mean that there is a one-to-one relationship between school training and ability to perform specific jobs; it is rather that formal education equips people with the minimum competence and commitment required by various modern occupations, which then may or may not require further specialized training. As Parsons puts it, the experience of schooling in the United States is like "a series of apprenticeships for adult occupational roles [1964:240, cited in Heller, 1969:225]." See also Kraus, 1973:30; Wilson, 1973:233.

The second way in which formal education is linked to occupation lies in the role of *educational credentials as an institutionalized device* for placing and remunerating individuals in various occupations. Some societies may conceivably prefer to allocate jobs and wages or to promote people on the basis of kinship relation, religious faith, or party loyalty, but in America as in most modern societies educational credentials serve the same purpose. Credentials for role allocation and remuneration for job performance, whether based on kinship, religious faith, political party, or education, are a matter of cultural definition and do not necessarily reflect the ability of particular individuals to perform the jobs allocated to them. The point to be emphasized is that the institutionalized device or strategy for occupational placement and remuneration should not be confused with technical competence for job performance (Collins, 1977; Jencks, 1972; McClelland, 1973).

Studies have documented the primary role of educational credentials in facilitating or impeding social mobility (Duberman, 1976; Duncan and Hodges, 1963:629–644; Fox and Miller, 1966:76–93; Heller, 1969:313–314; Hodges, 1964:259; Kraus, 1976:50). However, as I noted earlier, these certificates are less effective for Blacks than for Whites in America. When we compare Blacks and Whites who have similar education and similar family background, Blacks generally do not attain the same occupational status or receive the same wages as their White counterparts. Moreover, Blacks at any given class level desire at least as much education and social mobility as their White peers, but as a group they fail to achieve the same educational credentials as Whites. These differences in occupational and educational attainments are not merely due to differences in social mobility values and family background or to labor market discrimination; they remain even where many of these conditions are equal (Banks and McQuater, 1976). Rather, they are due in part to the operation of another institutionalized device—patron–client sponsorship for social mobility—which is characteristic of Blacks but not of Whites.

CLIENTAGE

Turner (1960) has suggested that some form of sponsorship traditionally functioned as an institutionalized device for social mobility in England and as an noninstitutionalized device in the United States. He notes, for example, that mobility into elite status in England is essentially through sponsorship, that the ideology underlying the English class system requires that existing elites grant elite status to some people not born into it but with the potential for achieving it. The potential elites are selected very early in their school career, given suitable training, and then admitted to full elite status. Turner contrasts this with the American class system in which he sees social mobility achieved through open contest. The American system espouses the ideology that everyone has the potential for elite status and can achieve it if only he or she has the proper motivation, perserverance, and training. Consequently, he says, future elites are not preselected but qualify for available elite positions through academic competitions. The winners of the school contest go on to become winners of the available elite positions in postschool society.

Heller (1969:314) suggests that coexisiting with the competition for academic credentials in the United States is a noninstitutionalized form of sponsorship known as "contact." The use of contact for moving up in the American status system is widely recognized and is known to work against members of the lower class who complain that what matters is not what you know (as reflected in your educational credentials and skills) but who you know.

Basically, English sponsorship elevates sponsorees to the same status as their sponsors; the American contact sponsorship sets no limits to the status attainable by the sponsorees. In contrast to both, a third type of sponsorship, based on patron–client relationship or *clientage*, expresses or reaffirms the subordinate status of the sponsoree or client and is not intended to raise him or her to the same status as the patron sponsor. In fact, sponsorship based on clientage may downplay the importance of educational credentials, which are stressed in the other forms of sponsorship.

The model of patron–client dyadic contract was initially employed by Foster (1961, 1963, 1967) to describe the processes of social organization in Tzintzuntzan, a Mexican peasant village. According to Foster (1967:217), clientage binds people of significantly unequal socioeconomic statuses or power control who, therefore, are obligated to exchange different kinds of goods and services. This model has proved analytically useful in studying feudal-like societies (Cohen, 1965, 1970; Maquet, 1970, 1971), semiurban communities (Whitten, 1965), and complex societies (Wolf, 1966), as well as in studying political processes in peasant societies (Powell, 1970) and in modernizing societies (Lemarchand, 1972; J.C. Scott, 1972). More recently Legg (1976) has suggested that the model can be used to study political processes in advanced industrial societies.

In an earlier work (Ogbu, 1974:54–58) I also suggested that patron–client dyadic contracts exist in modern industrial societies like the United States. I then attempted to show how patron–client relationships between primarily White teachers on the one hand and Black and Mexican–American parents and pupils on the other form the basis of interaction between low-income neighborhood residents and those of more affluent sections of the same city. My examination of the literature on Black–White relations in the United States and further reflection since I made this suggestion lead me to think that there are probably three variants or phases of clientage relevant to the experiences of Black Americans. I will designate the type of clientage described by Foster, which characterized Black–White relationships at the beginning of the twentieth century, as *classic clientage*. This bond later underwent significant changes, producing what I call *situational clientage*. Further changes in the system have occurred, especially since the 1960s, producing yet another variant, *collective clientage*. All three types coexist today but vary in degree of effectiveness as well as by geographical region and rural–urban location.

   Classic clientage dates back to the period of slavery. In many a plantation with a resident master there developed a close relationship between the master and his domestic slaves in which he exercised a fatherly responsibility toward the slaves, and the slaves reciprocated with filial loyalty and submission. This type of relationship came to be symbolized by the fictional affectionate and loyal character, Tom of Harriet Beecher Stowe's novel, *Uncle Tom's Cabin* (Ladenburg and McFeely, 1969:11; see also van den Berghe, 1967:81; Dollard, 1937/1957:387; Drake and Cayton, 1970:67; McCarthy and Yancey, 1973: 46–47; Powdermaker, 1939/1968:325).

   After emancipation the master–slave dyadic relationship in the South was transformed into a dyadic contractual relationship between White planters and Black tenant farmers. It was eventually extended to relationships between Blacks and Whites in general, especially after Reconstruction (1865–1877), when a new ruling White group emerged and used legal and extralegal mechanisms to disqualify Blacks from economic, political, and social participation on an equal basis with Whites (Bond, 1966; Tindall, 1949; Woodward, 1951). For Blacks clientage inevitably became the alternative channel to subsistence and economic advancement, to political influence and legal protection, and to social influence and community leadership (Dollard, 1957).

   Our best documentation of classic clientage comes from a number of ethnographic studies of rural and small urban communities in the South in the late 1920s and early 1930s (see Davis, Gardner, and Gardner, 1941/1965; Dollard, 1937/1957; Johnson, 1941; Powdermaker, 1939/1968; Raper 1929). There was then a break in the ethnographic studies until Hylian Lewis' (1954) study of another small Southern town, Kent, in 1948–1949. That, unfortunately, seems to be the last good ethnography of this phenomenon in the South. In the North ethnographic studies of Black–White relationships are rare. One exception was the study of Blacks in Chicago in the late 1930s and early 1940s by Drake and Cayton (1945/1970), and another was the study of the Black and White residents of a small town in Connecticut by Lee (1961) in the early 1950s. These two constitute the best ethnographies of the clientage system in the North. Nevertheless, there are references to the clientage system in the North and South in many published sources from the beginning of the twentieth century to the present. The following general outline of the patron–client relationship in both sections is based on the available ethnographic evidence and nonethnographic data.

   Terminologies varied from community to community, but White

members of the dyadic relationships were called "patrons," "angels," or simply "good white folks" (Davis, Gardner, and Gardner, 1941/1965:239; Dollard, 1937/1957:212; Johnson, 1941). Black clients were called "good niggers" by Whites, and were called by Blacks "the white man's niggers," "bad niggers," or "Uncle Toms" (Davis, Gardner, and Gardner, 1941/1965:23, 323; Dollard, 1937/1957:212; Drake and Cayton, 1970:67; Johnson, 1941:280; 1943:27; Lewis, 1954:252; Myrdal, 1944:678, 682; Powdermaker, 1939/ 1968:338). As is often the case in a society with this principle of social organization, not all potential patrons and clients were involved in dyadic contracts, but only those who desired to be. However, those who openly rejected the system were regarded as deviants, especially by the Whites. A White person who did not abide by the rules and tried to "fraternize" with Blacks was called a "nigger lover" and punished socially and economically (Myrdal, 1944:678). A Black who ignored the clientage rules was called a "bad nigger" or "uppity nigger" and was subjected to varying forms of harsh treatment (Davis, Gardner, and Gardner, 1941/1965; Myrdal, 1944; Powdermaker, 1939/1968).

The White patrons came primarily from the upper class and to a lesser extent from the middle class. Upper-class Whites wanted Black clients as a symbol of their aristocratic status and as a source of cheap labor. Middle-class Whites acquired Black clients as a means of easing their mobility into aristocratic status as well as a source of cheap labor. In return White patrons provided their clients with political and legal protection, with subsistence and other economic assistance, and with aid in times of personal and family crises (Davis, Gardner, and Gardner, 1941/1965:239, 273; Dollard, 1937/1957:212; Myrdal, 1944:591–93). The majority of the Black clients were from the lower class which, at the time, included most Blacks. But many clients also come from the middle and upper classes because they, too, depended on Whites for personal economic protection, such as in getting a loan from a bank, purchasing and retaining land and houses, and securing coveted positions in segregated public institutions controlled by Whites; for legal and political protection; and for financial support for development projects in Black communities, such as building and improving schools (Davis, Gardner, and Gardner, 1941/1965:273; Dollard, 1937/1957:262–263; Frazier, 1940:41; Myrdal, 1944:594; Powdermaker, 1939/1968:339).

Hylian Lewis's study of Kent, a pseudonym for a Southern town of 4000, indicates that the classic patron–client relationship continued to exist in the late 1940s. In Kent Whites controlled the political and economic resources and Blacks were forced to use informal and personalized relationships (clientage) as a channel to social, economic, and political advancements (Lewis, 1954:300–303). Whites saw Kent as a community with many "good niggers" or Black clients and many "good white folks" or White patrons. Blacks and Whites were said to have vested interests in maintaining the system. Although Lewis reports that he knew of no Blacks in Kent who were specifically called "Uncle Tom," a term widely used for Black clients, he also says that Blacks in

Kent recognized "Uncle Tomming" as a type of behavior and frequently referred to "Tomming" and "Charley-ing" around White people (p. 252). He explains that the absence of the individuals specifically designated as "Uncle Toms" was due either to the fact that local Blacks regarded "chronic 'white folks niggers'" (i.e., overzealous clients) as "deviants" or to the fact that every Black person in Kent had had at one time or another to "Uncle Tom" in order to survive. "In the latter case," he adds, "the obsequious or deferential behaviors to whites [would be] looked upon as a segmental [i.e., simulated] character rather than a dominant trait [p. 252n]." Even educated Blacks did not often escape clientage because their options were very limited. Many eventually capitulated to the system; often they used it pretentiously for personal or communal advancement (Dollard, 1957:263). This type of clientage continues to exist in the South, although it is decreasing in frequency and effectiveness (Poussaint and Atkinson, 1973:173).

As has been noted, ethnographic documentation of classic clientage in the North is an exception, though the relationship has existed there to a lesser degree than in the South. Even in the 1950s, Lee (1961:49–50, 98–100) found a widespread paternalism based on clientage in "Connecticut Town." The Whites there expressed this paternalism by saying that "things are done for them [i.e., Blacks] and they are helped when they need help [p. 98]." The paternalism extended to areas of employment, housing, social relations, and community projects. My own fieldwork in Stockton, California, in the late 1960s revealed the same kind of paternalism, including that in politics and the schools (Ogbu, 1974:54–58; see also Drake and Cayton, 1970; Farmer, 1968; Myrdal, 1944; Poussaint and Atkinson, 1973). "Uncle Tom" and "Mr. Charley" are terms more commonly used in the North to refer to Black clients and White patrons, respectively.

Black motives for entering clientage are the same in the North as in the South: in both regions Blacks depend on Whites for employment, wages, promotion, and the like and do not qualify for these rewards simply by possessing educational credentials judged sufficient for Whites (Drake and Cayton, 1970:387; Lee, 1961; Ogbu, 1974:55–58). The motives of Northern Whites seem to differ from those of Southern Whites in that the former do not enter clientage to enhance or validate their claims to aristocratic status. However, having Blacks in the client role expressing deferential and humble behavior confers on Whites of both regions a sense of status elevation. Furthermore, White employers and corporations derive cheap labor from the clientage, and White workers gain through greater chances for hiring and promotion under controlled competition from Blacks (see Adams, 1972; Perlo, 1975). A major difference between Northern and Southern clientage is that Northern clientage more frequently occurs on an ad hoc basis; the enactment is often *situational.* As Drake and Cayton (1970:387) describe it, in Chicago

> [if] working as servants [blacks] must be properly deferential to the white people upon whom they depend for meager wages and tips. In fact, they often have to overdo their act in order to earn a living; as they phrase it, they have to "Uncle Tom to Mr.

Charley" a bit more to survive. If they work in a factory, they must take orders from a
white managerial personnel and associate with white workers who, they know, do not
accept them as social equals.

This shift toward ad hoc or *situational clientage* indicates one of two fundamental changes that have occurred in the system. Even in the South the clientage has increasingly become situational with increasing urbanization and other forms of social change. In both North and South, situational clientage or "Uncle Tomming" is more common today than the classic clientage, particularly in the cities. The other important change that has occurred in clientage is the tendency for the government, especially the federal government, to assume the role of patron for the entire Black population, resulting in a sort of *collective clientage.*

The importance of the federal government as a collective patron can be seen in its role as an employer (including having a disproportionate number of Blacks in its armed forces), a sponsor of educational and other training programs, an advisor and protector of civil rights, and a distributor of subsistence assistance known as "welfare." Black dependence on the government not only for subsistence but for social mobility in the form of occupational mobility shows up in the changes that have taken place in the job ceiling since the 1960s because of extraordinary government supports. Between 1960 and the early 1970s, the number of Blacks employed in professional and technical jobs increased by 128%, although for the general population the increase was 49%. In the second highest-paying job category, namely, among managers, officials, and proprietors, the number of Blacks rose in the same period by nearly 100%, while for the general population the increase was only 23%. Most Black increases resulted from public and private affirmative action programs instituted from 1966, the year that Title VII of the Civil Rights Act of 1964 became law.

Several forces contributed to the breakdown of classic clientage and the emergence of the situational and collective forms. One was formal education, which taught Black people the American ideal of allocating social rewards or statuses on the basis of ability and training. This kind of teaching undermined the ideology of classic clientage, which stressed the importance of deferential behavior for the allocation of the same rewards. Therefore, as more and more Blacks became educated they rejected the clientage system, demanding to be evaluated and rewarded on the same basis as Whites (Dollard, 1937/1957:201; Johnson, 1941:281; Myrdal, 1944:596).

One option which became increasingly open to educated and uneducated Blacks dissatisfied with the classic clientage was migration. The growth of urban and industrial centers in the South and North created demands for unskilled and semiskilled labor that Blacks preferred to their more or less fixed tenant status in Southern agriculture (Bond, 1969:196, 229). The Depression and various wars fought by the United States in this century also acted to increase Black migration into the cities and into military service (Johnson, 1943:104ff; Myrdal, 1944; A.R. Ross, 1967:17). The migrants included middle- and upper-class Blacks who were skilled workers and professionals, and the latter became the preachers, teachers, doctors, lawyers, managers, and proprietors of the evolving, segregated urban ghettos. The size and heterogeneity of urban populations encouraged the establishment of segmental, transitory interpersonal relations (Wirth, 1968:26–45). As a result urban clientage came to be situational for most Blacks.

A third factor undermining classic clientage has been civil rights activities. Many civil rights organizations formed by Blacks and their White supporters since the first decade of the twentieth century have devoted their efforts and resources to the destruction or at least modification of traditional clientage through protests and boycotts against White business establishments, through legal suits challenging racial injustices, through pressure on local, state, and federal governments to protect the constitutional rights of Blacks, and through educational programs. Among the major civil rights organizations have been the National Association for the Advancement of Colored People (founded in 1905), the National Urban League (founded in 1911), the Southern Christian Leadership Conference, and the Student Non-Violent Co-ordinating Committee (both founded in the 1960s).

The final factor undermining classic clientage has been government actions, including civil rights legislations, executive orders, court enforcement of civil rights and constitutional rights of Blacks, and government programs to implement executive, legislative, and legal decisions guaranteeing these rights (see Adams, 1972; Burkey, 1971; Huff, 1974). Government efforts on behalf of Blacks have increased over several generations to the point where the government has now become the patron ensuring the legal, political, social, and economic protection of Blacks.

CLIENTAGE AND SPONSORED MOBILITY

Under each of the three forms of clientage social mobility takes place through sponsorship, but the nature of the sponsorship varies. Under classic clientage, Black individuals attained higher status in the wider society as well as in their segregated community through the support of White patrons rather than through their own *individual efforts* as reflected in their educational credentials. That is, Blacks were *given* higher social, economic, and political positions *as rewards for acting as good clients* rather than for their competence or productivity (Myrdal, 1944:594). To be a good client or a good "Uncle Tom" was to be properly deferential (servile, respectful, cooperative, and generally accommodating), to be dependent and dependable (whether real or feigned), and to be diplomatic and cautious.

The ethnographies cited earlier make it clear that after Blacks were excluded through legal and extralegal devices from competing with Whites on an

equal basis, clientage provided them with the only effective alternative channel for some degree of personal advancement (see Davis, Gardner, and Gardner, 1941/1965:273-274; Dollard 1937/1957:262; Johnson, 1934:27; Myrdal,
1944:594; Powdermaker 1939/1968:106-107, 339; Raper, 1929:83-84). For example, in the communities studied in the 1930s it was difficult if not impossible for a Black tenant-farmer to rise to the status of a farm owner without a
White patron who assisted him in getting a bank loan, provided him with
legal protection by ensuring that he obtained a proper title to the land and
that no one interferred with his rights to the property thereafter. Urban Blacks
desiring to buy homes or other property were similarly dependent upon White
patrons. Skilled Black workers and professionals also required the assistance
and protection of White patrons to advance in their fields (Davis, Gardner,
and Gardner, 1941/1965:273; Dollard, 1937/1957:262; Powdermaker, 1939/
1968:112, 330; Raper, 1929:84). Highly coveted positions within the Black
community itself, such as college presidencies, school principalships, teaching
jobs, and community leadership, were also attained through the sponsorship
of White patrons (Bond, 1966:278-279; Myrdal, 1944:594), who gave these
positions to Blacks who had rendered them personal services or were considered loyal and properly deferential. The attitudes of White patrons, Myrdal observes, put "a premium on the individual [Blacks] most inclined and
best gifted to flatter their superior whites, even if they [lacked] other qualities
[p. 594]." Powdermaker (1968:330-339) collected many stories from Black
landowners, professionals, and skilled workers of the flattery and tact they
had to employ "in order to get by."

Under classic clientage, many Blacks, especially the less educated and lower
class, accepted the necessity of deferential behavior and even taught the patterns to their children as the natural order of things (Frazier, 1940; Johnson,
1941). However, under the situational clientage of the North and of urban
centers, most Blacks of all classes deliberately "simulate" dependence or
deferential behavior in situations where they do not believe that they are
likely to be judged by the same criteria as Whites for allocation of social
rewards.

Under situational clientage educational credentials have acquired added
significance partly because the educational requirements of many jobs and
other status positions are more explicit and subject to public scrutiny. One effect is that Blacks tend to be *educationally overqualified* for their jobs and
other positions, in order to improve their standing in competition. That is, to
compete successfully for the same jobs Black applicants often have to have
more education than the White. In 1976, the year for which the latest data are
available, 52% more high school graduates and 23% more college graduates
among Black males than among White males were classified as having more
schooling than their jobs required. For females the proportions were 27%
more high school graduates and 0.92% more college graduates among Blacks
than among Whites. In 1960 (and evidently in earlier periods) the proportions

of Blacks in the overqualified category were probably greater (U.S. Commission on Civil Rights, 1978; see also Newman *et al.*, 1978). In general, however, Blacks find that they still have to "Uncle Tom" to Whites who control the specific situations in which they are hired or promoted, are appointed or elected to public offices, obtain loans to buy homes or move into White neighborhoods, and the like. Poussaint and Atkinson (1973:173) further add that Uncle Tomming includes maintaining a low profile on racial matters, that is, not being "too outspoken."

A few examples from incidents that took place in Stockton, California, during my fieldwork there in 1968–1970 will illustrate how sponsored mobility works under situational clientage. One incident concerned a local Black school administrator involved in organizing a coalition of civil rights groups considered "militant" by local Whites. When reporters arrived one day to interview leaders of the coalition after a school boycott, the Black administrator went into hiding for fear of losing his job if his superiors learned from the news media that he was involved in the movement.

The election and appointment of minority-group members to the local school board also serve as good examples of White sponsorship in Stockton. Before district voting was introduced in 1973 the general pattern was for Whites to appoint or elect a minority person who was acceptable to them; and being acceptable included not being "too outspoken" about racial matters and not advocating school integration by busing. The contrasting careers of two minority board members appropriately illustrate this pattern. One such candidate was sponsored and elected to the board in 1965. By 1969 he had violated the rule of clientage by being "too outspoken" about racial discrimination in the community. Furthermore, he was the only school board member to vote to integrate local public schools by busing in 1969. Although his actions earned him increasing support in minority areas, they cost him his White patronage. He was therefore forced to "retire" from the board, since he saw no chance of being re-elected. In contrast, another minority member of the board who had been appointed to 1968 decided to maintain a low profile on racial issues and to vote against the plan to integrate local public schools by busing. When approached by representatives from a coalition of 16 organizations of his own ethnic group and asked to vote for the integration plan, he refused, stating that he could do more for minorities by remaining on the school board. While his actions cost him the support of many minorities and their organizations, they increased his White sponsorship, so that in a subsequent election he was able to win the biggest vote in a field of nine candidates including seven Whites.

There were many such examples in education and other public and private institutions, where Blacks participated as employees or as appointed and elected officials. There was a tendency on the part of local Whites as well as local Blacks to think of Blacks in coveted social, political, and occupational positions as having achieved their status by playing "Uncle Tom," a generalization that is both exaggerated and unfair, yet had some basis in the social reality of Blacks in Stockton (see Ogbu, 1977).

Under collective clientage, Blacks look to the government as the patron guaranteeing their rights to employment, remuneration, promotion, and the like. Government sponsorship consists, then, in providing Blacks with extraordinary supports that Whites do not need in order to move into high-status jobs, earn higher wages, be promoted on the job, or buy a home in better sections of the city. The government currently provides these supports through civil rights and affirmative action policies and programs as well as special aids to education and job training. Educational credentials assume their greatest relevance to Black social mobility under collective clientage because the government in providing these supports insists that the sponsorees possess the appropriate educational training and ability. Thus, the essence of affirmative action policy seems to be to see that Whites who control the coveted social and occupational positions seek out and award them to *qualified blacks* and others who were previously excluded (Burkey, 1971:38–39; Ogbu, 1978:347).

The new sponsorship has proved very effective in accelerating Black social mobility by raising the height of their status system, by enlarging the pool of jobs available to Blacks at each occupational level, and by ensuring that Blacks are employed, promoted, and paid according to their educational credentials and on-the-job performance. The result of the new sponsorship can be seen from the fact that within 1 decade of its operation, the number of Blacks employed in the top-level occupational category—professional and technical jobs—increased by 128%, compared to an increase of 49% for the general population. The number of Black employees also increased by almost 100% in the second highest category, consisting of managers, officials, and proprietors; the increase for the general population in this category was only 23% during the same period (Brimmer, 1974:160; see also A. R. Ross, 1973). Most of the increases occurred from 1966, the year in which Title VII of the Civil Rights Act of 1964 (the Equal Employment Opportunities Act), the basis of affirmative action policy, became effective.

Education, Clientage, and Social Mobility in the United States

Under classic clientage, sponsorship was more important than educational credentials in the placement, remuneration, and promotion of Blacks. Many Blacks who got ahead were often the less academically qualified and the less competent but the more deferential. Blacks did not have to have the competence considered necessary for Whites seeking similar positions in the wider society, but they needed the support of powerful White patrons. Sponsorship under situational clientage has reversed this discrepancy between education and Black status position, so that Blacks tend to be *overqualified education-*

ally for their positions. Collective clientage appears to balance the relationship between educational qualification and Black status position partly by making government support for jobholders conditional upon appropriate educational credentials and demonstrated competence and partly by requiring that educational credentials be relevant to the position (Huff, 1974). Thus, while educational credentials for White job placement and remuneration have remained more or less constant the shifts described here have begun to make Black educational credentials similar to those of Whites.

In looking at the future, one can hypothesize that the long-term effect of affirmative action and similar programs—the new mode of sponsorship—is to institutionalize educational credentials to the same degree for Blacks and Whites as a strategy for social mobility. This institutionalization can be achieved through both raising the standard of Black school performance and convincing the Whites to accept Black educational credentials as of equal value to those of Whites. And when Black and White educational credentials become equal social currencies for occupational placement, remuneration, and on-the-job promotion, not only will the gap in rates of social mobility disappear but also the need for any form of sponsorship and clientage. Of course, there is also the possibility that the new collective clientage may become self-perpetuating because of vested interests in the new paternalism and dependency by the parties involved. But changes in the status system and mobility strategies among Igbo caste groups in Nigeria, described later, should give some support to the hypotheses I have made about the relative and changing roles of education and clientage in Black social mobility in the United States.

Caste, Change, and Social Mobility among the Igbos of Nigeria

CASTE AND CLASS STRATIFICATION IN PRECOLONIAL IGBO SOCIETY

Precolonial Igbo society was stratified by both caste and class. The caste system consisted of two groups—the dominant *diala* or freeborn and an outcaste, *osu*, group. In between was a semi-caste group, the *ohu* or slaves (Azikiwe, 1961:91–94; Basden, 1966:246–284; Green, 1947:23–24, 50–58; Horton, 1954; Leith-Ross, 1937; Meek, 1937:203–213; Nzimiro, 1972:25–27; Obi, 1963:79–80; Ogbalu, n.d.:72; Ottenburg, 1968:33–34, 1971:25–29; Uchendu, 1965:89–90). In every village or village group the *diala* controlled the political, economic, and social life of the community. *Diala* men sometimes married *ohu* women, and the offspring of such marriages were regarded as *diala*. However, neither *diala* not *ohu* would intermarry with *osu*, for if they did they automatically became *osu* themselves, as did all the children resulting from the marriage. Even sexual relations outside marriage were prohibited between *diala* and *osu*. The two castes were also residentially segregated, with the *osu* usually living on the outskirts of the village near the market or the shrines that they served. In clans or village groups where their number was relatively large, they were formed into separate villages. The *osu* were considered ritually polluting and could not share the same barber or cemetery with the *diala*, nor could they drink from the same cup or eat from the same plate (Leith-Ross, 1937:216–217; Uchendu, 1965:90).

The *osu* or cult slaves consisted of people (or their descendants) who were dedicated by *diala* to the latter's deities or people who on their own sought refuge or sanctuary at the shrines of particular deities for various reasons. The refugees were people who had committed abominations or other serious crimes for which they were likely to be put to death or those who were unable to defend themselves against powerful enemies. The sanctuary was effective because no one would harm an *osu* for fear of incurring the wrath of the deity that owned the *osu*. For this reason, too, crimes among the *osu* often went unpunished (Meek, 1937:213). However, because they were feared they were sometimes used by the *diala* elites to enforce decisions affecting members of the dominant caste, such as exacting fines levied by a village council on a recalcitrant *diala* (Green, 1947). The origins of the practice of dedicating people to the shrines as well as seeking sanctuary at the shrines are unclear; but in most cases the dedication and sanctuary were for life, and the person became a servitor or cult slave or "priest" to the deity. His or her *osu* status was passed on to the offspring.

Ohu consisted of slaves in the ordinary sense of the word (Meek, 1937:203; see also Horton, 1954; Nwachuku-Ogedengbe, 1975; Uchendu, 1975). The *ohu* and their descendants were regarded as property of specific *diala* individuals or families, who had acquired them through capture, purchase, or pawning. While they could be sold as property, *ohu* could also be redeemed and thereby become *diala*. Most *ohu* were members of their masters' households, although in some parts of Igboland their numbers were large enough to form separate quarters or separate villages (Basden, 1966; Horton, 1954; Nwachudu-Ogedengbe, 1975; Uchendu, 1975).

Each of the three groups was internally stratified by class, the class system of the *diala* being the most fully developed. The *diala*, who made up more than 90% of the population, had a class system based on wealth and membership in ranked title societies (as will be discussed later). The *diala* class system can be divided into roughly three categories, distinguished by male membership in the highest title societies, intermediate societies, and the lowest societies plus nontitled adult males. In village groups with the institution of chieftaincy or kingship, members of the chief's or king's council were drawn mostly from the holders of the highest titles.

The *osu* or cult slaves were also differentiated by class on the basis of wealth and, where they formed separate communities, their class system reflected membership in various grades of their own title societies. On the whole they were very poor, being dependent for their subsistence and other economic needs on the *diala* who had dedicated them to the deities and on the offerings made to the deities. The *osu* were required to work for their *diala* "owners" for 2 out of the 8 days in the Igbo week. The class system of the *ohu* or ordinary slaves was likewise less fully developed in areas where they formed separate communities with parallel title societies. Although they were permitted to have their own economic activities and to accumulate wealth, they generally worked for their *diala* owners for many more days than the *osu*. The *ohu* population was differentiated on bases other than class. For instance, a distinction was made between bought slaves and those born in the master's household, and these were in turn distinguished from other *ohu* who had accumulated enough wealth to achieve manumission and thereby acquire at least some status as *diala* (see Basden, 1966; Meek, 1937; Nwachuku-Ogedengbe, 1975; Uchendu, 1975:129–130).

Both *ohu* and *osu* were expected to be and were properly deferential in attitudes and behaviors toward the *diala*, but the two differed in matters of address. The *ohu* always referred to the *diala* who owned him as *onye-nwem* ("my owner"); and he used the same term for all free members of his master's household. For other *diala* males he used their titles derieed from membership in title societies, or he used the general term, *nnam-ukwu* ("my big father," "my male superior," "my master"). For *diala* women outside his master's household. For other *diala* males he used their titles derived from membership If a *diala* woman had taken a title based on the female title system, he called her by her title. Technically the *osu* did not belong to any *diala*: not to the *diala* who dedicated him to a shrine, nor to the *diala* who "owned" the shrine to which the *osu* was dedicated. The *osu* was the property of the shrine. The *osu* did not, therefore, address any *diala* as *onye-nwem* ("my owner"), but used the term *nnam-ukwu* ("my male superior") and *nnem-ukwu* ("my female superior"), or called the *diala* by his or her title. The *ohu* and the *osu* were regarded and treated more or less as grown-up children who were not capable of making important decisions for themselves. They were not expected to participate in communal discussions unless specifically called upon to do so. They were expected to show proper respect to every *diala*, including children; and violations of social etiquettes were severely punished.

TRADITIONAL IGBO STATUS SYSTEM

The most important index of the Igbo status system is precolonial days was membership in title societies, not a man's occupation as in the United States, because all Igbo men were farmers. In a given village group the title system consisted of several ranked titles. A man who took a particular title joined a society or club named after the title. He was then addressed by this title by other members of the community. If he took several titles, he belonged to as many societies. Usually a man began by taking the lowest title in his community and subsequently took others in order of their increasing prestige and expense. To join a society, that is, to take a title, the prospective candidate had to obtain the approval of the society members and thereafter had to pay an entrance fee and provide a feast for the members, and sometimes for the entire community (Basden, 1966:133–144; Green, 1947:48; LeVine, 1967:34; Meek, 1937:165–184; Ogbalu, n.d.:33; Ottenberg, 1968: 71–72; 1971:22–23; Uchendu, 1965:82).

Examples from a few localities in Igboland show both the general pattern and the variations within the title system. In Akpu (Aguata Local Government Council Area in Anambra State) the title system consisted of *Igwa-aka*, *Emume*, and *Ozo*. *Igwa-aka*, the lowest title in the village group, was open to all *diala*, but not to *ohu* or *osu*, who had demonstrated bravery in intervillage raids by capturing or killing a man from an enemy village. With the coming of the colonial adminstration, bravery was recognized as killing a specified "rare" bird or animal such as an eagle, lion, elephant, or crocodile. Having demonstrated his bravery in "war," the prospective candidate informed members of the *Igwa-aka* society of his desire to join; upon approval he paid an entrance fee and provided a feast for the society's members. *Emume* was open only to *diala; ohu* and *osu* were specifically prohibited from joining it. However, only *diala* who had accumulated enough wealth to pay a series of required fees and provide periodic feasts joined this society. Even more restricted in membership because of cost was the *Ozo* title society, which was also open only to the *diala*.

In Umuaka village group (Orlu Local Government Council Area in Imo State), the title system consisted of *Ngwuruobi, Ndi-ishi*, and *Ozo*, in order of prestige and expense. Taking the *Ozo* title involved payment of a large fee, slaughtering a big cow, and making feasts for members of the *Ozo* society and for the entire community for 16 days. *Osu* people in Umuaka village group could take the *Ozo* and other titles, but apparently they usually organized their own parallel societies instead. In the writer's own village group of Onicha (Ohaozara Local Government Council Area, Imo State), the title system consisted of *Isuji* (yam title), *Inwinyinya* (horse title), *Ohu-n'eri* (horse and cow title), and *Oju* or *Ozo* (a combination of yam, horse, and cow title) in order of prestige and cost. It seems that in this particular village group one could take other titles without first taking the yam title; at least this has been the experience of the writer, who has taken the second and third titles but not the first.

Membership in the title societies was not usually inherited, although wealthy parents sometimes paid for their sons to join in at least the lower-grade societies. Most men joined the societies *after* they had accumulated enough wealth on their own to pay the costs. In most parts of Igboland the wealth necessary to pay for title-taking was acquired primarily through farming and secondarily through trading and other minor economic activities.

Taking several titles and thereby joining several societies was a good economic investment in precolonial days, as members continued to share the fees paid by new members as long as they lived. A point to be stressed is that in general one first had to achieve economic success by having access to good farmlands, by having the proper skills in farming and other economic activities, and by having good luck, in order to rise in the status system. And the people most advantageously placed to achieve upward mobility were the *diala* who controlled the family, lineage, and communal farmlands as well as the labor of the *ohu* and *osu* (Basden, 1966:113–144; Green, 1947:48, 58; LeVine, 1967:34; Meek, 1937:165–184; Ogbalu, n.d.:32–33; Ottenberg, 1968: 71–72, 1971:23; Uchendu, 1965:82).

Among the *ohu* and *osu* the status system was less elaborate. Where *diala* and *ohu* lived in the same communities, the latter were not generally allowed to join the *diala* title societies and certainly were not admitted to societies whose membership led to political power and influence. However, *ohu* who lived in separate villages developed parallel, less expensive title societies. (This situation seems to have changed during colonial days, so that in some slave villages membership in title societies was more expensive than membership in similar societies in *diala* villages; see Horton, 1954:333.) The exclusion of the *osu* from membership in *diala* title societies was more nearly complete. However, they too sometimes had parallel title societies where they lived in separate villages. Membership in these *osu* title societies was less expensive and carried no prestige or privileges outside the *osu* village (Basden, 1966:248).

Both the *ohu* and the *osu* suffered considerable disadvantage in their access to resources for acquiring membership in the title societies. While farming was the principal means of accumulating wealth, both the *ohu* and the *osu* had no direct or legal rights to family, lineage, and communal farmlands (Obi, 1963:79–80). The *ohu* farmed such lands as he received from his *diala* master or was able to lease on his own. The *diala* who dedicated an *osu* (or his ancestors) to his deity was obligated to provide the *osu* with a piece of farmland that could be inherited by the latter's descendants (Basden, 1966:203). However, the land given to the *osu* was usually small and of poor quality. With few exceptions the *osu* and *ohu* did not control the economic resources required for social mobility in precolonial Igbo society. Their access to such resources depended largely on the willingness of their *diala* masters to reward them for their loyality, deference, and services.

RESTRATIFICATION UNDER WESTERN IMPACT

The traditional Igbo stratification, status systems, and status mobility strategies underwent important changes during the colonial period, roughly from 1900 to 1960. As elsewhere in Africa (c.f. Maquet, 1971; Mitchell, 1970) various categories of Europeans in colonial Igboland—administrators, missionaries, and traders—constituted a new dominant caste whose presence, values, and actions began to modify the traditional stratification. The new British ruling caste formally abolished the traditional distinctions between *diala, ohu,* and *osu* immediately after it came to power (Basden, 1966; Green, 1947; Leith-Ross, 1937; Meek, 1937; Ottenberg, 1971). This "emancipation" was successful in regard to the *ohu,* especially in communities where their number was small. They either migrated to new urban centers or assimilated into the lineages of their *diala* masters (Ottenberg, 1968:33–34). In communities with large *ohu* populations the distinction between them and the *diala* continues to date, although the *ohu* are no longer obligated to serve their former masters since they are now "free." Unfortunately, from the point of view of the *diala,* without voluntary manumission the *ohu* are still *ohu,* subject to as many disabilities as could still be imposed without inviting the intervention of the new ruling caste.

Emancipation had no visible effect on the invidious distinctions between the *diala* and the *osu,* regardless of the size of the outcaste population in a given locality. The two groups are still residentially segregated. Although rules about sexual relations have been somewhat relaxed, especially in urban centers, prohibitions against intermarriage still remain. In fact, in recent interviews I learned of two instances in the United States in the last few years in which *diala* heads of households intervened to stop potential marriages involving *diala* brides and *osu* grooms. I know of no instance involving a *diala* groom and an *osu* bride. I was informed that the main reason Igbos conduct extensive investigations into the backgrounds of prospective brides and grooms is to avoid a mixed marriage between the *diala* and the *osu.* However, in Nigeria some minor discriminatory practices against the *osu* have been dropped, so that, for example, in the cities the *osu* and the *diala* may now buy and sell seed yams to each other; they can share the same barber, drink and eat together, and be buried in the same cemetery. On the whole, colonial emancipation did not significantly change the relations between *diala* and *osu,* much less obliterate the caste line between them.

The persistence of the invidious distinctions between the *diala* and *osu* led the government of Eastern Nigeria in 1956 to try to legislate the caste system out of existence by passing an "Act of Ohu Emancipation and the Abolition of Osu Law" which combined features of the American Emancipation Proclamation of 1863 and India's Untouchable Offences Act of 1955. Among other things the new law prohibited calling any members of the respective groups *ohu* or *osu* (Azikiwe, 1961:91–94; Nzimiro, 1972:28; Obi, 1963:79). This legislation has not, however, proved any more effective than the previous one, according to informants. In fact, the subject of *osu* status in contemporary Igbo society has been a matter of public debate in the Nigerian press (see, for example, *Nigerian Sunday Times,* 1976; 10, 15).

EMERGENCE OF A NEW STATUS SYSTEM AND A NEW STATUS MOBILITY STRATEGY

Aspects of the traditional caste system that have changed most since colonial rule are the status system and social mobility strategies. Various classes of Europeans—colonial administrators, missionaries, and business people—introduced to the Igbos a new status system based primarily on occupation and clearly separated from both kinship and caste control. The new occupations making up the status system were also new to the *diala, ohu,* and *osu.* The colonial administration, for example, introduced "civil service jobs," for low-level jobs in agriculture, community development, courts or judiciary, education, health, public works, mining, and personal service; missionaries introduced jobs related to teaching, preaching, health, printing, and personal service; European business people needed clerks, messengers, interpreters, sales agents, guards, and domestic servants. Later the number, type, and level of these jobs open to Igbos increased, thus raising the height of the new status system and adding to the mobility within it. The Europeans also introduced an entirely new, nonindigenous institutionalized channel—formal education—for entering into and moving up within the new status system.

The new system and its mobility strategies were made available to the *diala, ohu,* and *osu* without distinction. But these groups did not respond in the same ways to the new situation. Initially the *diala* were reluctant to work for Europeans or attend their schools. The *diala* felt that serving other people as "houseboys" or working in other menial positions was more natural for the *ohu* and *osu,* and consequently they sent them whenever possible to work for the Europeans.

The *diala* often kept an even greater distance from the missionaries to whom they gave parts of the local "Evil Forests" to build their churches and schools. The Evil Forests were pieces of land set aside by each clan or village group for burying people who had died of dangerous diseases like leprosy and smallpox, for burying the *osu,* and for discarding fetishes and newborn twins (see Achebe, 1959:146–147). The *osu,* on the other hand, had nothing to lose through close association with the new residents of the Evil Forests, partly because they themselves were considered polluting and partly because the missionaries preached both spiritual and social redemption and equality. The *ohu* were also attracted to missionary education and religion because of the promise of social and spiritual rewards.

In general the *osu* were among the first Igbos to work for the Europeans as domestic servants, messengers, and in other menial roles, to learn English and the European way of life, to obtain formal education, and take up higher-level jobs as these became available to the "natives" in the colonial administration, missions, and commerce. As the pool of new jobs increased and educational credentials became the main channel to such jobs, the *osu* who had a head start in education maintained their lead also in occupational mobility. This trend continued after Nigeria gained independence in 1960 and Nigerians replaced British colonial administrators and later replaced European missionaries in high-level positions in mission schools, hospitals, and churches, and European personnel in some high-ranking jobs in the field of commerce. I have no statistics to back up this statement, but recent ethnographers (Nzimiro, 1972:28–29; Uchendu, 1965:90) and the Igbos I interviewed recently agree that the *osu* are today among the best educated, the top-level employed, and the wealthiest Igbos. To some extent the same is true of the *ohu* where the latter can be identified.

Status Systems, Mobility Strategies, and Social Mobility

In reviewing some aspects of social mobility in the United States and among the Igbos of Nigeria, I have indicated that these societies, stratified by class and caste, traditionally had unequal status systems and different strategies for status mobility among their component castes. These two factors made it virtually certain that the caste groups would differ in social mobility rates. When a status mobility strategy stresses and rewards individual efforts through education as it does for middle-class White Americans or through the accumulation of wealth as it did for the *diala* in precolonial Igbo society, members of the affected group come to value such striving, practice it, and teach it to their children. When the mobility strategy stresses and rewards successful clientage as it has traditionally done for Blacks in the United States and as it did for the *osu* and the *ohu* in precolonial Igbo society, members of the affected group also come to value or at least accept as inevitable the skills and behaviors associated with the strategy, practice them, and teach them to their children. I suggest therefore that when there are significant differences in social mobility orientations and efforts among different groups in society, we should look for at least part of the explanation in the reward system of that society.

I also indicated that (a) as the status system of the different castes in a society became more nearly equal, as they have through affirmative action and other programs in the United States or through the introduction of new occupations among the Igbos of Nigeria, and (b) as a common mobility strategy for the caste groups evolves, especially the institutionalization of educational credentials for all caste groups, the pace of social mobility increases in the subordinate caste. This stepped-up pace will eventually eliminate the gap in social mobility rates among the caste groups.

References

Achebe, Chinua
  1959 Things Fall Apart. Greenwich, Connecticut: Fawcett.
Adams, Arvil V.
  1972 Toward Fair Employment and the EEOC: A Study of Compliance Procedures Under

Title VII of the Civil Rights Act of 1964: A Report. Washington, D.C.: Government Printing Office.

Adams, Carol and Rae Laurikietis
1977   The Gender Trap: A Closer Look at Sex Roles: Book 1: Education and Work. New York: Academic Press.

Azikiwe, Nnamdi
1961   A Selection from the Speeches of Nnamdi Azikiwe. Cambridge: Cambridge University Press.

Banks, W. Curtis, and Gregory V. McQuater
1976   Achievement Motivation and Black Children. ICRD Bulletin Vol. 11, No. 4.

Basden, G. T.
1966   Niger Ibos. London: Cass.

Berreman, Gerald D.
1960   Caste in India and the United States. American Journal of Sociology 66:120–127.
1967   Caste in Cross-Cultural Perspective: Organizational Components. In Japan's Invisible Race: Caste in Culture and Personality. George DeVos and Hiroshi Wagatsuma, eds. Pp. 275–307. Berkeley: University of California Press.
1977   Social Inequality: A Cross-Cultural Paradigm. Department of Anthropology, University of California, Berkeley.

Bond, Horace Mann
1966   The Education of the Negro in the American Social Order. New York: Octagon Books.
1969   Negro Education in Alabama: A Study in Cotton and Steel. New York: Atheneum.

Brimmer, Andrew F.
1974   Economic Development in the Black Community. In The Great Society: Lessons for the Future. Eli Ginsberg and Robert M. Solow, eds. Pp. 146–163. New York: Basic Books.

Bullock, Henry Allen
1970   A History of Negro Education in the South: From 1619 to the Present. New York: Praeger.

Burkey, Richard M.
1971   Racial Discrimination and Public Policy in the United States. Lexington, Massachusetts: D.C. Heath.

Burma, John H.
1946   The Measurement of Negro Passing. American Journal of Sociology 52:18–22.

Cohen, Ronald
1965   Some Aspects of Institutionalized Exchange: A Kanuri Example. Cahiers D'Etudes Africaine 5:353–369.
1970   Social Stratification in Bornu. In Social Stratification in Africa. Arthur Tuden and Leonard Plotnicov, eds. Pp. 225–267. New York: Free Press.

Collins, Randall
1977   Some Comparative Principles of Educational Stratification. Harvard Educational Review 47:1–27.

Cox, Oliver
1945   Race and Caste: A Distinction. American Journal of Sociology 50:360–368.

Coxon, A. P. M., and C. L. Jones
1975   Introduction. In Social Mobility: Selected Readings. A. P. M. Coxon and C. L. Jones, eds. Pp. 9–19. Baltimore: Penguin.

Crockett, Harry
1966   Psychological Origins of Mobility. In Social Structure and Mobility in Economic Development. Neil J. Smelser and S. M. Lipset, eds. Pp. 291–303. Chicago: Aldine Press.

Davis, Allison, Burleigh B. Gardner, and Mary R. Gardner
1965   Deep South: A Social Anthropological Study of Caste and Class. Abridged. Chicago: University of Chicago Press. (First ed. 1941.)

Dollard, John
1957   Caste and Class in a Southern Town. Third ed. Garden City, New York: Doubleday. (First ed. 1937.)
Drake, St. Clair, and Horace Cayton
1970   Black Metropolis: A Study of Negro Life in a Northern City. Vols. 1 and 2. New York: Harcourt, Brace and World.
Duberman, Lucile
1976   Social Inequality: Class and Caste in America. Philadelphia: Lippincott.
Dumont, L.
1961   Caste, Racism and Stratification: Reflections of a Social Anthropologist. Contributions to Indian Sociology 5:20-43.
Duncan, Otis Dudley
1975   Patterns of Occupational Mobility Among Negro Men. *In* Racial Discrimination in the United States. Thomas Pettigrew, ed. Pp. 167-187. New York: Harper and Row.
Duncan, Otis Dudley, and Peter M. Blau
1967   The American Occupational Structure. New York: Wiley.
Duncan, Otis Dudley, and Robert W. Hodges
1963   Educational and Occupational Mobility: A Regressive Analysis. American Journal of Sociology 68:644.
Eckard, E. W.
1947   How Many Negroes Pass? American Journal of Sociology 52:498-500.
Epstein, Cynthia Fuchs
1971   Woman's Place: Options and Limits in Professional Careers. Berkeley: University of California Press.
Fallers, L. A.
1964   The King's Men. New York: Oxford University Press.
Farmer, James
1968   Stereotypes of the Negro and Their Relationship to His Self-Image. *In* Urban Schooling. Herbert C. Rudman and Richard L. Featherstone, eds. Pp. 135-149. New York: Harcourt, Brace and World.
Foster, George M.
1961   The Dyadic Contract: A Model for the Social Structure of a Mexican Peasant Village. American Anthropologist 63:1173-1192.
1963   The Dyadic Contract in Tzintzuntzan, II: Patron-Client Relationship. American Anthropologist 65:1280-1294.
1967   Tzintzuntzan: Mexican Peasants in a Changing World. Boston: Little, Brown.
Fox, Thomas, and S. M. Miller
1966   Intra-Country Variations: Occupational Stratification and Mobility. *In* Class, Status and Power. Second ed. Reinhard Bendix and Seymour Martin Lipset, eds. Pp. 574-581. New York: Free Press.
Frazier, E. Franklin
1940   Negro Youth at the Crossways. Washington, D.C.: American Council on Education.
Green, M. M.
1947   Ibo Village Affairs. New York: Praeger.
Haley, A.
1966   The Autobiography of Malcolm X. New York: Grove Press.
Heard, Nathan C.
1968   Howard Street. New York: Dial Press.
Heller, Celia S.
1969   Structured Social Inequality: A Reader in Comparative Social Stratification. New York: Macmillan.
HEW *see* U.S. Department of Health, Education, and Welfare.

Hodges, Harold M.
  1964   Social Stratification: Class in America. Cambridge Massachusetts: Schenkman.
Horton, W. R. G.
  1954   The Ohu System of Slavery in a Northern Ibo Village Group. Africa 24:311–334.
Huff, Sheila
  1974   Credentialing by Tests or by Degrees: Title VII of the Civil Rights Act and Criggs v. Duke Power Company. Harvard Educational Review 44:246–269.
Jencks, Christopher
  1972   Inequality: A Reassessment of the Effects of Family and Schooling in America. New York: Basic Books.
Johnson, Charles S.
  1934   Shadow of the Plantation. Chicago: University of Chicago Press.
  1941   Growing Up in the Black Belt: Negro Youth in the Rural South. New York: Schocken Books.
  1943   Backgrounds to Patterns of Negro Segregation. New York: Crowell.
Katzman, David M.
  1973   Before the Ghetto: Black Detroit in the Nineteenth Century. Urbana: University of Illinois Press.
Kraus, Irving
  1976   Stratification, Class and Conflict. New York: Free Press.
Ladenburg, Thomas J. and William S. McFeely
  1969   The Black Man in the Land of Equality. New York: Hayden Book Co.
Lee, Frank F.
  1961   Negro and White in Connecticut Town. New York: Bookman Associates.
Legg, Keith R.
  1976   Patrons, Clients, and Politicians: New Perspectives on Political Clientelism. Berkeley: Institute of International Studies, University of California.
Leith-Ross, Sylvia
  1937   Note on the Osu System Among the Ibo of Owerri Province, Nigeria. Africa 10:206–220.
Lemarchand, René
  1972   Political Clientelism and Ethnicity in Tropical Africa: Competing Solidarities in Nation-Building. American Political Science Review Vol. 66.
LeVine, Robert A.
  1967   Dreams and Deeds: Achievement Motivation in Nigeria. Chicago: The University of Chicago Press.
Lewis, Hylian
  1954   Blackways of Kent. Chapel Hill: University of North Carolina Press.
McCarthy, John D., and William Yancey
  1973   Uncle Tom and Mr. Charlie: Metaphysical Pathos in the Study of Racism and Personal Disorganization. In Race Relations: Current Perspectives. Edgar G. Epps, ed. Pp. 44–68. Cambridge: Winthrop.
McClelland, David C.
  1973   Testing for Competence Rather than for Intelligence. American Psychologist 29:1–14.
Maquet, Jacques
  1970   Rwanda Castes. In Social Stratification in Africa. Arthur Tuden and Leonard Plotnicov, eds. Pp. 93–124. New York: Free Press.
  1971   Power and Society in Africa. New York: World University Library.
Meek, C. K.
  1937   Law and Authority in a Nigerian Tribe: A Study in Indirect Rule. London: Oxford University Press.
Miller, Herman P.
  1971   Rich Man, Poor Man. New York: Crowell.

Miller, S. M.
  1960   Comparative Social Mobility. Current Sociology 9:1–89.
  1975   The Concept of Measurement of Mobility. *In* Social Mobility: Selected Readings.
         A. P. M. Coxon and C. L. Jones, eds. Pp. 21–31. Baltimore: Penguin.
Milner, Christina, and Richard Milner
  1972   Black Players: The Secret World of Black Pimps. Boston: Little, Brown.
Mitchell, J. C.
  1970   Race, Class, and Status in South Cental Africa. *In* Social Stratification in Africa. Arthur
         Tuden and Leonard Plotnicov, eds. Pp. 225–268. New York: Free Press.
Muller, Walter, and Karl Urlich Mayer
  1973   Introduction. *In* Social Stratification and Career Mobility. Walter Muller and Karl
         Ulrich Mayer, eds. Pp. 7–14. The Hague: Mouton.
Myrdal, Gunnar
  1944   An American Dilemma: The Negro Problem and Modern Democracy. New York:
         Harper.
National Advisory Commission on Civil Disorders
  1968   Report. Washington, D.C.: Government Printing Office.
Newman, Dorothy K. *et al.*
  1978   Protest, Politics, and Prosperity: Black Americans and White Institutions, 1940–1975.
         New York: Pantheon.
Nigerian Sunday Times
  1976   "Why, Why the "Osu" System: A Rejoinder. June 6. Pp. 10, 15.
Nwachukwe-Ogedengbe, K.
  1975   Slavery in Nineteenth-Century Aboh (Nigeria). *In* Slavery in Africa: Historical
         and Anthropological Perspectives. Suzanne Miers and Igor Kopytoff, eds. Pp. 133–154.
         Madison: University of Wisconsin Press.
Nzimiro, Ikenna
  1972   Studies in Ibo Political System: Chieftaincy and Politics in Four Niger States. Berkeley:
         University of California Press.
Obi, S. N. Chinwuba
  1963   The Ibo Law of Property. London: Butterworth.
Ogbalu, F. C.
  n.d.   Igbo Institutions and Customs. Onitsha, Nigeria: University Publishing Company.
Ogbu, John U.
  1974   The Next Generation: An Ethnography of Education in an Urban Neighborhood. New
         York: Academic Press.
  1977   Racial Stratification and Education: The Case of Stockton, California. IRCD Bulletin 12
         (3):1–27.
  1978   Minority Education and Caste: The American System in Cross-Cultural Perspective.
         New York: Academic Press.
Ottenberg, Simon
  1968   Double Descent in an African Society: The Afikpo Village-Group. Seattle: University of
         Washington Press.
  1971   Leadership and Authority in an African Society: The Afikpo Village-Group. Seattle:
         University of Washington Press.
Parsons, Talcott
  1964   The Social System. New York: Free Press.
Perlo, Victor
  1975   Economics of Racism, USA: Roots of Black Inequality. New York: International Pub-
         lishers.
Poussaint, Alvin, and Carolyn Atkinson
  1973   Black Youth and Motivation. *In* Race Relations: Current Perspectives. Edgar G. Epps,
         ed. Pp. 167–177. Cambridge, Massachusetts: Winthrop.

Powdermaker, Hortense
   1968   After Freedom: A Cultural Study in the Deep South. New York: Atheneum. (First ed.
          1939.)
Powell, John Duncan
   1970   Peasant Society and Clientelist Politics. American Political Science Review 64:411–425.
Raper, Arthur F.
   1929   Preface to Peasantry: A Tale of Two Black Belt Countries. Chapel Hill: University of
          North Carolina Press.
Rogoff, Natalie
   1953   Recent Trends in Occupational Mobility. Glencoe, Illinois: Free Press.
Ross, Arthur M.
   1967   The Negro in the American Economy. In Employment, Race, and Poverty: A Critical
          Study of the Disadvantaged Status of Negro Workers from 1865 to 1965. Arthur Ross
          and Herbert Hill, eds. Pp. 3–48. New York: Harcourt, Brace and World.
Ross, Arthur R.
   1973   Negro Employment in the South. Vol. 3; State and Local Governments. Washington,
          D.C.: U.S. Department of Labor.
Rossi, Peter H., and Michael D. Ornstein
   1973   The Impact of Labor Market Entry Factors: Illustrations from the Hopkins Social Ac-
          counts Project. In Social Stratification and Career Mobility. Walter Muller and Karl
          Ulrich Mayer, eds. Pp. 269–311. The Hague: Mouton.
Scott, James C.
   1972   Patron–Client Politics and Political Change in Southeast Asia. American Political Sci-
          ence Review 66:91–113.
Scott, Joseph W.
   1976   The Black Revolt: Racial Stratification in the USA. Cambridge: Schenkman.
Sjoberg, Gideon
   1960   The Preindustrial City: Past and Present. Glencoe, Illinois: Free Press.
Stack, Carol B.
   1974   All Our Kin: Strategies for Survival in a Black Community. New York: Harper and
          Row.
Thielbar, Gerald W. and Saul D. Feldman
   1972   Issues in Social Inequality. Boston: Little, Brown.
Thernstrom, Stephan
   1973   The Other Bostonians: Poverty and Progress in the American Metropolis 1880–1970.
          Cambridge: Harvard University Press.
Tindall, George B.
   1949   The Campaign for the Disenfranchisement of Negros in South Carolina. Journal of
          Southern History 15:212–234.
Tuden, Arthur, and Leonard Plotnicov
   1970   Introduction. In Social Stratification in Africa. Arthur Tuden and Leonard Plotnicov,
          eds. Pp. 1–29. New York: Free Press.
Tumin, Melvin M.
   1970   Mobility, I: Patterns and Structures. In Readings on Social Stratification. Melvin M.
          Tumin, ed. Pp. 294–295. Englewood Cliffs, New Jersey: Prentice-Hall.
Turner, Ralph H.
   1960   Sponsored and Contest Mobility and the School Systems. American Sociological Review
          Vol. 35, No. 5.
Uchendu, Victor C.
   1965   The Igbo of Southeast Nigeria. New York: Holt, Rinehart and Winston.
   1975   Slaves and Slavery in Igboland, Nigeria. In Slavery in Africa: Historical and Anthropo-
          logical Perspectives. Suzanne Miers and Igor Kopytoff, eds. Pp. 121–132. Madison:
          University of Wisconsin Press.

U.S. Commission on Civil Rights
  1968   Mobility in the Negro Community: Guidelines for Research on Social and Economic
          Progress. Clearinghouse Publications, No. 11. Washington, D.C.: Government Printing
          Office.
  1978   Social Indicators of Equality for Minorities and Women. Washington, D.C.: Govern-
          ment Printing Office.
U.S. Department of Health, Education, and Welfare
  1969   Toward a Social Report. Ann Arbor: University of Michigan Press.
Valentine, Bettylou
  1978   Hustling and Other Hard Work: Life Styles in the Ghetto. New York: Free Press.
Van den Berghe, Pierre
  1967   Race and Racism: A Comparative Perspective. New York: Wiley.
Warner, W. Lloyd
  1936   American Caste and Class. American Journal of Sociology 32:234–237.
Warner, W. Lloyd, et al.
  1941   Color and Human Nature: Negro Personality Development in a Northern City. Wash-
          ington, D.C.: American Council on Education.
  1965   Introduction: Deep South—A Social Anthropological Study of Caste and Class. In Deep
          South: A Social Anthropological Study of Caste and Class. Allison Davis, Burleigh B.
          Gardner, and Mary R. Gardner, eds. Pp. 3–14. Chicago: University of Chicago Press.
  1970   A Methodological Note. In Black Metropolis: A Study of Negro Life in a Northern City.
          St. Clair Drake and Horace R. Cayton, eds. Vol. 2, Pp. 669–782. New York: Harper and
          Row.
Weber, Max
  1946   Class, Status, and Party. In Max Weber: Essays in Sociology. H. H. Gerth and C. W.
          Mills, eds. and trans. Pp. 180–195. London: Oxford University Press.
Whitaker, Ben, ed.
  1973   The Fourth World: Victims of Group Oppression. New York: Schocken Books.
Whitten, Norman E.
  1965   Class, Kinship, and Power in an Ecuadorian Town: The Negros of San Lorenzo. Stan-
          ford: Stanford University Press.
Wilson, H. Clyde
  1973   On the Evolution of Education. In Learning and Culture: Proceedings of the 1972 An-
          nual Spring Meeting of the American Ethnological Society. Solon T. Kimball and Jac-
          quetta Hill-Burnett, eds. Pp. 211–244. Seattle: University of Washington Press.
Wirth, Louis
  1968   Urbanism as a Way of Life. In Classic Essays on the Culture of Cities. Richard Sennett,
          ed. Pp. 143–164. New York: Appleton-Century-Crofts.
Wolf, Eric
  1966   Kinship, Friendship, and Patron–Client Relations in Complex Societies. In The Social
          Anthropology of Complex Societies. Michael Banton, ed. Pp. 1–35. London: Tavistock.
Woodward, C. Vann
  1951   Origins of the New South, 1877–1913. Baton Rouge: University of Louisiana Press.

PART

V

INEQUALITY IN SOCIALIST SOCIETIES

14

MARTIN KING WHYTE

Destratification and Restratification in China

The quest for greater social equality is surely one of the most powerful political impulses of our age. For millions around the globe, this quest is identified with Marxian socialism, which is seen as an ideology and political program making possible economic development without the inequalities and entrenched privileges of capitalism. To date, however, socialist regimes have not been very successful "equalizers." True, they generally succeed in eliminating the privileges of the existing "exploiting classes," but subsequently they have shown a tendency to introduce new and complex forms of inequality and concentration of power, rather than gradually limiting them, as they originally pledged.

The experience of the Soviet Union is the most dramatic in this regard. Lenin (1917/1943) wrote buoyantly in *State and Revolution,* on the eve of his assumption of power in 1917, of the prospect of minimal inequality, with all positions in society performed for "workingmen's wages." Yet, even before his death, Lenin in power became a forceful advocate of "necessary" incentives and privileges for those holding positions of authority and expertise. By the early 1930s, Stalin completed the repudiation of the "deviation" of egalitarianism, and the basic institutions of the Soviet system of stratification were established: an elitist educational system; a set of material incentives and bonuses to serve as the primary motor for higher industrial production; a massive bureaucratic and terror machine to control the masses; a network of special stores, health facilities, vacation resorts, and other such things to cater to the needs of the elite; and even a graded system of uniforms for various

309

SOCIAL INEQUALITY
Comparative and Developmental Approaches

kinds of civil servants.[1] Some partial measures to reduce the rigid hierarchies erected during the Stalin years took place under Khrushchev, but nonetheless today anyone who would use the Soviet Union as evidence for the proposition that socialism leads to increased social equality would have to engage in some pretty inspired verbal gymnastics.[2]

Still, the lessons to be drawn from the Soviet case are not entirely clear. The familiar (if not tired) approaches usually labeled "functionalism" and "conflict theory" in the sociological study of stratification in the West lead to different analyses.[3] The functionalist view argues that a structure of inequality (i.e., stratification) is necessary and valuable, since without it people would not be motivated to undertake the training and preparation for various positions needed in a complex society, to assume the burdens of difficult and demanding posts, and to perform in their jobs in a highly motivated way. Since modernizing and industrial societies have a complex network of occupational and authority hierarchies, an involved set of material, power, and status differentials is unavoidable. Seen in this light, Soviet authorities may have arbitrarily introduced some particularly dastardly forms of inequality, but the present, very unequal form of Soviet society confirms the Western view that an elaborate system of stratification is one of the "imperatives" of industrialization, and that the early Bolsheviks were foolish to think they could do without such a system.

The familiar counter to this argument, the conflict view, is that inequality and stratification are fundamentally and inherently exploitative and unjust, at least as they have existed up to now. Purely and simply, they represent ways in which certain powerful groups manage to control and oppress less powerful groups. All such ruling groups promote ideas about the necessity and legitimacy of existing forms of inequality, but these should be seen as the self-serving rationalizations for exploitation that they are. In all complex societies

[1]The classic study of the move away from egalitarianism in the Soviet Union is Barrington Moore, *Soviet Politics: The Dilemma of Power* (1959). For an analysis of stratification in Russia in the late Stalinist period, see Alex Inkeles (1950:465–479). For an analysis of the contemporary system of entrenched privileges in the U.S.S.R., see Mervyn Matthews (1978).

[2]One common theme in analyses of Soviet stratification is that greater income equality than in capitalist societies may have been achieved, but that this was done through concentrations of power and of privileges associated with power that are much greater than under capitalism, so that political position determines economic rewards, rather than the reverse (Goldthorpe, 1966:648–659). The classic statement of the primacy of political power in Soviet stratification is, of course, Milovan Djilas, *The New Class* (1957). However, in recent years scholars have even disputed whether incomes are more equally distributed in the Soviet Union than under capitalism. F. L. Pryor (1972:639–650) argues that incomes in the U.S.S.R. are more equally distributed than in Britain and America, but less equally than in other East European countries. Peter Wiles (1974) argues that incomes of nonagricultural workers in the U.S.S.R. are about as unequally distributed as in Britain, so that the overall Soviet income distribution is probably more unequal if the depressed Soviet rural population is taken into account. The issue cannot be properly studied until comprehensive income distribution statistics are released for the Soviet Union.

[3]See the classic debates between Kingsley Davis and Wilbert Moore on the one hand and Melvin Tumin on the other in Bendix and Lipset, 1966; also G. Lenski, 1966.

existing inequalities are in this sense "irrational" and could certainly be sharply reduced, if not eliminated. Through this prism, the Soviet experience is seen as a failed or sidetracked experiment, or simply as a cruel and hypocritical hoax. For those who argue this point from a socialist rather than an anarchist view, the conclusion is often that, for a variety of historical, geopolitical, psychological, and other reasons, "real" socialism was never really tried in Russia, which instead succumbed to revisionism, state capitalism, social imperialism, or some such "deformity."

For many of those who, in spite of the failure of egalitarianism in the Soviet Union, remain unconvinced of the validity of the functionalist argument, China in the period since the Cultural Revolution has seemed to offer fresh hope. Before that time the Chinese case did not look all that different from the Soviet one, with the pre-1949 economic and political elite dispossessed but a new, complex set of hierarchies and privileges installed. Military officers, high cadres, intellectuals, and other groups enjoyed a variety of material and nonmaterial benefits, and an elitist and highly competitive educational system tended to assure that those who already possessed privileges in the new society would have privileged children as well. Then in a series of dramatic reforms and programs begun in the early 1960s and culminating in the Cultural Revolution (1966–1969) and its aftermath, a thorough attempt was made to restructure Chinese society along more egalitarian lines. It is with the nature of those changes and their subsequent fate that we are concerned here.

Destratification

The egalitarian tide began to gather force before the Cultural Revolution. Mao Tse-tung in 1963–1965 was already expressing grave concern about the social consequences of the existing educational system, arguing that schooling was too long and complex, thus divorcing students from the realities of labor and contact with the masses while motivating them to become members of the bureaucratic or intellectual elites. He called for shortened schooling, more practical courses, and more physical labor in the curriculum, and promoted such novel ideas as letting students whisper answers to each other in class and doze off during boring lessons (Mao, 1969a:42–44, 1974:242–252). With characteristic bluntness, Mao proclaimed, "The present schooling system, curriculum, and methods of teaching and examination must all be changed because they trample people underfoot. . . . One cannot [should not] read too many books. . . . Should one read too many of them. . . one would become a bookworm, a dogmatist, or a revisionist [Mao, 1969a:43–44]." Experiments with shorter periods of schooling began, student labor stints were increased, and increasing stress was placed on political activism and class background, rather than grades, in educational selections. In 1965 Mao also criticized the Ministry of Public Health as the "Ministry of Urban Lords" for its disproportionate concentration of resources on urban health problems, and he initiated a redirection of investment and personnel toward rural health care, resulting eventually in a new set of institutions, including "barefoot doctor" paramedical personnel and cooperative health insurance systems in the countryside (Mao, 1969b:20). In 1965 ranks were also eliminated from the Chinese armed forces, and Mao and some other leaders made more and more statements arguing that if the existing system of inequality were not transformed further, China would succumb to "revisionism" (i.e., Soviet-style socialism) and foresake the egalitarian ideals for which the revolution had been fought. The next year the Cultural Revolution brought this emerging critique to a dramatic climax, as millions of student and worker radicals took to the streets against the existing elite they called "capitalist roaders" and "bourgeois powerholders." Educational institutions at all levels, mass associations, and even the Chinese Communist party itself ceased to function while contending factions struggled for positions of dominance in this new revolution.

When the dust cleared 3 years later (thanks in good measure to the vigorous "dustpans" wielded by teams of workers and soldiers sent to suppress the disorders), many institutions had been altered significantly. The most far-reaching changes occurred in education, a realm of obvious importance for determining whether or how existing inequalities would be transmitted over generations. My sketch of the reforms introduced will be brief, as more detailed treatments exist elsewhere (see, e.g., Pepper, 1978).

First, the length of schooling was shortened at all levels. Primary schooling was reduced from 6 to 5 years, secondary or middle schooling from 6 to 4 or 5, and university level programs were shortened from 4–6 years to 3–3½ years generally. Second, the curriculum was modified. Subjects and themes that were considered unessential or bourgeois were dropped, and the remaining academic program was pared back to allow for increased doses of labor, military training, and political study. In many secondary schools students began to spend 2 or 3 months or more every year working on farms or in factories, in contrast with the 2 or 3 weeks or so they spent before the Cultural Revolution. The theme of "open-door schooling" was extolled, with students combining theory with practice inside and outside the classroom, and being urged to become enlightened manual laborers rather than to strive for entrance to higher schooling and to the ranks of white-collar workers. Third, China abandoned the previous system of having "keypoint" primary and secondary schools that received extra resources, the most qualified teachers, and the best students (the latter recruited in urban areas by citywide, standardized entrance examinations). Special schools for the children of military officers and high cadres were also disbanded. Subsequently all schools as well as students were supposed to be considered equal. Students had to attend primary and middle schools in their immediate neighborhood, with no entrance examinations involved.[4] Energetic efforts were made to universalize educational access in both rural and urban areas, the ideal being at least primary school completion in the former, and at least lower middle school completion in the latter. Fourth, within schools the examinations that Mao Tse-tung had branded "surprise attacks" against students were modified or abandoned, and although homework, quizzes, and grades remained, it became official policy to promote students regardless of how they did on such exercises. Fifth, the universities, after they reopened in 1970–1972, were similarly transformed. Not only was the period of study shortened, but some universities were in fact closed entirely as "bourgeois citadels," and others were "dispersed" to the countryside to forge closer ties with the peasant masses. Within the remaining universities the same "open door" emphasis prevailed, with students spending substantial periods each year in manual labor and in social investigations in factories and on farms, or in workshops run right on campus. Graduate training on a systematic basis ceased, although a few students were apparently kept on in apprenticelike training after graduation.

University students were selected by a method that was perhaps the most novel part of these reforms. It became virtually impossible in most fields to go directly from secondary school to the university. Instead, secondary school graduates were required to go out and put down roots in society—a few in factories or the military, but most in rural communes or state farms, which absorbed 17 million urban youths in the period 1968–1978. University students were then to be selected from youths who had spent at least 2 years at their posts. Initially no examinations were to be held for the selection process, nor were student academic records to be inspected. Instead, individuals were to apply through their work units and then had to pass through stages of discussion and nomination by their work mates, approval by the local party authorities, and then a final screening by the university. Labor enthusiasm, class background, and political activism were supposed to be the primary criteria, rather than intelligence or academic ability. Initially, there was not even a rule that the entrants be secondary school graduates, although by 1973 the problems of teaching university-level material to large numbers of students who were only primary school graduates led to stipulations that candidates should have the equivalent of at least lower middle schooling, and to a controversial effort to make the final university screening stage into a more rigorous examination procedure.[5] This reformed selection process attempted

[4]Where there were not enough teachers and places in the neighborhood middle schools for all who wanted to attend, a system of recommendation from lower-level schools, considering criteria such age, class labels (see n. 6), political activism, and family economic circumstances was used to select students, instead of entrance examinations.

[5]After 1973 there was an attempt by radical leaders to repudiate these screening exams, during which they popularized as the model applicant Chang T'ieh-sheng, who was said to have turned in a blank examination paper and to have protested that he had been too busy integrating himself with the peasants to cram for the exam (Whyte, 1977).

to reduce or eliminate the advantage that the urban, educated classes had enjoyed via the standardized university entrance examinations of the pre-1966 period and to fill universities with a new breed of "worker–peasant–soldier" students of good class backgrounds.[6] These new students were expected to return to their work or military units after graduation, rather than using university training as a route of entry into the privileged elite. The egalitarian wave did not, however, lead to a massive expansion of university enrollments; in fact, in the early 1970s Chinese universities had only about half as many students as they had had at their peak before the Cultural Revolution, although in the meantime the number of middle school graduates had expanded dramatically.[7] Finally, education was deemed to be too important a matter to be left in the hands of the educational bureaucrats, and revolutionary committees dominated by members of military or worker propaganda teams sent in from the outside (but also including representatives of teachers, students, and administrators) took over the administration of schools from principals and chancellors.

These reforms involved several policy changes. First, they stressed quantity over quality. The lower levels of education were rapidly expanded while the highest levels were contracted, and the conception of schools as being primarily concerned with the detection and channeling of talented young minds was rejected. At all levels the new system shifted emphasis away from book and classroom learning toward new forms of practical training that, it was hoped, would make students less likely to think of themselves as a privileged stratum. In terms of manpower policy, these reforms seem to reflect the conviction that what a developing society like China needs most is not primarily highly trained experts but a mass of well-motivated manual workers with some basic level of education and technical skill. Even the choosing of the select minority who would receive advanced education was based on criteria that were designed to inhibit elitist aspirations—things like labor enthusiam, relations with the masses, class background, and political activism rather than intelligence and academic aptitude. In this regard it is not inappropriate to see the Chinese reforms as a revolutionary effort to find an alternative to the educational meritocracies of other modern societies.

This same egalitarian urge swept through other areas of society. Take the case of the policy toward cadres, the leading personnel in the bureaucratic system created by the Chinese Communists. In the Cultural Revolution itself

---

[6]Class background labels refer to designations given each family in China on the basis of the family's economic position just before 1949. They became increasingly important after 1962 in judging and stigmatizing or rewarding individuals. Although the labels have no relationship to current jobs or economic standing, they remained in use, inherited through the male line (Kraus, 1977:54–74); however, see also, p. 325).

[7]University enrollments rose from 200,000 in 1972–1973 to 584,000 in 1976–1977, but in 1959–1960 there had been 810,000 students. In comparison, the number of middle school students increased from 14 million in 1965–1966 to 35 million in 1972–1973, and then to 58.3 million in 1976–1977. See Whyte (1975:694) and Pepper (1977:815–816).

most leading cadres were severely attacked as "bourgeois powerholders" and "capitalist roaders." Some had their houses ransacked by Red Guards, lost their posts, and were confined to "cowsheds" (often small closets or bathrooms in their organizations) while they examined their errors. In several localities their domestic servants were turned out en masse as vestiges of exploitation, and a system of ration coupons for industrial products distributed according to salary (which benefited leading cadres and other high-income groups) was abolished. Separate dining halls for leading personnel were eliminated, along with the special schools for cadre children already noted. In a number of places ranking cadres were forced to move out of their spacious and well-furnished apartments and into humbler quarters, while several families of ordinary workers moved into their former abodes. Many cadres and specialists who were classified as members of the "national bourgeoisie" (i.e., former owners of industrial and commercial property) had their bank accounts confiscated, lost their privately owned homes, and were demoted to menial and low-paying jobs. The network of special party and cadre training schools designed to select and train the elite within this elite also ceased operating, and large numbers of cadres were sent to live among the peasants in distant villages in an effort to purge them of their bureaucratic ways (see Chen, 1973). After 1969 a new network of "May 7th cadre schools" was set up to send the cadres to the countryside in rotation (initially for 1–3 years, later for only 6 months generally) for agricultural labor and political study designed to "reeducate" them. Cadres in production units were required to spend regular periods (say, 1 day a week) laboring at ordinary work posts in their own units. Throughout society, a modified form of administration was introduced, the revolutionary committee, in which administrators shared power with representatives of their subordinates and outside workers or soldiers. In general these reforms were designed to prevent cadres in various sectors of society from becoming an elitist "new class," with vested interests separate from those they led (see Pfeffer, 1973).

Many of these same policies were applied to intellectuals. Both those trained under the old society and abroad and those trained in China after 1949 were portrayed as arrogant and impractical, concerned more with fame and professional prerogatives than with the needs of production or the opinions of the masses. They too were required to transform their attitudes through stints at manual labor and in May 7th cadre schools. They were told to be willing to serve the state in any capacity in which they were needed rather than zealously planning their ascent up a career ladder in their special fields. They were castigated for being overly concerned with useless theory, and directed to learn the practical skills of ordinary workers and peasants. Many, in fact, were shifted permanently to manual labor jobs. Teachers were told to cease acting like dictators of the classroom, and students were encouraged to "go against the tide" and criticize teachers who made ideological errors. Doctors were criticized for lording it over nurses and hospital attendants, and some hospitals implemented role reversals, with doctors mopping floors and nurses

(but apparently not attendants) performing operations. Royalty fees for journalists and writers were eliminated in favor of a straight salary system. Most
existing works in literature and the arts were denounced as bourgeois
"poisonous weeds," and new, more politically pure works, such as the model
revolutionary operas, took their place. In general an amateur ethic was
stressed, with poetry, short stories, and paintings increasingly produced by
ordinary workers, peasants, and soldiers in their spare time. Individual credits
for academic, literary, and artistic work increasingly gave way to collective
and anonymous creations.

Other privileged sectors of Chinese society were also affected. Overseas
Chinese—those who had relatives abroad or had themselves returned from
abroad to live in China—had enjoyed a series of special privileges. They could
receive remittance payments from overseas relatives and use these and special
ration coupons to buy goods not available to others, often in special stores
with restricted access. Special housing was provided in a number of areas for
returned Overseas Chinese, and in some places individuals could use funds
sent from overseas to purchase privately owned apartments much superior in
quality to those occupied by ordinary citizens. Special schools were created to
help returned Overseas Chinese youths adapt to the Chinese system of education and to prepare them for the university examinations, and such students
were also given some preference in university selection and were made eligible
to attend a number of special universities established especially for them. In
general Overseas Chinese were given special consideration in education, access to jobs, and other advantages, with an Overseas Chinese Affairs Commission looking out for their interests. Most of these privileges were swept
away as a result of the Cultural Revolution. The Overseas Chinese Affairs
Commission was disbanded, and the special stores, rations, and schools
disappeared. Some of the special private housing was apparently also confiscated and given over to ordinary families to live in. Chinese with relatives
abroad could still receive remittances, but in a period of intense suspicion of
those with "overseas ties," some were pressured to cut off these ties and refuse
to receive the special funds that set them off from their neighbors and fellow
workers.

Not the least of the consequences of this egalitarian surge was a modification of the wage and incentive system. Even before the Cultural Revolution
the incentive systems used in industrial enterprises had come under attack,
and existing piece rate and bonus systems were denounced for "putting
material incentives in command" (over politics) and enticing workers toward
revisionism with "sugar-coated bullets." These systems were almost universally discarded in favor of straight time-rate (i.e., fixed wage) systems, with
workers expected to be motivated to produce more by the operation of moral
incentives and group pressure. The existing system of differentiated ranks and
wages remained, but now reflected seniority primarily, rather than productivity or related factors. And most urban workers and other employees were

"frozen" in their existing ranks, with no large-scale promotions occurring after 1963. In 1975 even the remaining fixed wage system fell under attack in the campaign to criticize "bourgeois right." Using quotations from Mao Tse-tung, the documents of this campaign pointed out the similarities between China's eight-grade industrial worker's wage scale and systems used in industrial capitalism. Although they argued that the socialist principle of distribution according to work had to be followed, they claimed that unless efforts were made to gradually restrict the range of material differentials, these inequalities would spawn revisionism and an eventual restoration of capitalism (see Yao, 1975). Urban wages were virtually frozen while rural pay scales were allowed to increase gradually, a plan intended to reduce the urban–rural income gap, one of the "three differences" the Chinese, as good Marxists, were pledged to eliminate (the other two being the worker–peasant and the mental–manual labor differences). In the countryside, a number of time–rate and other more egalitarian work point systems and other reforms were pushed in an effort to reduce inequality within villages. Throughout Chinese society, systems of distribution and selection increasingly turned away from an emphasis on knowledge, skill, and individual productivity and toward a stress on political activism, labor enthusiasm, and class background.

All these changes did not result in a society without inequality and stratification. In fact most of these reforms did not affect income distribution in major ways, but were aimed primarily at reducing the privileges, prestige, and favorable mobility opportunities of advantaged groups in society. They were accompanied in the Chinese media by arguments that such differentials and privileges were not a necessary feature of socialism or a developing economy, but were in fact the first foot in the door of revisionism and capitalist restoration. The altered system was seen as more suitable for generating the mass labor enthusiasm and mobilization of popular will that were needed to develop China's economy.

Several features of the Chinese social scene when compared with the Soviet Union gave some analysts hope that a way had been found to avoid abandoning the egalitarian ideals of the revolution in the pursuit of economic development. First, the Chinese revolution had been a mass revolution that developed in the countryside, rather than emerging from a small urban conspiratorial elite. As such the need for, and skill in, mobilizing the laboring masses should have been more developed in China, and the impulse to control those masses as "undisciplined" and to cater to the interests of urban elites should have been less compelling. Second, China could learn by observing the "negative experiences" of the Soviet Union, and in fact Mao and others had reacted against the social consequences of trying to introduce the "Soviet model" into China in the 1950s. Third, China has built a much more intensive and pervasive organizational system than exists in the Soviet Union. With more total state control over nonagricultural employment there is less need to rely on material incentives to allocate personnel than in the more free Soviet labor market, and within Chinese work units it may be easier to mobilize group pressure in support of production and other goals, without using material incentives.[8] Also, some would argue that China's more backward economy and huge population simply make a manpower policy stressing geared-down schooling and an emphasis on mobilizing the masses of manual laborers more suitable, especially since advanced technology and science can be borrowed from abroad when needed rather than developed afresh at considerable cost. For reasons such as these, the post-Cultural Revolution reforms seemed to offer new hope or evidence that more egalitarian social arrangements could be adopted and sustained.

Restratification

All of such discussion now appears increasingly academic if not silly. Only a few months after Mao's death in 1976, a new leadership set about dismantling the egalitarian reforms of the previous decade with enthusiasm and perhaps even glee. Mao's fears that his programs might be swamped by "revisionism" after his death appear justified, for the revisions are occurring on a wholesale and rapid basis. In the wake of the purge, a month after Mao's death, of the "gang of four" (Mao's widow, Chiang Ch'ing, and three of his other radical supporters), the new leaders have utilized the campaign against them to justify their attempt to turn the clock back to the 1960s, if not the 1950s. My account of these changes can only be preliminary, as the situation is still in flux, with dramatic revelations occuring almost daily.

In education the pace of dismantling the egalitarian reforms has been particularly swift. As early as 1973–1975 there were efforts to tighten classroom discipline, to place more stress on academics, and to restore university entrance examinations, although in 1975–1976 this "reverse tide" was attacked. Since Mao's death the emphasis on educational quality and standards has won the day. The reduced, 10-year sequence of primary and secondary schooling has not been abandoned, although now students start a year earlier, at age 6. Nor has the goal of universalizing lower levels of schooling been repudiated. But the network of key-point primary and secondary schools and universities has been restored (actually there are several nested networks—a national one, provincial ones, and city and other local ones) and is once again receiving extra resources, the best teachers, and the most up-to-date curricular innovations. The neighborhood principle of student enrollment is being abandoned, at least at the secondary school level, in favor of restored citywide entrance examinations to select the most qualified students to attend the key-point schools. Within schools the "open-door" emphasis is being cut back by declar-

---

[8]For an argument on the lesser importance of material incentives in China, see Riskin (1975). For a description of the uniquely penetrating organizational system in China, see Whyte (1974).

ing once again that "the main task of students is to study,"[9] so that they spend, at most, only a few weeks a year at manual labor, as they did before the Cultural Revolution. The curriculum is being strengthened, with basic science courses, foreign languages, and other discarded or reduced subjects restored and upgraded, and in some cases even introduced into primary schools. The curriculum and textbooks are to be standarized, on a nationwide basis, rather than being adapted to the situation and needs of local communities and production units. Quizzes and exams are being stressed, with students once again in danger of failing and not being promoted. Needless to say, Mao's "whispering the answers" and "dozing off in class" are no longer in vogue. Respect for teachers has become a prominent theme. Strict control of teacher allocation and other educational matters is being placed back in the hands of the Ministry of Education bureaucracy. What is more, for the first time an explicit system of tracking within schools is being lauded, with students given tests and then sorted into "fast," "average," and "slow" classes in order to facilitate maximum learning (*People's Daily*, 1978f).[10]

Perhaps more important, students now know that a select minority among them have the prospect of going directly to the university and escaping assignment to the countryside. The sending out of youths for farm labor is gradually being abandoned, but many urban secondary school graduates for some time to come will still have to serve a stint in the countryside. But now most new university students will be selected directly from secondary schools, and those who display particular brilliance can even be selected for the university before they complete middle school. University selection once again hinges primarily on standardized entrance examinations, the first of which was given in December 1977. Scores on these exams are the major, although not the exclusive, criterion for selection, and it is interesting to note that special age and marital status waivers were provided to enable middle school graduates of 1966–1967 to sit for the first exams, apparently on the grounds that they were the final classes to emerge before the Cultural Revolution reforms debased the quality of schooling. Large numbers of disbanded or dispersed universities have been reestablished, and selected institutions have been directed to take in groups of nonboarding day students in order to increase enrollments as rapidly as possible, although this policy obviously increases the advantage urban youths have over rural ones in gaining entrance.

At the university level as well, time away in communes, factories,

---

[9]The phrase refers to part of Mao's May 7, 1966 directive: "This [policy] holds good for students, too. While their main task is to study, they should in addition to their studies learn other things, that is, industrial work, farming, and military affairs. They should also criticize the bourgeoisie [p. 7]." This directive was used in the Cultural Revolution and afterward to justify a shift away from pure academics. Now by merely moving the emphasis back to the first clause, the entire policy emphasis has been shifted back to what it was previously.

[10]For the decision restoring centralized control to the Ministry of Education, see *British Broadcasting Corporation* (hereafter *BBC*), 1978a. On the standardized tests, see *Hsinhua News Bulletin* (1978b:31).

political study, and other activities is to be curtailed so that students can master academics. The period of university education has been lengthened, generally back to 4 years for liberal arts programs and 5 years for science programs. Furthermore, new graduate students are being enrolled through examinations on a systematic basis for the first time since the Cultural Revolution. Also, the principle that graduates should return to their original production units after graduation has now been revised to apply to only a few regular colleges (primarily in agriculture and forestry), but mainly to graduates of the separate network of work unit-run technical schools, the rural "May 7th colleges" and the "July 21st workers' colleges." Graduates of most university programs can now be assigned to positions in the professions and the bureaucracy without apology. There have even been references to the possibility of introducing new kinds of tests as a way of allocating graduates to suitable work positions outside. So the new type of university student is to be quite different from the political and labor activist of earlier years, a fact that has already led to tensions between freshmen and more advanced students in several institutions.[11]

The lot of cadres has also changed. Already in the early 1970s some of the more extreme actions against them were reversed. In many cases they were restored to their jobs, switched back to their more spacious apartments, with their mass "tenants" ejected, and allowed to hire servants again if necessary to cope with the burdens of their work. Their stays in cadre farms were generally reduced to 6-month periods, and since 1977 this system of "May 7th cadre schools" has been dismantled. Those cadres who are members of the "national bourgeoisie" have had their private homes restored to them, their original work posts and salaries given back, and their bank accounts reimbursed, with interest.[12] The network of party and cadre schools designed to train cadres for positions of political and professional leadership has been restored to full operation with fanfare (*Peking Review*, 1977b:6-14). Proper utilization of cadre skills, respect for their authority, trusting them with individual responsibilities, granting them regular promotions (on the basis of performance and not just seniority), and strict organizational discipline are all themes re-emphasized today, although abuses of cadre power are also being attacked (*People's Daily*, 1977f, g; *BBC*, 1978g).[13] In major sectors of society (schools, factories, production brigades, research institutes, and so forth) the

---

[11]The reference to job placement examinations is in Teng Hsiao-p'ing (1978b:9); see also *BBC*, 1978c. On the tension between the different cohorts of students, see Agence France Presse dispatch, Peking, March 22, 1978, published in Hong Kong.

[12]On this change, see Foreign Broadcast Information Service, (hereafter *FBIS*) (1979c:G-5; 1979c:E-17; and 1979e:E-7).

[13]Another recent article (*Red Flag*, 1978:78-80) even pointed out the benefits of the "Taylor system of scientific management" used in early industrial capitalism as a method for managers to get the most work out of their workers. The Taylor system has often been attacked by Western Marxists as a core symbol of capitalist exploitation (see Braverman, 1974).

revolutionary committee form of administration, with its representatives of the masses and outside workers and soldiers, has been junked in favor of a return to a system of individual directors or managers supervised by party committees such as existed before the Cultural Revolution. The "gang of four's" contention that the high incomes and authority of leading cadres inevitably lead them to act like revisionists (an argument curiously close to Djilas's new class thesis) has been labeled as absurd (*Enlightenment Daily*, 1978a; *People's Daily*, 1977c; *Red Flag*, 1977:61–64). There have even been suggestions that leading cadres in production units be offered material bonuses and promotions as rewards for increasing production (*FBIS*, 1979b:J–1; *Peking Review*, 1978g:8, 1978i:21; *People's Daily*, 1978g:4).[14] Finally, there are unconfirmed reports that the restoration of ranks in the military is under consideration (*South China Morning Post*, 1978b).[15]

For intellectuals the shift in emphasis from "red" to "expert" has had dramatic consequences. The Chinese public is being told that the "gang of four" considered all intellectuals virtual class enemies, but that in fact intellectuals are patriotic individuals whose contributions will be vital to the "four modernizations" even if many of them refuse to concern themselves with political matters. Official regulations now specify that at least five-sixths of their working time be devoted to work in their specialties, with manual labor, political study, and other activities confined to the remainder, and preferably to their spare time (*Peking Review*, 1977a:9).[16] Large numbers of intellectuals who had been assigned to manual labor and other jobs not in keeping with their training, in line with the previous emphasis on "jacks of all trades" and the subordination of professional concerns to politics, are now being shifted back to work for which they were trained. Doctors and nurses have been restored to their original roles and their "necessary division of labor" is being lauded. Intellectuals are promised better conditions for their work, including more research funds and equipment, research assistants, and contact with foreign scholars. In some localities, at least, those who make outstanding contributions are being promised access to better housing, preference in getting their children transferred back from the countryside, and special consideration in getting spouses working elsewhere transferred to work in the same place.[17] Basic theoretical research is very much back in vogue. The most prominent current model among intellectuals is a 45-year-old mathematician

[14]Industrial managers are also being threatened with material or penal sanctions for mismanagement and negligence that harm production.

[15]The *South China Morning Post*, on May 5, 1978, reported that the restoration of ranks was under discussion within the Chinese army. On May 23, 1978, the Hong Kong *Wen Hui Pao*, a Communist paper, carried a cryptic denial by a Chinese military spokesman that such a change had occurred.

[16]Teng Hsiao-p'ing (1978a:15) went further, advocating that scientists be able to devote full time to their work.

[17]On the model efforts of Szechwan province in this regard, see *People's Daily* (1978d). On other localities, see *Ta Kung Pao* (1977) and *FBIS* (1979e:K–1).

named Chen Ching-jun, who spent 15 years shut up in his office and library trying to prove (so far with only partial success) the "Goldbach conjecture," which states that every even number larger than 2 can be represented by the sum of two primes (*Peking Review*, 1978a:30). It would be hard to imagine a more perfect counter to the previous stress on intellectuals plunging into manual labor among the masses and solving immediate production problems. Academic titles have been restored, pay raises for teachers and researchers have been carried out or promised, and a few teachers have been promoted to "special grade" status above the regular 11-grade salary rank system, in reward for outstanding achievements in teaching (rather than, say, for political purity or simply seniority) (*BBC*, 1978f).[18] Furthermore, more than 100,000 "rightists," many of them intellectuals who were purged in 1957 for criticizing party rule, have now been pardoned and in many cases restored to work (*Wen Hui Pao*, 1978a).

Banned and disgraced writers and artists have come out of the woodwork and resumed their activity, and both works and themes, domestic and foreign, that were prohibited between 1966 and 1976 are being seen in bookstores and on stage once again. Individual authorship credits are being given more widely again, and the system of royalty payments has been restored.[19] In the arts, but even more so in science, the role of the single creative individual is once again lauded. The autonomy of researchers and research directors is being stressed, and special science classes are being run for party cadres who have to supervise such individuals.[20] Intellectuals are also being recruited into the Communist party in increased numbers. All of these changes find curious reflection in the content of official propaganda in China. Posters that used to show sweaty representatives of the laboring masses advancing from victory to

[18] An informant in Hong Kong who returned from a trip to China in 1978 claimed he was told that the pay for such special grade teachers could range up to 250 yuan a month, or five to six times what the average schoolteacher makes.

[19] Personal communication from Chinese visiting scholars (1979). The royalty payments are apparently different from those used in the West in providing fees calculated by the number of characters written rather than by the number of copies of the book or article sold.

[20] See, for example, the following statements:

> However, we must not underestimate or deny the role of the individual in the scientific–technological field. In science and technology, the hard work and creativity of an individual is extremely important [*FBIS*, 1977a:E–8].

> Some research should be done together with the masses now, and some research has to be done by the professionals alone [*FBIS*, 1977b:E–5].

> The history of science shows what great results can be produced in the field of science from the discovery of a genuinely talented person! . . . There must be a division of responsibilities and a system of individual responsibility at each post from top to bottom. . . . We should give the directors and deputy directors of research institutes a free hand in the work of science and technology according to their division of labor. . . . We must not look askance at them. Party committees should get acquainted with their work and examine it, but should not attempt to supplant them [Teng Hsiao-p'ing, 1978a:16–17].

victory have an addition, usually in the front row—a slim figure with a lab coat and glasses but no perspiration, smiling broadly at being returned to his proper place in official esteem.

Overseas Chinese similarly see a sharp change in policies that affect them. Again the changes predate Mao's death, although the pace has accelerated since then. Beginning in 1972 exit visas were granted on a large scale to those who wished to join kin abroad. The Overseas Chinese Affairs Commission has been restored, and an effort made to re-establish the privileges and special consideration these people enjoyed before 1966. Where confiscated, their private homes and better quality public flats are to be returned to them, and there are reports that their kin abroad will once again be able to send funds to purchase them private housing. Skilled personnel of Chinese extraction willing to come to China are reportedly being promised a number of benefits: provision of well-equipped laboratories, guarantees that husbands and wives will be assigned to work in the same place, and promises that they can leave China again when they wish. The network of special primary and middle schools catering to returned Overseas Chinese is being reestablished, two special universities for Overseas Chinese have reemerged, and youths from such families are being promised a certain preference in competition for places in ordinary universities. Special ration cards and purchasing privileges for Overseas Chinese have been restored. They are also being promised that they will not be automatically suspect politically because of their ties abroad, that their ability to receive remittances will not be interfered with, and that they will receive equal or preferential treatment in admission to the Communist Youth League, the Communist party, the army, and sensitive work posts. Chinese still abroad are once again being encouraged to invest funds in development projects within China, at promised rates of interest substantially higher than those available to citizens in China (Ching, 1978; *People's Daily*, 1978b; *BBC*, 1978b; *Wen Hui Pao*, 1978a).[21]

For the average Chinese, the first general wage adjustment in 14 years was carried out in late 1977. The exact effects of this wage reform on inequality are difficult to ascertain. Apparently many of these raises were concentrated among those in low ranks with long periods of work, which suggests further equalization. At the same time another set of raises was being granted in recognition of performance and contributions, which may suggest more inequality, and we have already noted the movement of many specialists back into high-paying positions (*Peking Review*, 1978e:17; *Beijing Review*, 1979b:39, *People's Daily*, 1978a).[22] The Maoist restriction to fixed time–rate

---

[21]The author saw a notice in Canton announcing the re-establishment of special overseas remittance purchasing certificates and special stores as of April 1, 1978.

[22]Chinese authorities also announced the reinstatement of a 1963 innovation award system that had been discontinued since the Cultural Revolution: those who originate technical innovations that improve production are eligible for prizes of up to 10,000 yuan (*Beijing Review*, 1979c:8).

monthly wages has also been waived in favor of units adopting systems of piece rates or time rates with bonuses, which would also seem to foster inequality. In fact, the Chinese press is now filled with stories of "closet material incentivists," firms that restored such schemes in 1972–1974 in spite of official disapproval (*Peking Review*, 1978b:6–8; *People's Daily*, 1978g). Furthermore, there are the special "above grade" and professor and researcher promotions referred to earlier, which are clearly not based on the principle of raising the lowest, as well as a recent report that worker grades above grade eight may be formally instituted (*Ta Kung Pao*, 1978b:2; *Peking Review*, 1978e:16). In 1979 a new set of wage increases was announced, clearly targeted toward those already receiving high pay and thus increasing their advantage (*FBIS*, 1979k).

Since urbanites are being promised that their wages will regularly be adjusted upward from now on in recognition of increases in productivity, there is some danger that the income gap between city and countryside will be enlarged. Whether this happens or not depends on a number of factors whose implications are not yet entirely clear. Although rural grain taxes have apparently been reset from the fixed levels of the previous 2 decades to new levels based on the average grain yields of the years 1971–1975, which might suggest a higher tax rate, the government announced that after 1979 the price it pays localities for grain delivered above the tax quotas will be raised, while the prices of manufactured inputs for agriculture, such as chemical fertilizer, pumps, and tractors, will be reduced (*Peking Review*, 1978j:13). These price changes will improve the terms of trade between city and countryside. However, if there are decreasing marginal returns from the use of such modern inputs, so that expenditures on them increase faster than grain yields increase, then rural incomes may still suffer. In fact, a study of over 2000 production teams (the lowest level of the commune structure) in several provinces over the period 1965–1977 showed that this is just what had been happening, so that payment for peasant labor declined 20% on the average in those terms of spite of their general increase in production (*Enlightenment Daily*, 1978b). It remains to be seen whether the announced price changes and other policies are sufficient to offset the forces working to increase the rural–urban income gap.

Within the countryside increasing inequality is quite clearly being officially encouraged. Crop specialization is being fostered much more actively, so that communes well endowed to grow cash crops or situated to supply urban markets will prosper disproportionately. Efforts in the preceding period to raise the accounting unit up from the production team of 20–40 households to the production brigade of 200–500 households (often an entire village), thus standardizing payment within this larger unit, have been criticized, and localities are being encouraged to decentralize back to the team level. Within the team, piece rates and other incentive remuneration systems, which benefit the strong and able, have been tolerated at least since 1971. More recently, there has even been a far-reaching effort to encourage the fixing of production quotas and rewards for work groups within the production team, a policy intended to foster more income diversity and competition within the team itself. In general, the previous effort to place administrative limits on the maximum income particular families and rural subgroups could earn has been denounced as an irrational policy (*FBIS*, 1979c:E–18, 1979g:E–7, 1979i:K–1; *People's Daily*, 1979a).[23]

On a more general note, the system of class background labels used for 3 decades as one important criterion for determining access to opportunities and privileges seems in the process of being dismantled. The previous policy was intended in part to improve the social position of groups oppressed before 1949 (those labeled poor peasants, lower-middle peasants, workers, and so forth) and to discriminate against former elites (those labeled capitalists, merchants, landlords, rich peasants, and so forth—labels all based on individual and family status before 1949). Now the order of the day is individual performance rather than social background, and in 1979 the government declared that, except in special cases, bearers of landlord, rich peasant, and other "negative" labels would be reclassified innocuously as "commune members" or "workers" and their offspring given equal consideration for education, jobs, and other benefits (*FBIS*, 1979f:E–17, G–5; *People's Daily*, 1979b). Of course, it will take more than decrees from Peking to eliminate the social stigma of class background that has been fostered for a generation.

Admittedly not all the post-Cultural Revolution policies have been repudiated and not all the previous ones restored. Special schools for cadre children and separate dining halls for cadres have not been reported, at least in explicit form. Primary and secondary schooling have been kept at the shortened, 10-year length, and political and other criteria still may play some role in university students' selection. Moral incentives and political work have not been rejected, but only confined to a reduced role. Still, on balance, one must be impressed with the comprehensiveness of this attempt to turn the clock back and with the dramatic speed with which it has been implemented, beginning even before Mao was safely ensconced in his crystal sarcophagus.

---

[23]*FBIS* (1979j:E–12) demonstrates the advantages of using dialectical reasoning in its discussion of two different strategies for reducing income disparities within the countryside:

> The first is going backward, that is, as the "gang of four" advocated, using restrictions to prevent well-to-do production teams from advancing so that poor teams can catch up. That would not narrow the gap. Even if the gap could be narrowed that way [sic], it would only lead everyone into the dead end of common poverty. We must not do this. The other way leads us forward. First we must admit the gap exists, oppose egalitarianism, permit and encourage some commune members from advanced units with high collective incomes to receive more income and live better lives in order to serve as examples to lead the poorer production teams forward, to encourage them, and to make them see that there is hope ahead.

We must examine some of the reasons given for this restratification of Chinese society.

Analysis

The arguments used by China's new leaders and in the Chinese press fall into several categories, not all of which are of much interest to us here. For instance, the previous egalitarian surge is described as a wrongheaded deviation fostered by the "gang of four" in violation of Mao's true wishes. It is not made very clear why, if this is so, Mao failed to tell the Chinese that himself at any time during his final decade. Much of the discussion in the press involves going back and citing Marx, Engels, Lenin, Stalin, and Mao to prove that the sorts of incentives and differentials now being fostered are in keeping with the Marxist canons. Like most such doctrinal exercises, this produces little enlightenment, since all these fathers of the faith made contradictory statements on equality and remuneration at various times. In any case, most of the oracular statements cited are so vague that they can cover a variety of sins as well as a few virtues. For instance, Maoists and modernizers can all agree with the standard formula that under socialism distribution should be carried out according to work contributions, rather than absolutely equally. But they cannot agree on meaningful criteria for comparing the work contributions of political leaders, professors, lathe workers, and peasants, and therefore they disagree about whether, according to this formula, there should be more or less inequality than there is at present.

If we descend a level below such ideological formulas, we find that most of the arguments relied on in introducing restratification are ones quite familiar, if not dear, to every Western social scientist; we are back in the lexicon of functionalism. Fundamentally China's new leaders are telling their people and us that material, power, and status differentials are functional and necessary for the parts they play in "the four modernizations," that is, in the drive to transform China into an economically developed society. The reduction of these "reasonable" differentials in the previous decade is said to have done grievous harm to China's economy and social fabric. Let us review some of the specific charges here.

In education it is claimed that the reformed system was turning out low-quality and even semiliterate graduates. The combination of de-emphasis on tests, entrance exams, and academics generally plus no failures, the harassment of teachers, and few prospects for advancement to the university after middle school meant that students had little motivation to study their lessons, and thus many did not bother. Even those who were motivated found that the short period of study, much of it spent out in labor and other activities, and also the stress on political credentials, made it difficult or even politically risky to learn much in their studies. At the university level the new students were so diverse in background and so burdened with "open door" activities that they could not even master middle-school level technical skills.[24] In any case, the Cultural Revolution hiatus in university training (no graduates were produced for the 7 years between 1966 and 1972, and longer in many institutions) and the termination of systematic graduate training meant that China was deprived of a new generation of highly trained experts that would be needed even to keep abreast of developments in advanced countries.

On a different note, the reformed university selection system turned out to be prone to a number of abuses. The previous entrance examination system might be considered a "bourgeois dictatorship of marks," but it must be kept in mind that in China as elsewhere, standardized examinations were introduced in an effort to detect real talent at all levels in society and to prevent university places from being monopolized by offspring of the wealthy and powerful. With standardized examinations gone and replaced by a system of recommendations from local units, the opportunities for using "pull" increased substantially. Cases both of local cadres getting their offspring or kin nominated and of higher cadres pulling strings to get their own children admitted "by the back door" have been noted in the press and seem to have occurred on a large scale. Thus, it is not even clear how much this reformed selection system served its original purposes of broadening the opportunities

---

[24]Chou Jung-hsin, Minister of Education in 1975, was hounded out of office by the radicals for making this and other criticisms, and he subsequently died in disgrace. However, the scientific and technological group of the Shanghai Municipal Revolutionary Committee subsequently tested college graduates about to be assigned to work in various scientific and technological departments to see if they had mastered basic knowledge that *middle school* students should know. The results were not encouraging: 68% flunked mathematics, 70% flunked physics, 76% flunked chemistry, and some could not answer even a single question in their specialty (*People's Daily*, 1977d).

On the new academic emphasis, we find quotes such as the following:

Examinations, which were indiscriminately looked down upon with contempt, now are used as an effective means to raise academic levels and arouse the students' interest in study [FBIS, 1977:E–20].

Socialist colleges . . . are not ladders for a privileged stratum to climb. In a socialist society, the people all have equal rights to go to college, quite different from the old China. But socialist society is still not communism and the differences in the level of education between rural and urban schools, a relic of history, still exist. The gap is being narrowed step by step, but the only way to eliminate it completely is to develop primary and secondary education in the rural areas and raise their educational standards—all this on the basis of a steady growth in production. It cannot be done by changing the principle of selecting the best students [*Hsinhua News Bulletin*, 1978a:17].

Last year in selecting students quite a few cadre and intellectual children got good grades in the examination, had good political performance, and in accordance with the selection principles, were admitted to universities. . . . Old cadres are precious resources of the revolution, intellectuals are laboring people, and if their excellent offspring are accepted into the universities in accord with the party's policy, that will aid the early realization of the four modernizations, and that is the correct embodiment of the party's proletarian line [*People's Daily*, 1978i].

for offspring of ordinary workers and peasants to attend college, or enrolling primarily public-spirited diligent laborers.[25]

The wholesale criticism of cadres is said to have produced at least three different kinds of problems. Many cadres were apparently so intimidated by the harsh treatment they received and by the mercurial shifts in higher policies that they became indecisive and refused to take initiative and exercise responsibility within their units. Others descended into factional activity, cultivating ties and recruiting supporters to protect themselves and to attack their local opponents. In response to such factional activity, the abolition of "bourgeois" rules and regulations, the persecution of their leaders, and the power exercised in their units by untrained outsiders, many subordinates became cynical, indifferent, or simply lazy. In other words, a general crisis of authority resulted, and the recent changes are an effort to recreate decisive leadership and willing followership.[26]

As for intellectuals, it is argued that most were intimidated or made resentful. They felt they were treated as if they were tantamount to class enemies. Not only were their contributions not appreciated but they were in danger of being branded with various "labels" and transferred for "re-education" if they tried to devote their energies to their specialties. And many were transferred to work inappropriate to their training, others worked listlessly, and some feigned illness to withdraw from work altogether. Thus, even the expertise of those intellectuals China did possess was not well utilized, leading the country to fall further below the scientific and intellectual levels of the rest of the world.[27] The most serious problems were seen for the future.

[25]In the *People's Daily* (1977d) we see the following statement about the "gang of four": "They opposed academic examinations and stressed 'recommendations,' which provided an opportunity for those who wanted to enter college through the back door."

[26]On cadre factionalism and favoritism, see *People's Daily* (1977b). On the hesitant mood of cadres, witness this view:

> They dare not boldly take the lead in doing things, but adopt the attitude of "go slow, wait and see, and then act." They want to make sure of everything before they take any action, like wanting to touch the stones in the river when they cross it. Whenever they run into problems, in order to play it safe they invariably say that it is necessary to wait until the situation becomes clear. They will not take action until the arrival of documents with official seals from the "Red chieftains" [BBC, 1978d].

[27]Witness the following view:

> Some college graduates who were trained to do scientific and technical work were instead assigned to be purchasers, salesmen, storehousekeepers, typists or cooks. Some people who specialized in rocket launching, for example, were assigned to be doorkeepers. Some majoring in automatic control became butchers, and teachers of mathematics and those who knew foreign languages were made to fuel gas sellers or bakers [BBC, 1978e].

One-third of all postliberation university graduates in Liaoning province were said to be assigned to such inappropriate work; 8000 technicians were in this situation in Peking alone, and 5000 in Anhwei province. The statement that China has lost ground relative to the rest of the world is frequently voiced, for example in Teng Hsiao-p'ing's report to the National Science Conference (1978a).

With no new highly skilled experts being trained in China, and with earlier generations discouraged from working on basic theory, the foundation for future scientific progress and the solution of technological problems would be seriously undermined. In literature and the arts the production of a limited range of wooden and repetitious works was seen as leading to mass boredom and interfering with the potential of these media to inspire and entertain the masses. The radical policy also cut China off from much that was useful in her own heritage and in Western culture. For these reasons the renewed effort to fully utilize people in their fields of training and give them rewards and praise is being lauded as necessary and justified.[28]

The withdrawal of privileges from Overseas Chinese within China had led to resentment among those affected, and prompted tens if not hundreds of thousands to apply to leave China when it became possible to do so after 1972.[29] The post-Cultural Revolution policies had also affected the flow of remittances into China, cut off the stream of Chinese born abroad coming to give their services to their ancestral homeland, and had a negative influence on the support China enjoyed within Overseas Chinese communities in other countries. The reinstatement of privileges is deemed necessary to restore the positive contributions that Overseas Chinese can make to China's cause both at home and abroad (FBIS, 1978c:H-3; People's Daily, 1978b).

It is also claimed that the post-Cultural Revolution reforms caused serious problems among urban workers. The absence of material incentives and sanctions keyed to production results and of prospects for raises led many workers to have low levels of commitment to their enterprises, and to dawdling on the job, absenteeism, petty pilferage, and even to factional protests

[28]On policies in literature and the arts, see Peking Review (1978d:7–10). On the virtues of restoring the titles of researchers, we learn that:

> This important policy measure would enhance the sense of responsibility of people in technical posts, bring into fuller play the wisdom and resourcefulness of scientific and technical personnel, and encourage them to exert themselves in bringing science and technology in China up to advanced world levels [FBIS, 1977b:E-8].

Similarly, on the issue of restoring titles for teachers and raising their pay:

> This decision will encourage teachers to make full use of their initiative and creativity in the service of socialist education and will encourage them to be "Red and Expert," thus making a greater contribution to the movement to modernize [FBIS, 1978a:E-20, E-21].

The claim that there is a danger in restoring differentials based upon job and rank is rejected:

> In hospitals in our country, the political standing of doctors, nurses, and attendants is the same, all being workers, whether engaged in physical or mental labor. The relationship between them is one of revolutionary comrades and mutual cooperation. There is no such thing as "the bourgeois ladder" in our country [Peking Review, 1978f:20].

[29]In 1973–1974 about 60,000 people came to Hong Kong from China on the basis of exit visas. By 1976–1977 this number had tailed off, partly under British pressure, to 30,000 people per year, but in the first 4 months of 1978 more than 20,000 legal immigrants arrived in Hong Kong (South China Morning Post, 1978a, 1978c).

and strikes that disrupted production and caused large monetary losses. In the urban service trades low pay and status combined with the absence of incentives and penalities led to a lack of diligence and poor service to customers, in spite of their being required to repeatedly study Mao's (1971) article, "Serve the People." The countryside does not seem to have been as severely affected by such problems, but nonetheless in some places peasants are reported to have responded to egalitarian work-point systems by working poorly or by leaving agriculture to look for outside income earning prospects. In general, throughout society remuneration is now judged to have been insufficiently related to work results to have the necessary stimulating effect on production. The population is now being told frankly that equality must take a back seat to production.[30]

In general, then, the arguments presented since 1976 assert that needed authority and incentive systems had been undermined during the previous decade, so that people in many walks of life had little motivation to work hard and received no penalty for sloughing off, for unruliness and factionalism, or for other undesirable behavior. The pervasive state control over the nonagricultural labor market may have made economic rewards for taking various jobs less essential than in a capitalist society or the Soviet Union, but the bureaucratic allocation system has apparently not found a way to ensure that once placed in jobs people will work hard and increase their skill levels. The penetrating organizational system and mobilized group pressure seem to become routinized and incapable of motivating workers to efforts without the aid of material incentives. The system of the previous decade, premised on the idea that by reducing inequality the maximum labor effort of the masses of ordinary workers and peasants would be unleashed, apparently led in practice to fairly sloppy efforts at all levels of society. The population is

---

[30]See, for example, the following statements:

To each according to his work encourages the laborer to plunge into his work, and this will help raise labor productivity and thus increase social products. Moreover, exercising supervision over the individual amount of labor and the amount of consumption is helpful in stamping out indolence, parasitic behavior, and misappropriation of state assets [People's Daily, 1977a].

One should not judge whether a distribution system is good or bad simply on the basis of whether it is equal or unequal; one should primarily do so by considering what role it plays in the development of production. . . . We have never given first place to the question of equality, which is not the objective of the proletarian revolutionary struggle [People's Daily, 1977h].

Workers who have performed special deeds should receive comparatively high pay commensurate with their labor [Peking Review, 1978e:17].

The incentives being advocated are not all positive. A number of articles advocate cuts in pay for poor workers, with justification such as the following:

To safeguard the socialist system for which countless revolutionaries have laid down their lives, it is imperative to take effective measures against those who sponge on socialism [Beijing Review, 1979d:7].

being told that restoration of differentials and privileges is not only essential for China's modernization but will not have the effect of aggravating social cleavages and conflicts.

There are several objections that can be raised to the essentially functionalist arguments of the period since 1976. First, in spite of the horror stories in the Chinese press about poor discipline, lack of motivation, work stoppages, waste, and other problems, the Chinese economy did not do badly in the post-Cultural Revolution period. In fact, over the years 1964–1974 industrial output grew at a rate of about 10% a year, and agricultural output at perhaps 3%, quite impressive figures. It is true that the industrial growth rate was cut roughly in half in 1974–1977, and that in these years agriculture grew very little at all, but it is not clear whether we should blame the distribution and incentive policies of 1966–1976 for this drop, or elite political conflict, earthquakes and droughts, or perhaps other problems.[31] In any case the Chinese economy for a time seemed to be progressing fairly well under the destratification regime. Perhaps it can be argued that the Chinese economy could have done better or that the real danger was further down the destratification road, particularly given the "gutting" of the educational system. Still, the vivid rhetoric about the economic harm done in the recent past has no exact fit with the visible evidence. (We should keep in mind that in the Cultural Revolution the radicals told similarly lurid stories about the harm revisionist policies had done to the economy, although the preceding years had also been good ones economically.)

Second, given the familiarity of the Chinese functionalist arguments, those who do not find them persuasive in other contexts may well wonder whether all the current restratification measures are really required for China's development programs, and what effect they will have on the major sectors of society that do not benefit from them, particularly peasants and poorly educated urbanites. Third, critics of functionalism may note that perhaps some other motivations are involved besides simply a concern for China's economic progress. Revenge and spite are not out of the question. Of the group of five top leaders in post-Mao China, one, Teng Hsiao-p'ing, was purged not once but twice at the behest of China's radical leaders with Mao's blessing, in addition to having had a daughter tortured and permanently disabled. Turning the tables and having the last laugh may not be completely alien considerations to him. One other member of this group, Yeh Chien-ying, the former minister of defense and now chairman of the National People's Congress, has a son-in-law who is China's foremost pianist. During the Cultural Revolution the son-in-law was arrested and subjected to "struggle" meetings during which his arm was broken, acts Yeh was then unable to prevent (*Ta Kung Pao*, 1978a). It may be supposed that even such a venerable old gentleman as Yeh Chien-ying gains some pleasure from getting back at the

---

[31]I follow here some points made in a personal communication (1978a) from Nicholas Lardy, although the interpretation is my own. See also his article (1978b).

radicals. And of course there are large numbers of cadres and intellectuals who were purged and vilified in the Cultural Revolution but then restored to their posts in the years 1970-1976, but without all their former status and perquisites. One may entertain the thought that such people formed a powerful constituency for restratification, whether or not this policy will serve the interests of China's modernization. Finally, we cannot be certain that Humpty Dumpty can be put back together again. In view of all the alterations in people's lives in the last decade, the new incentive systems may not have the effect on popular motivations that they once might have had. Furthermore, we cannot say with any assurance that the policy of restratification will be permanent and will not be succeeded by another dialectical swing toward destratification as segments of China's leadership become concerned anew about the social consequences of these distribution policies.[32]

Conclusion

Perhaps, then, we cannot accept China's embrace of the functionalist theory of stratification without some skepticism. But it should be quite clear that in post-Mao China restratification and its functionalist justifications are the order of the day, after a decade of experimentation with more egalitarian forms. Only time will tell whether these policies lead to as complex a set of privileges and differentials as exist in the Soviet Union. Perhaps China's recent experience does not "prove" that such inequalities and privileges are necessary in any complex society, any more than the Soviet case did. But for the present the Chinese case can no longer be pointed to as evidence that the functionalist arguments are wrong, and that socialism can provide a formula for realizing economic development without compromising the commitment to social equality. Those who still wish to cling to the faith will have to look elsewhere than to China for their proof.

ACKNOWLEDGMENTS

William Parish, Suzanne Pepper, and Andrew Walder supplied useful comments on an earlier version of this chapter.

[32]The Chinese press has carried a number of articles that admit there is resistance at lower levels to putting many of these policies into practice. See, for example, FBIS (1978b; 1979a:H-4, 1979h:E-15, E-16); Peking Review (1978h:15-17); and People's Daily (1978c, 1978e, 1978k). The first source criticizes the view that providing convenient living accomodations for intellectuals is "serving bigwigs."

References

BBC (*see* British Broadcasting Corporation)
Beijing Review (*see also* Peking Review)
    1979a   No. 1. Pp. 28–29. Jan. 5.
    1979b   No. 2. P. 39. Jan. 12.
    1979c   No. 5. P. 8. Feb. 2.
    1979d   No. 8. P. 7. Feb. 23.
Bendix, R., and S. M. Lipset, Eds.
    1966   Class, Status, and Power. Second ed. New York: Free Press.
Braverman, Harry
    1974   Labor and Monopoly Capital. New York: Monthly Review Press.
British Broadcasting Corporation (BBC), Summary of World Broadcasts, Far East.
    1978a   FE/5737/BII/8–10. Feb. 11.
    1978b   FE/5739/BII/3. Feb. 14.
    1978c   FE/5753/BII/8–10. March 2.
    1978d   FE/5806/FII/9. May 6.
    1978e   FE/5810/BII/6. May 11.
    1978f   FE/5812/BII/7. May 13.
    1978g   FE/5816/BII/6. May 18.
Chen, Jack
    1973   A Year in Upper Felicity. New York: Macmillan.
Ching, Frank
    1978   Peking Is Seen Opening Avenue for Investment. Asian Wall Street Journal. P. 1. May 5.
Djilas, Milovan.
    1957   The New Class. New York: Praeger.
Enlightenment Daily (Peking)
    1978a   Feb. 20.
    1978b   Dec. 7.
Foreign Broadcast Information Service (FBIS) (Washington, D.C.), Daily Report, People's Republic of China.
    1977a   P. E–8. Sept. 26.
    1977b   P. E–8. Oct. 5.
    1977c   P. E–5. Oct. 18.
    1977d   P. E–20. Nov. 3.
    1978a   Pp. E–20 and E–21. March 18.
    1978b   P. H–1. March 29.
    1978c   P. I–3. Apr. 7.
    1979a   P. H–4. Jan. 2.
    1979b   P. J–1. Jan. 15.
    1979c   Pp. E–18 and G–5. Jan. 24.
    1979d   P. E–17. Jan. 25.
    1979e   Pp. E–7 and K–1. Jan. 29.
    1979f   Pp. E–17 and G–5. Feb. 1.
    1979g   P. E–7. Feb. 6.
    1979h   Pp. E–15 and E–16. Feb. 13.
    1979i   P. K–1. Feb. 14.
    1979j   P. E–12. Feb. 23.
    1979k   Pp. L–11 and L–12. Oct. 31.
Goldthorpe, John
    1966   Social Stratification in Industrial Society. *In* Class, Status, and Power. Second ed. R. Bendix and S. M. Lipset, eds. Pp. 648–659. New York: Free Press.

Hsinhua News Bulletin (Hong Kong)
   1978a P. 17. May 13.
   1978b P. 31. May 16.
Inkeles, Alex
   1950   Social Stratification and Mobility in the Soviet Union. American Sociological Review
         15:465–479.
Kraus, Richard
   1977   Class Conflict and the Vocabulary of Social Analysis in China. China Quarterly 69:54–
         74.
Lardy, Nicholas
   1978a Personal communication.
   1978b Recent Chinese Economic Performance and Prospects for the Ten-Year Plan. In
         Chinese Economy Post-Mao, Vol. 1. Pp. 48–62. Joint Economic Committee, Congress
         of the United States. Washington, D.C.: U.S. Government Printing Office.
Lenin, V. I.
   1943   State and Revolution. New York: International Publishers. (First ed. 1917.)
Lenski, Gerhard
   1966   Power and Privilege. New York: McGraw-Hill.
Mao Tse-tung
   1966   The May 7th Directive. Peking Review, No. 32. P. 7. Aug. 5.
   1969a Instructions Given at the Spring Festival Concerning Educational Work [Feb. 13,
         1964]. Current Background, No. 891. Pp. 42–44. Oct. 8.
   1969b Instruction on Health Work [June 26, 1965]. Current Background, No. 892. P. 20. Oct.
         21.
   1971   Serve the People [Sept. 8, 1944]. Selected Readings from the Works of Mao Tse-tung.
         Peking: Foreign Languages Press.
   1974   Talks with Mao Yuan-hsin (1964–66). In Mao Tse-tung Unrehearsed. S. Schram, ed.
         Pp. 242–252. Harmondsworth, England: Penguin Books.
Matthews, Mervyn
   1978   Privilegein the Soviet Union. London: George Allen & Unwtn.
Moore, Barrington
   1959   Soviet Politics: The Dilemma of Power. Cambridge: Harvard University Press. Peking
         Review (see also Beijing Review)
   1977a No. 40. P. 9. Sept. 30.
   1977b No. 43. Pp. 6–14. Oct. 21.
   1978a No. 1. P. 30. Jan. 6.
   1978b No. 7. Pp. 6–8. Feb. 17.
   1978c No. 12. P. 15. March 24.
   1978d No. 17. Pp. 7–10. Apr. 28.
   1978e No. 33. Pp. 16–17. Aug. 18.
   1978f No. 38. P. 20. Sept. 22.
   1978g No. 41. P. 8. Oct. 13.
   1978h No. 43. Pp. 15–17. Oct. 27.
   1978i No. 46. P. 21. Nov. 17.
   1978j No. 52. P. 13. Dec. 29.
People's Daily (Peking)
   1977a Feb. 27.
   1977b Oct. 7.
   1977c Oct. 8.
   1977d Oct. 23.
   1977e Oct. 26.
   1977f Oct. 31.

1977g   Dec. 7.
1977h   Dec. 21.
1978a   Jan. 2.
1978b   Jan. 4.
1978c   Jan. 23.
1978d   March 13.
1978e   March 16.
1978f   Apr. 23.
1978g   May 5.
1978h   May 6.
1978i   May 24.
1978j   May 27.
1978k   Dec. 27.
1979a   Jan. 4.
1979b   Jan. 29.
1979c   Feb. 4.
Pepper, Suzanne
    1977   An Interview on Changes in Chinese Education After the "Gang of Four." China
            Quarterly, No. 64. Pp. 815–816.
    1978   Education and Revolution: The "Chinese Model" Revised. Asian Survey 18:847–911.
Pfeffer, Richard
    1973   Leaders and Masses. In China's Developmental Experience. M. Oksenberg, ed. Pp.
            157–174. New York: Praeger.
Pryor, F. L.
    1972   The Distribution of Non-Agricultural Labour Incomes in Communist and Capitalist
            Nations. Slavic Review 31:639–650.
Red Flag (Peking)
    1977   No. 11. Pp. 61–64.
    1978   No. 5. Pp. 78–80.
Riskin, Carl
    1975   Workers' Incentives in Chinese Industry. In China: A Reassessment of the Economy.
            Pp. 199–224. Joint Economic Committee, Congress of the United States. Washington,
            D.C.: U.S. Government Printing Office.
South China Morning Post (Hong Kong)
    1978a   P. 1. May 4.
    1978b   P. 1. May 5.
    1978c   P. 1. May 25.
Ta Kung Pao (Hong Kong)
    1977   P. 1. Nov. 8.
    1978   P. 1. Apr. 24.
Ta Kung Pao English Edition (Hong Kong)
    1978   P. 2. May 11.
Teng Hsiao-p'ing
    1978a   Speech at the National Science Conference. Peking Review, No. 12. P. 15. March 24.
    1978b   Speech at the National Educational Work Conference. Peking Review, No. 18. P. 9.
            May 5.
Wen Hui Pao (Hong Kong)
    1978a   P. 1. May 13.
    1978b   P. 1. May 23.
Whyte, Martin King
    1974   Small Groups and Political Rituals in China. Berkeley: University of California Press.
    1975   Inequality and Stratification in China. China Quarterly, No. 64. Pp. 684–711.

1977 A Tale of Two Models. Contemporary China 1:19–20.
Wiles, Peter
1974 Distribution of Income, East and West. New York: Elsevier.
Yao Wen-yuan
1975 On the Social Basis of the Lin Biao Anti-Party Clique. Peking Review, No. 10. Pp. 5–10.

15

WLODZIMIERZ WESOLOWSKI
TADEUSZ KRAUZE

Socialist Society and the Meritocratic Principle of Remuneration

Meritocracy has been discussed in Western sociology for many years. The concept of a meritocratic society has two distinct meanings. In the first version it denotes the ascent to power of a new stratum. In the second and more restricted version it refers to the mechanism for allocating people to various social positions, especially those conferring unequal rewards of income, power, and prestige.

A French sociologist, Alain Touraine (1969, 1977), envisages the coming of postindustrial society, which will possess distinctively new features, the most outstanding being a tremendous accumulation of knowledge. In it, knowledge would play a role equivalent to that of capital in industrial society. Postindustrial society would be a programmed society, governed by a "technocratic class." This class would impose on society a type of "historicity," a particular mode of perceiving social reality and its dynamics. The technocratic class would govern society using the power of large organizations: economic, political, and cultural. The central conflict in postindustrial society would be that between decision makers who monopolize knowledge and power, and those lacking control over these resources.

Daniel Bell (1973) is less dramatic in his exposition of the basic features of postindustrial society. He stresses the accumulation of knowledge as Touraine does, and discusses the new role played by men of science both in technological development and societal transformation. He foresees the domination of society by a coalition of elites rather than by one elite. This coalition would include a political elite and elites of wealth and knowledge.

337

SOCIAL INEQUALITY
Comparative and Developmental Approaches

At a more specific level, Bell discusses a framework for achieving a just distribution of income in postindustrial society, a problem similar to one considered in this chapter. Bell favors a distribution of income that would be achieved within his broader conception of "tempered meritocracy."

A book, or rather a pamphlet, by Michael Young, "The Rise of Meritocracy" (1959), deserves praise for illuminating problems that had been felt but not clearly expressed by others. The critical question he raises is: What are the consequences of strictly applying the meritocratic principle in allocating people to jobs and positions of leadership? Young's book may be viewed as a critique of the belief that one principle can suffice as the basis for the overall organization of society. The core concern of Young's book is the role of the IQ in allocating people to various social positions. The satirical flavor of the book is directed against overgrown bureaucracy and especially the misuse of IQ testing. Rather than examining the importance of IQ, we shall consider levels of education as having greater relevance for the discussion of meritocracy.

Two topics for discussion present themselves to Marxist sociologists at the outset: first, the relationship between the concepts of meritocratic society and socialist society; and second, the relationship between the meritocratic and socialist principles of remuneration. There has yet to be a serious discussion of the first relationship, although in sociological literature it is possible to find critical essays by Marxist writers on meritocratic and postindustrial societies. Several analyses contrast the significant differences implicit in the conceptions of these two types of social order (Birnbaum, 1969; Gvishiani, 1972). It would be difficult to reject the conclusions in the cited essays that, at the global level, these theories diverge substantially. On specific issues, nevertheless, one can find certain areas of agreement. For example, both conceptual schemes stress the role of science in shaping the contours of society.

The focus of this chapter is not a comparative analysis of the two global theories, but rather a specific analysis comparing meritocratic and socialist principles of remuneration. It is puzzling that current Marxist literature does not attempt to compare these two principles of remuneration in a systematic way, since their similarities are readily apparent to anyone acquainted with both sociological theory and the literature on sources of inequality in earnings.

The vast Western literature on mechanisms governing the distribution of earnings (Psacharopoulos, 1977; Sahota, 1978; Taubman, 1975) is not related to theoretical concepts embodied in global theories of meritocratic societies. Two types of studies, one attempting to explain specific regularities governing the distribution of earnings and the second seeking to analyze the main trends of societal development, have not been theoretically connected to each other. The human capital theory (Becker, 1964; Mincer, 1970; Thurow, 1975), an example of the first type of study, investigates education as the main determinant of earnings without relating it to any broader theory of social order.

From Marx's writings one can infer that his concept of "socialist remuneration" is reconcilable with meritocratic remuneration. The meritocratic principle is implicit in Marx's writings, although it is subject to more general values to be realized in socialist society. Within the Marxist framework and in present-day socialist societies, the meritocratic principle of distribution of earnings can be seen as a means for achieving an important goal of these societies, namely social justice. This method of achieving social justice will not be applicable to future communist societies, in which the meritocratic principle would probably cease to operate.

In his later works, Marx was very careful to distinguish between the socialist and communist stages of development. One can maintain that during the first stage socialist society is, in a sense, a meritocratic society, although this opinion is not commonly held among Marxists. Unequal distribution based on "merit" can be seen by a Marxist as a "just" distribution under specific historical constraints. The conjunction of the concepts of socialism and meritocracy gives rise to specific problems and creates certain intellectual tensions that we will now explore.

Socialist and Meritocratic Principles of Remuneration

THE SOCIALIST PRINCIPLE

The socialist principle of remuneration evolved from certain remarks contained in Marx's *Critique of the Gotha Programme* (1938). Arguing with Lasalle's proposal that in socialist societies workers should receive the "proceeds of their labor," Marx was reflecting on the complicated mechanisms of socialist economy and the constraints imposed on the ideal of "equity." He wrote:

> The right of the producers is proportional to the labour they supply; the equality consists in the fact that measurement is made with an equal standard, labour.
> But one man is superior to another physically or mentally and so supplies more labour in the same time, or can labour for a longer time; and labour, to serve as a measure, must be defined by its duration or intensity, otherwise it ceases to be a standard of measurement. This equal right is an unequal right for unequal labour [1938:9].

In their theory of capitalist economy, Marx and Engels stressed the necessity for differentiating between simple and complex labor and, consequently, between corresponding levels of remuneration. In the *Critique of the Gotha Programme* Marx stated, for the first time, the necessity for applying these rules in the first stage of the development of socialist society. Because socialist society emerges from the womb of bourgeois society, it retains many bourgeois features (and "bourgeois rights"), including a principle of remuneration inherited from capitalism. In the first stage of socialist society there is no possibility of implementing the communist formula, "from each according to his ability, to each according to his needs."

Engels (1934) supplied the following rationale for the elimination of inequality in pay in future communist societies:

> In a society of private producers, private individuals or their families pay the cost of training the skilled worker; hence the higher price paid for trained labour power also comes first of all to private individuals; the clever slave is sold for a higher price, and the clever wage earner is paid higher wages. In a socialistically organized society, these costs are born by society, and to it therefore belong also the fruits, the greater values produced by skilled labour. The labourer himself has no claim to extra payment.

It can be assumed that Engels' argument sounded romantic to his contemporaries, and it still does to many of us today. One should bear in mind, however, that in a society where education is free and provides access to interesting and psychologically rewarding jobs, grounds exist for questioning pay differentials between, for example, university professors and unskilled laborers.

The concept of "socialist remuneration" evolved from Marx's ideas. It reads: "From everybody according to his ability, to everybody according to his work." As a step toward putting the formula into operation, it is said that the phrase "according to his work" has two aspects, one referring to the "quality" and the other to the "quantity" of work. Quality of work pertains to the level of qualifications, responsibility, and all aspects that comprise the "vertical" dimension of work, which reflects individuals' unequal levels of expertise, knowledge, talent, and creativity. While the quality of an individual's work may remain constant, the quantity of work can vary according to the amount of effort he or she exerts. The concept of quantity indicates, for example, the number of unit products manufactured by a worker during a unit of time.

As they constructed their economic systems, socialist countries developed a special device for setting wage and salary differentials. At the conscious level this device was thought to implement the formula "from everybody according to his ability, to everybody according to his work," but seen from another perspective it can be interpreted as an unconsciously evolved mechanism for implementing a version of the meritocratic principle. The device in question is the schedule of earnings (Kordaszewski, 1963; Krencik, 1962), which determines the wages paid the entire labor force in the nationalized sector and public institutions. These schedules were constructed in the particular ministries by teams of people specialized in setting wages, and they are subject to approval by the National Planning Commission and the Ministry of Labor.

Three composite factors were used in constructing these schedules:

1. Level of education, specific occupational skills, and experience during the occupational career.
2. Creativity and effort. (Both creativity and effort were taken into account in pay schedules for nonmanual employees, while effort was considered primarily in the pay schedules for manual workers.)

3. Responsibility and risk. (Responsibility was taken into account in pay schedules for managers and supervisory personnel.)

In preparing schedules of earnings each component was weighted. The greatest weight was given to formal education, although in certain cases long practical training and experience acquired on the job could be substituted for formal education. Because great emphasis is presently placed on formal education, many enterprises have developed plans to increase the formal education of employees who essentially have had only practical training.

THE MERITOCRATIC PRINCIPLE

The meritocratic principle of remuneration, by contrast, has not yet been fully conceptualized and put into operation. From numerous sources one can infer that the essence of the formula consists of relating inputs (i.e., individual investments) to outputs (i.e., individual rewards). In Young's initial formulation (1959) input was understood as "IQ plus effort," and output was seen as earnings, power, and prestige. This formulation seems rather vague. For the purpose of empirical research an attempt should be made to define the meritocratic principle in a more precise way. It may be understood, for example, as relating the level of education (an independent variable) to the level of earnings (a dependent variable) (cf. Bowles and Gintis, 1976, and Persell, 1977).

It seems that the meritocratic principle of the distribution of earnings can be formulated in three different ways, all of them closely related to the socialist principle of remuneration.

The first formulation is the narrowest and, consequently, the simplest to test. According to it, levels of earnings are monotonically related to levels of education. The correlation between education and earnings can be taken as the indicator of the extent to which the meritocratic principle operates in the distribution of earnings.

In the second formulation of the meritocratic principle, levels of earnings are monotonically related to the "quality of work," which encompasses several factors. These factors are level of education, specific occupational skills, training acquired on the job, responsibility, risk, and so on. The best label for all these factors might be either "level of skill" or "level of qualifications," which denotes a concept closely related to "quality of work" as understood in Marxist literature (Kordaszewski, 1963; Krencik, 1962).

The third and broadest meaning of the meritocratic principle consists in the monotonic relation of earnings to a composite scale of quality and quantity of work. At first glance, inclusion of the quantity of work (understood as exertion at work) has little relation to the meritocratic principle, although one could argue that greater exertion at work, resulting in a larger output, constitutes a special type of "merit."

These three formulations of the meritocratic principle are, we believe, presented here for the first time. Their close correspondence to the socialist principle of remuneration results from the particular modes of their operationalization.

We tend to accept the first and second formulations of the meritocratic principle for the purpose of research on earnings distribution in socialist society. There is no theoretical reason or practical need to equate the meritocratic principle with the socialist principle of remuneration. What we argue for is their close association and considerable conceptual proximity. The socialist principle, being a broader one, includes both these versions of the meritocratic principle.

The close dependence of earnings on education and qualifications is socially perceived in Poland (and very likely in other socialist countries) as a "proper," that is, normatively sanctioned, relationship. There is no name for the meritocratic principle in everyday language, but the concept is latent whenever people discuss "just" or "fair" earnings. The meritocratic concept would be seen not as conflicting with the socialist moral code but as one of its components.

In the value system of Polish society, education and competence have always been held in high esteem, much higher than power or wealth. This specific value structure has been documented in several research reports (Koralewicz, 1974; Sarapata and Wesolowski, 1961; Wesolowski and Slomczynski, 1968). On the basis of these investigations one can conclude that in present-day Polish socialist society there exists widespread support for the meritocratic principle. The high esteem in which education is held is strengthened by the supposedly rational and universalistic character of the schedules of earnings. Therefore, differentiation of pay based on education and skill is perceived as being legitimate, superior to, and more just than that based on private capital, the arbitrary personal assessments of managers, or pure political power.

Principles of Remuneration in Present Socialist Societies

Both socialist and meritocratic principles operate in a broad social context and are not the exclusive determinants of earnings. At least two mechanisms modify their operation: the labor market and social conventions.

LABOR MARKET DEMAND AND ECONOMY

In Poland seemingly irrational differences in wages exist among the branches of industry, and sometimes within a given industry. For example, toolmakers with equivalent education and qualifications receive higher pay in heavy than in light industry. A more extreme case is provided by the differentiation of wages and salaries between those working in established industrial enterprises and those working on the construction of new ones. This is illustrated by the double pay received by employees of high-priority steel mills and automobile factories. Such deviations undermine both the socialist and meritocratic principles of remuneration. However, these discrepancies are tolerated because of the important goal of rapid economic development of socialist society. A good example is provided here of a conflict between goals and principles as they are put into practice.

The situation described previously is aggravated by the fact that in most occupations the demand for workers exceeds the supply. Rapid economic growth intensifies this problem and creates a high rate of turnover in the labor force.

SOCIAL CONVENTIONS, CUSTOMS, AND THE LEGACY OF THE PAST

Operation of the meritocratic principle is constrained by the social and cultural heritage of a given society. Certain historically established patterns of remuneration may have no rational justification at the present time. In Poland, for example, for many generations it was taken for granted that nonmanual work was more valuable than manual work. Also, until recently, the division into nonmanual and manual work was paralleled by a clear division of education levels, a division that contributed to a pronounced demarcation between the working class and the intelligentsia. The postwar industrialization and modernization of Polish society resulted in an expansion of the number of white-collar workers with low educational levels, and a simultaneous increase in the number of skilled workers with comparable, and often higher, educational levels. In this situation some groups of white-collar workers felt deprived of their "proper" social position and salary, ignoring the fact that their educational attainment was lower than that of certain skilled workers. Such views exemplify the burden of fossilized forms of social consciousness. In defense of their interests, some white-collar workers present these views as allegedly justifiable on the basis of the meritocratic principle. A displacement of meritocratic criteria from the educational dimension to the traditional manual/nonmanual division can be observed here.

This example indicates the role of social conventions in determining pay structures in both socialist and capitalist societies. In 1946, Barbara Wooton, an English economist, remarked, "All wages are to be explained more in terms of conventions than as a result of strictly economic factors. This is not, of course, a final explanation, since it is necessary to inquire how these conventions came to be established, and how in the course of history they change."

In his book, *Inequality of Pay*, Henry Phelps Brown (1977) discusses the well-known correlation between occupational prestige and income, asking whether prestige is determined by income or whether the direction of causal influence is reversed. He reports that, at least for some occupations, income level is socially allocated on the basis of occupational prestige. However, Sarapata (1963), conducting research in Poland, found that for certain occupations, such as teacher and nurse, respondents postulated remuneration that more closely reflected occupational prestige than actual income. This result shows that occupational prestige is important in conventional thinking about "just" remuneration.

THE ROLE OF THE EGALITARIAN ETHOS

In socialist countries the ideology of equality interacts with remuneration principles in a specific way, leading to a narrowing of the range of pay differences.

Socialist and meritocratic principles of remuneration do not address the issue of minimal and maximal levels of pay but only the internal arrangement of pay scales within unspecified boundaries.

Viewed in historical perspective, wage policies in socialist countries have reduced the range of pay. Nevertheless, establishing an adequate range has remained an open theoretical and practical question. Serious attempts have been made to establish the lower boundary of the pay scale; however, the question of setting an upper limit, although raised and discussed, has not been resolved.

It appears that determining the range of earnings is not easy. At least three elements should be incorporated in any rational proposal to set the range of pay: (1) the motivational potential of pay differences as a factor leading to the increase of educational attainment; (2) popular opinion as to what constitutes a "just" pay structure; and (3) the necessity for controlling spontaneous processes that could lead to the petrification of still existing inequalities (the perpetuation of inequality under the guise of the meritocratic principle).

In conjunction with the egalitarian ethos, specific social policies play a part in determining the allocation of goods to various groups. In some cases the allocation of certain goods is based on family needs rather than on work. We shall consider several examples of the relationship between such policies and the meritocratic principle.

In the area of educational policy, a proportional increase in the level of education in all groups serves socialist development, but is neutral with respect to the meritocratic principle. However, increases in education of those with relatively high incomes who are already in the labor force will increase the level of meritocratic allocation. In Poland, about 25% of occupationally active people who began work in 1945 upgraded their formal education at some time after entry into the labor force. A substantial proportion increased their education in order to keep their jobs; they felt threatened by competition from younger and better educated workers entering the labor market.

Several policies related to health, education, and general welfare are also neutral with respect to the meritocratic and socialist principles of remuneration. Among them are socialized medicine, recreational services, and privileges accruing to children from peasant and working-class families at competitive entrance examinations to schools of higher education.

In general, it can be said that specific social policies concerned with the allocation of goods and services can intensify, be neutral, or hinder the operation of the meritocratic principle.

Some Empirical Illustrations

In this section we discuss certain measurement problems pertaining to the operation of the meritocratic principle and the prevalence of the egalitarian ethos.

The first problem is a methodological one. It consists of devising and then applying an index appropriate for measuring the extent to which the meritocratic principle operates in a given society. Such a measure would be useful, since one can assume that in almost all contemporary societies the meritocratic principle operates to some extent. The question is to what extent.

It is easier to find a measure for the first (simpler) version of the meritocratic principle than for the second, more complex one. In Tables 15.1 and 15.2 we present data on the operation of the simple version of the meritocratic principle. Table 15.1 presents the actual distribution and Table 15.2 the model distribution of education and income in three large cities in Poland.

In each cell of Table 15.1 we find the number of male household heads who earn the amount specified in the column heading and have the educational level specified in the row heading. The correlation coefficient for this

TABLE 15.1
Education and Earnings in Three Polish Cities: Number of Male
Household Heads in Each Category

Education	Midpoints of earnings per month (in 100 zlotys)						
	9	15	25	35	45	70	N
Complete higher	0	19	68	88	38	16	229
Incomplete higher	1	22	48	22	7	0	100
Complete secondary	3	118	280	56	21	4	482
Incomplete secondary	5	195	212	31	4	0	447
Complete elementary	12	366	243	24	3	0	648
Incomplete elementary	18	266	97	2	2	0	385
Totals	39	986	948	223	75	20	2291

Source: Adapted from Wesolowski and Slomczynski, 1968:Table 5, p. 188.

TABLE 15.2
Assignment of Male Household Heads to Income Categories According to Meritocratic Principle

Education	Midpoints of earnings per month (in 100 zlotys)						
	9	15	25	35	45	70	N
Complete higher	0	0	0	134	75	20	229
Incomplete higher	0	0	11	89	0	0	100
Complete secondary	0	0	482	0	0	0	482
Incomplete secondary	0	0	447	0	0	0	447
Complete elementary	0	640	8	0	0	0	648
Incomplete elementary	39	346	0	0	0	0	385
Totals	39	986	948	223	75	20	2291

Source: Marginals of Table 1.

table is .51. Table 15.2 presents the model distribution of earnings and education for the same population. The model allocates persons to cells according to marginal values, so that the resulting distribution shows the maximal possible extent of realization of the meritocratic principle. The coefficient of correlation for Table 15.2 is .88. It should be noted that the value of this coefficient must be substantially smaller than 1, since the distributional constraints on education and income (expressed as the marginal values of Table 15.1) need to be satisfied. The degree to which the meritocratic principle is at work within the population is measured by the ratio of the actual correlation coefficient to the maximal correlation coefficient. The value of this ratio is .63.

The aforementioned measurement procedure has been proposed by Krauze and Slomczynski (1980) and utilizes data that are easily obtainable. We believe that when applied to many countries and to various periods in their development, it will provide interesting substantive results. Other methods need to be developed to study the operation of various principles of remuneration. They, for example, should allow one to assess both the extent to which the second version of the meritocratic principle and the socialist principle of remuneration operate. The task of defining and measuring the appropriate variables needed for the construction of composite scales seems quite difficult, since the appropriate measurement technique must take several dimensions into account.

Tables 15.3 and 15.4 supply evidence illustrating egalitarian attitudes. Table 15.3 compares actual and postulated earnings; the latter are defined as those that the respondents regard as appropriate to their own occupations. Differences between the socio-occupational groups with respect to their claims for higher wages and salaries are not large. The table shows that professionals

TABLE 15.3
Earnings Postulated as Appropriate for Own Occupation

	Average monthly earnings (in zlotys)		Differences between postulated and received earnings (in percentages)
	Actually received	Postulated as appropriate	
Professionals	7412	9430	27
Office employees	5437	6748	24
Technicians	5155	6348	23
Foremen	5020	6313	26
Service workers	4339	5840	35
Skilled workers	4337	5934	37
Semiskilled workers	3863	5665	47
Unskilled workers	3378	4658	38

Source: Unpublished data from a survey of male household heads, Lodz, 1976. Sample, 1000 persons.

TABLE 15.4
Postulates Pertaining to Differences in Earnings (in percentages)

Postulates	Socio-occupational categories					
	Production managers	Technicians	Foremen	Skilled workers	Unskilled workers	Total
Differences should be increased	—	2.4	0.9	1.4	1.6	1.2
Differences should remain at present level	56.8	34.1	28.7	15.7	19.6	26.9
Wage levels should be changed for certain occupations	11.7	14.6	25.7	17.9	22.9	19.5
Highest pay should be decreased or lowest increased	15.6	14.6	19.8	27.8	34.4	23.8
Highest pay should be decreased and simultaneously the lowest increased	15.6	34.1	24.7	35.7	19.6	27.6
No response	—	—	—	1.4	1.6	0.7
Number in each category	N = 51	N = 41	N = 101	N = 140	N = 61	N = 394

Source: B. Blachnicki, 1978:193–205, and Table 2.

and white-collar employees are more restrained in their claims than are manual workers.

If the postulated earnings (Table 15.3) were implemented, the resulting distribution would have a smaller value of the Gini index of inequality (cf. Sen, 1973:29–31) than the existing distribution.

A rather strong egalitarian ethos, manifested at least at the level of verbal behavior, is confirmed by the data provided in Table 15.4 from a small-scale research project conducted in one factory (Blachnicki, 1978), in which 394 employees were interviewed. The postulate that differences in salary should be increased was agreed to by no more than 2.4% of the respondents in each socio-occupational group under study. A high proportion of respondents in each group selected the following statements: "Highest pay should be decreased or the lowest pay increased" or "Highest pay should be decreased and simultaneously the lowest pay increased."

Conclusions

Though stressing the prevalence of the egalitarian ethos in Poland, we would hesitate to overstate its influence. The egalitarian ethos does not affect the meritocratic principle as such (except for the limiting case of complete equalization of pay), but it may decrease the range of pay. If such a decrease occurs, the meritocratic and socialist principles must operate within a relatively narrow range.

References

Becker, Gary S.
   1964   Human Capital. New York: Columbia University Press.
Bell, Daniel
   1973   The Coming of Post-Industrial Society: A Venture in Social Forecasting. New York: Basic Books.
Birnbaum, Norman
   1969   The Crisis of Industrial Society. Oxford: Oxford University Press.
Blachnicki, Boguslaw
   1978   Economic Inequality in the Consciousness of Industrial Employees. In Social Structure. Polish Sociological Association, ed. Pp. 193–205. Wroclaw: Ossolineum.
Bowles, Samuel, and Herbert Gintis
   1976   Schooling in Capitalist America. New York: Basic Books.
Brown, Henry Phelps
   1977   The Inequality of Pay. Berkeley: University of California Press.
Engels, Friedrich
   1934   Herr Eugen Duhring's Revolution in Science (Anti-Duhring). New York: International Publishers.
Gvishiani, Dzhermen Mikhailovich
   1972   Organizatsiia i upravlenie [Organization and Management]. Moscow: Nauka.

Koralewicz, Jadwiga
  1974 System wartosci a struktura spoleczna [Value System and Social Structure]. Wroclaw and Warsaw: Ossolineum.
Kordaszewski, Jan
  1963 Placa wedlug pracy [Remuneration According to Work]. Warsaw: Ksiazka i Wiedza.
Krauze, Tadeusz, and Kasimierz Slomczynski
  1980 Meritocratic Allocation According to Education and Status. Mimeographed.
Krencik, Wieslaw
  1962 Badania polityki zatrudnienia i plac w gospodarce socialistycznej [Research on Employ-ment and Wage Policy in a Socialist Economy]. Warsaw: PWN.
Marx, Karl
  1938 Critique of the Gotha Programme. New York: International Publishers. (First ed. 1875.)
Mincer, Jacob
  1970 The Distribution of Labor Incomes: A Survey with Special References to the Human Capital Approach. Journal of Economic Literature, Vol. 3, No. 1.
Persell, Caroline Hodges
  1977 Education and Inequality: A Theoretical and Empirical Synthesis. New York: Free Press.
Psacharopoulos, George
  1977 Economics of Education: An Assessment of Recent Methodological Advances and Em-pirical Results. Social Science Information 16(3/4):351-371.
Sahota, Gian Singh
  1978 Theories of Personal Income Distribution: A Survey. Journal of Economic Literature 16: 1-55.
Sarapata, Adam
  1963 Iustum Pretium. Polish Sociological Bulletin, No. 7.
Sarapata, Adam, and Wlodzimierz Wesolowski
  1961 The Evaluation of Occupations by Warsaw Inhabitants. American Journal of Sociology 66:581-591
Sen, Amartya
  1973 On Economic Inequality. Oxford: Clarendon Press.
Taubman, Paul J.
  1975 Sources of Inequality in Earnings: Personal Skills, Random Events, Preferences Toward Risk and Other Occupational Characteristics. Amsterdam: North Holland.
Thurow, Lester C.
  1975 Generating Inequality: Mechanisms of Distribution in the U.S. Economy. New York: Basic Books.
Touraine, Alain
  1969 La Société post-industrielle. Paris: Editions du Seuil.
  1977 The Self-Production of Society. Derek Coltman, trans. Chicago: University of Chicago Press.
Wesolowski, Wlodzimierz, and Kazimierz Slomczynski
  1968 Social Stratification in Polish Cities. In Social Stratification. J. A. Jackson, ed. Pp. 175-211. Cambridge: Cambridge University Press.
Wooton, Barbara
  1946 Appendix IX to Minutes of Evidence Taken Before the Royal Commission on Equal Pay. London: Her Majesty's Stationery Office.
Young, Michael
  1959 The Rise of Meritocracy. Baltimore: Penguin.

EPILOGUE

KATHLEEN M. ZARETSKY

Discussing Inequality

The chapters in this volume were distributed in advance to all participants in the symposium, many of whom had not previously met or communicated with one another. Late in the summer of 1978 these social anthropologists, and the occasional sociologist, assembled at the castle in Austria which was once the home of the Lichtensteins but which now serves as the summer conference center of the Wenner-Gren Foundation for Anthropological Research. There followed 7 days of discussions, broken midway by a day of rest and recuperation in Vienna. There were morning and afternoon sessions, all held at a huge, circular conference table on the second floor of the castle.

As rapporteur, one of my responsibilities was to keep a record of the proceedings. Accordingly, I took extensive notes, comprising in fact two kinds of records of the symposium. On the one hand I kept handwritten notes of the flow of the discussion: of its substance, its arguments, its digressions. These notes, together with the tape recordings of the same sessions, provided me with a pool of information about the content of the conference—a pool so vast as to be overwhelming. I kept, though rather less diligently, another kind of handwritten record as well: an off-the-cuff rendering of the social dynamics of the conference roundtable itself. The latter set of notes is too personal and too impressionistic to merit detailed attention, yet to ignore these notes entirely would do an injustice to the social reality within which the intellectual currents of the conference moved. Initially, for example, discussion was impaired by jet-lag, the newness and strangeness of the setting, the inflexibility

351

SOCIAL INEQUALITY
Comparative and Developmental Approaches

of the schedule, by such extraneous intrusions as dealing with lost luggage, and the fact that some participants promptly came down with colds and laryngitis. Soon, however, routines were established and adapted to, recurrent patterns of interaction appeared, factions developed as did characteristic kinds of disagreements, characteristic clusters of allies and opponents, and a certain degree of predictability in the focus of the discussions. Some participants consistently supported the positions espoused by particular others despite apparent contradictions between those and their own positions, some consistently opposed the positions of others despite apparent agreement with their own. Some participants were Marxists; others were not. Some Marxists were doctrinaire; others were not. Some participants were eminent; others were not. There was a considerable range of age. There were 4 women and 16 men. Some people seemed to play to specific audiences: to impress the famous among us, for example. Others were intimidated by the presence of those same personages and participated considerably less in discussion than they might have under other circumstances. All of these factors played their roles in determining the direction, substance, and dynamics of the discussions.

There was little agreement. Everyone arrived with a point of view, put this point of view forth whenever it was his or her turn or inclination to speak, and departed with the same point of view apparently unaltered. And yet the discussions were by-and-large lively and good-natured. Genuine interest was taken by virtually all participants in the information and ideas put forth by others present. The organizer had defined the topic of the symposium very broadly (see Preface to this volume), and perhaps as a result of that the range of the information and ideas brought and presented was broad indeed. I think that we each found it to be difficult but interesting for 20 people to talk about everything, and all at the same time.

The substance of the discussion was too diverse and often too complex as well, to do it justice in a few pages, and I shall therefore not attempt to do so here. Instead, I shall simply try to convey something of the quality of that discussion by making a few comments about the kinds of issues that were characteristically raised, the kinds of disagreements that recurred, and the occasional expressions of consensus of the part of the participants.

From the beginning there was considerable fundamental and continuing disagreement on the defining characteristics and key mechanisms of the topic at hand, social inequality itself. This situation was perhaps intensified by the attention early in the proceedings to social inequality in nonstratified societies. Though these are the kinds of societies that fall especially within the social anthropologist's realm of expertise, there was sharp disagreement on the basic issue of the presence or absence of inequality in such societies, not least because no final agreement could be reached on what constitutes evidence for inequality and on the extent to which one can speak of "degrees" of inequality. Much of this discussion involved the relative status of women in the division of labor and sex roles in unstratified societies—a discussion which turned on the question of the possibility of complementarity of sex roles versus the inevitability of institutionalized inequality in the presence of differen-tiated sex roles. The argument then became one concerning the biases of the original ethnographers, as well as of later interpreters of the data. If unequal access to material wellbeing is not at issue, it was argued, the estimation of psychic and political inequality is at least open to challenge, perhaps espe-cially if a situational approach is adopted, as was consistently pressed for by several participants.

Marshall Sahlins put forth another kind of argument when he elegantly and at length described for Fiji a hierarchy of the intrinsic and consensual sort advocated by Louis Dumont (1970) as underlying certain social systems, notably that of India. Because this kind of hierarchy transcends the ordinary kind of evidence adduced for inequality, and as most other symposium members proved to be skeptical of Sahlins' and Dumont's theoretical position, a certain oppositional unanimity emerged here in what had been theretofore a rather disputatious forum.

When the discussions shifted to stratified societies, most participants seemed to be more comfortable, and they promptly embarked upon a round of disagreement about the relative importance of modes of production, dis-tribution, accumulation, inheritance, consumption, and so forth. The role of power and force formed part of this debate as well. The issue of progressive development through time in the degree and complexity of political and economic inequality brought some agreement, but at the expense of a certain loss in sensitivity to the down-to-earth ethnographic and situational realities of inequality, for the discussions frequently were conducted at a high level of abstraction, involving generalizations not only about entire social systems but also about types of social systems and spanning great ranges in time and social evolution or development.

On the whole, people found it easier to discuss inequality in stratified rather than in unstratified societies. This seemed to be based on the fact that the evidence for inequality is relatively clearcut when it takes the form of un-equal access to material wellbeing, the ideological rationalizations for the social order are ethnographically relatively explicit with reference to ranking, and the experiential or psychic disadvantages of inequality are readily discern-ible in concrete instances. A significant point raised here was that although the material disadvantage of inequality affects those low on a hierarchical scale, one can argue that the psychic disadvantages affect all by inflicting debased status (at least as defined by the elite, hegemonic subculture) on those at the bottom, and the illusions, dependencies, vulnerabilities, and anxieties of in-flated status on those of the elite subculture. Thus, highly stratified societies are physically damaging to those on the bottom, and they are psychically damaging across the board: for those who ride the tiger and fear to dismount or be unseated, as well as for those who comprise that tiger.

Discussion of the role of ideology in stratified societies led the symposium back to one of its very earliest topics: the social attribution of intrinsic char-acteristics to individuals which justify their placement in a system of unequal reward. Acquired status differs conceptually from this mode of assignment by intrinsic status, but it was also argued that the reasons given for achieved status may also ultimately entail the attribution of inborn qualities. For example, a society based on merit may produce a kind of birth-ascribed differentiation by hindsight, with formal education, for instance, providing the major mechanism for the translation of such differences into inequalities. Such retroactive realization of ascribed qualities disassociates them from group membership (i.e., from birth ascription) and they thus undercut the potentially egalitarian ties of community.

Among the most lively sessions of the symposium were those devoted to discussions of papers drawing on material from contemporary China and Poland. Detailed information about the planning that organizes the development of equality and inequality in these societies and about the character of the everyday experience of their citizens took the assertion of a socialist alternative out of the realm of ideology and ideals to which some participants were wont to keep it, and placed it firmly before us as intricate and recalcitrant reality. This discussion brought up clearly as well as the issue of equity versus equality as a long-range goal for those primarily concerned about inequalities of the immediate present. It was apparent that equity, or the strain toward equity, is the best one can hope for—and *is* the best hope—in large-scale industrial systems. This position, however, was strongly and cogently challenged as a panacea by those participants (most notably, no doubt, John Bodley) holding the vision that a scaling down of the institutional structures of large-scale systems could bring about realization of the egalitarian potential inherent in small-scale existence, and that this is the last, best hope for egalitarian society and even for human survival.

Although inequality can be described as a more or less neutral logic of organization in society, it is obvious that it is extremely difficult to talk about it without evaluation: the evaluative ideology that defines and justifies the social reality for the privileged in every stratified society; that which defines and decries it for the dispossessed in every such society; the evaluation by the observer or analyst of the material and nonmaterial consequences of unequal status; the potential evaluation of any system of inequality from within and from without as entailing not only inequality but also injustice. Most participants in this conference did not hesitate to make this kind of judgment—that one of them demurred in fact had a unifying effect on the others—and indeed almost all believed it to be a positive responsibility of the social scientist not only to identify, but also to work toward the diminishment of that inequality which results in injustice. There was not, however, clear agreement on what constitutes injustice, for domination and exploitation are not unitary phenomena, and the perception of injustice is itself open to cultural bias.

Such discussions produced self-critical moments when, for example, a cautionary note was struck about the location of all the participants in an academic world characterized by competitive individualism and hierarchy, and attention was directed to the potential for both blindness and bias therein. Antidotes were proposed as well, ranging from simple heightened awareness to participation in egalitarian collectivist political activity, but consensus, needless to say, was not forthcoming.

There was a general uneasiness among participants with quantification as a method for research and analysis, and there were frequent calls for more and better ethnohistorical accounts. Perhaps this was expectable in a symposium made up largely of anthropologists, but surely it was unusual in the field of social inequality and stratification studies. Given the level of abstraction which often characterized our discussions, the partipants remained, finally, quite empirical. When confronted with either complex arrays of numbers or elaborately conceived theoretical abstractions, participants tended to respond doubtfully at best. When, for example, Martin Orans was asked to comment on a particularly abstruse presentation (one which involved, however, ethnographic material from Oceania with which he is familiar), he described his reaction by referring to the *Peanuts* cartoon in which Lucy asked Linus what he saw in the shapes of the clouds they were watching overhead. Linus replied that he saw things such as a map of British Honduras and an image of the stoning of Stephen with the apostle Paul standing to one side. When Lucy turned to Charlie Brown with the same question he answered, "Well, I was going to say I saw a ducky and a horsie, but I changed my mind! [Schulz, 1961:57]." There was, in fact, considerable respect among the conferees for "horsies and duckies." Orans and others did not hesitate to describe them or ask others to do so, and the phrase became a watchword of the symposium.

In sum, then, there was throughout a tension between the satisfying closure offered by resort to large-scale theoretical formulations, and the final, cruel honesty of specific contextual, situational, empirical analyses. The strength of anthropology in remaining true to the density and complexity of human experience was evident, as the pull of universalizing theory was offset by careful description of concrete cases and by the suspicion with which easy generalization was greeted. The diversity of experience and perspective represented in the discipline and in its representatives at the symposium clearly is part of that strength. The political and social concern of those present at this particular assemblage was clear as well. Although the discussion frequently focused on more or less neutral structural matters, always lurking in the background, and frequently coming to the fore, were individuals and individual values—the final human measure of our science.

References

Dumont, Louis
1970 Homo Hierarchicus: The Caste System and Its Implications (M. Sainsbury, translator). London: Weidenfeld and Nicolson.
Schulz, Charles M.
1961 Peanuts Every Sunday. New York: Holt, Rinehart and Winston.

Index

357

STUDIES IN ANTHROPOLOGY

Under the Consulting Editorship of E. A. Hammel,
UNIVERSITY OF CALIFORNIA, BERKELEY

Andrei Simić, THE PEASANT URBANITES: A Study of Rural-Urban Mobility in Serbia

John U. Ogbu, THE NEXT GENERATION: An Ethnography of Education in an Urban Neighborhood

Bennett Dyke and Jean Walters MacCluer (Eds.), COMPUTER SIMULATION IN HUMAN POPULATION STUDIES

Robbins Burling, THE PASSAGE OF POWER: Studies in Political Succession

Piotr Sztompka, SYSTEM AND FUNCTION: Toward a Theory of Society

William G. Lockwood, EUROPEAN MOSLEMS: Economy and Ethnicity in Western Bosnia

Günter Golde, CATHOLICS AND PROTESTANTS: Agricultural Modernization in Two German Villages

Peggy Reeves Sanday (Ed.), ANTHROPOLOGY AND THE PUBLIC INTEREST: Fieldwork and Theory

Carol A. Smith (Ed.), REGIONAL ANALYSIS, Volume I: Economic Systems, and Volume II: Social Systems

Raymond D. Fogelson and Richard N. Adams (Eds.), THE ANTHROPOLOGY OF POWER: Ethnographic Studies from Asia, Oceania, and the New World

Frank Henderson Stewart, FUNDAMENTALS OF AGE-GROUP SYSTEMS

Larissa Adler Lomnitz, NETWORKS AND MARGINALITY: Life in a Mexican Shantytown

Benjamin S. Orlove, ALPACAS, SHEEP, AND MEN: The Wool Export Economy and Regional Society in Southern Peru

Harriet Ngubane, BODY AND MIND IN ZULU MEDICINE: An Ethnography of Health and Disease in Nyuswa-Zulu Thought and Practice

George M. Foster, Thayer Scudder, Elizabeth Colson, and Robert Van Kemper (Eds.), LONG-TERM FIELD RESEARCH IN SOCIAL ANTHROPOLOGY

R. H. Hook (Ed.), FANTASY AND SYMBOL: Studies in Anthropological Interpretation

Richard Tapper, PASTURE AND POLITICS: Economics, Conflict and Ritual Among Shahsevan Nomads of Northwestern Iran

George Bond, Walton Johnson, and Sheila S. Walker (Eds.), AFRICAN CHRISTIANITY: Patterns of Religious Continuity

John Comaroff (Ed.), THE MEANING OF MARRIAGE PAYMENTS

Michael H. Agar, THE PROFESSIONAL STRANGER: An Informal Introduction to Ethnography